Matthew's Non-Messianic Mapping of Messianic Texts

Biblical Interpretation Series

Editors-in-Chief

Paul Anderson (*George Fox University*)
Jennifer L. Koosed (*Albright College, Reading*)

Editorial Board

A. K. M. Adam (*University of Oxford*)
Nijay Gupta (*Portland Seminary*)
Amy Kalmanofsky (*Jewish Theological Seminary*)
Jennifer Knust (*Duke University*)
Vernon Robbins (*Emory University*)
Annette Schellenberg (*University Wien*)
Johanna Stiebert (*University of Leeds*)
Duane Watson (*Malone University*)
Christine Roy Yoder (*Columbia Theological Seminary*)
Ruben Zimmermann (*Johannes Gutenberg-Universität Mainz*)

VOLUME 188

The titles published in this series are listed at *brill.com/bins*

Matthew's Non-Messianic Mapping of Messianic Texts

Evidences of a Broadly Eschatological Hermeneutic

By

Bruce Harold Henning

BRILL

LEIDEN | BOSTON

The Library of Congress Cataloging-in-Publication Data is available online at http://catalog.loc.gov
LC record available at http://lccn.loc.gov/2020046598

Typeface for the Latin, Greek, and Cyrillic scripts: "Brill". See and download: brill.com/brill-typeface.

ISSN 0928-0731
ISBN 978-90-04-44416-4 (hardback)
ISBN 978-90-04-44418-8 (e-book)

Copyright 2021 by Koninklijke Brill NV, Leiden, The Netherlands.
Koninklijke Brill NV incorporates the imprints Brill, Brill Hes & De Graaf, Brill Nijhoff, Brill Rodopi, Brill Sense, Hotei Publishing, mentis Verlag, Verlag Ferdinand Schöningh and Wilhelm Fink Verlag.
All rights reserved. No part of this publication may be reproduced, translated, stored in a retrieval system, or transmitted in any form or by any means, electronic, mechanical, photocopying, recording or otherwise, without prior written permission from the publisher. Requests for re-use and/or translations must be addressed to Koninklijke Brill NV via brill.com or copyright.com.

This book is printed on acid-free paper and produced in a sustainable manner.

Contents

Acknowledgments IX
References and Abbreviations X

1 **Introduction** 1
   1.1 The Contribution of This Study 1
      1.1.1 *A Brief Summary of the Central Thesis* 1
      1.1.2 *The Importance of a Fulfillment Key in Matthew* 2
   1.2 Significance of This Thesis in Matthean Studies and Its Relationship to Current Trends 5
      1.2.1 *Generalizing Matthew's Hermeneutical Paradigm* 5
      1.2.2 *The Overlap of Matthew's Ecclesiological and Messianic Hermeneutic* 7
      1.2.3 *The Effect of Matthew's Theology of Discipleship on His Hermeneutic* 9
      1.2.4 *Matthew's General Approach as Broadly Eschatological* 13
   1.3 Method 14
      1.3.1 *Intertextuality* 16
      1.3.2 *Cognitive Linguistics* 28
   1.4 Summary of Thesis and Case Studies 42

2 **Matthew's Non-Messianic Use of the Eschatological Shepherd** 45
   2.1 Introduction 45
   2.2 The Contribution of Ezek 34 47
      2.2.1 *Matt 9:36 by Itself Does Not Allude to an OT Text* 47
      2.2.2 *Matt 9:36 and 10:6 Do Allude to Ezek 34* 48
      2.2.3 *Ezek 34 Would Have Been Understood as Messianic* 49
      2.2.4 *Ezek 34 Is Evoked in Matt 9:36 and 10:6 to Depict Major Literary Characters* 63
   2.3 The Contribution of Jer 23:1–6 68
      2.3.1 *Matt 9:36 and 10:6 Do Allude to Jer 23:1–6* 68
      2.3.2 *"Shepherds" Are Royal and Prophetic Figures of the Messiah* 70
      2.3.3 *Matthew Portrays the Disciples as "Shepherds"* 77
   2.4 The Contribution of Zech 10:2–4 83
      2.4.1 *The Possibility That Matt 9:36 and 10:6 Allude to Zech 10:2–4* 83
      2.4.2 *The Combination of the Messiah and General Eschatological Rulers Suggests the Allusion* 84

2.4.3 *Zech 10:2–4 Uniquely Resonates with the Complex Portrayal of the Apostles as Oppressors Who Execute God's Judgment* 88
2.5 Conclusion 91

3 Matthew's Non-Messianic Use of Isaiah's Vineyard Care-Givers 93
3.1 Introduction 93
3.2 Isaiah 5:1–7 96
    3.2.1 *Overview of Contents* 96
    3.2.2 *Agency Potential* 97
    3.2.3 *Eschatological Potential* 99
    3.2.4 *Messianic Potential* 101
    3.2.5 *Summary of Isaiah 5:1–7* 102
3.3 Ezekiel 15, 17, 19 103
    3.3.1 *Overview of Contents* 103
    3.3.2 *Connection to Isa 5:1–7* 104
    3.3.3 *Agency* 105
    3.3.4 *Eschatology* 106
    3.3.5 *Messianism* 107
    3.3.6 *Summary of Ezek 15, 17, 19* 109
3.4 2 Baruch 36–40 109
    3.4.1 *Overview of Contents* 109
    3.4.2 *Connection to Isa 5:1–7* 110
    3.4.3 *Agency* 111
    3.4.4 *Eschatology and Messianism* 111
    3.4.5 *Summary of 2 Baruch 36–40* 112
3.5 Ps 80 113
    3.5.1 *Overview of Contents* 113
    3.5.2 *Connection to Isa 5:1–7* 114
    3.5.3 *Agency* 115
    3.5.4 *Eschatology* 116
    3.5.5 *Messianism* 116
    3.5.6 *Excursus: What If the WTP Alludes to Ps 80?* 118
    3.5.7 *Summary of Ps 80* 121
3.6 John 15:1–8 121
    3.6.1 *Overview of Contents* 121
    3.6.2 *Connection to Isa 5:1–7* 122
    3.6.3 *Agency* 122
    3.6.4 *Eschatology* 123
    3.6.5 *Messianism* 123
    3.6.6 *Summary of John 15:1–8* 124

3.7 Matt 21:33–45 125
    3.7.1 *Overview of Contents* 126
    3.7.2 *Connection to Isa 5:1–7* 126
    3.7.3 *Agency* 127
    3.7.4 *Eschatology* 133
    3.7.5 *Messianism* 135
3.8 Conclusion 136

4 Matthew's Non-Messianic Use of Temple-Construction Imagery 139
4.1 Introduction 139
4.2 Matt 21:42–43 142
    4.2.1 *Matt 21:42–43 Evokes Imagery of Eschatological Temple Construction* 143
    4.2.2 *Matt 21:42–43 Portrays the Disciples as Eschatological Temple Builders* 149
    4.2.3 *The Image of an Eschatological Temple Builder Was a Messianic Concept* 155
4.3 Matt 16:18 Portrays the Disciples as the Messianic Temple Foundation 160
    4.3.1 *Matt 16:18 Evokes Imagery of Eschatological Temple Construction* 161
    4.3.2 *Matt 16:18 Portrays the Disciples as the Eschatological Temple Foundation* 165
    4.3.3 *The Image of the Eschatological Temple Foundation Was Seen as Messianic* 169
4.4 Matt 7:24–27 Portrays the Disciples as Messianic Temple Builders 172
    4.4.1 *The Prevalence of Temple Imagery* 174
    4.4.2 *The Possible Allusion to Isa 28 Would Support This Building Being the Temple* 176
    4.4.3 *The Connection to Matt 16:18 Suggests This Building Is the Temple* 177
4.5 Conclusion 178

5 Matthew's Non-Messianic Use of the Herald in Isa 61:1–3 180
5.1 Introduction 180
5.2 Ambiguities in the Original Context 181
5.3 Diversity in Relevant Jewish Literature 186
    5.3.1 *Sirach 48* 186
    5.3.2 *Tg Isa 61:1* 187

     5.3.3   *Tg Num 25:12*   188
     5.3.4   *1QH^a 23:14–15*   189
     5.3.5   *11Q13 2:9*   190
     5.3.6   *4Q521*   192
     5.3.7   *Luke 4:16–30*   194
     5.3.8   *Luke 7:22*   197
  5.4 The Contexts of Matthew's Uses Do Not Suggest an Exclusively Messianic Hermeneutic   198
     5.4.1   *Matt 5:3–4*   198
     5.4.2   *Matt 11:5*   207
  5.5 Conclusion   211

6 **Conclusion**   213
  6.1 Variety within the Case Studies Reveals Matthew's Overall Hermeneutic   213
  6.2 Matthew's Hermeneutic May Occur Elsewhere   216
  6.3 The Case Studies Demonstrate "Messianic" Should Be Stretched to "Eschatological"   216
  6.4 Possible Explanations   217

Bibliography   221
Modern Author Index   249
Subject Index   254
Ancient Sources Index   256

Acknowledgments

The following volume comes from my PhD thesis at Trinity College – Bristol / University of Aberdeen and benefited from the support of many. I would like to thank my wife, Anna, and my three children, Griffith, Bonnie, and Freda for lovingly cheering me on. Your devotion and faith in me have been a gift from God and a constant source of strength. I am also thankful for my parents, Terry and Sandra Henning, who have faithfully supported and encouraged me in this research project. The fellowship of my home assemblies, Curtis Gospel Chapel and Carriage Hill Bible Chapel, have also been inspirational. Moody Theological Seminary and Emmaus Bible College have been an immense help in providing resources. My advisor Professor John Nolland, as well as my secondary advisor Dr. David Turner, deserve many thanks for insightfully and graciously providing feedback and stimulating my thinking. I praise God for you all and consider it an honor to be disciples together on the mission of our Lord and savior, Jesus Christ. To him be the glory.

References and Abbreviations

Translations are the author's, unless otherwise noted. Abbreviations follow Billie Jean Collins, Bob Buller, and John F. Kutsko, *The SBL Handbook of Style: For Biblical Studies and Related Disciplines*, 2d ed. (Atlanta: SBL, 2014) or occur as follows:

EGGNT	Exegetical Guide to the Greek New Testament
LBS	Linguistic Biblical Studies
NCBC	New Cambridge Bible Commentary
NIDNTTE	Silva, Moisés, ed. *New International Dictionary of New Testament Theology and Exegesis*. 5 vols. Grand Rapids: Zondervan, 2014
NIVAC	New International Version Application Commentary
NSBT	New Studies in Biblical Theology
PNTC	Pillar New Testament Commentary
ZECNT	Zondervan Exegetical Commentary on the New Testament

CHAPTER 1

Introduction

1.1 The Contribution of This Study

1.1.1 A Brief Summary of the Central Thesis

While commentators frequently observe Matthew's messianic use of non-messianic texts, attention must also be given to Matthew's non-messianic use of messianic texts. In other words, despite Matthew's often-noticed ingenuity for seeing the messiah in places modern interpreters do not detect any messianic elements, he strangely "misses low-hanging fruit" by passing on the opportunity to use seemingly messianic texts to inform his reader about Jesus' identity. My thesis examines some of these occurrences as case studies to demonstrate that Matthew's hermeneutical paradigm must be wider than Christology. Instead of his hermeneutic being narrowly messianic, in which texts from the Hebrew Bible function as unique identifiers of one person as *the* messiah, this research project argues Matthew's hermeneutic of fulfillment is better described as "broadly eschatological." This present work seeks to nuance the way Matthew's hermeneutic of fulfillment is understood by widening his interpretive paradigm from the common Christological "key" to one which, while allowing for the obvious significance of Christology, also accounts for other eschatological figures and themes. In other words, Matthean scholars have often proposed that the key to understanding Matthew's concept of fulfillment is the premise "Jesus is the messiah." The problem with this key is that it does not open enough doors. Instead, one which does unlock these same doors, as well as others, is the broader eschatological paradigm "The kingdom of heaven is at hand" (Matt 4:17).[1] The primary difference between these two approaches is that the former involves a one-to-one mapping of the scriptural figure (the messiah), whereas the latter allows the eschaton's actualization through a variety of figures, regardless if God (as the ultimate source) or any others as his agents (particularly Jesus and/or the disciples) are utilized, or indeed if agency is not in focus at all. The benefit of this latter paradigm is that it not only explains the messianic uses, but also the occasions in Matthew's

---

1 Unless otherwise noted, NT references are either my own translation or are from Barbara Aland et al., eds., *The Greek New Testament*, Fifth Revised Edition (Stuttgart, Germany: Deutsche Bibelgesellschaft, 2014).

Gospel which do not map agents to any particular figure or which map agents to figures besides Jesus, particularly the disciples.

I will argue for a "broadly eschatological" hermeneutic by examining four case studies in order describe Matthew's general hermeneutic, allowing for elements of variation and consistency in his approach. The first three of these cases surprisingly map a potentially messianic image or figure to the disciples (chapter 2 – eschatological shepherding; chapter 3 – eschatological vineyard workers; chapter 4 – concepts connected to eschatological temple building), while the last does not seem to pick up on the agent (chapter 5 – the eschatological herald) but emphasizes the results of the new age.[2] Thus, we should broaden the common description of Matthew's hermeneutic as "messianic" to the category "eschatological," as evidenced by references to texts often perceived as messianic and yet which do not map the messianic image to Jesus.

1.1.2 *The Importance of a Fulfillment Key in Matthew*

As an exploration of the way fulfillment works in Matthew, the current research touches a central nerve in Matthean studies. With more than double the quotations of other canonical gospels and hundreds of allusions,[3] the gospel of Matthew is distinguished in its extensive use of the Hebrew Scriptures. Though these references function in a variety of ways,[4] it is Matthew's fulfillment use,

---

2 However, we will see in chapter 5 that the potentially messianic image of the eschatological herald may be in view in Matthew's allusions to Isa 61, but this depends on the debated issue of the extent to which the surrounding context of a source text is meant to be significant for understanding the allusion. See 1.3.1.3 for further discussion.

3 John Nolland, *The Gospel of Matthew: A Commentary on the Greek Text* (NIGTC; Grand Rapids: Eerdmans, 2005), 29; Grant R. Osborne, *Matthew* (ZECNT; Grand Rapids: Zondervan, 2010), 38. David L. Turner, *Matthew* (BECNT; Grand Rapids: Baker Academic, 2008), 17 has a convenient chart based on UBS' index of quotations and index of allusions and verbal parallels, though this is far from exhaustive (e.g. Isa 61:1–3 in Matt 5:3–4 is absent).

4 Emerson Powery, *Jesus Reads Scripture: The Function of Jesus' Use of Scripture in the Synoptic Gospels* (BibInt; Leiden: Brill, 2003) examines the function of Jesus' use of Scripture as presented in the Synoptic gospels and categorizes them as either "literal," "accommodation," "modernizing," or "eschatological." Craig L. Blomberg, "Matthew" in *Commentary on the New Testament Use of the Old Testament*, ed. G. K. Beale and D. A. Carson (Grand Rapids: Baker Academic, 2007), 1–100 categorizes different uses of major citations and allusions. Nolland lists the following uses: "(1) to retell the OT story as context for the coming of Jesus; (2) to straightforwardly claim the fulfillment of previously unfulfilled prophecy (some texts are treated as specifically messianic) – sometimes Matthew achieves a concreteness of focus by finding significance in specific details; (3) to claim the eschatological fulfillment of prophecy that has thus far had only a partial and inadequate historical fulfillment (the line between this and the previous category is a blurred one); (4) to identify important biblical patterns as being reiterated in connection with Jesus; (5) to identify fundamental ethical principles of abiding significance; (6) to provide paradigms from the history of God's people which are

which claims an event of the gospel's narrative fulfills a previous scriptural text "fulfilled" that has attracted the bulk of scholarly consideration.[5] While not all agree with France's assessment that "the central theme of Matthew's gospel is fulfillment,"[6] clearly Matthew strongly emphasizes the subject. Whether or not it indicates the controlling idea of the gospel, Matthew's foregrounding of fulfillment in the first couple chapters with his now-famous quotation formulas sets the tone of the rest of the gospel.

However, though Matthew clearly concerns himself with the topic of fulfillment, the way the Scriptures come to find this fulfillment in the events of Matthew's narrative has often puzzled interpreters. In fact, of the early fulfillment texts in the first two chapters of Matthew, the one that has proven to be the simplest turns out to be Matt 2:5–6,[7] which the reader finds in the mouth of the primary antagonists in Matthew – the religious leaders of Israel! With such a complicated phenomenon lying within a major theme in one of the most discussed books of the New Testament, the disagreement among scholarship comes as no surprise. The explanations of how Matthew can come to his conclusions from the Old Testament fall into four categories. First, some argue that Matthew's seemingly bizarre use of the Scriptures demonstrates that he does not worry about their original meaning.[8] Second, on the opposite end

---

pertinent to the present situation (for Matthew the paradigmatic seems to shade into the prophetic, probably at times in terms of eschatological reiteration) ... (7) to appeal to an element of the ideal future that is promised in order to criticise the status quo; and (8) to locate a foundation in a divine self-declaration for arguing for a particular view" (*The Gospel of Matthew*, 36). My project is interested in uses (2), (3), and (6) which he notes are not discrete categories. In each of these senses the Scriptures are "fulfilled" in the events of Matthew's narrative.

5   For a review of the literature in the last quarter of the twentieth century, see Donald Senior, "The Lure of the Formula Quotations: Re-assessing Matthew's Use of the Old Testament with the passion Narrative as test case" in *The Scriptures in the Gospels*, ed. C. M. Tuckett (BETL; Leuven: Leuven University, 1997), 89–115. See also J. R. Daniel Kirk, "Conceptualizing Fulfillment in Matthew" *TynBul* 59.1 (2008): 77–98.

6   Richard T. France, *The Gospel of Matthew* (NICNT; Grand Rapids: Eerdmans, 2007), 10. This is most thoroughly articulated in his *Matthew: Evangelist and Teacher* (Grand Rapids: Zondervan, 1989), 166–205, where he calls fulfillment Matthew's "preoccupation" and "central focus of his theology" (166). Cf. his monograph *Jesus and the Old Testament: His Application of Old Testament Passages to Himself and His Mission* (Downers Grove, IL: InterVarsity Press, 1971).

7   Though it is introduced with γέγραπται and does not mention πληρόω, the result is the same.

8   E.g. Vernon McCasland, "Matthew Twists the Scriptures" *JBL* 80 (1961): 143–48; Lidija Novakovic, "Matthew's Atomistic Use of Scripture: Messianic Interpretation of Isaiah 53.4 in Matthew 8.17" in *Biblical Interpretation in Early Christian Gospels: Volume 2: The Gospel of Matthew*, ed. Thomas R. Hatina (LNTS; London: T&T Clark, 2008), 147–62 who points to the originator as Henry J. Cadbury, "The Titles of Jesus in Acts," in *The Beginnings of Christianity,*

of the spectrum some argue that Matthew's uses are not in fact strange and that his usage can be discovered from an exegesis of the original text.[9] Third, and more moderately, some advocate Matthew pointing back to the original intention of the Scripture, but that he reveals not the human author's intention, but the *sensus plenior* of the divine author.[10] A fourth perspective, which is similar though distinguishable from the third, sees Matthew's use as differing from the original meaning without making recourse to a hidden divine intention, and yet allows for no violence to be done to the original meaning since the language of "fulfillment" indicates that the referent in the OT text functions as a type or figure of the event in Matthew's narrative.[11]

As widely as these positions differ, they all recognize that Matthew has some underlying agenda. In views 1, 3, and 4, Matthew's hermeneutical key informs him of the significance of the passages in question. Yet even the second view, which sees Matthew's use as revealed in the exegesis of the original text, does not necessarily exclude Matthew from "reading backwards" so as to assure that his "exegesis" arrives where he knows it should. In other words, even if we are to think of Matthew doing "exegesis" as he reads the First Testament, we are still left with the question of why he chooses to incorporate the Scriptures he does. In the second view, Matthew's underlying hermeneutical paradigm does not work as a key to unlock otherwise hidden meanings of the text, but as a sieve which allows him to sift through Old Testament texts to find the ones relevant for his Gospel. Thus, though views three and four dominate the current

---

ed. F. J. F. Jackson and K. Lake (London: Macmillan, 1933), 369–70; Morna D. Hooker, *Jesus and the Servant: The Influence of the Servant Concept of Deutero-Isaiah in the New Testament* (London: SPCK, 1959).

9   E.g. John H. Sailhamer, *The Meaning of the Pentateuch: Revelation, Composition, and Interpretation* (Downers Grove, IL: InterVarsity, 2010); Walter C. Kaiser Jr., *The Uses of the Old Testament in the New* (Eugene, OR: Wipf and Stock, 2001).

10 E.g. William Lasor, "Prophecy, Inspiration, and *Sensus Plenior*," *TynBul* 29 (1978): 49–60; Donald A. Carson "Matthew" in *The Expositor's Bible Commentary: Vol. 8*, ed. Frank E. Gaebelein (Grand Rapids: Zondervan, 1984), 92; Douglas J. Moo and Andrew David Naselli, "The Problem of the New Testament's Use of the Old Testament" in *The Enduring Authority of the Christian Scriptures*, ed. Donald A. Carson (Grand Rapids: Eerdmans, 2016), 702–46 (who advocates *sensus plenior* along with a canonical approach).

11 E.g. "Typological fulfillment is neither allegory nor *sensus plenior*, and in contrast to predictive fulfillment, it does not necessarily maintain that the prophet is looking into the distant future and prophesying about something outside his own historical context. Rather, typological fulfillment in the life of Jesus refers to the *fullest expression of a significant pattern of events*" (James M. Hamilton Jr., "'The Virgin Will Conceive': Typological Fulfillment in Matthew 1:18–23" in *Built Upon the Rock: Studies in the Gospel of Matthew*, ed. Daniel M. Gurtner and John Nolland (Grand Rapids: Eerdmans, 2008), 233, emphasis original; Cf. Kirk, "Conceptualizing Fulfillment in Matthew," 77–98).

ideological landscape and represent the approach of this current work,[12] *all* perspectives acknowledge some aspect in which Matthew's interpretation somehow involves a hermeneutical paradigm.

The above perspectives can be illustrated by considering the famously complicated use of Hos 11:1 in Matt 2:15. The first view argues that Matthew does not care or does not know that Hos 11 is about the historical exodus. Matthew takes Hos 11:1 out of context to make his point. The second view seeks to demonstrate that the original context of Hos 11 does indeed concern the future restoration Matthew describes, so that Matthew actually cites the original meaning of Hos 11.[13] The third view sees Hos 11 as having two meanings since it ultimately comes from two authors – human and divine. Matt 2:15 refers to the fuller meaning intended by God for a later fulfillment. The fourth view argues that Matthew only recognizes one meaning of Hos 11 – the historical exodus – but he sees this as prefiguring Matthew's concerns. However, all of these positions see Matthew reading Hos 11 with the agenda of looking for information about the messiah, and thus can be classified as a Christological hermeneutic.

1.2 Significance of This Thesis in Matthean Studies and Its Relationship to Current Trends

1.2.1 *Generalizing Matthew's Hermeneutical Paradigm*
Since Jesus occupies the center stage of Matthew from beginning to end, readers should expect that the fulfillment motif has much to say about his identity, particularly as he is proclaimed in the first verse, Χριστοῦ υἱοῦ Δαυὶδ υἱοῦ Ἀβραάμ. These two themes – fulfillment and Christology – so overlap that many propose the latter as the foundation for the former. An underlying assumption that Jesus is, for example, the typological fulfillment of Israel or David, does make Matthew's seemingly bizarre use of the OT understandable. Several scholars emphasize that Matthew views the Scriptures as being fulfilled in the events of his narrative because of his conviction that Jesus is the messiah. For example, France asserts Matthew's Christocentric hermeneutic thus,

---

12 Though position four seems slightly more likely than three, this will not affect this current research project.
13 E.g. Michael Shepherd, *A Commentary on the Book of the Twelve: The Minor Prophets* (Grand Rapids: Kregel Academic), 94–95; John H. Sailhamer, "Hosea 11:1 and Matthew 2:15" *WTJ* 63 (2001): 87–96.

> It is, I believe, precisely the thorough-going nature of Matthew's conviction that in Jesus all God's purposes have come to fulfillment which has led him to use the text in the subtle ('artificial'?) way that we find in the formula-quotations, and to search for aspects of 'fulfillment' in texts which would seem to the modern interpreter to have no reference beyond their original historical setting.[14]

Luz agrees,

> The center of the fulfillment is the word πληρόω. It is a "christological" word. Apart from the story of Jesus there is no "fulfillment" of the scriptures in the entire NT (with one exception). For the evangelist πληρόω is also important outside our quotations. Just as Jesus has "fulfilled" the prophetic predictions by his life, he has also fulfilled the Law and Prophets by his perfect obedience (5:17; cf. 3:15). Thus Matthew programmatically emphasizes the fulfillment of the entire Bible by Jesus' story and behavior.[15]

Carlston and Evans follow this same trajectory,

> Matthew understands Jesus in continuity with Judaism, its Scripture and its history. Jesus is seen as 'fulfilling' the foundations of Judaism, at least as those foundations are rightly understood ... So far as it is 'prophecy,' it is fulfilled in the teaching, career, and person of Jesus ... All three strands – Law, Prophecy, and Wisdom – are Christologically understood.[16]

Most recently, Schreiner states

> The term πληρόω should thus be understood in an eschatological sense: Jesus becomes all that the Law and Prophets have pointed to. He is the terminus, the telos of the Scriptures ... All of the promises made in the OT, all of the predictions spoken, are now 'filled up' in Jesus Christ. He fulfills the Law and the Prophets by becoming the one to whom the Law

---

14 France, *Matthew: Evangelist and Teacher*, 182.
15 Ulrich Luz, *Matthew 1–7: A Commentary on Matthew 1–7* (Hermeneia; Minneapolis, MN: Fortress Press, 2007), 130.
16 Charles E. Carlston and Craig A. Evans, *From Synagogue to Ecclesia* (WUNT; Tübingen: Mohr Seibeck, 2014), 333–34.

and Prophets point. Jesus is the end of the law, the satisfaction of all of Israel's history.[17]

To be sure, scholars vary in their descriptions of this hermeneutic, but many see Christology, for various reasons, as the key which unlocks Matthew's use of the First Testament.[18] One can clearly see how this Christological emphasis arises from the so called "fulfillment-quotations" in Matthew as these redactions to Mark all emphasize the person and ministry of Jesus.[19] An impressive line of scholars stands behind this approach with convincing arguments. This present study argues not that the above is incorrect, but that it is incomplete. A wider approach that accounts for all the data is in order. An eschatological hermeneutic is here proposed since it allows for the messianic uses as well as those exemplified in this research's case studies.

1.2.2 The Overlap of Matthew's Ecclesiological and Messianic Hermeneutic

The current trends emphasizing Christology do not always exclude ecclesiological interests. On the one hand, the very fact that the story of the Scriptures

---

17 Patrick Schreiner, *Matthew, Disciple and Scribe: The First Gospel and Its Portrayal of Jesus* (Grand Rapids: Baker Academic, 2020), 39. Schreiner seems to equate "eschatological" with "Christological" here. This often happens in the literature, but our examination of the subject requires differentiating the terms.

18 The literature is vast. Notable treatments include Georg Strecker, *Der Weg der Gerechtigkeit: Untersuchung zur Theologie des Matthäus* (FZPhTh; Göttingen: Vandenhoeck & Reuprecht, 1971), 82–85; Robert H. Gundry, *The Use of the Old Testament in St. Matthew's Gospel, With Special Reference to the Messianic Hope* (NovTSup; Leiden: Brill, 1967), 208–15; Willhelm Rothfuchs, *Die Erfüllungszitate des Matthäus-Evangeliums: Eine biblische-theogische Untersuchung* (BWANT; Stuttgart: Kohlhammer, 1969), 89–133; Richard S. McConnell, *Law and Prophecy in Matthew's Gospel: The Authority and Use of the Old Testament in the Gospel of St. Matthew* (Basel: Friedrich Reinhardt, 1969), 133–38; Barnabas Lindars, *New Testament Apologetic: The Doctrinal Significance of the Old Testament Quotations* (London: SCM Press, 1961), 259–56; Richard Beaton, *Isaiah's Christ in Matthew's Gospel* (SNTSMS: Cambridge: Cambridge University Press, 2002), 86–121; Jean Miller, *Les citations d'accomplissement dans l'Évangile de Matthieu: Quand Dieu se rend present en toute humanité* (AnBib; Rome: Editrice Pontificio Instituto Biblico, 1999). A discussion of these variations is not necessary for our research and would be repetitious. For a discussion of the variations of this Christocentric hermeneutic in Matthew, see Nicholas Piotrowski, *Matthew's New David: A Socio-Rhetorical Study of Scriptural Citations* (NovTSup; Leiden: Brill, 2016), 5–8. Others see Christology as the purpose of the references to Scripture, but do not describe this as a key. Instead, they claim the original intention of the referred-to text was to predict the messiah ("view 2" described above).

19 Senior, "Lure," 86–115 rightly points out that undue attention should not be given to these, though he concludes that other uses essentially fit the same paradigm.

lines up in such a way that they climax with Jesus means that Matthew and his community inherit the Bible *vis-a-vis* their competitors.[20] Moreover, Matthew often uses Scripture in such a way that Jesus' followers correspond to Israel and inherit her promised blessings.[21] Though scholars debate the exact relationship between Israel and Jesus' followers, few would deny that the references to the OT somehow link Jesus' followers with Israel.

Though treatments of Matthew's fulfillment motif have explored how this informs his Christology and Ecclesiology, investigation of how these themes converge has been wanting. Piotrowski's recent monograph explores the overlap between Christology and Ecclesiology in Matthew's use of Scripture and argues that Matthew's early quotation formulas provide information about Jesus' followers. His perception of the lacunae in this significant theme in Matthean scholarship warrants being cited at length. Speaking of the benefit of looking into the formula quotations for Christological matters, he raises his concern thus,

> There appears to be a tacit agreement that Matthew's use of the OT, most explicitly in his formula-quotations, is primarily and nearly exclusively meant to support his Christology. Yet despite the great deal of attention paid to Matthew's use of the OT, not all the data can be explained in christological terms. Christology alone does not seem to be a sufficiently broad enough category ... There seems to be another function, broader than yet encompassing christological concerns for the formula quotations ... The actual ecclesiological *content*, not just the ecclesiological usage, of these quotations has been overlooked. The question also remains as to what *effect* the content of these specific texts likely had on Matthew's first audience. Do they traditionalize and legitimize the rest of Matthew's ecclesiological vision, or do they, themselves, in what they affirm, *contribute* to Matthew's ecclesiological vision?[22]

---

20 E.g. Luz, *Matthew*, 1:130, "Matthew, the Jewish Christian, whose community has intensively suffered through the separation from Israel, emphasizes the Jesus community's fundamental claim to Israel's Bible." J. Andrew Overmann, *Matthew's Gospel and Formative Judaism: The Social World of the Matthean Community* (Minneapolis: Ausburg, 1990), 74 affirms the same thought but is more concerned to place Matthew within Judaism.

21 E.g. France, *Jesus and the Old Testament*, 60–67. So also Richard B. Hays, *Echoes of Scripture in the Gospels* (Waco, TX: Baylor, 2016) in which each chapter considers the use of the Old Testament in reference to Israel, Christ, and the Church.

22 Piotrowski, *Matthew's New David*, 10–11, emphasis original.

INTRODUCTION

Piotrowski is on to something. This present study strongly agrees that "Christology alone does not seem to be a sufficiently broad enough category." Along with Piotrowski, this study adds an "amen" to there being significant overlap between ecclesiological and christological matters in Matthew's use of the Old Testament. Moreover, the fuzzy line between these two concerns in Matthew extends farther than to what Piotrowski finds. In the above-cited section, he finds reason for looking to ecclesiological matters because "a few of the quotes were not recognized in the first century to be messianic."[23] But we will shortly see (1.2.3) that Matthew sees great continuity and overlap between Jesus and his disciples, so why assume that passages traditionally understood as messianic uniquely map to Jesus?

This study examines times when First Testament texts are evoked which were easily seen as messianic, as indicated by their original context and/or their history of interpretation. Surely these would have been seen as likely candidates to provide Matthew support for his theology that Jesus is the fulfillment of Israel's long-awaited hopes of a coming messiah. However, several of these traditionally messianic texts do not serve such a function in Matthew. Instead, Matthew evokes these passages for other purposes. When the messianic image gets mapped in Matthew, sometimes the target is surprisingly Jesus' disciples. Sometimes, Matthew picks up a messianic figure from the Old Testament – and the mapping does not clearly land anywhere. The passage's use as a messianic 'prooftext' seems to be of no interest.

1.2.3   *The Effect of Matthew's Theology of Discipleship on His Hermeneutic*

Matthew's centerpiece is the person of Jesus and his unique status as the messiah and son of God. However, some Matthean scholars claim that Ecclesiology also stands at the center of the gospel. These two themes are hardly mutually exclusive. Much of Matthean scholarship focuses on commitment and learning by the disciples, especially as a paradigm for later followers.[24] Especially with its long ethical instruction in chapters 5–7 and description of community life in chapter 18, we can easily see Matthew as presenting a "manual for discipleship."[25] But this should not overshadow the fact that the disciples are described as having a (unique?) role with significant privileges and responsibilities. Meier plausibly suggests that Jesus drew his understanding of

---

23   Piotrowski, *Matthew's New David*, 10.
24   E.g. Ben Cooper, *Incorporated Servanthood: Commitment and Discipleship in the Gospel of Matthew* (London: Bloomsbury, 2013); Stephen C. Barton, *Discipleship and Family Ties in Mark and Matthew* (SNTSMS; Cambridge: Cambridge University Press, 1994); Jeannine K. Brown, *The Disciples in Narrative Perspective* (Leiden: Brill, 2002).
25   Nolland, *Gospel of Matthew*, 21.

discipleship from the Elijah-Elisha narrative,[26] meaning that the disciples not only learn from Jesus but are also being trained to carry on his mission.[27]

Moreover, Jesus' role and the role of the disciples highly overlap. This can be seen even with a cursory reflection on several of Jesus' significant functions in Matthew – forgiving, teaching, healing, exorcising, ruling – all of which are all shared with the disciples. They too are called to forgive (e.g. Matt 18:15–20), teach (28:19–20; cf. 16:19?), heal and exorcise (10:1), and even rule (19:28). Though Wilkins rightly concludes that the focus of discipleship in the ancient world "was not upon 'learning,' or upon being a 'pupil,' but upon adherence to a great master" he then qualifies this by saying "μαθητής carried the general / technical associations of adherent, with the type of discipleship determined by the one leading."[28] As described in Matthew, the "type of discipleship," even at a cursory overview, involves participating in many of the same activities. Moreover, the readers' awareness of the overlap between Jesus' role and that of the disciples continues to increase as attention is paid to a closer reading of Matthew. Others have noticed this before. Dodd, for example, writes, "In primitive Christian messianic doctrine, then, there are these two inseparable moments: the Messiah is identified with the People of God as their 'inclusive

---

26   John P. Meier, *A Marginal Jew: Volume 3: Companions and Competitors* (ABRL; New York: Doubleday, 2001), 44–49. Cf. Josephus *Ant.* 8:354. See also Paul R. Trebilco, *Self-Designations and Group Identity in the New Testament* (Cambridge: Cambridge University Press, 2002), 224. Elisha being Elijah's disciple is similar to how Josephus describes Joshua as a disciple of Moses (*Ant.* 6:84).

27   The missional aspects of discipleship in Matthew can be seen regardless of one's view of the relationship between Jesus' followers and Israel. However, a post-supersessionist perspective particularly highlights this aspect. For example, "If the transfer of God's βασιλεία means the disciples are entrusted with the task of conveying God's will to humanity (cf. 16.19; 28.20) and thus of guiding people to the kingdom of heaven, the missionary task of the community also comes into view here. With regard to 12.46–50, it is further to be observed that this is not just about distinguishing the disciples from the crowds; rather, the disciples are more specifically presented before the forum of the ὄχλοι as the family of Jesus and thereby as models to the ὄχλοι. In the missionary perspective outlined here, the Church does not appear as an entity that enters into competition with Israel. Rather, the Church relates to Israel positively in its missionary task" (Matthias Konradt, *Israel, Church, and Gentiles in the Gospel of Matthew*, transl. Kathleen Ess (Waco, TX: Baylor, 2014), 331–32).

28   Michael Wilkins, *Discipleship in the Ancient World and Matthew's Gospel*, 2d ed. (Eugene, OR: Wipf and Stock, 2015), 220. Similarly, Terence L. Donaldson argues "The distinctive character of discipleship for Matthew is determined by (1) the person to whom disciples give their allegiance and (2) the nature of the relationship established between disciples and teacher" ("Guiding Readers – Making Disciples: Discipleship in Matthew's Narrative Strategy" in *Patterns of Discipleship in the New Testament*, ed. Richard Longenecker (Grand Rapids: Eerdmans, 1996), 33).

representative': he is set over against the People of God as sovereign Lord."[29] But the most thorough investigation of this concept in Matthew remains Kynes' monograph, *A Christology of Solidarity*.[30] Space does not allow for a full discussion of his book, but we can consider two exemplary insights to cement the connection between Jesus and his disciples as a significant theme in Matthew.[31]

After discussing the application of promises to Israel to both Jesus and the disciples in the Sermon on the Mount, Kynes concludes

> As the light of the world, as the city on a hill, and as those who can call God 'Father,' the new community of the kingdom is described in terms reminiscent of those used of Israel. But significantly, in each of these cases the disciples come to share in a position which already belonged to their Master, for he himself was the light shining into a dark world (cf. 4:15, 16), the ideal representative of a restored Israel (cf. especially 3:1–4:11), and the true Son of God (3:17–4:11). Thus, *the identity of the disciples is grounded in that of Jesus himself; and only through their relationship with him do they participate in the role of Israel*.[32]

However, the conclusion that the Sermon on the Mount presents Jesus as the avenue through which the disciples can inherit Israel's blessings is not clear from the text itself. A simpler explanation would focus on the announcement of the kingdom's arrival (4:17). This entails the fulfillment of the prophets' long-awaited promises which from several eschatological texts benefit only an "Israel within Israel." Still, Kynes' overall point that Matthew transfers the same

---

29   Charles H. Dodd, *According to the Scriptures: The Sub-Structure of New Testament Theology* (London: Nisbet, 1952), 121.

30   William L. Kynes, *A Christology of Solidarity: Jesus as the Representative of His People in Matthew* (Lanham, MD: University Press of America, 1991). Furthermore, the connection between the messiah and his people is often discussed in relation to the son of man in Dan 7, where this figure maps לְעַם קַדִּישֵׁי עֶלְיוֹנִין (v 27).

31   Regarding his Matthean scope, Kynes writes "We have not attempted to demonstrate the *distinctiveness* of Matthew's christology, but have sought to show only that this representative role is a part of his presentation. Placing the evangelist's christology in its broader New Testament context suggest itself as a possible area of further research" (*Christology of Solidarity*, 4). The same approach is advocated in this project.

32   Kynes, *Christology of Solidarity*, 55–56, emphasis added. He concludes regarding the concept of sonship on pg 195, "Jesus is the Son of God, but his disciples, too, become sons of the Father: twenty times in Matthew (only once in Mark; four times in Luke) Jesus refers to God as the Father of his disciples. Furthermore, this filial relationship with God is predicated *only* of Jesus' disciples. Suggesting a connection between Christology and discipleship: those who become disciples of the Son of God share in his relationship with the Father" (emphasis original).

imagery for Israel to both Jesus and his disciples strongly illustrates the overlap presumed between the two.

Kynes' discussion of the disciples' miracles powerfully demonstrates the commonality between Jesus and his disciples. His explanation of Peter walking on the water in chapter 14, though it has not influenced subsequent literature, seems convincing. He explains

> The logic of the request, then, assumes an understanding on the part of the disciples that they are to share in Jesus' authority and miracle-working power. Peter acts on this assumption and, in faith, steps out of the boat at Jesus' bidding. His temporary success in v. 29 demonstrates that his conviction is well-grounded. The figure who appeared on the sea is the same Lord who had given his disciples authority to cast out demons and to heal (10:1) and power to perform miracles (δυνάμεις) in his name (cf. 7:22). The lesson of the loaves, that Jesus could enable his disciples to carry out his commands, is grasped by Peter in a spectacular way.[33]

This explanation not only has the advantage of taking the bestowal of authority in 10:1 seriously, but it also addresses the often-neglected question of why Peter's question follows his realization that it is Jesus walking on the water. Peter's logic is εἰ σὺ εἶ, κέλευσόν με ἐλθεῖν (14:28) and this presumes that he shares, to some extent, in the miraculous abilities present in Jesus. Moreover, this may also explain Jesus' frustration (Τί δειλοί ἐστε, ὀλιγόπιστοι; in 8:26) and similar times when Jesus expects them to do the miraculous (e.g. δότε αὐτοῖς ὑμεῖς φαγεῖν in 14:16).

This overlap of the responsibility of the disciples with that of Jesus is a common feature in Matthew's gospel. Discipleship entails being "yoked" with Jesus (cf. 11:28–30), which suggests an intimate connection and unity in work.[34] The Matthean Jesus puts it simply, ἀρκετὸν τῷ μαθητῇ ἵνα γένηται ὡς ὁ διδάσκαλος

---

33 Kynes, *Christology of Solidarity*, 70. He is not alone in this interpretation, however. He quotes A. Schlatter, *Der Evangelist nach Matthaus* (Regensburg: Pustet, 1959), 470–71, "Indem auch Petrus ermachtigt wird, das Schiff zu verlassen und sich neben Jesus zu stellen, wird freilich gesagt, dass auch der Junger an der Macht Jesu Anteil habe. Jesus verdeutlicht den Jungern nicht nur an sich selbst die allmachtige Gegenwart Gottes und sieht darin nicht einen ihm allein gegebenen Besitz, den er eifersuchtig zu huten habe. Vielmehr wird das Verlangen des Jungers erfullt und er soll da stehen, wo Jesus steht."

34 The OT and Apocrypha do not speak of yoking animals together, so the idea in Matt 11:29 may not be a connection alongside of Jesus. However, if this is the case, a unity of purpose would nonetheless still be in view.

INTRODUCTION 13

αὐτοῦ καὶ ὁ δοῦλος ὡς ὁ κύριος αὐτοῦ (10:25). This current project argues that this overlap is so central to Matthew's thinking that it has affected his hermeneutic.

1.2.4   *Matthew's General Approach as Broadly Eschatological*
Others have examined the phenomenon of Jesus' followers fulfilling a prediction traditionally reserved for the messiah. Two recent examples deal with this topic explicitly. Quek discusses the application of Ps 2:8–9 in Rev 2:26–27, arguing that "it is the messianic understanding of the psalm that allows it to be applied to the corporate body of believers."[35] He argues that Rev 2 functions similarly to 4Q174 3:18–21 where the singular "anointed one" of Ps 2:2 is interpreted as "the chosen ones of Israel." After discussing the inadequacy of the "corporate solidarity" paradigm,[36] he argues instead this phenomenon results from the nature of the Davidic covenant as providing corporate protection. Quek's analysis intriguingly offers parallels to Rev 2:26–27 to show this is not a unique phenomenon and wisely avoids "corporate solidarity." However, though the explanation from the Davidic covenant is plausible in the cases he examines (since Ps 2 has resonances of 2 Sam 7), it lacks sufficient explanatory power to account for this phenomenon when a connection to 2 Sam 7 is more remote or non-existent. An explanation that addresses the many times this situation occurs in various contexts would be preferable. The current research examines Matthean texts, but the broad approach may work for other texts as well.

Beers' recent monograph also studies this phenomenon, by exploring both citations and allusions to the "servant" of Isa 40–66 in Luke-Acts.[37] She concludes that Luke

---

[35]   Tze-Ming Quek, "'I will give Authority over the Nations': Psalm 2.8–9 in Revelation 2.26–27" in *Early Christian Literature and Intertextuality: Volume 2: Exegetical*, ed. Craig A. Evans and H. Daniel Zacharias (LNTS; London: T&T Clark, 2009), 178.

[36]   The older concept of 'corporate solidarity' is widely rejected today. J. S. Kaminsky, *Corporate Responsibility in the Hebrew Bible* (Sheffield: Sheffield Academic, 1995), 1–29 reviews the history of the concept and A. Perriman, "The Corporate Christ: Re-assessing the Jewish Background," *TynBul* 50.2 (1999): 241–63 critiques the concept in application to the messiah. See also Raju D. Kunjummen, "The Things Concerning Himself, Beginning with Moses: The Messiah's Suffering and Subsequent Glory" in *Reflections from the Emmaus Road: Essays in Honor of John H. Fish III, David A. Glock, and David J. MacLeod*, ed. Franklin S. Jabini, Raju D. Kunjummen, and Mark R. Stevenson (Dubuque, IA: Emmaus Bible College, 2018), 175–76.

[37]   Holly Beers, *The Followers of Jesus as the 'Servant': Luke's Model from Isaiah for the Disciples in Luke-Acts* (London: T&T Clark, 2016).

appears to see the Isaianic servant as a composite figure (across chs. 40–66) and to sense both individual (i.e. of Jesus) and corporate (i.e. of the disciples) 'fulfillment' of it, portraying especially Jesus in the gospel in Isaianic terms (e.g. Isa 61.1–2 in Lk. 4.18–19), but also hinting narratively that the disciples will take up or continue Jesus' servant role. This singular-plural fluidity is not a contradiction in terms, for in Isaiah the most frequent use of servant imagery points to Israel, and Jesus' role as servant thus equals his enactment of faithful Israel's mission.[38]

This perspective meshes well with the current research. Beers' work explores texts which could easily have been viewed as messianic and yet Luke applies them non-messianically to Jesus' followers. However, besides focusing on a different gospel (and thus, at least potentially, a different hermeneutic of fulfillment), this current study considers non-messianic references to a variety of 'messianic' texts and images and thus argues that the phenomenon does not result from a peculiar way of understanding one idea or passage (or sets of passages – i.e. the "servant songs" or the "Davidic covenant"), but from a different overall method of how Scripture is understood to be fulfilled.

Thus, the above material has briefly sketched out major ways scholars have understood the complicated subject of fulfillment in Matthew. Virtually all rightly see Christology at the heart of not only Matthew but also its fulfillment motif. A subgroup also rightly stresses Ecclesiology within Matthew, with some interest in tying this to the explanation of fulfillment. This study seeks to push this conversation forward by demonstrating that the mapping schemes in Matthew are not as exclusively messianic as often claimed and that a wider approach (a broadly eschatological hermeneutic) better explains the data. Attention to a variety of case studies will reveal that this does not result from a peculiarity of the referred text, but comes from a more generalizable hermeneutical paradigm. Analyzing the data of these case studies with a concern for the relation of Christology, Ecclesiology, and eschatological fulfillment requires first setting forth a method of inquiry, to which we now turn.

1.3 Method

Establishing Matthew's broad eschatological hermeneutic involves examining several case studies, each of which rests upon the methodological presuppositions discussed here. Before exploring each of these significant components in

---

38 Beers, *Followers of Jesus*, 177.

some detail, the larger picture of how these pieces fit together can be briefly first summarized. The research in the case studies of this project roughly fit the following pattern: First, a passage is selected in which a non-messianic use of a potentially messianic text or image seems possible. By "messianic text" we will want to include both those passages which themselves point forward to the coming of an eschatological deliverer or ruler,[39] as well as passages which are understood this way in subsequent uses, even if messianic features are absent in the original text. If the same background text(s) or image(s) occur elsewhere in Matthew, we note those passages also and, in general, examine them after sufficiently treating the first occurrence via the following steps. This first step is relatively simple, only requiring knowledge of commonly proposed intertexts, and thus does not need elaboration in the following sections. Second, we will examine the intertextual background(s) to discover what Matthew might have desired to communicate to his audience. This requires looking into theories of intertextuality and allusion for the definition (1.3.1.1), identification (1.3.1.2), and function (1.3.1.3) of intertextual references. Third, relying on Watson's metaphor of a conversation, we will listen to different voices for how Matthew might have understood the text(s).[40] This involves some exegesis of the original source text, as well as a consideration of how the passage was understood by later interpreters, paying particular attention to how and when a messianic interpretation is taken. The approach of this current project seeks to avoid confusing Matthew's likely understanding of a passage with both modern exegesis of that passage as well as how other ancient interpreters took it. While these possible trajectories of interpretation must be noted, we must allow room for Matthew to align with or diverge from them. Fourth, we consider the Matthean text itself to see how Matthew 'interacts' with the voices from the previous step, particularly in regards to how he maps the potentially messianic figures. The exegesis of the Matthean text, besides utilizing more 'traditional' elements (grammatical analysis, consideration of historical and literary context, etc.), will also include aspects of narrative criticism, though occasionally redaction criticism is used as well. The examination of allusions and references to the First Testament will also incorporate a perspective from cognitive

---

39 Defining "messiah" is notoriously difficult. See Matthew Novenson, *The Grammar of Messianism: An Ancient Jewish Political Idiom and Its Users* (Oxford: Oxford University Press, 2017) for the most recent thorough discussion. However, we are only concerned with the way Matthew understands the term. While a precise definition is not fully agreed upon by scholars, the promised royal king who will deliver his people from their enemies, usher in the age of eschatological blessing, and rule over the people of God will suffice as a definition for our purposes.

40 Francis Watson, *Paul and the Hermeneutics of Faith*, 2d ed. (London: Bloomsbury, 2015).

linguistics for a more robust method of analyzing Matthew's intertextuality. Many elements of the above procedure are well known, but two matters call for elaboration – intertextuality (1.3.1) and cognitive linguistics (1.3.2).

1.3.1   *Intertextuality*
Interest in intertextuality and allusion theory greatly increased in biblical studies with Hays' *Echoes of Scripture in the Letters of Paul*[41] and since that bursting of the flood gates, studies in this field continue to rise with no signs of abating. Since the literature on methodology in this area has increased with such a wide variety of approaches advocated, space does not allow for a summary and evaluation of major positions, nor is repeating the well-done overviews found elsewhere necessary.[42] This research seeks to focus on the text and not become too distracted by debating method. Still, a brief justification of the definition, identification, and function of allusions utilized in this study will help track its argumentation.

1.3.1.1   Definition
Perri's definition of allusion from over 40 years ago continues to be cited in the literature and represents the approach taken in this work. She defines allusion as

> a conscious attempt on the author's part to remind readers of an earlier text, so that through their reflection on that text, the present author's meaning is enhanced in some way. In order for the allusion to be successful, the audience must *recognize* the sign, *realize* that the echo is deliberate, *remember* aspects of the original text to which the author is alluding, and *connect* one or more of these aspects with the alluding text in order to get the author's point.[43]

---

41   Richard Hays, *Echoes of Scripture in the Letters of Paul* (New Haven: Yale University Press, 1989).
42   For example, see the summaries in Kenneth D. Litwak, "Echoes of Scripture? A Critical Survey or Recent Works on Paul's Use of the Old Testament" *CRBS* 6 (1998): 260–88; Leroy A. Huizinga, "The Old Testament in the New, Intertextuality and Allegory" *JSNT* 28.1 (Sep 2015): 17–35; *Reading the Bible Intertextually*, ed. Richard B. Hays, Stefan Alkier and Leroy A. Huizenga (Waco, TX: Baylor, 2009), 3–34. Several different recent approaches are summarized in *Exploring Intertextuality: Diverse Strategies for New Testament Interpretation of Texts*, ed. B. J. Oropeza and Steve Moyise (Eugene, OR: Cascade, 2016) and *Practicing Intertextuality: Jewish and Greco-Roman Exegetical Techniques in the New Testament*, ed. B. J. Oropeza and Max Lee (Eugene, OR: Cascade, forthcoming).
43   Carmela Perri, "On Alluding" *Poetics* 7.3 (1978): 301, emphasis original. This definition uses "echo" synonymously with "allusion." Though some differentiate the two, this has not reached a consensus, so I will not make a distinction between them.

Two features of this definition warrant comment. First, Perri's mention of meaning being "enhanced *in some way*" is sufficiently vague to account for the wide uses of allusion encountered in biblical studies. For example, while not exhaustive (and perhaps overly formulaic), Beale recommends analyzing an author's use of the OT by placing it in one of *twelve* categories.[44] An allusion simply invites comparison of texts and interpreters must allow for a wide variety of effects from these comparisons. "*Enhanced* in some way" also accounts for the non-essential nature of allusions in creating surplus meaning. France creatively describes these as "bonus points" which are not necessary for understanding the primary thrust of an author.[45] In his inaugural volume to the "Through Old Testament Eyes" commentary series, Andrew Le Peau illustrates this feature with the film *Toy Story*'s allusions to *Star Wars*. He notes that though many miss these references, they are nonetheless present and add depth to the film.[46] The creators anticipate a wide variety of viewers and though many, particularly children, will not get the references, they can still follow the film's plot. The "bonus points" feature of allusions stems from their nature as indirect references and the assumed intention of an author to communicate necessary points overtly with an audience. A necessary reference, if the author wishes his whole audience to make the connection, would have to be made explicit with a direct reference. Moyise puts it simply, "it makes no sense to say that an author *intended* a particular meaning when she or he has withheld the information that would make such a meaning possible for the readers."[47] However, this approach assumes another feature of Perri's definition which is under debate, the locus of meaning for an allusion.

Perri's definition includes the author ("a conscious attempt on the author's part") as well as the reader (being successful means "the audience must

---

[44] They are: "Direct Fulfillment of Old Testament Prophecy"; "Indirect fulfillment of Old Testament Prophecy"; "Affirmation That a Not-Yet Fulfilled Old Testament Prophecy Will Assuredly Be Fulfilled in the Future"; "Analogical or Illustrative Use of the Old Testament"; "Symbolic Use of the Old Testament"; "Abiding Authority Carried Over from the Old Testament"; "Proverbial Use of the Old Testament"; "Rhetorical Use of the Old Testament"; "The Use of an Old Testament Segment as a Blueprint or Prototype for a New Testament Segment"; "Alternate Textual Use of the Old Testament"; "Assimilated Use of the Old Testament"; "Ironic or Inverted Use of the Old Testament." G. K. Beale, *Handbook on the New Testament Use of the Old Testament: Exegesis and Interpretation* (Grand Rapids: Baker, 2012), 55–94.

[45] Richard T. France, "The Formula-Quotations of Matthew 2 and the Problem of Communication," NTS 27.02 (1981): 233–251.

[46] Andrew T. Le Peau, *Mark Through Old Testament Eyes: A Background and Application Commentary* (Grand Rapids: Kregel, 2017), 14–15.

[47] Steve Moyise, *Evoking Scripture: Seeing the Old Testament in the New* (London: T&T Clark, 2008), 130, emphasis original.

recognize ... realize ... remember ... connect").[48] But some have contested an audience's ability to hear scriptural echoes. Christopher Stanley argues that emphasizing the audience of the New Testament diminishes the likelihood that they would detect intertextual usage beyond the explicit reference of the author since biblical texts were expensive and 80–90% were illiterate.[49] However, the situation does not appear to be as bleak as Stanley paints it.[50] The most significant observation concerning the audience and the ability to pick up biblical allusions is the importance of the repeated, communal nature of learning and teaching. One can easily expect Matthew's envisioned audience to have a wide range of understanding, and those who are "scribes discipled for the kingdom of heaven" can "bring out treasure" (Matt 13:52; cf. 28:18–20) for the less knowledgeable in the audience. Regardless of the debates concerning Matthew's relationship to Judaism,[51] he and his community clearly view themselves as committed to the abiding authority of the Scriptures (e.g. Matt 5:17) and we can safely assume that they would have continued to reread them as a source of guidance.[52] We can easily apply Watson's observation concerning

---

48 William Irwin, "What is an Allusion?" *Journal of Aesthetics and Art Criticism* 59.3 (2001): 289 describes three views: intentionalist, which he says is too strong since it does not leave room for failed allusions; internalist, which he says does not allow for audience's misunderstanding a coincidence; and hybrid, which is the view he advocates.

49 Christopher D. Stanley, *Arguing with Scripture: The Rhetoric of Quotations in the Letters of Paul* (New York: T&T Clark, 2004), 41, 44–45. His concern is with Pauline epistles, but these arguments can apply for Matthew with some modification.

50 Others give a higher literacy rate, e.g. Alan Millard, *Reading and Writing in the Time of Jesus* (Sheffield, Sheffield Academic Press, 2001), 154–84; John F. Sawyer, *Sacred Languages and Sacred Texts* (London: Routledge, 1999), 44–58. Also, the use of opisthographs and palimpsests would have made possession of literature much cheaper (Harry Y. Gamble, *Books and Readers in the Early Church: A History of Early Christian Texts* (New Haven: Yale, 1995), 231). Furthermore, there does seem to be a canon within a canon in the first century. Susan E. Docherty, "New Testament Scriptural Interpretation in its Early Jewish Context" *NovT* 57.1 (2015): 7 lists Genesis, Deuteronomy, Isaiah, and the Psalms. So, purchasing all of what is now identified as "The Hebrew Bible" is not necessary. Moreover, others have rightly stressed the role of orality and "oral texts" used by "illiterate" people. E.g. John H. Walton and D. Brent Sandy, *The Lost World of Scripture: Ancient Literary Culture and Biblical Authority* (Downers Grove, IL: IVP Academic, 2013); James D. G. Dunn, *Jesus Remembered: Christianity in the Making* (Grand Rapids: Eerdmans, 2003).

51 The view assumed in this research is that there was a significant amount of connection still with the synagogue and fits comfortably with Overmann, *Matthew's Gospel and Formative Judaism* and David Sim, *The Gospel of Matthew and Christian Judaism* (Edinburgh: T&T Clark, 1998). However, little of the research in this study rests on the view.

52 Stanley's point regarding the expense of manuscripts becomes even less potent depending on a community's emphasis on oral communication.

Paul to our situation.[53] Though we can imagine his conversion to Jesus was dramatic, no reason exists to suppose that Matthew,[54] like Paul, would have stopped being a reader and learner of Scripture, albeit from his perspective as a disciple of Jesus. Moreover, the nature of the Gospel of Matthew, both in its content and intricacy, strongly suggests that this is a document intended to be consistently reread, so much so that it has been argued that Matthew saw himself as writing Scripture.[55] The above observations go a long way in addressing the concern regarding the ability for Matthew's audience to pick up on indirect references to the First Testament. Subtle, or 'quiet,' allusions are entirely possible in Matthew since the author expects the referring text and referred-to text to be reflected upon deeply and continuously.

Others contest the view that an allusion must fit in the framework of an author communicating to an audience from concerns from literary criticism. Hays lists five possibilities for the locus of an echo: the author's mind, the readers, within the text itself, in one's own personal act of reading, and in a community of readers. He then states that his purpose is "hold them all together in creative tension."[56] This perspective continues throughout his recent work on allusions in the gospels ("the meaning of a text cannot be strictly delimited by the original intentions of the author"[57]) and suggest why his own criteria (discussed shortly) are used so infrequently in his own work. This approach has been criticized as generating fanciful readings which cannot be falsified.[58] In contrast, this project commits to viewing a valid allusion as one that was intended by the author for the audience, even if only part of the audience picks up on it or gradually apprehends it. The separation between a conscious

---

53 Watson, *Paul and the Hermeneutics of Faith*, xxv.
54 This statement assumes that the apostle Matthew wrote our gospel, but the argument would work as long as the author was committed to the continuing teaching role of Scripture (cf. 5:17–20).
55 Roland Deines, "Did Matthew Know He Was Writing Scripture?" (Parts 1 and 2) *EuroJTh* 22.2 (2013): 101–09; 23.1 (2014): 3–12.
56 Hays, *Echoes of Scripture in the Letters of Paul*, 26. Contra Stanley E. Porter, "Allusions and Echoes" in *As It Is Written: Studying Paul's Use of Scripture*, ed. Stanley Porter and Christopher Stanley (Atlanta: SBL, 2008), 36; Cf. H. Daniel Zacharias, "Matthew's Presentation of the Son of David: Davidic Tradition and Typology in the Gospel of Matthew" (PhD Dissertation; University of Aberdeen, 2015), 12–13.
57 Hays, *Echoes of Scripture in the Gospels*, 136. Cf. Richard B. Hays, *Conversion of the Imagination: Paul as Interpreter of Israel's Scripture* (Grand Rapids: Eerdmans, 2005), 169, 179.
58 E.g. Paul Foster, "Echoes without Resonance: Critiquing Certain Aspects of Recent Scholarly Trends in the Study of the Jewish Scriptures in the New Testament" *JSNT* 38.1 (2015): 96–111.

author's intent and his or her "latent meaning" or "willed type"[59] is not always clear, yet we should still see them as part of the "author's meaning," so long as they remain evident from the text. Thus, this study will see an allusion as an author's (allowing for his or her latent meaning and willed type, as embedded in the text) enhancement in some way (non-essential and without predefined expectations as to how the referring and referred-to text relate) of a text to a reader (allowing for a community of readers who are rereading both the referring and referred-to text and who are able to instruct one another).

1.3.1.2   Identification

Since an allusion is tied to the author's intention, the text he or she wrote, and what can be expected of the audience to eventually apprehend, how do interpreters know they have correctly identified an allusion and are not just seeing shapes of clouds in the sky? Though the detection of legitimate allusions remains more on the art side of exegesis than the science, attempts have still been made at constructing criteria for identifying allusion in a systematic way. Hays' influential *Echoes of Scriptures in the Letters of Paul* introduced the most well used.[60] Others critiqued them,[61] which led to Hays' later clarification.[62] Though scholars continue to call for more precise guidelines in assessing allusions,[63] Hays' criteria at this point nevertheless remain the most common and other approaches mostly reorganize Hays' original seven.[64]

The first criterion is *availability*. The scriptural echoes considered in the research is easily meet this test (see above on the nature of the audience),

---

59 For "latent meaning," see Mitchell Kim, "Respect for Context and Authorial Intention: Setting the Epistemological Bar" in *Paul and Scripture: Extending the Conversation*, ed. Christopher D. Stanley (Atlanta: SBL, 2012), 121. For "willed type," see E. D. Hirsch, Jr., *Validity in Interpretation* (New Haven: Yale Press, 1967), 24–67 and Douglas J. Moo, "The Problem of Sensus Plenior" in *Hermeneutics, Authority, and Canon*, ed. Donald A. Carson and J. D. Woodbridge (Grand Rapids: Zondervan, 1986), 189.

60 29–31.

61 *Paul and the Scriptures of Israel*, ed. Craig A. Evans and James A. Sanders (JSNTSup; Sheffield: Sheffield Academic, 1993); Stanley Porter, "The Use of the Old Testament in the New Testament: A Brief Comment on Methodology and Terminology" in *Early Christian Interpretation of the Scriptures of Israel: Investigations and Proposals*, ed. Craig A. Evans and James A. Sanders (JSNTSup; Sheffield: Sheffield Academic, 1997), 79–96.

62 *Conversion of the Imagination* (Grand Rapids: Eerdmans, 2005), 34–38.

63 E.g. Foster, "Echoes Without Resonance," 96–111 and Stanley E. Porter, "Allusions and Echoes" in *As It Is Written: Studying Paul's Use of Scripture*, ed. Stanley E. Porter and Christopher Stanley, [Atlanta: SBL, 2008], 29–40).

64 E.g. Christopher A. Beetham, *Echoes of Scripture in the Letter of Paul to the Colossians* (Leiden: Brill, 2008), 28; Brian J. Abasciano, *Paul's Use of the Old Testament in Romans 9.1–9: An Intertextual and Theological Exegesis* (London: T&T Clark, 2005).

INTRODUCTION 21

especially since we will consider biblical texts from well-known portions, such as Isaiah, Psalms, and Jeremiah. However, we will also consider the understanding of these passages in Second Temple texts and potentially later Jewish writings, particularly the Targums. We can be less certain if these texts were available to Matthew and his audience, especially those whose date comes later. What we might at first consider to be an allusion to Scripture might be better understood as an allusion to a later understanding of that passage. However, if we say the allusion is to the biblical text with the interpretation manifested in a later writer or if we say the allusion is to the text of the later writer will not ultimately make much difference.

We will not want to confuse modern exegesis of an OT text with what would have made sense to Matthew and his readers, and later interpretations may indicate the way Matthew would have understood the scriptural text. On the other hand, even if a use of a text in the history of interpretation post-dates Matthew or there is insufficient reason to think it was available to Matthew, examining these passages is still beneficial. Watson's metaphor of a conversation between Paul, Scripture, and other interpreters can easily be applied to Matthew. Other readings can highlight the similarities between a biblical author and his contemporaries. Watson writes "Through their common concern with the interpretation of scripture, Pauline and non-Pauline writings constitute a single intertextual field, rather than indicating an immediate 'parting of the ways' between two monolithic entities labelled 'Christianity' and 'Judaism.'"[65] Comparison with other Second Temple literature also helps identify ambiguities in the Scripture since it identifies areas of disagreement. To use Iser's terminology,[66] comparing Paul's interpretation with his contemporaries' locates the "gaps of meaning" between the text and reader. For our research, this means that we will often examine the "original"[67] scriptural context, see how other interpreters handled the passage to look for exegetical ambiguities, and then turn to Matthew to see his contribution to the discussion.

The issue of availability also raises questions about the nature of Matthew's scriptural text. Menken argues Matthew used a revised LXX which is closer to

---

65 Watson, *Paul and the Hermeneutics of Faith*, 527.
66 E.g. Wolfgang Iser, *Prospecting: From Reader Response to Literary Anthropology* (Baltimore: John Hopkins, 1989), 10. Though I find the terminology from this reader-response approach helpful, this does not indicate commitment to its ideological underpinnings.
67 By this I mean the biblical text as Matthew probably would have had it. We will not be concerned much with the history of original composition to canonical form.

the Hebrew.[68] Gundry argues Matthew uses the Hebrew.[69] When he seems to be taking from Mark, it appears that Matthew has retained that version.[70] Our analysis will not require one particular view here, especially since we are mostly concerned with allusions and not direct citations. Rather than assuming a position here, this study will consider both the MT and the LXX as possibilities and note relevant textual variants. If an argument depends on one variant reading over another, we will have to be relatively hesitant since we have not staked out a side on this debate.[71]

The second criterion in Hays' list is *volume*. This refers to the similarity between the referring text and the referred-to text. Hays clarifies that this refers to "the degree of verbatim repetition of words and syntactical patterns" and notes that it depends on the "distinctiveness, prominence, or popular familiarity of the precursor text."[72] He illustrates how the volume of an allusion may still be loud without a long section of text being repeated with the examples of "Our Father," or "self-evident truths" or "I have a dream."[73] The criterion of volume can be further nuanced with what Abasciano calls "contextual verbal coherence." By this he means "the presence of common vocabulary in the broader OT context – not just the verse alluded to – also heightens the likelihood that an allusion is present."[74] Moreover, volume can consist of conceptual repetition, though lexical repetition provides for greater volume.[75]

The third criterion is *recurrence / clustering*. An allusion is more likely if an author has already activated the source text in the reader's mind. If an author alludes to a text frequently, the probability that a proposed allusion to that same text is valid only increases. This criterion comes from a phenomenon called "priming." Bob Synder explains this as "a process whereby the recall of a particular memory causes the low-level activation of other associated

---

68 Maarten J. J. Menken, *Matthew's Bible: The Old Testament Text of the Evangelist* (Leuven: Peeters, 2004), 6–10, 279–83.

69 Robert Gundry, *The Use of the Old Testament in St. Matthew's Gospel* (Leiden: Brill, 1975), 147–85.

70 Maarten J. J. Menken, "Deuteronomy in Matthew's Gospel" in Deuteronomy in the New Testament, ed. Steve Moyise and Maarten J. J. Menken (LNTS; London: T&T Clark, 2007), 42–62. For a brief but convincing evaluation, see Nolland, *The Gospel of Matthew*, 29–33 and Piotrowski, *Matthew's New David*, 247–51.

71 For a similar approach, see W. J. C. Weren, *Studies in Matthew's Gospel: Literary Design, Intertextuality and Social Setting* (Leiden: Brill, 2014), 100.

72 Hays, *Conversion of the Imagination*, 35–36.

73 Hays, *Conversion of the Imagination*, 36.

74 Abasciano, *Paul's Use*, 29 n. 99.

75 Michael B. Thompson, *Clothed with Christ: The Example and Teaching of Jesus in Romans 12:1–15:3* (Eugene, OR: Wipf and Stock, 2011), 31.

memories (a context), without this process necessarily becoming conscious."[76] Once the readers' minds have started activating a text as significant, they are more likely to continue making connections to that text. Abasciano adds to this criterion what he calls "contextual allusive density."[77] The smaller the distance between the allusions to the same source, the greater the likelihood it will continue to be used. This criterion is only a positive test, however, and cannot be used negatively to deny a proposal since it is possible for an author to allude to a particular text only once.

The fourth criterion for determining the validity of an allusion is *thematic coherence*. Hays asks "Does the proposed precursor text fit together with the point Paul is making?" and then explains what this means for the purpose of his study, "Paul is not just randomly proof-texting in his allusions to Isaiah but that Isa 40–55 is fundamentally formative for his understanding of what God is doing in the world through the proclamation of the gospel: God is revealing his eschatological righteousness, ending the exile of his people, and bringing the Gentiles to see and understand."[78] As noted earlier, however, interpreters must allow for a variety of uses, even including contrastive allusions.[79] If we can identity an overall scheme to explain how Scriptures are used in a given text (e.g. Hays), this increases the likelihood that an allusion has been rightly detected. But the multifaceted ways a writer might incorporate a text warn against using this criterion negatively. This current study requires proceeding carefully with this principle and warns against assuming a particular transference scheme or how we might expect two texts to cohere. In considering passages which were often considered "messianic" the principle of thematic coherence could potentially suggest that these are only rightly evoked if the proposed messiah figure finds its fulfillment in Jesus. But this assumption is what is being called into question in the current study! We will often find that a potential allusion has expected thematic coherence in that it fits Matthew's eschatological fulfillment scheme, but that the connection between the messianic figure and the disciples is unexpected. This does not necessarily contradict the principle of thematic coherence. Instead, it challenges us to think afresh the paradigm of fulfillment.

---

76 Bob Snyder, *Music and Memory: An Introduction* (Cambridge, MA: MIT Press, 2000), 262, cited in Lundhaug, *Images of Rebirth*, 39.
77 Abasciano, *Paul's Use*, 29 n. 100.
78 Hays, *Conversion of the Imagination*, 38–40.
79 E.g. Craig A. Evans "Listening for Echoes of Interpreted Scripture" in *Paul and the Scriptures of Israel*, ed. Craig A. Evans and James A. Sanders (JSNTSup; London: Bloomsbury, 2015), 51 argues that when Paul inverts who the enemies of God are in his reference, he displays a biblical hermeneutic seen in Isa 28.

The fifth of Hays' criteria is *historical probability*. Here we are concerned with whether the resulting interpretation fits Matthew's context or if it is anachronistic. This is not to deny that the proposed reading might be new and diverge from other Second Temple literature since Matthew is not bound to simply reproduce earlier interpretations. Watson's metaphorical conversation helps us in this regard. We should not be surprised if there are times when Matthew nods his head in agreement with other interpreters in the conversation, but neither should we be surprised if Matthew speaks up in disagreement or with a new perspective. Still, if a reading would be highly unlikely for a Jewish believer in Jesus in the first century, the proposed allusion is likely eliminated.

Sixth, Hays presents the criterion of *the history of interpretation*. If early interpreters identified these same proposed echoes, this adds legitimacy to the proposal. However, Hays rightly warns that "The Christian tradition early on lost its vital connection with the Jewish interpretive matrix in which Paul had lived and moved; consequently, later Christian interpreters missed some of Paul's basic concerns."[80] Thus, later writers can confirm a proposal, but we should not require this for identification. Moreover, we can invoke Watson's metaphorical conversation here too. Though Matthew has much in common with other texts from Second Temple Judaism, there are obviously significant differences – but these do not prohibit the usefulness of the conversation. So too with other texts from the early church. Bates has rightly pointed out that the apostolic fathers often evidence the hermeneutic of NT writers.[81] While we can value the approach of reading Matthew as a Second Temple text,[82] we must at least extend the same courtesy to later Christian writers.

The seventh and last of Hays' criteria is *satisfaction* and gauges the extent to which "the resultant reading ... is clarified and enhanced by an awareness of the proposed intertexts."[83] However, while we can examine the other criteria in a preliminary fashion to establish the allusion before proceeding its analysis, we will only know if an allusion is satisfying after hearing the proposal in its entirety. As indicated by Perri's definition above, allusion is about enhancing an author's meaning. A proposed allusion's validity is proportionate to its ability to do just that.

---

80   Hays, *Conversion of the Imagination*, 43.
81   Matthew W. Bates, *The Hermeneutics of the Apostolic Proclamation: The Center of Paul's Method of Scriptural Interpretation* (Waco: Baylor: 2012).
82   E.g. Anders Runeson, *Divine Wrath and Salvation: The Narrative World of the First Gospel* (Minneapolis: Fortress, 2016).
83   Hays, *Conversion of the Imagination*, 44.

1.3.1.3 Function

Ben-Porat's often-cited description of an allusion describes it as "a device for the simultaneous activation of two texts ... [which] results in the formation of intertextual patterns whose nature cannot be predetermined."[84] By "activating" a text in addition to the one being written, an author invites comparison between the two. However, scholars debate the function of how the referred-to text relates to the referring text, especially regarding the role of the surrounding context of the referred-to text. Our previous discussion has explained the approach taken here that the author and audience can be expected to have had access to the source text. But would they have seen that surrounding context as providing significant insights for understanding how the allusion is to function? Currently a wide spectrum of positions on this issue exists in biblical studies. This study will lean toward the maximalist end which sees the context of the alluded-to text as highly significant, though the complexities are so involved that space does not allow for a thorough defense of this stance. Still, we can consider a summary of the two ends of this spectrum along with a brief evaluation.

On one side of the spectrum, some argue that NT writers have an atomistic use of Scripture, such as Hatina.[85] He argues against source-oriented approaches which pay careful attention to the exegesis of the referred-to text in allusions and citations.[86] He laments,

> Instead of focusing on the salient features of Mark' narrative, such as prominent themes and the plot, from which one might determine an interpretive paradigm, the source-oriented practitioner subverts this process by assuming that the hermeneutical key is to be found in Mark's exegesis of Scripture ... the preoccupation with cryptic or at least subordinate scriptural references renders this approach highly speculative.[87]

---

84   Ziva Ben-Porat, "The Poetics of Literary Allusion" *PTL* (1976): 105–28.
85   Other examples include Novakovic, "Matthew's Atomistic Use of Scripture"; Cadbury, "The Titles of Jesus in Acts," 369–70; Hooker, *Jesus and the Servant*; Donald Juel, *Messianic Exegesis: Christological Interpretation of the Old Testament in Early Christianity* (Philadelphia: Fortress Press, 1992); Peter Enns, *Inspiration and Incarnation: Evangelical and the Problem of the Old Testament*, 2d ed. (Grand Rapids: Baker Academic, 2015).
86   E.g. Rikki E. Watts, *Isaiah's New Exodus in Mark* (Grand Rapids: Baker, 1997); Joel Marcus, *The Way of the Lord: Christological Exegesis of the Old Testament in the Gospel of Mark* (SNTW; London: T&T Clark, 2004).
87   Thomas R. Hatina, *In Search of a Context: The Function of Scripture in Mark's Narrative* (JSNTSup; London: Sheffield, 2002), 46.

Not only does Hatina insist that priority must be given to the narratival aspects of a text, but he decries those who incorporate a source-oriented approach as one among many. According to Hatina, examining the referred-to text of an allusion or citation only detracts from where focus belongs – narrative criticism. He supports this view by drawing an analogy from lexicography, in which meaning is determined not by etymology but by usage.[88] Hatina argues further that "atomistic exegesis ... was the norm in early Jewish interpretation."[89] Furthermore, he points to the difficulty of knowing which elements of the referred-to context would be significant if they are not explicitly stated.[90] As we will see, another side to this debate has interacted with these concerns. Space does not allow for a full response, but relevant issues to consider in answering these objections would include intertextuality being an aid to (not replacement of) exegesis and narrative criticism; the effect of an allusion over against an explanation (the lexicography comparison proves too much – if only the new context matters then there is no purpose in signaling a text, even by citation, that comes from elsewhere); variation within Jewish hermeneutics and Instone-Brewer's study of the contextual awareness of the biblical authors;[91] and the difficulty and imprecision of knowing which elements in a source text are significant does not mean they are not used.

On the other side of the spectrum, some scholars argue that the NT greatly relies on the context of their OT references. We can take Hays as an example here.[92] Emphasizing NT authors' commitment to Scripture, he argues that the

---

88   Hatina, *In Search of a Context*, 2–3, 161.
89   Hatina, *In Search of a Context*, 42.
90   Hatina, *In Search of a Context*, 161.
91   See David Instone-Brewer, *Techniques and Assumptions in Jewish Exegesis before 70 CE* (TSAJ; Tübingen: Mohr Siebeck, 1992). However, Moyise, *Evoking Scripture*, 14 rightly observes that the contextual use he examines is not the same as modern historical-critical exegesis. For a response to the atomistic understanding in light of early Jewish techniques, see G. K. Beale, "Did Jesus and the Apostles Preach the Right Doctrine from the Wrong Texts? Revisiting the Debate Seventeen years Later in the Light of Peter Enn's Book *Inspiration and Incarnation*" *Them* 32.1 (Oct 2006): 18–43. The use of a metaphorical conversation with other Second Temple texts goes a long way in safeguarding that we are not assuming modern exegesis in considering the way the Matthean Jesus understood the source text.
92   His approach follows in the wake of Dodd, *According to the Scriptures*. Other examples of exegetes who see the wider context of a reference as highly significant include France, *Jesus and the Old Testament*; Douglas Moo, *The Old Testament in the Gospel Passion Narratives* (Sheffield: Almond Press, 1983); J. Ross Wagner, *Heralds of the Good News: Isaiah and Paul in Concert in the Letter to the Romans* (Leiden: Brill, 2003); Kaiser, *The Uses of the Old Testament*; G. K. Beale and D. A. Carson, eds., *Commentary on the New Testament Use of the Old Testament*, (Grand Rapids: Baker Academic, 2007).

most appropriate "encyclopedia of production"[93] is the Jewish Scriptures as opposed to Greco-Roman contexts. Citations, allusions, and echoes point an audience to reread the Scriptures to comprehend their significance in light of the coming of the messiah. Illustrated with the conversation on the road to Emmaus, Hays emphasizes that Jesus taught a new hermeneutic. Drawing on Hollander, he describes the significance of "metalepsis," defined as

> a literary technique of citing or echoing a small bit of a precursor text in such a way that they reader can grasp the significance of the echo only by recalling or recovering the original context from which the fragmentary echo came and then reading the two texts in dialogical juxtaposition. The figurative effect of such an intertextual linkage lies in the unstated or suppressed points of correspondence between the two texts.[94]

For Hays, a maximalist approach to context stems from two sources, one literary and the other theological. His proposal of metalepsis comes from both Jesus' new hermeneutic (i.e. Luke 24:25–27) as well as literary theory and his reliance upon Hollander and Hays' own examples. However, this dependence on a literary theory deemphasizes the control of the author (see discussion of Perri's definition above in 1.3.1.1). Those who advocate an author-centered approach to meaning should thus tread carefully as they borrow methodology from scholarship based on different presuppositions. However, the theological considerations for metalepsis have more merit since, as we have seen in 1.2.1, NT authors are highly interested in typology and fulfillment.

However, Hays goes too far in emphasizing the newness of the hermeneutic of Christ-followers. Though they come to different conclusions, they have much in common with other Second Temple interpreters and, according to the narratives in the canonical gospels and Acts, have enough similarities with unbelievers to effectively converse over the Scriptures. But Hays' most significant claim is that OT references function as metonymy, in which one small part is meant to represent the larger whole. We can grant that, since we are envisioning readers who continue to read both the OT and Matthew, eventually the referred-to text would be encountered in context and seen in light of its new explanation. However, the crux of the matter is how much of the OT context

---

93   This is from Umberto Eco, *Semeiotics and the Philosophy of Language* (Bloomington: Indiana University Press, 1986).
94   Hays, *Echoes of Scripture in the Gospels*, 11. Also called "transumption," Hays is pulling from John Hollander, *The Figure of Echo: A Mode of Allusion in Milton and After* (Berkeley: University of California Press, 1984), 133–49.

Matthew evokes (even if only latently) to understand and enhance his writing. Even with an approach more toward the maximalist end, the thorny matter of which elements of the referred to text are relevant for understanding an allusion still persists. One can contrast, for example, the use of Israel's history in *Wisdom of Solomon*, which is contextual in that it reflects on the larger narrative of the Pentateuch and yet significantly glosses over its record of the nation's moral failures,[95] with Paul's references to the same narrative, but which focuses on different details (e.g. Rom 9:6–13). The use of allusion results in "intertextual patterns whose nature cannot be predetermined"[96] and so we must be content with a certain amount of ambiguity and subjectivity and yet some method of constraint in knowing which elements of the surrounding source context is necessary.

To summarize our survey of central issues surrounding the identification and function of an allusion, we will see allusions as the following: purposeful devices left by the author which invite a variety of comparison to the referred to-text; identifiable by Hays' seven criteria with nuances and caveats included from others working in the field of allusion; and signals to consider the broader context of the referred-to text, though we will want to consider the history of interpretation to safeguard confusing our exegesis with what would have made sense to Matthew. Knowing how much of a referred-to text or its later interpretation are relevant for the allusion requires further attention. To this end, we will make use of the field of cognitive linguistics, especially Cognitive Metaphor Theory and Blending Theory. These fields require a discussion since their terminology and concepts are used throughout the study.

1.3.2 *Cognitive Linguistics*

Though our study of Matthean allusions to the OT will incorporate the above research from the field of intertextuality, we will also join with scholars who utilize insights and terminology from cognitive linguistics – Cognitive Metaphor Theory (AKA Conceptual Metaphor Theory) and especially Blending Theory (AKA Integration Network Theory). These concepts will give more precision to our discussion, but will not play a foundational role in the following study.[97]

---

95 See Watson, *Paul and the Hermeneutics of Faith*, 353 and John M. G. Barclay, *Paul and the Gift* (Grand Rapids: Eerdmans, 2015), 204 for a discussion of the significance of this omission.

96 Ben-Porat, "The Poetics of Literary Allusion," 108.

97 Examples of those who use Cognitive Metaphor Theory and Conceptual Blending in biblical studies include Bonnie Howe, *Because You Bear This Name: Conceptual Metaphor and the Moral Meaning of 1 Peter* (Leiden: Brill, 2006); Mary Therese DesCamp, *Metaphor and Ideology: Liber Antiquitatum Biblicarum and Literary Methods Through a Cognitive Lens*

The argument for an eschatologically broad hermeneutic from the following case studies can stand without reference to cognitive linguistics. But we will incorporate this field of study for its useful framework in thinking through the effects of an allusion on a text and its definitions will hopefully provide clarity and consistency. Readers who are eager to move on to the case studies or who are suspicious of attempts to mix exegesis with social sciences can move on to the next chapter and still capture the essence of the argument. However, I am persuaded that Conceptual Metaphor Theory, and particularly Blending Theory, can be a powerful tool in the hand of the biblical exegete, especially those concerned with issues of intertextuality.

1.3.2.1 Cognitive Metaphor Theory / Conceptual Metaphor Theory

The seminal work on conceptual metaphor within cognitive linguistics is Lakoff and Johnson's *Metaphors We Live By*,[98] which has spawned a movement with wide acceptance.[99] This approach has been so influential that Gerard Steen humorously states regarding the history of the study of metaphor, "in the beginning was Aristotle. Then there were the Dark Ages, which lasted until 1980. And then there was Lakoff ..."[100] Cognitive Metaphor Theory emphasizes the role of experiences to create categories in the mind and argues "metaphors, metonymies, and images are based on experience, often bodily

---

(Leiden: Brill, 2007); Elizabeth R. Hayes, *The Pragmatics of Perception and Cognition in MT Jeremiah 1:1–6:30: A Cognitive Linguistics Approach* (BZAW; Berlin: de Gruyter, 2008); Hugo Lundhaug, *Images of Rebirth: Cognitive Poetics and Transformational Soteriology in the Gospel of Philip and the Exegesis of the Soul* (NHMS; Leiden: Brill, 2010); Beth M. Stovell, *Mapping Metaphorical Discourse in the Fourth Gospel: John's Eternal King* (LBS; Leiden: Brill, 2012); Robert H. von Thaden, Jr., *Sex, Christ, and Embodied Cognition: Paul's Wisdom for Corinth* (ESEC; Atlanta: SBL Press, 2017); Aleksander Gomola, *Conceptual Blending in Early Christian Discourse: A Cognitive Linguistic Analysis of Pastoral Metaphors in Patristic Literature* (Berlin: de Gruyter, 2018); Gregory R. Lanier, *Old Testament Conceptual Metaphors and the Christology of Luke's Gospel* (LNTS; London: T&T Clark, 2018).

[98] George Lakoff and Mark Johnson, *Metaphors We Live By* (Chicago: University of Chicago Press, 1980). For overviews of Conceptual Metaphor Theory, see George Lakoff, "The Contemporary Theory of Metaphor" in *Metaphor and Thought*, 2d ed., ed. Andrew Ortony (Cambridge; Cambridge University Press, 1993), 202–51; Zoltán Kövecses, *Metaphor: A Practical Introduction*, 2d ed. (Oxford: Oxford University Press, 2010); Vyvyan Evans and Melanie Green, *Cognitive Linguistics: An Introduction* (Edinburgh: Edinburgh Press, 2006), 296–304.

[99] There are a few detractors, however, e.g. Stephen Kessler, *Theories of a Metaphor Revised: Against a Cognitive Theory of Metaphor: An Apology for Classical Metaphor* (Berlin: Logos Verlag, 2018).

[100] Gerard Steen, "Metaphor and Language and Literature: A Cognitive Perspective," *Language and Literature* 9.3 (2000): 261, quoted in Lundhaug, *Images of Rebirth*, 23.

experience."[101] This view explores the way metaphor works in the human mind and is broader than a given text and even culture, asserting that our minds work the way they do because we learn by comparing unknown ideas with known ones.[102] Previously known subjects are depicted as possible "source domains" which are used to describe a new entity, called a "target domain." According to this theory, "The generalizations governing poetic metaphorical expressions are not in language, but in thought: they are general mappings across conceptual domains ... the locus of metaphor is not in language at all, but in the way we conceptualize one mental domain in terms of another," or "cross-domain mapping."[103]

However, though most proponents of Cognitive Metaphor Theory emphasize bodily experience as the information for a source domain, some have used the theory to understand the use of metaphor from elsewhere. Zinken explains, "There is, however, a type of imagination which does not project physical experiences onto abstract domains, but seems to be rather culturally grounded, and which is very important in the linguistic interpretation of the world. This type of imagination is realized in what I call *intertextual metaphor*." He then lists the following examples: "Jim is a pig"; "Scientific progress leads to new Frankensteins"; and "There are too many unknown variables in this equation."[104] These metaphors arise, not from previous farm experiences, reading Mary Shelley, or algebra, but from tropes inherited from culture. Similarly, our approach regarding Matthean allusions to messianic texts will focus on source domains that do not come from experiences, but from an assumed background of Scripture, thus emphasizing the *text* of Zinken's inter*text*ual metaphor even more than he requires.[105]

---

[101] George Lakoff, *Women, Fire, and Other Dangerous Things: What Categories Reveal about the Mind* (Chicago: University of Chicago Press, 1987), xiv.
[102] Evans and Green, *Cognitive Linguistics: An Introduction*.
[103] Lakoff, "Contemporary Theory," 203.
[104] Jörg Zinken, "Ideological Imagination: Intertextual and Correlational Metaphors in Political Discourse" *Discourse & Society* (2003): 509.
[105] Cognitive linguistics, with its emphasis on the way meaning is created in the mind (as opposed to the text) can be contrasted with functional linguistics, which emphasizes the way a particular text operates (e.g. Michael A. K. Halliday, *An Introduction to Functional Grammar* (London: Arnold, 1985)). However, the two are not necessarily mutually exclusive, e.g. Alan J. Cienki, Barbara Josephine Luka, and Michael B. Smith, *Conceptual and Discourse Factors in Linguistic Structure* (San Diego: CSLI Publications, 1995); Sally Rice and John Newman, *Empirical and Experimental Methods in Cognitive/Functional Research* (Stanford, CA: CSLI Publications, 2010). See Stovell, *Mapping Metaphorical Discourse*, 50–53 for an overview for how the two approaches can converge.

Though we will find Cognitive Metaphor Theory a helpful tool in analyzing Matthew's use of the OT, a word of clarification is in order. While we are using a theory about metaphor, this does not require seeing the different images in the subsequent chapters *merely* as metaphors. In fact, recall that Cognitive Metaphor Theory describes the way the mind creates meaning and thus extends far beyond the study of "traditional" metaphor. Since we will be examining times when Matthew evokes eschatological passages, and Matthew presents the significance of Jesus' coming as, in some way, starting this time period (e.g. Matt 4:17), the events in Matthew's gospel go beyond analogy to corresponding scriptural images and texts. They *fulfill* the OT. This is not to say, however, that all of Matthew's uses of the OT are in this category. Especially if a non-eschatological text is evoked, Matthew may only be making a comparison by way of analogy. But in the following case studies, the mappings between the target domain and the source domain go beyond analogy or metaphor and are in the category "fulfillment."

Though Cognitive Metaphor Theory pays attention to how elements from a source domain map to a target domain, it also acknowledges that this mapping often carries over other connotations from the source domain. Aspects which transfer from the source domain but are not explicit mappings are called "entailments" or "inferences."[106] But this does not mean that every feature connected to a source domain functions as an entailment. This phenomenon is called "partial metaphorical utilization."[107] There are features of the source domain which are irrelevant to the statement being made about the target domain. Cognitive Metaphor Theory calls the use of aspects of a source domain "highlighting" and the non-use of other aspects "hiding."[108] Kövecses illustrates with a discussion of the LOVE → NUTRIENT[109] metaphor, such as "I'm starved for affection" or "She is sustained by love."[110] He explains,

> The source domain of nutrient utilizes such aspects of the concept as the desire for nourishment (*starved*), the positive effects of being well nourished (*sustained*) ... However, many things in connection with nutrients are left out of this picture. For example, no reference is conventionally

---

106   E.g. See discussion in Evans and Green, *Cognitive Linguistics*, 298.
107   Kövecses, *Metaphor*, 103.
108   Lakoff and Johnson, *Metaphors We Live By*, 10–13; Kövecses, *Metaphor*, 92–93; Evans and Green, *Cognitive Linguistics*, 303.
109   This is standard notation in cognitive metaphor theory, in which the metaphor "key" is capitalized. Sometimes the mapping is represented with an arrow, as here. Sometimes it is written out, e.g. "LOVE IS A NUTRIENT."
110   Kövecses, *Metaphor*, 92–93.

made to the idea that nutrients come into the body from outside, that we digest nutrients in order to process them, that eventually some of the nutrient goes out of the body ... In sum, in the same way as metaphorical highlighting of the target is partial, metaphorical utilization of the source is partial as well. Given a source domain, only certain aspects of it are conceptually utilized and activated in the comprehension of the target domain.[111]

Some of the entailments of a source domain simply cannot map to the target because doing so would violate the underlying imagery. This is based on what is called the "invariance principle," which requires that the scheme of the mapping be consistent. When the invariance principle prohibits a feature of the source domain from mapping, Lakoff calls this "target domain override."[112] However, some features do not violate the invariance principle and *could* map, yet fail to do so. Kövecses explains that, "each source is associated with a main meaning focus (or foci), and it is this that determines what gets mapped from the source; items outside the main meaning focus do not get mapped onto the target."[113] This speaks to our earlier concerns regarding metalepsis and the relevance of the context of an alluded passages for understanding the new context. Using Cognitive Metaphor Theory in application to allusions suggests that not all of the alluded-to context is relevant, but only those aspects which are within the main meaning focus will map to the target domain. The understanding of main meaning focus can be imprecise and depend on the subjective interpretation of the interpreter. Though this does not definitively answer the contextual debate from earlier regarding how much of the alluded-to context is relevant for the alluding context, it nonetheless provides helpful parameters. But though this field of study is helpful, for a more thorough analysis of the intricacies within the specific use of a metaphor, we can gain further precision by turning to Blending Theory.

1.3.2.2 Blending Theory / Integration Network Theory

Blending Theory also considers mapping and pays careful attention to targets and sources, but its use for the current research lies in allowing for a greater level of complexity.[114] It does so by positing that the connection of two ideas

---

[111] Kövecses, *Metaphor*, 94.
[112] Lakoff, "Contemporary Theory of Metaphor," 215–16.
[113] Kövecses, *Metaphor*, 307; cf. 138–40.
[114] The higher learning curve involved with Blending Theory may explain why it has not taken off quite like the simpler and more generic Cognitive Metaphor Theory. Not all intertextual research would equally benefit from Blending Theory (only a portion of the

triggers the imagination to create a whole new mental space, called a "blend" which, though similar to its sources, is yet something new. The seminal text for this approach is Fauconnier and Turner's *The Way We Think*.[115] Their basic scheme involves at least four elements: two inputs (similar to Cognitive Metaphor Theory's target and source domains), as well as a generic space and a blended space.[116] The most significant aspect of Integration Network Theory is the fourth space, called the "blend," which Fauconnier and Turner explain thus, "structure from two input mental spaces is projected to a new space ... Blends contain generic structure captured in the generic space but also contain more specific structure and they can contain structure that is impossible for the inputs."[117]

As noted above, Conceptual Blending parallels Cognitive Metaphor Theory in that it tracks mappings from one space to another.[118] But it also attends to the new mental space that is created with a different set of relations. Blending Theory calls this new concept that only arises after two scenarios converge an "emergent structure." Fauconnier and Turner define this as what "arises in the blend that is not copied there directly from any input. It is generated in three ways: through *composition* of projections from the inputs, through *completion* based on independently recruited frames and scenarios, and through *elaboration* ('running the blend')."[119] Blending Theory's use of emergent structure is thus well suited for our inquiry because allusions go beyond simple "this is

---

insights from the theory are used here), but still, in general, this perspective seems to deserve a greater utilization in biblical studies than it has received.

115 Gilles Fauconnier and Mark Turner, *The Way We Think: Conceptual Blending and the Mind's Hidden Complexities* (New York: Basic Books, 2002). Overviews of this theory can be found in Pierre Van Hecke, "Metaphor and Conceptual Blending" in *Metaphor in the Hebrew Bible*, ed. Pierre van Hecke (Leuven: Leuven University Press, 2005); Gilles Fauconnier and Mark Turner, "Conceptual Integration Networks" in *Cognitive Science* 22.2 (1998): 133–87; Seana Coulson and Todd Oakley, "Blending Basics" in *Cognitive Linguistics*, 11 3/4 (2000): 1–22.

116 "Generic space" is far less important for this study than "blended space." Fauconnier and Turner, *The Way We Think*, 47 explain "generic space" thus, "at any moment in the construction of the network, the structure that inputs seem to share is captured in a generic space, which in turn maps onto each of the inputs. A given element in the generic space maps onto paired counterparts in the two input spaces." The "Generic space" consists of aspects of the source and target domains which overlap and describes the "world" which both domains share. It can be thought of as the work-space where things are thought through before reaching a conclusion.

117 Fauconnier and Turner, *The Way We Think*, 47.

118 For an example of blending theory applied to Psalm 23, see Gomoloa, *Conceptual Blending in Early Christian Discourse*, 13, figure 1.

119 Fauconnier and Turner, *The Way We Think*, 48, italics original.

that" equations and invite creative comparison. Gomoloa explores how this emergent structure is explicated in the rest of Ps 23 – besides the identity mappings above, the imagery extends with lying down in green pastures, drinking water from still waters, etc.[120]

Moreover, though Ps 23 eventually explicates the emergent structure after prompting the audience to blend a shepherding input with the author's situation, a text does not need to explicitly state the emergent structure within a blend. Coulson and Oakley consider the following description of a political ad:

> In 1998 an African American man named James Byrd Jr. was chained to a pickup truck and dragged to his death in Texas by three white men. In 2000, in the midst of a tight presidential campaign, a television advertisement featured the voice of James Byrd Jr.'s daughter. The ad presented grainy, black and white footage of a pickup truck with Texas plates, a chain tied to the bumper, dragging unseen cargo. Focused on the license plate and the chain, the camera follows the truck as it slowly pulls away. In the voiceover, Byrd describes her father's gruesome death, as well as Texas governor, George W. Bush's refusal to sign legislation strengthening laws against racially motivated attacks known in the U.S. as hate crimes. When Bush refused to back the legislation, Byrd recalls she felt "as if my father had been killed all over again."[121]

Coulson and Oakley explain how the ad was considered "distasteful and unfair" because, though the ad only gave facts concerning a murder, Bush's political statements, and a testimonial from Byrd's daughter about her feelings, something more implicit is at play. The ad prompts the audience to imaginatively create an emergent structure within a blend, in which Bush is mapped to the three white men in the truck, as if Bush caused the death of Byrd.[122] Thus, although a text may explicitly build an emergent structure, as with Ps 23, it does not have to. Blending Theory's consideration of the new world created by

---

120   Gomoloa, *Conceptual Blending in Early Christian Discourse*, 12–15.
121   Coalson and Oakley, "Blending Basics," 175.
122   Coalson and Oakley, "Blending Basics," 176. Similarly, Fauconnier and Turner, *The Way We Think*, 330 explain that we often reject creating blends because we know there will be a tight connection between inputs – e.g. many would not blend an oppressed minority with an endangered species because, though there are significant similarities, the result would be insulting. The examples of the political ad and the endangered species demonstrate how an emergent structure is created in a blend that goes beyond the explicitly stated comparisons since the clear offensiveness lies in the implied correspondences (entailments).

the merging of different concepts allows us to analyze how these "new characters" interact in the new space of the blend and thus provide us with a powerful tool for considering the effect of evoking Scripture for Matthew's portrayal of his narrative. Like Cognitive Metaphor Theory, this continues to allow room for subjectivity and imagination, but still provides some parameters.

Thus, the power of Blending Theory is its careful attention to the new world (the "blend" and its emerging structure) evoked when two or more sources are compared to create meaning. For our context, we care about the new world comparing the events of Matthew's narrative with the scriptural texts to which he alludes creates. Furthermore, Blending Theory contains several "governing principles" to describe the way the new blend is constructed.[123] The beauty of the theory is that it goes beyond asserting the creation of a new space with its own characters and rules when two or more sources are compared, to the exploration of how this new world is made. This is important for us as we seek to understand the blend and its emergent structure in Matthean allusions and will provide some sophistication in knowing how we are to construct the new world created by comparing an event in Matthew's narrative with a scriptural text. Because we will work with textual blends and thus a smaller subset of what Fauconnier and Turner consider, not all their governing principles warrant attention. The three most relevant for our research are the following:

- The Topology Principle: "Other things being equal, set up the blend and the inputs so that the useful topology in the inputs and their outer-space relations [the way elements relate independently of the blend[124]] is reflected by inner-space relations [the new relationships which are at play within the blend]."[125] In other words, the relationships from the sources should be preserved as closely as possible in the constructed blend. In the example of Ps 23, this means that the relationships between the sheep and the shepherd from the source domain are consistently used in the blend.[126]

- The Pattern Completion Principle: "Other things being equal, complete elements in the blend by using existing integrated patterns as additional

---

[123] The total list is "the Topology Principle; the Pattern Completion Principle; the Integration Principle; the Maximization of Vital Relations Principle; the Intensification of Vital Relations Principle; the Web Principle; the Unpacking Principle: and the Relevance Principle." Fauconnier and Turner, *The Way We Think*, 325–36.

[124] In Ps 23 this would be the way sheep and shepherds relate as well as the way David and YHWH relate.

[125] Fauconnier and Turner, *The Way We Think*, 326.

[126] Fauconnier and Turner, *The Way We Think*, 126–34 discuss several different kinds of networks. In a single-scope network, the topology from only one domain is transferred to the blend. In double-scope networks, the elements from the topology from both domains are transferred.

inputs. Other things being equal, use a completing frame that has relations that can be the compression versions of the important outer-space vital relations between the inputs."[127] This addresses "elaboration" / "running the blend" in creating an emergent structure. In the political ad example, this explains why the audience ends up picturing Bush as Byrd's murderer.

- The Integration Principle: "Achieve an integrated blend ... [this] allows its manipulation as a unit, makes it more memorable, and enables the thinker to run the blend without constant reference to the other spaces in the network."[128] This principle can compete with the Topology Principle since the relationships in the different sources can conflict. In such a case, we adjust to create a wholistic, consistent blend. For the Ps 23 example, the topology from the source domain that shepherds would watch over sheep for financial gain or kill them for food fails to map because this would create a disintegrated blend.

There is give and take with these, and Blending Theory notes that the principles can exclude one another (note the repetition of "other things being equal" above), but these governing principles will aid in our construction of a blend when Matthew compares something in his narrative to one or more scriptural texts.

Like Cognitive Metaphor Theory, Blending Theory also works well in intertextual analysis. Though Blending Theory comes later and enjoys a higher degree of sophistication, it comports well with Ben-Porat's often cited definition (see 1.3.1.3). The use of Blending Theory thus coincides well with intertextuality, so much so that Lundhaug proposes the term "intertextual blending."[129] This study will find these concepts useful because we will want to focus on the imaginative new world created when Matthew compares the situation in the narrative of his story with an Old Testament background. We will certainly want to focus on mappings that Matthew explicitly makes, but we will also want to attend to the implicit ones. Blending Theory's emergent structure and governing principles will aid us in this endeavor.

Blending Theory will be useful for our studies for two other primary reasons. We have just seen that it allows for the complexity of the emergent structure within the blend, but it also helps in analyzing the complicated input spaces which generate the blend. Beyond the relatively simple four element scenario described above, Conceptual Blending also examines "multiple-scope blends" in which several different input spaces, in various relations to one

---

127   Fauconnier and Turner, *The Way We Think*, 328.
128   Fauconnier and Turner, *The Way We Think*, 328–29.
129   Lundhaug, *Images of Rebirth*, 47.

another, all contribute to the same imaginative blended space.[130] Fauconnier and Turner illustrate this with the Grim Reaper, who is the combination of several inputs, such as an individual dying, death as a killer, and reapers as harvesters. Building on Lakoff and Kövecses, they also provide the example of the metaphor of ANGER IS HEAT and imagine the cartoon Elmer Fudd "turn[ing] red, beginning at his feet and climbing thermometer-like to his head, at which points smoke would blow out of his ears."[131] This easily understood image represents a multi-scope blend which draws from several different sources. The idea of multiple source inputs will be useful for the present research because we are considering highly complex metaphors in which large backgrounds are evoked to portray a situation in Matthew's narrative. This is especially so since we are considering allusions, which, unlike citations, do not necessarily specify only one OT reference as the source domain,[132] and can draw on general ideas, formed by several contributing scriptural texts. Lundhaug explains

> With both conceptual and intertextual blending what we are modelling are the mental interpretive processes of combining and creating connections between mental spaces that become active in working memory, cued by sensory input derived from reading or hearing the texts under scrutiny. In both cases we may have integration networks that are single-, double-, or multiple-scope, with a potentially infinite number of input spaces. Moreover, since they are all mental spaces, we may also have hybrid integration networks that include both conceptual and intertextual input spaces.[133]

Multi-scope blends provide a framework for how we can account for multiple allusions. This research project's emphasis on authorial intent will necessarily require a cap to be placed on how many references lie behind a text (so, not infinite). However, we must still make room for the possibility that an author evokes a complicated network of texts and ideas, provided that each potential allusion satisfies the criteria discussed above. The possibility that a text alludes to more than one intertext seems plausible in light of Integration Network Theory's multi-scope blends. Moreover, this phenomenon has recently received

---

130 See Fauconnier and Turner, *The Way We Think*, 279–98.
131 Fauconnier and Turner, *The Way We Think*, 302.
132 Though this seems to generally be the case, I am not denying that citations can evoke multiple sources. See below for further discussion.
133 Lundhuag, *Images of Rebirth*, 48.

attention in a two-volume series on composite citations.[134] Bobichon's discussion of Justin Martyr's *Dialogue with Trypho* and *Apology* is particularly helpful for our study since he demonstrates that not only does Justin produce composite allusions, but that his Jewish opponent is claimed to have recognized these references and their significance.[135] Granted, this precedent does not prove that Matthew has the same approach. But it does confirm the possibility of the validity of using multi-scope blends to investigate more than one potential intertext in an allusion.

Besides allowing for complexity in the blended space and the input spaces, Blending Theory also focuses on the complexity within the connections/mappings themselves, called "Vital Relations." The overall thesis of this project argues for a broadly eschatological hermeneutic which emphasizes the arrival of the eschaton, whether the means is God himself, the messiah, some other agent(s), or is unspecified. For those case studies in which agents besides *the* messiah fulfill the messianic figure, Blending Theory's treatment of Vital Relations will provide us with helpful concepts. We have already noted that the mappings in this study extend beyond analogy due to Matthew's paradigm of fulfillment. Blending Theory will provide a greater level of sophistication here, particularly in making the overall thesis statement more precise since we are interested in why Matthew makes the decisions he does in unexpected mappings of messianic images. Fauconnier and Turner list the most frequent kinds of Vital Relations as identity, time, space, cause-effect, part-whole, representation, role, analogy, disanalogy, property, similarity, category, intentionality, and uniqueness.[136] The most important of these for our study are "identity" and "role." Moreover, each of these compressions or Vital Relations has their own complexities. The complications surrounding "identity" and "roles" are particularly significant. Fauconnier and Turner explain,

> Identity may be the most basic Vital Relation … [it] is taken for granted as primitive, but it's a feat of the imagination … The complexity of identity

---

134 *Composite Citations in Antiquity: Volume One: Jewish, Graeco-Roman, and Early Christian Uses*, ed. Sean A. Adam and Seth M. Ehorn (LNTS; New York: T&T Clark, 2016) and *Composite Citations in Antiquity: Volume Two: New Testament Uses*, ed. Sean A. Adams and Seth M. Ehorn (LNTS; New York: T&T Clark, 2018).

135 Philippe Bobichon, "Composite Features and Citations in Justin Martyr's Textual Composition" (158–81). Maarten J. J. Menken's article in the second volume, "Composite Citations in the Gospel of Matthew" (34–61), focuses on whether Matthew has purposefully combined his citations or if they were in his source, and thus does not contribute to the subject at hand.

136 Fauconnier and Turner, *The Way We Think*, 96–101.

connections across spaces leads to phenomena like referential opacity, which have long vexed philosophers of language. Identity connectors do not have to be one-to-one across inputs. 'If he were twins, he would hate himself' prompts for a new network in which one person in one input space has *two* identity counterparts in the other space. In the blend, the twins are counterparts by identity of the single person in the first input space ... But identity can link less specific elements – in particular, roles. In understanding 'In France, the president is elected for a term of seven years, while in the United States *he* is elected for a term of four years,' we connect as identical the role *president* in the French space and the role of *president* in the American space, and this is why we can use 'he' in this way.[137]

We can diagram the referential opacity in these examples with a double mapping, as follows:

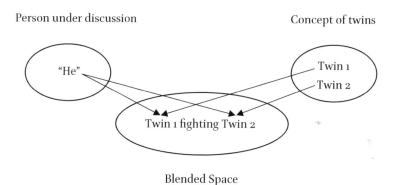

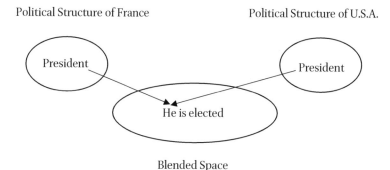

FIGURE 1   Examples of Vital Relations and Referential Opacity

---

137   Fauconnier and Turner, *The Way We Think*, 95–96, italics original.

Our use of Conceptual Blending's Vital Relations to explain "broad mapping" is not a first-time use. For example, Elizabeth Hayes has used these tools of Vital Relations in Conceptual Blending in her analysis of the use of Isa 42 in Matt 12. She argues that the role of "justice bringer" in Isa 42 links to the role of "justice bringer" in Matt 12, but that this does not require the ontological identity (the value) to be the same.[138] The concept of "justice bringer" does not get mapped as a Vital Relation of identity, but of role, and thus has a kind of referential opacity. In the context of Isa 42, Hayes sees the value of this role being Israel, but in Matt 12 Jesus fulfills the same role.[139] This allows her to agree with H. G. M. Williamson that "Jesus fulfils, but does not thereby exhaust the prophecy."[140] However, in our study, we will consider the evidence of referential opacity within the same document – unlike Hayes' example where Isaiah maps an image one way and Matthew another, our study examines times when Matthew maps a messianic image a certain way in one passage and then changes the mapping scheme in another of text. Like Williamson, we will see that in several case studies, various images which were seen as messianic – eschatological shepherd, vine care-giver, temple foundation, temple builder – are best seen as roles. Though Jesus is a value for these roles in Matthew, he is not the only value. Instead, it will be seen that Jesus shares the place of value for these roles with the disciples.

The above is only a brief introduction to this vast field of study. While we will spend the majority of our energy on more traditional features of exegesis, likely more familiar to the reader, the previous discussion of cognitive linguistics prepares us for concepts relied upon occasionally throughout the following case studies. Specifically, Blending Theory will be helpful in providing us with a more robust and scientific approach concerning three areas. First, it will aid us in examining the new world created by the intertextual reference (the governing principles which create the emergent structure in the blend). We will not only be concerned with matching elements in the NT text with corresponding

---

138 Elizabeth R. Hayes, "The One Who Brings Justice: Conceptualizing the Role of 'The Servant' in Isaiah 42:1–4 and Matthew 12:15–21" in *Let Us Go Up to Zion: Essays in Honour of H. G. M. Williams on the Occasion of his Sixty-Fifth Birthday*, ed. Iain Provain and Mark Boda (SVT; Leiden: Brill, 2012), 148.

139 Hayes, "The One Who Brings Justice," 98–99 also categorizes the mapping as "analogy." While there are similarities between the figures in Isa 42 and Matt 12, this categorization seems misleading in light of the fulfillment motif discussed above.

140 H. G. M. Williamson, *Variations on a Theme: King, Messiah and Servant in the Book of Isaiah*, Didsbury Lectures (Carlisle: Paternoster Press, 1998), 142–43; Hayes, "The One Who Brings Justice," 150.

elements from the First Testament, but we also want to attend to the creative new world resulting from the combination of these two domains. Elements for which we cannot draw a line to an OT precursor are still significant in analyzing how Matthew adapts the OT. Sometimes the Matthean Jesus will run the blend for us and explicate elements that emerge in the blend.

For example, Jesus' use of Isa 5 in the Wicked Tenant Parable explicitly draws attention to new figures which play an important role – the servants, the son, and the farmers (see 3.7). At other times, new elements which arise from running the blend are not explicated but are nonetheless significant. Such will be the case in the use of the builders of Ps 118. Though this quoted text only mentions incompetent builders and then the incorporation of the once-rejected stone, the completion principle implies new builders who do recognize the value of the stone, and these implicatures require attention as they are mapped to the disciples (see 4.2.2). Continuing along the spectrum, we will also consider *uncertain* implicatures, when it is not clear how much an audience is intended to run the blend. For example, the emergent structure created by the allusions to Isa 61 may (but not must) imply something about the identity of the one(s) heralding the good news of the kingdom (see 5.4.1.2). Incorporating Blending Theory into these discussions will give us a greater degree of sophistication in considering the extent to which we should attend to these elements which otherwise may be missed if our concern were only to see what bits of the NT passage can be paired with an explicit element in the alluded to text.

The other features of Blending Theory introduced earlier will also be relevant for our case studies. The category of multi-scope blends will alert us to the potential of several source domains, whether explicit OT texts or interpretive trajectories which all can provide a significant backdrop against which we should understand the NT text. Since we want to include the author and his intentions within the locus of meaning, we must limit how many source domains operate in the blend, but if a suggested domain meets the criteria of an allusions described above, we need not reject it. Furthermore, we will also want to attend to the nature of the mappings themselves (the Vital Relations). This will particularly help in navigating the complications from portraying disciples in messianic imagery, while still maintaining Matthew's clear conviction that the title of "the messiah" only goes to Jesus. Though we can profitably use various Vital Relations to analyze metaphor and intertextuality, our purposes specifically focus on identity and role since we are concerned with the non-messianic use of traditionally messianic texts and want to trace the mappings of the messianic figure into the blend.

1.4 Summary of Thesis and Case Studies

The chapter began by stating the current work's thesis as the following:

> Matthew's hermeneutic of fulfillment is broadly eschatological as opposed to narrowly messianic. The common description of Matthew's hermeneutic as "messianic" needs to be broadened to the category "eschatological," as evidenced by references to texts often perceived as messianic and yet which do not map the messianic image to Jesus.

We are now in a position to restate the thesis with the terminology and concepts of Conceptual Blending to gain further precision. The thesis is as follows: The Matthean Jesus creates multiple scope networks from source domains which have a figure who was traditionally seen as the messiah. Yet the emergent structures in these blends do not always map this figure by the Vital Relation of identity to Jesus. Instead, the Vital Relation is at times one of role, such that the blend maps the messianic figure to Jesus' disciples. At other times, Matthew does not explicitly map the messianic figure and. Instead, he is mapped at most only as an entailment, subtly in the emergent structure through the governing principle of Pattern Completion. In other words, the predominate theory of Matthew's Christocentric hermeneutic must be nuanced because it does not include times when the Matthean Jesus creates a conceptual blend in which he evokes a messianic text as a source domain and:

(1) maps various elements into the blend, but does not explicitly map the messianic figure himself.

OR

(2) maps a messianic figure from a source domain
(3) and maps the disciples from the target domain to that figure.[141]

Moreover, the diversity of these scenarios in different source domains and different target domains shows that this phenomenon is not due to an obscurity in one particular reference, but reflects an important aspect of Matthew's hermeneutical approach. Either of the above scenarios demonstrates the difficulty of simply labeling Matthew's paradigm of fulfillment as 'Christological,' and

---

[141] Chapter 5 will argue for (1) regarding the use of Isa 61. Chapters 2, 3, and 4 will argue for (2) and (3) regarding the use of the eschatological shepherd, the vine care-givers, and temple related imagery respectively.

thus the general description of 'broadly eschatological' holds more explanatory power.

Chapter 2 will consider our first case study regarding Matt 9:36 and 10:6. Three source domains will be considered, Ezek 34, Jer 23, and Zech 10. We will see that Ezek 34 should be labeled "messianic" in both its own textual features as well as its history. Yet the role of eschatological agent, often accomplished by the messiah, maps (via the Vital Relation of "role") to the disciples in Matt 10:6. Jer 23 will also be considered as a likely, though probably secondary, source domain, which results in a direct mapping (via the Vital Relation of "identity") of its plural shepherds (v 4) to the disciples. Zech 10, the quietest echo of the three, seems to function similarly. It mentions several "mighty rulers" connected to the messiah who map (via the Vital Relation of "identity") to the disciples in the Mission Discourse.

In the second case study of chapter 3, we will see Isa 5 is the primary intertextual background for the Wicked Tenant Parable (Matt 21:33ff) and though the text itself has very few possible messianic elements, several instances in the history of its interpretation demonstrate how easily the image was used to address agency, eschatology, and messianism. With Isa 5 alone as the source domain, no specific messianic figure presets itself to map into the blend, and yet we can find the messiah in the hermeneutical milieu surrounding Isaiah's vineyard. Furthermore, in this blend, the disciples accomplish the messianic role of taking care of God's vineyard. We also will consider the possibility of Ps 80 as a secondary source domain, in which case there is a specific figure, the בן ("the branch"/"son"), who easily could have been viewed as the messiah as he is vital to the flourishing of the vineyard. Here too this messianic image maps to the disciples.

In chapter 4, our third case study, we will consider images connected to eschatological temple construction. We will see two different components of this image as messianic – the temple builder and the temple stone. Matt 21:42–43 and 16:18 use both elements and we will see the messianic potential for both in the alternating references to Jesus (stone in 21:42–43; builder in 16:18). This shows that both images contain messianic potential, and in each text the disciples occupy the space of the other element. In all of the case studies considered, a text/image has varying levels of messianic features, but the history of interpretation demonstrates how easily the messiah could be read into the passages.

In the first three case studies we will see a non-messianic hermeneutic since Matthew maps these potentially messianic images to the disciples, but the fourth case study in chapter 5 will evidence a broadly eschatological hermeneutic in a different way. Complications will arise when considering both the mapping of a messianic figure from the source domain into the blend, as well as the mapping of the disciples from the target domain. In considering Isa 61:1–3 as the background of Matt 5:3–4 and 11:5, we will investigate if the source domain should be labeled "messianic." Though both the textual features and its later uses do not suggest as clear of a messianic picture as is often presented, we will still conclude that there are sufficient indications that Matthew could have taken the text that way and thus mapped a messianic figure into the blend. The mapping from the target domain into blend is similarly more complicated than the other case studies. In neither of the Matthean texts will we see a clear mapping of the disciples into the blend. Yet, a good case can be made that this happens via the blending theory's governing principles. If this does not prove persuasive, evidence still exists of a non-messianic use of a messianic text in that Matthew could have taken advantage of the opportunity to say something about Jesus' identity, but instead uses a messianic passage to inform his readers of the nature of the coming eschaton. Each of these case studies has its own unique features, but they all suggest a pattern requiring Matthew's hermeneutic to be described as broadly eschatological as opposed to narrowly messianic.

CHAPTER 2

Matthew's Non-Messianic Use of the Eschatological Shepherd

2.1   Introduction

When Matthew describes the crowds as ἐσκυλμένοι καὶ ἐρριμμένοι ὡσεὶ πρόβατα μὴ ἔχοντα ποιμένα (9:36) and then proceeds to state Jesus' commission πορεύεσθε δὲ μᾶλλον πρὸς τὰ πρόβατα τὰ ἀπολωλότα οἴκου Ἰσραήλ (10:6), most commentators see the Hebrew Scriptures as a significant backdrop.[1] The verses contribute to Matthew's shepherding motif, an aspect of his Christology which has recently received scholarly attention. Chae's monograph, *Jesus as the Eschatological Davidic Shepherd*, argues that Ezek 34 as the background for Matthew's shepherding imagery explains the significance of Jesus being a healer and teacher.[2] Willitts' *Matthew's Messianic Shepherd King* argues that the imagery contains a significant political component, including a restoration of the land to the twelve tribes of Israel.[3] Baxter's *Israel's Only Shepherd* argues that the political use of the term demonstrates the Gospel of Matthew is more properly aligned with Jewish use of the metaphor and thus shows an earlier stage of the "parting of the ways" than is often assumed.[4] Zacharias' *Matthew's Presentation of the Son of David* argues Jesus being a Davidic shepherd explains his non-militarism, humility, and rejection.[5]

---

1   E.g. W. D. Davies and Dale C. Allison Jr., *A Critical and Exegetical Commentary on the Gospel according to Saint Matthew* (ICC; London: T&T Clark International, 2004), 2:148; Turner, *Matthew*, 262; Nolland, *Gospel of Matthew*, 407; France, *Matthew*, 372; Keener, *Gospel of Matthew*, 308–9.

2   Young Chae, *Jesus as the Eschatological Davidic Shepherd: Studies in the Old Testament, Second Temple Judaism, and in the Gospel of Matthew* (WUNT; Tübingen: Mohr Siebeck, 2006).

3   Joel Willitts, Matthew's Messianic Shepherd King: In Search of the Lost Sheep of the House of Israel (BZVW; Berlin: Walter de Gruyter, 2007).

4   Wayne Baxter, *Israel's Only Shepherd: Matthew's Shepherd motif and His Social Setting* (LNTS; London: T&T Clark, 2012).

5   H. Daniel Zacharias, *Matthew's Presentation of the Son of David: Davidic Tradition and Typology in the Gospel of Matthew* (London: Bloomsbury, 2016). Schreiner, *Matthew, Disciple and Scribe*, 65–130 gives an excellent summary of the Davidic theme in Matthew in light of recent research and focuses on the application of this image to Jesus as Shepherd, concluding that Jesus is the "royal shepherd," "the ministering shepherd," "the merciful shepherd," "the shepherd judge" and the "sacrificial shepherd" (113).

Though these works helpfully contribute to the study of Matthew's use of Scripture, even the titles demonstrate a narrower messianic approach. According to these titles, Jesus alone is the eschatological Davidic shepherd, or shepherd king, or Israel's *only* shepherd. While each work notes the motif has applications for the disciples, this is only secondary and there is no focus on what this might mean for understanding Matthew's paradigm of fulfillment. This chapter explores potential scriptural source domains for Matt 9:36 and 10:6 and argues that Matthew evokes passages which would have been understood as containing substantial messianic components. Yet, remarkably, Matthew's interests in these passages lies elsewhere. Here at least, the allusions do not establish the identity of the messiah but primarily cast *the apostles* as characters in the story of God's eschatological restoration of Israel. Because Matthew could have easily evoked these texts for Christological purposes, but instead picks up on other features of the text and maps them to the disciples, this poses significant problems in describing his hermeneutic as Christocentric. This chapter will demonstrate that the way Matthew interprets eschatological Scripture allows for other significant characters to function as God's agents.[6] As explained in the previous chapter, we are concerned with times when the Matthean Jesus creates a conceptual blend in which he:

(1) maps a messianic figure from a source domain
and (2) maps the disciples from the target domain to that figure.[7]

Step (2) for this current case study comes easily as the disciples are clearly the ones being sent in 10:6, but (1) will require the lion's share of our attention as we explore how Matthew and his readers would have likely understood the images from the source domains. This chapter considers three possible scriptural source domains for the image of eschatological shepherding in Matt 9:36 and 10:6, namely Ezek 34, Jer 23:1–6, and Zech 10:2–4. Matt 9:36 and 10:6 certainly may create a multi-scope blend and allude to all three of these passages. After all, Matthew can refer to multiple texts in his quotations (e.g. Matt 2:6 / Mic 5:2, 2 Sam 5:2), cases which Richard Hays argues are "a matter neither of accidental misquotation from memory nor of simple dependence on some otherwise

---

6 Though the word "agent" could refer to someone who accomplishes a task, this research uses the word more narrowly as one who does the mission of another who sent him. Mostly this is used as YHWH accomplishes his purposes through instrumental agents, those whom he sends to work on his behalf.
7 Another option outlined in the introduction was for Jesus to evoke a potentially messianic text as a source domain, map various elements into the blend, but not explicitly map the messianic figure himself, a possibility which will be explored in chapter 5.

unknown textual tradition … [but rather they] function as allusive, hermeneutically constructive compositions."[8] If there is no reason to require a single referent in a quotation, how much less for an allusion, provided the arguments for the proposed allusions are convincing. Still, though Matthew can allude to all three passages, the argument of this chapter does not require him to do so. If one had to pick only one source domain, Ezek 34 is the best option. But Jer 23 very well may be in view also and Zech 10 may provide a quiet echo. These second two additional intertexts would result in a different kind of mapping and Vital Relations than Ezek 34, yet the argument of this chapter only requires each of the potential mapping schemes to be non-messianic, and we will see that such is indeed the case. We will explore each of these potential backdrops to see what emerges and what each would contribute to the Mission Discourse.

2.2   The Contribution of Ezek 34

2.2.1   *Matt 9:36 by Itself Does Not Allude to an OT Text*
Matt 9:36 has several potential backdrops in the Jewish Scriptures, with Num 27:17, 1 Kgs 22:17, 2 Chron 18:16, and Judith 11:19 having the most lexical correspondence, as seen in the table below:

TABLE 1   Greek Parallels to Matt 9:36

Matt 9:36	ὡσεί	πρόβατα		μὴ	ἔχοντα	ποιμένα
Num 27:17	ὡσεί[a]	πρόβατα	οἷς	οὐκ	ἔστιν	ποιμήν
1 Kgs 22:17	ὡς	ποίμνιον	ᾧ	οὐκ	ἔστιν	ποιμήν
2 Chron 18:16	ὡς	πρόβατα	οἷς	οὐκ	ἔστιν	ποιμήν
Jdt 11:19	ὡς	πρόβατα	οἷς	οὐκ	ἔστιν	ποιμήν

a   Codex Alexandrinus has the variant ὡς, which would make it identical to 2 Chron 18:17 and Judith 11:19.

There are possible connections between these contexts and Matt 9:36. One could envision Num 27 as having relevance for Matthew's argument. This text established Joshua as the successor of Moses, and this could cohere with Matthew's new Moses motif. Still, not much lies in its favor.[9] The context of

---

8   Hays, *Echoes of Scripture in the Gospels*, 186–87.
9   This could possibly be confirmed by Deut 18:15–18. Dale Allison, *The New Moses: A Matthean Typology* (Minneapolis: Fortress Press, 1993), 214–17 considers this possibility, but concludes

1 Kgs 22 (= 2 Chron 18) is even more difficult to see as relevant for Matthew, where Micaiah reluctantly prophesies the outcome of Israel and Judah's alliance against Syria. Jdt 11 describes Judith's assurance to Holofernes regarding Babylon's successful attack against Jerusalem because of their sin. Though this could possibly connect with Matthew's portrayal of Israel as in a state of spiritual exile for her sin and helpless from judgment, it requires too much ingenuity to be likely. Moreover, the expression has wider use even outside the Scriptures of Israel as evidenced by the Babylonian proverb, "a people without a king (is like) sheep without a shepherd."[10] Thus, the wide usage of this saying mitigates against the possibility of the allusion to any of the above in Matt 9:36. The phrase by itself is most likely a general saying and not a specific allusion.[11] If Matt 9:36 does allude to any or all of the above, this would not necessarily discredit the argument here that Ezek 34 and Jer 23 are the primary backdrops. Yet the unlikeliness of these connections allows other allusions to enjoy the bulk of the readers' attention as they reflect on the OT significance of this expression. For those concerned with the improbability of Matthew overbearing his readers with too many echoes, the unlikeness of the above allusions clears room for Ezek 34 and Jer 23, and perhaps even Zech 10, to be purposeful and legitimate references.

Though Matt 9:36 alone probably does not allude to an OT text, when we connect the nearby clause πορεύεσθε δὲ μᾶλλον πρὸς τὰ πρόβατα τὰ ἀπολωλότα (10:6) to the phrase in 9:36, the volume sufficiently increases to evoke the Jewish Scriptures' prophetic portrayal of eschatological renewal in shepherding terms.

2.2.2 Matt 9:36 and 10:6 Do Allude to Ezek 34

Scholars have successfully argued that Matt 9:36 and 10:6 allude to Ezek 34.[12] We should expect this passage to create a louder echo than Jer 23 since it treats the same subject in thirty-one verses that Jeremiah does in six. Indeed, if interpreters can only hear one echo in Matt 9:36 and 10:6, Ezek 34 will probably be

      the reference is too vague to specifically evoke Num 27. He notes that the connection to Num 27 is more likely in Mark 6:34 since it is connected with the feeding of the five thousand (vv 35–44) which has similarities with Moses providing manna (Num 11).

10   Wilfred Lambert, *Babylonian Wisdom Literature* (Winona Lake, IN: Eisenbrauns, 1996), 232.

11   Contra Willitts, *Matthew's Messianic Shepherd-King*, 122–24, who sees significance in the occurrence of the expression in Num, 1 Kgs (= 2 Chron), but not in Judith or the Babylonian proverb.

12   Gundry, *Use of the Old Testament*, 32–33; Heil, J. P. "Ezekiel 34 and the Narrative Strategy of the Shepherd and Sheep Metaphor in Matthew," *CBQ* 55 (1993): 700–02 (who argues Ezek 34 stands behind all of Matthew's use of shepherding imagery); Willitts, *Matthew's Messianic Shepherd*, 123–4; Baxter, *Israel's Only Shepherd*, 143–150.

the choice. Furthermore, if, with many scholars, we see Ezek 34 as an expansion of Jer 23:1–6[13] then we can anticipate the same eschatological and messianic components (see in section 2.3). As with the Jeremiah text, so too Ezek 34:1–10 decries the poor shepherding of the shepherds, but the explicit statement in v 5, מִבְּלִי רֹעֶה; διὰ τὸ μὴ εἶναι ποιμένας increases the volume of the echo in Matt 9:36, as does Ezekiel's description of the sheep as הָאֹבֶדֶת; ἀπολωλός in v 4 (cf. Matt 10:6). The description of YHWH searching for the sheep in Jer 23:3 finds its counterpart in Ezek 34:11–16 and Jeremiah's messianic portion in 23:5–6 parallels Ezek 34:23–24. For these reasons, Ezek 34 probably creates the loudest echo with Matt 9:36 and 10:6.

2.2.3 Ezek 34 Would Have Been Understood as Messianic

Turning to the source domain, our concern is to explore how Matthew would have understood the shepherd image which maps to the disciples. This requires an examination of the textual features of Ezek 34 as well as listening to "conversation partners" as other users of Ezek 34 handle the text. Doing so will demonstrate that Ezek 34:23–24 contains sufficient elements to warrant thinking Matthew would have viewed this as messianic. We will take some time to listen to Matthew's conversation partners since they not only confirm that Ezek 34 had a messianic interpretation, but also demonstrate the variety of ways a later user of the passage might map the messiah into the blend. The benefit of making this investment will appear (especially in 2.2.4.2) when we see how the history of interpretation suggests some interpretive options for considering the logic of the mapping scheme in Matt 10:6.

2.2.3.1 Textual Features in Ezek 34:23–24 Suggest a Messianic Interpretation

Some understand Ezekiel as having little or no interest in messianism.[14] Yet features from the text of 34:23–24 suggest Matthew would have understood the shepherd there as the messiah. First, v 23 describes him as "one shepherd" (רֹעֶה אֶחָד; ποιμένα ἕνα[15]). In the next section, we will see that Jer 23 refers to several eschatological shepherds. Block sees the significance of Ezekiel's description of one shepherd in contrast to the situation of Jer 23:4, stating

---

13   Block, *Ezekiel*, 2:282; Zimmerli, *Ezekiel*, 2:214. Leslie Allen, *Ezekiel 20–48* (WBC; Nashville, TN: Thomas Nelson, 1994), 161 sees Jer 23:1–2 as the background, but vv 3–6 as less certain.
14   E.g. "Memories of an autocratic monarchy that served its subject badly were so bitter, and the constraints of political realism were so compelling, that messianic exuberance was necessarily absent" (Allen, *Ezekiel 20–48*, 195).
15   Codex Alexandrinus has the variant ἕτερον. This variant probably stresses his difference from the shepherds of 34:1–10.

The reference to 'one shepherd' ... goes beyond Jeremiah 23:4, which has Yahweh installing responsible shepherds (plural) to replace the present exploitative and irresponsible rulers. In announcing a single ruler Yahweh seeks a reversal of the division of Israel into northern and southern kingdoms that occurred after the death of Solomon (1 Ki. 11–12). Like the rest of the prophets, Ezekiel perceived the nation as one and recognized as legitimate only the dynasty reigning from Jerusalem.[16]

The use of the same title in 37:24, רוֹעֶה אֶחָד; ποιμὴν εἷς, confirms this explanation since it follows on the heels of two sticks being joined as one to show the reunification of Israel and Judah (37:15–22). Block does not explain his comments that this "goes beyond Jer 23:4," but nothing in Ezek 34 sets aside Jeremiah's prediction of other eschatological rulers. The fact that there is "one shepherd" emphasizes the reunification of the kingdom and does not contradict Jeremiah's prediction. Other leaders operating in a different capacity does not negate the existence of one primary leader. Instead, the fact that Ezekiel's shepherd is *the* one over the reunified country demonstrates his supremacy. Alone, this does not require him to be the messiah, but we can hardly imagine Matthew seeing anyone else fulfilling this role.

Second, he is "my servant David" (in both v 23 and v 24 – עַבְדִּי דָוִיד; τὸν δοῦλόν μου Δαυιδ, though τὸν δοῦλόν μου is lacking in v 24 LXX). Jer 30:9 and Hos 3:5 also refer to an eschatological David. Some have seen the reference to David as signifying the restoration of the Davidic dynasty, but not a specific messiah per se. The expression וַהֲקִמֹתִי עֲלֵיהֶם רֹעֶה אֶחָד could indicate a resurrection of the historical David since קום carries the meaning "resurrect" elsewhere (e.g. Isa 26:14).[17] However, the verb also denotes installment to office, most significantly in Jer 23:4–5.[18] Given the connection between these two texts, a similar

---

16   Block, "Bringing Back David," 173.
17   The LXX's ἀναστήσω is used in this sense often. BDAG, 83. קום; ἀναστήσω also occurs with the eschatological David in Jer 30:9. A resurrected David is a minority view, but still has its adherents (e.g. John F. Walvoord, "The End Times" in *Understanding Christian Theology*, ed. Charles R. Swindoll and Roy B. Zuck (Nashville: Thomas Nelson, 2003), 1355–56. Mowinckel observes that this view is unlikely because of the scarce references to resurrection in the OT, as well as the phenomenon of calling a Davidide David in Ps 132:10 (Sigmund Mowinckel, *He That Cometh: The Messiah Concept in the Old Testament and Later Judaism*, trans. G. W. Anderson, (New York: Abingdon, 1954), 163). Some have also seen the reference to David as signifying the restoration of the Davidic dynasty, but not a specific messiah per se, a situation which seems more likely in Jer 23 and 33 than Ezek 34 and 37.
18   Block, "Bringing Back David," 175, n. 24. There may be more significance besides simple installment, however. As we will see, he is also described as נָשִׂיא, which comes from נשׂא, "lift up." Though the use of the title itself does not require making the etymological

understanding of קוּם is likely. In this understanding, David is not being resurrected, but a David-like figure is being put into a position. Since the covenant of 2 Sam 7:12–14 / 1 Chron 17:10–14 (cf. Ps 89:3–4) probably lies in the background, which describes a future king as the descendent of David, arising after David "rests with his fathers" (v 12), the installment to office view is most probably correct. In fact, the Davidic covenant may have had such popular familiarity that the mention of "my servant David" might purposefully allude to the use of the expression in 2 Sam 7:5, 8, which is also strengthened by the correspondence of קוּם appearing in both contexts (cf. Ezek 34:23 and 2 Sam 7:12).[19]

The third messianic feature of the shepherd is that he is "leader among them"[20] (v 24 – נָשִׂיא בְתוֹכָם; ἐν μέσῳ αὐτῶν ἄρχων). At first, this might argue against a messianic understanding since Ezekiel often uses נָשִׂיא in seeming distinction from מֶלֶךְ. He uses נָשִׂא in reference to Zedekiah (12:10, 12; 21:25) and reserves מֶלֶךְ for Jehoiachin (1:2). We can explain this by seeing only the latter as the legitimate king.[21] Alternatively, the distinction may stem from Ezekiel's emphasis on YHWH alone as true king, seen as early as the throne scene of ch 1.[22] However, any view that strictly differentiates נָשִׂיא and מֶלֶךְ runs into difficulty in 7:27 and 19:1.[23] נָשִׂיא also refers to one from Egypt, as well as Gog (called נְשִׂיא רֹאשׁ in 38:2, 3, and 39:1). But the last section contains the term's

---

connection, the proximity of וַהֲקִמֹתִי and עֲלֵיהֶם may draw this out. Still, the possibility is only slight and nothing in the argument here rests on it.

19 Johanan ben Zaccai may also provide an example of referring to the messiah with one of the names of the good kings of Judah when he states, "set a throne for Hezekiah, king of Judah, who is coming" (*Ber.* 28b). See further discussion in William Horbury, "Messianism in the Old Testament Apocrypha" in *King and Messiah in Israel and the Ancient Near East: Proceedings of the Oxford Old Testament Seminary*, ed. John Day (JSOTSup; Sheffield: Sheffield Academic, 1998), 424.

20 E. A. Speiser rightly notes that the traditional Western translation "prince" is "the least likely of the attempted translations" ("Background and Function of the Biblical Nasi" *CBQ* 25.1 (1963): 111).

21 Ralph H. Alexander, "Ezekiel" in *The Expositor's Bible Commentary: with the New International Version*, ed. Frank E. Gaebelein (Grand Rapids: Zondervan, 1986), 6:780; Lamar E. Cooper, *Ezekiel* (NAC; Nashville: Broadman & Holman, 1994), 116.

22 Paul M. Joyce, "King and Messiah in Ezekiel" in *King and Messiah in Israel and the Ancient Near East: Proceedings of the Oxford Old Testament Seminar*, ed. John Day (London: Bloomsbury, 2013), 333–37; Timothy S. Laniak, *Shepherds after My Own Heart: Pastoral Traditions and Leadership in the Bible* (NSBT; Downers Grove, IL: InterVarsity, 2006), 160. Iain Duguid rightly concludes, "According to Ezekiel 34, the expected change in Israel's governance will be accomplished not so much through a change in the nature of the *office* but through a change in the nature of the *occupant*" (*Ezekiel and the Leaders of Israel* (VTSup; Leiden: Brill, 1994), 47, emphasis his).

23 Cooper, *Ezekiel*, 116 argues the terms are being used in a more general sense in 7:27. The first two lines seem to be in synonymous parallelism, so that נָשִׂיא and מֶלֶךְ are equivalent. So Greenberg, *Ezekiel 1–20*, 156–57.

predominate usage, in which a figure related to the new temple vision receives the title 18 times (44:3, 45:7, 8, 16, 17, 22, 46:2, 4, 8, 10, 12, 16, 17, 18, 48:21 [twice], and 22 [twice]).[24] Elsewhere in the Hebrew Scriptures, נָשִׂיא denotes one of a position less than מֶלֶךְ.[25] However, 1 Kgs 11:34 shows this is not absolute and the two terms are connected in Ezek 37:24–25. If נָשִׂיא does emphasize subservience, it would no more rule out a messianic identification than the usage of the word עֶבֶד. Zimmerli's commentary is on target, suggesting מֶלֶךְ is avoided, but only to "describe the dignitary in an archaically solemn fashion by means of a genuine ancient Israelite title, which avoids an outworn everyday word current in the international world."[26] Furthermore, the LXX's more general uses of ἄρχων diminishes this possibility of seeing this figure as a king since it translates terms such as שַׂר (over 240×), רֹאשׁ (over 100×), נָשִׂיא (over 90×), and מֶלֶךְ (almost 20×).[27] The term is more general than βασιλεύς and the comments above address concerns as to why the latter is not used here. Hence, the title נָשִׂיא; ἄρχων points in the direction of the figure being the messiah.

Thus, the three features of this text's figure (1) being the "one" shepherd, (2) being called "My servant David," evoking the Davidic covenant and depicting him as a righteous Davidide, and (3) being described is a "ruler," suggest the text itself has the messiah in view. Indeed, in light of the many connections between David and Jesus in Matthew, we can easily imagine Matthew drawing a line between these two here.

2.2.3.2 The Interpretation History of Ezek 34 Suggest a Messianic Understanding

The textual features discussed above in Ezek 34:23–24 suggest these two verses at least would have been viewed messianically and a consideration of some later uses will confirm this understanding. However, the way the messiah gets

---

[24] Cooper, *Ezekiel*, 390 argues he is a representative of the messiah. The connection between the Davidic Shepherd and the temple "prince" is disputed.

[25] *HALOT*, 727. Joyce, "King and Messiah in Ezekiel," 330 states "it is the technical term for the leader of a clan, and is always used of authorities in subordination to a greater authority." Speiser observes that its uses are either in the pre-monarchial period or Ezekiel and afterwards and this suggests its difference from מֶלֶךְ ("Background and Function," 111), but he rightly notes that in Exod 22:27 (cf. Gen 34:2), it approximates the same role (115). See *DCH*, 2:772 for a full listing of uses and referents, ranging from Abraham to Simeon Bar Cosiba to angelic beings.

[26] Walther Zimmerli, *Ezekiel: A Commentary on the Book of the Prophet Ezekiel* (Philadelphia: Fortress Press, 1979), 2:218, 277–79. Block's take is similar, that Ezekiel avoids מֶלֶךְ to emphasize the figure's distinction from other then current kings. Block, "Bringing Back David," 176.

[27] Silva, *NIDNTTE*, 1:414.

mapped into the blend has complications and variations. While some later texts which handle Ezek 34 demonstrate that the figure in vv 23–24 could be mapped directly to the messiah, other texts considering Ezek 34 use the chapter in general messianically, but make no specific recourse to vv 23–24. In this scenario, the messianic elements of the text (2.2.3.1) do not enter the picture. Ezek 34 presents YHWH's shepherding activity in rescuing the lost sheep of Israel. But the messianic figure only appears *after* this restoration and his work is simply described as "shepherding." As Block observes regarding the messianic figure,

> Remarkably, he plays no part in the restoration of the nation. He neither gathers the people nor leads them back to their homeland. Unlike other prophets, Ezekiel makes no mention of the Messiah as an agent of peace or righteousness, these being attributed to the direct activity of God.[28]

Later interpreters pull from the description of YHWH's shepherding activity and map these to the messiah. The logic of this move is not entirely clear. This could result from a "broadly eschatological" paradigm, or mapping via the Vital Relation of "role," in which information is gleaned about the messiah because he is the assumed instrumental agent of YHWH. Alternatively, the interpreter may conflate the two shepherding ministries of YHWH and the messiah in Ezek 34 so that the shepherding work of YHWH in the wider context of the entire chapter transfers to the messiah described in vv 23–24. We will consider three texts which evidence a messianic understanding of Ezek 34, but pull from the description of shepherd YHWH: 1 Enoch 89, Psalms of Solomon 17, and Matt 25. In this category, 1 Enoch stands by itself as it describes the messiah, but Ezek 34 only provides information about God as shepherd. Pss. Sol. 17 and Matt 25 both use Ezek 34 to depict the messiah as shepherd, yet the relevant details come from the section concerning YHWH and not vv 23–24.[29]

---

28 Daniel I. Block, "Bringing Back David: Ezekiel's Messianic Hope" in *The Lord's Anointed: Interpretation of Old Testament Messianic Texts*, ed. Philip E. Satterthwaite, Richard S. Hess and Gordon J. Wenham (Grand Rapids: Baker, 1995), 183. However, he cites Jer 23:5–6 as an example of the messiah being an agent of righteousness. But we will see in 2.3 that the figure there is only installed after the false shepherds are punished and the people are restored to their land.

29 4Q504 ("The Words of Heavenly Lights") also merits attention, but since both the allusion to Ezek 34 and its figure being the messiah are so unclear, drawing conclusions from it seems unwise. It is a collection of prayers for each day of the week. The fourth fragment contains a prayer for the fifth or sixth day. It is both a prayer for restoration as well as a praise for God's past dealings with Israel. Lines 5–8 combine several ideas which are found in Ezek 34. The text reads

But before considering these examples, we should attend to usages in the history of interpretation which seem to have vv 23–24 specifically in view. This will confirm the above section which identified messianic elements of the text, though we will not be able to say with any certainty if later interpreters came to this conclusion for the same reasons as us. Three passages warrant discussion as examples of this category: *Targum Jonathan*, 2 Esdras 2, and John 10, though the last has the clearest messianic use of Ezek 34:23–24. However, as will be shown below, *Targum Ezekiel* obviously has Ezek 34:23–24 in mind, but it is not clear that it sees the passage messianically, while 2 Esdras 2 clearly has the messiah in view, but it is not certain that Ezek 34 is alluded to.

Targum Jonathan renders Ezek 34:24 וַאֲנָא יוי אֱהֱוֵי לְהוֹן לֶאֱלָהּ וְעַבְדִי דָוִיד **מַלְכָּא** בֵּינֵיהוֹן "And I, Adonai, I will be God to them and my servant David will be **king** among them."[30] A textual variant exists in the place of interest (in bold) and it is not clear if the Targumist originally translated נָשִׂיא with מַלְכָּא or רבא. However, evidently someone along the line of transmission used מַלְכָּא, and the argument here does not require the מַלְכָּא reading to be original, since we are concerned with how later interpreters understood the passage. Still, the Targum of the parallel passage of 37:25 has וְדָוִד עַבְדִי מַלְכָּא לְהוֹן לְעָלַם, and here it uses מַלְכָּא without any variants for נָשִׂיא, perhaps due to the influence of 34:24.[31] Thus, regardless whether מַלְכָּא or רבא is the correct reading in 34:24, Tg Ezekiel sees the Davidic "leader" as a king in 37:24–25 and, at the least, so does someone in the transmission of Tg Ezekiel 34:24. This "strengthening" of the Hebrew נָשִׂיא points toward a messianic interpretation.

> ותבחר בשבט יאודה ובריתכה הקימותה לדויד להיות כרעי נגיד על עמכה וישב על כסא ישראל לפניך כול הימים.
>
> "And you chose the tribe of Judah, and established your covenant with David so that he would be like a shepherd, a prince over your people, and would sit in front of you on the throne of Israel forever." (Martinez and Tigchelaar translation). The passage's correspondences with Ezekiel 34:23–24 include הקימותה, לדויד, and כרעי. Though מלך is not used, the concept of kingship is there with the expression וישב על כסא. Furthermore, though נגיד is used (which does not occur in Ezek 34) and not נשיא, there is semantic overlap since both often refer to of a position less than king. The phrase לדויד may, like Ezek 34, refer to an eschatological Davidide, or it may simply concern the historical David. For the former interpretation, see John J. Collins, "Messianism in the Maccabean Period" in *Judaisms and Their Messiahs at the Turn of the Christian Era*, ed. Jacob Neusner, William S. Green, and Ernest S. Frerichs (Cambridge: Cambridge University Press, 1987), 105; For the latter, see Kenneth Pomykala, *Davidic Dynasty Tradition in Early Judaism: Its History and Significance for Messianism* (Atlanta: Scholars Press, 1995), 174.

30 Targum translations are mine unless otherwise noted.

31 The LXX uses ἄρχων here, which consistently translates נָשִׂיא throughout Ezekiel, though it is used for other words as well (שַׂר in 17:12, 22:27; שָׂטִים in 27:8; נָגִיד in 28:2; אַיִל in 31:11; נְסִיכֵי in 32:30) and most noticeable for מֶלֶךְ in 28:12 and 37:22.

Levey has argued that Tg Ezekiel reflects the views of R. Johanan b. Zakkai, who replaced messianism, due to its dangerous implications with Rome, with Merkabah mysticism.[32] His argument depends on a comparison with more overtly messianic interpretations in *Targum Jonathan*, other possible messianic texts (17:22, 21:32, and 29:21) which give no implications of a messiah in the translation, and משחא being absent from Tg Ezekiel. However, Damsma has rightly responded that being less overtly messianic does not mean messianism is being avoided, that a non-messianic interpretation of 17:22, 21:32 and 29:21 better fits the original intent, and that the absence of the actual word משחא does not mean a messianic concept does not occur.[33] Of the 31 uses of מלכא in Tg Ezekiel, three refer to the king of Judah, thirteen to the king of Babylon, two to the king of Tyre, and six to the king of Egypt.[34] This usage of the highest political authority in the land, coupled with the eschatological context and Davidic terminology, argues that the targumist probably had the messiah in view, though this perspective is not as overt as in other targumic translations of other biblical texts.

2 Esdras 1–2 (5 Ezra), commonly thought to be a later Christian insertion to 2 Esdras, also employs shepherding imagery messianically in 2:34. The text reads "Ideoque vobis dico gentes, quæ auditis, et intelligitis, Expectate pastorem vestrum, requiem æternitatis dabit vobis: quoniam in proximo est ille, qui in fine sæculi adveniet." ("Therefore, I say to you gentiles/nations who hear and understand, look for your shepherd. He will give eternal rest to you: for he is near, at the end of the world to come."[35]) This figure seems to be the messiah, who occurs elsewhere in the text, namely 7:26 and 12:32 which are the only places where "Christus" appears.[36] The difficulty with 2:34 for our purposes is that the allusion to Ezek 34 is not clear. Though the proposed source text applies to Israel, and 2 Esdras 2:34 addresses the promise to the gentiles (gentes), this is because Israel rejected the Lord's command (v 33). Furthermore, the promise of "eternal rest" (requiem æternitatis) parallels Ezek 34:25, following

---

32   Samson Levey, *The Targum of Ezekiel: Translated, with a Critical Introduction, Apparatus, and Notes*. (The Aramaic Bible. Edinburgh: T&T Clark, 1987), 4. He also presents this argument in "Targum to Ezekiel" *HUCA* 46 (1975): 144. Block similarly states "the Targum refuses to recognize the Messiah anywhere in Ezekiel," ("Bringing Back David," 168).

33   Alinda Dasma, "The Merkabah as a Substitute of Messianism in Targum Ezekiel?" *VT* 62.4 (2012): 515–33.

34   19:3, 5, and 6 are about lion imagery, part of "a lamentation for the princes (נְשִׂיאֵ) of Israel" (19:1). The uses in 34:24, 37:22, 24, 25 concern the eschatological Davidide in question.

35   Translation mine.

36   For a review of all messianic portions, see Michael E. Stone, "The Messiah in 4 Ezra" in *Judaisms and their Messiahs at the Turn of the Christian Era*, ed. Jacob Neusner, William S. Green and Ernest Frerichs (Cambridge: Cambridge University, 1987), 209–24).

on the heels of the messianic text, in which a בְּרִית שָׁלוֹם; διαθήκην εἰρήνης is promised.[37] Somewhat strangely, this contradicts other statements in 2 Esdras where the messiah's kingdom is said to come to an end (7:29, 12:34). Chae further observes that the reference in 2 Esdras 2:16 to raising the dead and concern for God's name corresponds with Ezek 36:22–23 and 37:1–14, which increases the likelihood of an Ezekielian allusion.[38]

Ezek 34 is clearly evoked in John 10, where the messianic implications are obvious. Manning analyzes several correspondences between the two, concluding they "share three phrases, eleven key words, five close synonyms, and four weaker synonyms. The amount of verbal parallelism demonstrates that John is not merely drawing on everyday shepherd life."[39] Moreover, it draws from both the chapter as a whole and the messianic section (vv 23–24), so that, when the former is the source domain, YHWH as shepherd maps to Jesus but when the source text is particularly the messianic section, that figure maps directly to Jesus.[40] In particular, the expression εἰς ποιμήν (John 10:16) echoes the messianic texts of Ezek 34:23 (ποιμένα ἕνα) and 37:24 (ποιμὴν εἷς). Manning suggests that this double mapping "is intended to communicate Jesus' messianic identity in divine and human terms."[41] He further points to the following controversy surrounding Jesus' statement ἐγὼ καὶ ὁ πατὴρ ἕν ἐσμεν (John 10:30) as support.[42] Carson sees the same significance, referring to the prologue's connection between the Word and God.[43] Caution is in order here. As we will

---

37 In the MT, this is promised "to them" (לָהֶם), but in the LXX it is given "to David" (τῷ Δαυιδ).

38 Chae, *Jesus as the Eschatological Davidic Shepherd*, 159. However, if this passage has been added later with Christian influence, then this may account for the presence of the messianic shepherd and other NT shepherd passages would make the allusion to Ezek 34 less likely. In particular, Stanton has argued that 5 Ezra has been greatly influenced by Matthew (Graham Stanton, "5 Ezra and Matthean Christianity in the Second Century" *JTS* 28.1 (1977): 67–83). If so, this may also explain the statement concerning rest (cf. Matt 11:28).

39 Gary T. Manning Jr., *Echoes of a Prophet: The Use of Ezekiel in the Gospel of John and in Literature of the Second Temple Period* (LNTS; London: T&T Clark, 2004), 112–13.

40 This observation has been made before, though without the precision of Blending Theory. See M. Deeley, "Ezekiel's Shepherd and John's Jesus: A Case Study in the Appropriation of Biblical Texts," in *Early Christian Interpretation of the Scriptures of Israel: Investigations and Proposals*, ed. Craig A. Evans and James A. Sanders (JSNTSup; Sheffield: Sheffield Academic, 1997), 264; Craig R. Koester, *Symbolism in the Fourth Gospel: Meaning, Mystery, Community* (Minneapolis: Fortress Press, 1995), 27–28.

41 Gary T. Manning, "Shepherd, Vine and Bones: The Use of Ezekiel in the Gospel of John" in *After Ezekiel: Essays on the Reception of a Difficult Prophet*, ed. Paul M. Joyce and Andrew Mein (New York: T&T Clark, 2011), 30.

42 Manning, "Shepherd, Vine and Bones," 30–31.

43 Donald A. Carson, *The Gospel according to John* (PNTC; Grand Rapids: InterVarsity Press, 1991), 382.

see, Pss. Sol. 17 will make a similar mapping from YHWH to the messiah, but it is unlikely that the figure there should be understood as divine. Instead, the mapping there is probably via the Vital Relation of "role." Again we will see this in the examination of Matt 25 where "divine identity" is more possible than Pss. Sol. 17 but less likely than John 10. Though judging the conjectures that the Johannine Jesus maps YHWH from Ezek 34 to himself because he shares in that divine identity is difficult, that it picks up on a major theme of that gospel, as well as the immediate pericope, and since others besides Jesus (i.e. the disciples) are not associated with the function of the good shepherd in John makes it probable.

Thus, if Tg Ezek has the messiah in view – which seems likely but not certain – and if 2 Esdras 2 contains a legitimate allusion to Ezek 34 – which seems less likely but far from impossible – then along with John 10 we have three examples of later writings taking up the figure in Ezek 34:23–24 and mapping him to the messiah. This should not be surprising given the messianic components discussed in 2.3.2.1.

However, other Second Temple texts, 1 Enoch 89, Pss. Sol. 17, and Matt 25, clearly have the messiah in view and allude to Ezek 34, yet they do not draw their information about his identity or function from vv 23–24. This yields the conclusion (especially from Pss. Sol. 17 and Matt 25) that it may not even matter if Ezek 34:23–24 would have been seen as messianic, since authors can evoke the broader context and map it to the messiah (if the deity of the messiah is in view, then this can be via the Vital Relation of "identity"; alternatively, "role" would describe the mapping if the messiah's deity is not being considered).

The *Animal Apocalypse* (*1 Enoch* 85–90), ca. 163 BCE,[44] considers the messiah and evokes Ezek 34, yet the messianic portion (vv 23–24) does not play any role in the discussion. The passage uses shepherding imagery thoroughly to describe the history of Israel, from creation to the eschaton in nine periods. Like Ezek 34, it portrays the exile as a time when Israel is ravaged by wild beasts (89:58). Though this text discusses leaders in Israel, including Moses, Joshua, and Ezra, they are described as sheep (e.g. 89:16, 31, 39), who can become rams (e.g. 89:45, 48) who eventually turn into white bulls in the eschaton (90:37–39). The *Animal Apocalypse* only depicts YHWH as shepherd, whom it calls called "the Lord of the Sheep" (89:16). This contrasts with Ezek 34 since in the *Animal Apocalypse*, no human agent, not even the messiah, receives the status of shepherd. Chae's conclusion seems correct, "The fact that the vision avoids calling any leader figure 'shepherd' accentuates God's status as the one and only

---

[44] George W. E. Nickelsburg, *1 Enoch 1: A Commentary on the Book of Enoch, Chapters 1–36; 81–108* (Hermeneia; Minneapolis: Fortress, 2001), 360–61.

'Lord of the Sheep' over Israel."[45] 1 Enoch 90:37 may refer to a messianic figure when it describes a white bull with large horns after the restoration, whom all the other animals fear and petition.[46] This bull's significance, however, does not particularly lie in any actions. Nickelsburg states "His importance lies in his patriarchal status and not in any explicit messianic function. Indeed, different from all the divine agents we have discussed [elsewhere in *1 Enoch*], this figure receives no commission or delegation of authority, nor is he the recipient of revelation."[47] His messianic status may be supported by the several correspondences between the passage and the Son of Man in Dan 7:13–14,[48] though of course scholars dispute the identity of that figure. Some have offered other proposals,[49] but if the white bull is a messianic figure, and if the *Animal Apocalypse* adapts Ezek 34, the portrayals of Israel as an attacked flock of sheep and YHWH as a shepherd map over but the messianic text of vv 23–24 appears to have been neglected. It makes no mention of another shepherd besides YWHW, nor does anything from vv 23–24 stand out in the passage. Thus, the use of Ezek 34 in *Animal Apocalypse* can be labeled "messianic," though only the general, eschatological features of the whole chapter seem to be in view.

Pss. Sol. 17 similarly incorporates a messianic use of shepherding imagery but with unexpected mapping schemes. It contains two places which employ shepherding imagery from OT sources. The first (v 24) describes a ῥάβδος, evoking a shepherd's staff and alluding to Ps 2 as seen in the reference to σκεύη

---

45 Chae, *Jesus as the Eschatological Davidic Shepherd*, 101. Though the actual term "shepherd" is not used of Jewish leaders, Gentile kings receive this title (89:59ff) and Jewish leaders, while remaining sheep, still function as shepherds in their positions of leadership over the sheep.

46 Other Enochic scholars who take this view include Michael Knibb, *The Ethiopic Book of Enoch: Introduction, Translation and Commentary* (Oxford: Oxford University, 1978), 2:216; Gabriele Boccaccini, *Middle Judaism: Jewish Thought, 300 B.C.E. to 200 C.E.* (Minneapolis: Fortress, 1991), 134; Jonathan A. Goldstein, "How the Authors of 1 and 2 Maccabees Treated the 'Messianic' Promises," in *Judaisms and their Messiahs at the Turn of the Era*, ed. Jacob Neusner, W. S. Green, and E. S. Frerichs (Cambridge: Cambridge University, 1987), 72–73.

47 George W. E. Nickelsburg, "Salvation without and with a Messiah" in *Judaisms and their Messiahs at the Turn of the Christian Era*, ed. Jacob Neusner, William S. Green, and Ernest Frerichs (Cambridge: Cambridge University, 1987), 56.

48 Daniel C. Olson, *A New Reading of the Animal Apocalypse of 1 Enoch: 'All Nations Shall Be Blessed': With a New Translation and Commentary* (SVTP; Leiden: Brill, 2013), 29–30.

49 Olson, *A New Reading*, 26 argues against a messianic understanding since the earlier discussion of David and Solomon (89:45–50) do not anticipate a coming Davidic ruler and since the white bulls receives no uniquely messianic traits. See discussion of other interpretations there.

κεραμέως in v 23 (LXX).⁵⁰ However, the figure in view at this point in Pss. Sol. 17 is God. The psalmist petitions him (κύριε, ὁ θεός in v 21) to raise up a king (v 21) and to cleanse Jerusalem (v 22), and the discussion of this latter action utilizes vocabulary from Ps 2 (Pss. Sol. 17:24). Thus, tracing the mapping lines into the blend, we surprisingly find that in this first echo, the messianic portion of Ps 2 applies not to the human king, but to God. The second section (Pss. Sol. 17:40–41) seems to evoke Ezek 34. This second section applies shepherding imagery to the Davidic king (v 21), who is called χριστὸς κυρίου (v 32, cf. the title of ch 18 and 18:7).⁵¹ This text has sufficient similarities with Ezek 34 to suggest an allusion is being made. It states ποιμαίνων τὸ ποίμνιον κυρίου ἐν πίστει καὶ δικαιοσύνῃ καὶ οὐκ ἀφήσει ἀσθενῆσαι ἐν αὐτοῖς ἐν τῇ νομῇ αὐτῶν. ἐν ἰσότητι πάντας αὐτοὺς ἄξει. Besides the ποιμ stem, Ezek 34 also shares ἄγω related words – ἐξάγω, συνάγω, and εἰσάγω all occur in v 13. Moreover, Ezek 34 also describes the sheep with ἀσθενέω (v 4). There may also be a thematic parallel between βοσκήσω αὐτὰ μετὰ κρίματος in v 16 and ποιμαίνων ... ἐν ... δικαιοσύνῃ in Pss. Sol. 17:40.⁵²

Yet none of these alluded texts in Ezek 34 come from the messianic section (vv 23–24). Here we have a reversal of the surprising mapping scheme noted above. Pss. Sol. 17:24 describes God as shepherd, using language from a messianic text (Ps 2); Pss. Sol. 17:40–41 describes the messiah as shepherd, but instead of using the messianic portion (Ezek 34:24–25), it pulls from the generally eschatological material where only YHWH's agency is in view. Though Pss. Sol. 17:24 clearly has the messiah in view, nothing suggests Ezek 34:23–24 is understood messianically. As noted earlier, the psalmist may have felt comfortable mapping the YHWH portions of Ezek 34 to his description of the messiah because he took vv 23–24 messianically and he assumes the shepherding work of one is done by the other. But that the mapping is via the Vital Relation of "role," a "broad eschatological paradigm" which rests on the premise that the messiah is God's agent, sent to do his will is just as likely.

---

50 BDAG, 902. Ps 2:9 LXX has ποιμαίνω as the main verb. The MT has תְּרֹעֵם, "you will break," (from רעע) but apparently the LXX understood the vocalization to be תִּרְעֵם (from רעה).

51 Extant Greek mss have χριστὸς κύριος, but this is probably a translation error, as in Lam 4:20. See Kenneth R. Atkinson, "On the Use of Scripture in Development of Militant Davidic Messianism at Qumran: New Light from *Psalm of Solomon 17*" in *The Interpretation of Scripture in Early Judaism and Christianity: Studies in Language and Tradition*, ed. Craig A. Evans (JSPSS: Sheffield: Sheffield Academic, 2000), 107 n5.

52 However, κρίμα may have a negative connotation in Ezek 34:16 if the antecedent of αὐτά is τὸ ἰσχυρόν, which is the closest. But the antecedent could be the Τὸ ἀπολωλός, in which case βοσκήσω αὐτὰ μετὰ κρίματος would be positive.

Matt 25 presents a similar scenario.[53] This instance is of utmost interest because it comes from the same author as the texts in question (Matt 9:36 and 10:6), though assuming Matthew always uses the same scriptural text uniformly would be a mistake. Examining Matthew's allusion in ch 25 to the same text provides the clearest evidence that Matthew could have seen Ezek 34 as messianic, though his concerns lie elsewhere in 9:36 and 10:6. It also provides us with an instance of a broad eschatological framework, which we will eventually see being employed in the use of Ezek 34 in Matt 9:36 and 10:6 (discussed in 2.2.4.2).

Matthew 25:31–46 concludes Jesus' eschatological discourse (ch 24–25) as the final of four "parables" (two servants in 24:45–51, ten virgins in 25:1–13, and three servants in 25:14–30), though this climax only has one verse containing parabolic elements.[54] In v 32, as the Son of man on his glorious throne, Jesus will separate πάντα τὰ ἔθνη into two groups, ὥσπερ ὁ ποιμὴν ἀφορίζει τὰ πρόβατα ἀπὸ τῶν ἐρίφων. Several biblical backdrops, particularly Dan 7:9–14,[55] lie behind the larger unit, but Matt 25:32 alludes to Ezek 34. Several features point in this direction: Matt 9:36 and 10:6 have already evoked the text in connection with Matthew's shepherd motif; both Matt 25:31–46 and Ezek 34 distinguish between πρόβατα and ἐρίφων (cf. Ezek 34:17[56]), and Matthew includes the relatively surprising title ὁ βασιλεύς in vv 34 and 40, which is explained if Ezek 34:24 and 37:24 are in the background.[57]

---

53 Only brief mention can be made of Matt 18:11–14. The echo of Ezek 34 is much quieter, if it exists at all. But if so, then it too portrays the eschatological shepherd being mapped to different individuals. V 14 describes God the Father in this role. V 11 puts the son of man there, though the verse is probably not original (Bruce Manning Metzger, United Bible Societies, *A Textual Commentary on the Greek New Testament, Second Edition a Companion Volume to the United Bible Societies' Greek New Testament* (4th Rev. Ed.) (London; New York: United Bible Societies, 1994), 34). Furthermore, the overall context suggests the disciples are those who seek reconciliation, meaning they too are shepherds in this sense.

54 Graham N. Stanton, "Once More: Matthew 25:31–46" in *A Gospel for a New People: Studies in Matthew* (Edinburgh: T&T Clark, 1992), 221–30 argues it is best understood as "apocalyptic discourse."

55 Joel 4:1–3 (LXX) is also likely. The passage has similarities with *1 Enoch* and though some see Matthew's dependence on it (see Bird, *Are You the One Who is to Come?* 92), it is far from certain that *1 Enoch* would have been available to Matthew (for different perspectives on this issue, see *Parables of Enoch: A Paradigm Shift*, ed. Darrell Bock and James Charlesworth (London: Bloomsbury, 2013)).

56 The LXX has Ἰδοὺ ἐγὼ διακρινῶ ἀνὰ μέσον προβάτου καὶ προβάτου, κριῶν καὶ τράγων. The syntax of Ezek 34:12 also has similarities with Matt 25:32, though the restoration of the text has complications. See Nolland, *Matthew*, 1025 n213.

57 The Dan 7 connection prepares the reader for this (i.e. v 14), as well as Matthew's earlier (2:2) and later statements (21:5, 27:11, 29, 37, 42). Yet Nolland is correct in saying "the uses in in 25:34, 40 are in a class apart" (Nolland, *Matthew*, 1027). This is understandable,

A brief overview of some complexities will demonstrate that though Matt 25:31–46 does allude to Ezek 34, it is far from a straightforward fulfillment of that text. Instead, Jesus puts his unique spin on this eschatological passage and takes it in surprising directions. Ezek 34 most likely only considers a Judahite audience. But Matthew envisions a judgment of πάντα τὰ ἔθνη (v. 32).[58] Most see worldwide judgment,[59] and thus the scope of judgment here surpasses the one in Ezekiel 34. Complications also arise in considering how the actions of Ezek 34 map to Matt 25:31–46. The actions in Ezek 34 which cause the shepherd to distinguish (שָׁפַט in vv 17, 20, 22; διακρινῶ in vv 17, 20 and κρινῶ in v 22) the animals of his flock include taking the best pasture and water for themselves and spoiling the rest (vv 18–19) as well as forcing out the weak so as to make them prey (vv 21–22). The shepherd in Matt 25:31–46 distinguishes (v 32 ἀφορίσει αὐτοὺς ἀπ' ἀλλήλων) the animals based on whether or not they gave food to the hungry, water to the thirsty, took in the stranger, clothed the naked, visited the sick, and came to the imprisoned (repeated four times in vv 35–36, 37–39, 42–43, 44; the last is abbreviated). Ezekiel's shepherd punishes antagonistic actions and saves the persecuted. But Matthew 25's shepherd punishes neglect and saves, not the persecuted (though that is implied with their description in v 40), but the ones who care for the needy. Moreover, Matthew specifies that those who receive the six actions above are τούτων τῶν ἀδελφῶν μου τῶν ἐλαχίστων and therefore Jesus considers the actions as done to him (v 40, cf. 45). Scholars debate the identity of this group[60] and though

---

however, if Ezek 34 is in view. Recall the discussion of נָשִׂיא in 3.3.2.1 where this title overlaps with מֶלֶךְ.

58   A similar phenomenon has occurred in 2 Esdras 2.
59   Some dispensationalists also see πάντα τὰ ἔθνη as gentiles being judged for their treatment of the Jewish people, particularly the Jewish evangelists of the tribulation. Stanley Toussaint, *Behold Your King: A Study of Matthew* (Grand Rapids: Kregel, 1980), 290–91; Eugene W. Pond, "Who are the Sheep and the Goats in Matthew 25:31–46?" *BSac* 159 (July–Sept 2002): 288–301; John F. Walvoord, *Matthew: Thy Kingdom Come* (Chicago: Moody, 1974), 200. In this understanding, Matthew has put quite a unique spin on Ezek 34.
60   For an argument for the particularist position, see Stanton, "Once More," 207–30 (from whom I take my terminology); Keener, *Gospel of Matthew*, 605–56. For the universalist, see Davies and Allison, *Matthew*, 3:428–29. For an attempt to blend the two, see John P. Heil, "The Double Meaning of the Narrative of Universal Judgment in Matthew 25.31–46," *JSNT* 69 (1998): 3–14. In a universalist interpretation, they are anyone in need and this provides for a more natural mapping of the Ezekielian scheme. But in a particularist interpretation, they are specifically Jesus' disciples carrying his message. In this approach, the goats are judged, not so much for their cruelty but for their rejection of the gospel message (cf. Matt 10:14–15). This would so complicate the transfer from Ezekiel to Matthew that it makes it less likely, though not impossible, this feature of the Ezekielian scheme is being mapped.

some interpretations require a more complicated mapping scheme than others, none are simple.⁶¹

Thus, when considering the Christological use of Ezek 34, we are within our bounds to expect a complicated fulfillment of the shepherd. We had seen earlier that Matthew probably would have viewed vv 23–24 as messianic. This portion emphasizes shepherding but without elaboration, repetitiously stating וְרָעָה אֶתְהֶן אֵת עַבְדִּי דָוִיד הוּא יִרְעֶה אֹתָם וְהוּא־יִהְיֶה לָהֶן לְרֹעֶה (v 23).⁶² Besides the several uses and forms of רעה, it ascribes no specific actions to the Davidic under-shepherd. Instead, the larger unit focuses on YHWH's actions. Block observes a chiasm in vv 4 and 16, in which YHWH undoes the selfish actions of the negligent shepherds.⁶³ Then, he is the one who separates and metes out punishment and salvation to his flock. The whole unit concludes with an abrupt emphasis of the shepherd's transcendency as divine in v 31.

Again, how the Matthean Jesus gets from Ezek 34 to the messiah doing the tasks attributed to YHWH is not clear. We could explain this mapping scheme by seeing Matthew as using a broader eschatological paradigm in which YHWH is the primary agent of establishing the kingdom and assume he will use secondary agents. In this approach, the messianic features of vv 23–24 are surprisingly unnecessary. While we may safely assume that Matthew and his readers would have seen vv 23–24 as significant for understanding the messianic identity of Jesus, nothing in the text of Matt 25 picks up on that messianic portion. We will see the likeliness of this approach when Matt 9:36 and 10:6 are considered below.

Alternatively, Matthew could map Ezek 34:17–22 to Jesus via vv 23–24. In other words, רעה is the one verb associated with the work of the messiah in

---

61   While allusions are rarely, if ever, determinative in preferring competing interpretations, the allusion to Ezek 34 in Matt 25:31–46 points in the direction of the universalist interpretation. This does not solve the debate, but it is a strike against the particularist position. If Jesus evokes Ezek 34 here, which condemns some of the flock for its selfishness and lack of compassion, then it would be strange for Jesus to use language which could so easily align with this but mean something else. However, not all particularist interpretations of this passage see the significance of the sheep's actions in receiving the gospel message. For example, France writes "This passage thus expands on the message of 10:40–42: how people respond to Jesus' representatives is both a sign of their attitude to him and the basis for their reward" (*Matthew*, 965) and yet states "to draw that conclusion does not establish that the 'sheep' are commended because their treatment of disciples reveals their positive attitude to Jesus himself" (*Matthew*, 958–9).

62   The LXX reduces this repetition by only having ποιμανεῖ αὐτούς, τὸν δοῦλόν μου Δαυιδ, καὶ ἔσται αὐτῶν ποιμήν.

63   Daniel I. Block, *The Book of Ezekiel: Chapters 25–48* (NICOT; Grand Rapids: Eerdmans, 1998), 291.

Ezek 34:23–24, but the previous text explains what shepherding looks like. Though word concerns care for the needy, it also ironically entails meting out punishment (v 16 - ; אֶרְעֶנָּה בְמִשְׁפָּט βοσκήσω αὐτὰ μετὰ κρίματος).[64] However, v 23 creates a progression from the previous unit. After YHWH judges the flock, then he installs the messianic shepherd. But in either of the above two approaches, the actions of YHWH from the broader chapter of Ezek 34 are understood messianically.[65] Thus, though the history of interpretation does not provide abundant evidence that Ezek 34:23–24 was seen as a messianic prophecy, we have seen good evidence from Tg Ezek, 5 Ezra, John 10, *The Animal Apocalypse*, Pss. Sol. 17, and Matt 25 that some interpreters understood Ezek 34, whether specifically from vv 23–24 or from the broader chapter, as describing the messiah as an eschatological shepherd.

2.2.4 Ezek 34 Is Evoked in Matt 9:36 and 10:6 to Depict Major Literary Characters

2.2.4.1 Ezek 34 Depicts Characters besides the Apostles

The allusion in Matt 9:36 and 10:6 to Ezek 34 sheds light on several of Matthew's characters. As with Matt 25:31–46, it also presents Jesus as God's true shepherd. The statement in 9:36–37 concludes a major section in which Matthew presents Jesus' words (ch 5–7) and deeds (ch 8–9). Ezek 34:1 has portrayed the eschatological shepherd as healer (particularly YHWH, though since the Davidic under-shepherd is his servant in vv 23–24, he likely has the same role).[66] This

---

64 Assuming the antecedent is "the strong."
65 There are other conceivable explanations for how this mapping is made. Perhaps Matthew records Jesus fulfilling this role because he sees him as the embodiment of YHWH (cf. discussion of John 10). Cf. Hays, *Echoes of Scripture in the Gospels*, 70–71, 189. This is supported if Prov 19:17 stands behind the text. However, the association with Jesus and his disciples from ch 10 seems more likely. Turner has argued that the expression θρόνου δόξης (Matt 25:31) has an extensive background and though sometimes it speaks of God's heavenly reign, Matthew's Deuteronomistic worldview suggests the expression should be understood in light of apocalyptic passages which portray it as "the restored Davidic throne as the center of eschatological judgment, leading to justice and righteousness, the restoration of Israel, and the blessings of the nations." (David Turner, "'His Glorious Throne': The Future of Israel and the Gentiles according to Matthew." Paper presented at SBL 11/19/2016, pg. 9.) The expression is rich with messianic expectations, especially in light of Dan 7. Thus, while it is possible that Matt 25 presents Jesus as divine, his identity as the messiah is more likely center stage. This does not make the explanation of Jesus being YHWH impossible, but if a simpler one exists it is to be preferred. This explanation also runs into difficulty when it is called to mind that the throne of Matt 25:31 is shared with his disciples (cf. 24:47, 25:21, 23 and 34).
66 See "The Davidic Shepherd as the 'Therapeutic Son of David'" in Chae, *Jesus as the Eschatological Davidic Shepherd*, 279–324.

coheres with Matthew's statement concerning Jesus in the previous verse (9:35), θεραπεύων πᾶσαν νόσον καὶ πᾶσαν μαλακίαν (cf. Ezek 34:16). But as the discussion of Jer 23 will show, nothing within the text of the allusion overtly ties Jesus to the shepherd figure. Of all the characters portrayed in Ezekielian terms, Jesus receives the least attention (though this changes in Matt 15:24). That interpreters (rightly) detect a reference to Jesus as shepherd reveals readers' tendency to "run the blend" in the construction of an emerging structure to make implicit mappings.

The greedy shepherds of Ezek 34 similarly map to the leaders of Israel in Matthew's narrative by "running the blend." Matthew describes the crowds with the participles ἐσκυλμένοι and ἐρριμμένοι (Matt 9:36). Several commentators and translators accept a softer meaning, such as "harassed and helpless" (ESV).[67] However, the background of Ezek 34 suggests we see a more vivid image.[68] The former verb has a weaker sense elsewhere in the NT (e.g. "bothered" in Mark 5:35, Luke 7:6, 8:49). It originally meant "flayed"[69] and such a violent meaning fits well here in light of backgrounds like Ezek 34:8 where beasts prey on the flock. The latter can mean either "thrown" or "put down," and though other usage in connection with animals on the ground[70] may favor a softer connotation, the Ezekielian intertext suggests a harsher connotation such as "wasted away" or "discarded."[71] The possible meanings "banish" or "abandon" would also fit nicely in this context.[72] The passive voice of the participles hides the agent of these verbs, but Matthew's larger portrait of Israel's leaders blames them for actively destroying Israel (e.g. 2:16–18, 23:31–35). However, the previous pericope which describes the interaction between the Pharisees and the crowds (9:32–34) illustrates the leaders' heartless attitude toward the people's healing. Like Ezekiel, Matthew blames the leaders for both actively damaging and failing to respond with compassion (i.e. vv. 1–10). Moreover, Matt 10:16 portrays the disciples' enemies as wolves. Though these animals do not occur in Ezek 34, they do in Ezek 22:27 as a description of the nations' rulers (שָׂרֶיהָ; ἄρχοντες). The original context does not clarify if this term refers to prophets and priests (see vv 23–28), but in either case both Ezekiel

---

67 Nolland, *Gospel of Matthew*, 407; Davies and Allison, *Matthew*, 1:98–99.
68 Gundry, *The Use of the Old Testament*, 32.
69 BDAG, 933.
70 BDAG, 906. LSJ, 1572 also lists Dioscorides Pedanius, De materia medica 1.29 and 4.169 in which animals lie down for hibernation.
71 LSJ, 1572. The entry also lists "cast out of house or land" which could possibly correspond with the description of the people as straying and lost (Ezek 34:4).
72 Franco Montanari, *The Brill Dictionary of Ancient Greek* (Leiden: Brill, 2015), 1881.

and Matthew describe Israel's rulers as vicious animals (cf. Matt 7:15 where false prophets are λύκοι ἅρπαγες).

2.2.4.2 Ezek 34 Depicts the Apostles as Healers

Matt 9:36 hints at the relevance of Ezek 34 for understanding the disciples. As the text is part of the conclusion of chs 8–9, which provides examples of Jesus' extensive ministry of compassion, it highlights the limitations of Jesus' work in Israel. Though he has accomplished much, healing πᾶσαν νόσον καὶ πᾶσαν μαλακίαν in πόλεις πάσας καὶ τὰς κώμας (Matt 9:35), the next verse demonstrates the limitations of this hyperbole as much more remains to be done. Certainly Matthew does not attribute inadequacy to Jesus. Instead, the nature of God's mission, here described as eschatological shepherding, requires more than one agent. Thus, he proceeds with a command for prayer for further workers (though the imagery switches from shepherding to harvesters, an image which we will explore in chapter 3).

But Matt 10:6 does explicate the connection between the disciples and eschatological shepherding in Ezek 34. Though it does not directly call the disciples ποιμένες or use them as the subject of ποιμαίνω, by activating Ezek 34 as an intertextual background, he clearly maps them into the blend. Wayne Baxter argues "Nowhere does Matthew call the disciples 'shepherds' or even explicitly associate the verb ποιμαίνω with them. In fact, Jesus sends them out, not as shepherds per se, but as 'sheep in the midst of wolves'. Hence for Matthew ... Jesus is uniquely the Shepherd of God's people Israel."[73] On the contrary, the shift in imagery does not negate their previous position as shepherds since a simple and consistent mapping of figures cannot be assumed. One cannot argue that the many references to Jesus as shepherd means that he is not also the lamb (e.g. John 1:29, 10:14). Imagery is far more flexible than what Baxter allows. Furthermore, the lack of explicit connection with the ποιμεν- word group is an argument from silence. The disciples are only sent to τὰ πρόβατα τὰ ἀπολωλότα οἴκου Ἰσραήλ and the sheep of Ezek 34 are described with ἀπόλλυμι three times (vv 4, 16, 29).[74] In Ezek 34, the most frequent verb used to describe the shepherd's action or the false shepherds' inaction, besides βόσκω or ποιμαίνω, is ἐκζητέω (vv 6, 8, 10, 11, 12; ζητέω in vv 4, 12, 16).[75] Matt 10:6 uses πορεύομαι, which is not found in Ezek 34, so although no lexical correspondence exists, a conceptual echo is formed since "going to lost sheep" approximates "searching for lost sheep." To borrow terminology from Blending Theory,

---

73 Baxter, *Israel's Only Shepherd*, 147.
74 אבד in vv 4, 16. This last verse is not within the parable however.
75 The MT has more variety. It uses בקש in vv 4, 8 16, דרש in vv 8, 10, 11, and בקר twice in v 12.

this is a clear case of the Pattern Completion Principle or "running the blend."[76] The apostles are to go to the lost sheep, and in the imaginative new world created by comparing the task of the Mission Discourse with Ezek 34, this results in the disciples being shepherds.

Moreover, 10:1 describes their ability θεραπεύειν πᾶσαν νόσον καὶ πᾶσαν μαλακίαν, which aligns them with the ministry of Jesus described with precisely the same expression (9:35).[77] Chae convincingly argues that the use of Ezek 34 stands behind Matthew's connection of Jesus as the son of David and Jesus as healer.[78] In addition to examining other uses of Ezek 34 (as was considered earlier), he points to the use of חָבַשׁ; Καταδέω in Ezek 34:4, 16, רָפָא; σωματοποιέω in v 4, חָזַק; ἐνισχυω in vv 4, 16, as well as the context of Matt 8–9. While Matthew never calls the disciples the "sons of David," they do occupy the role of healing shepherds. Besides Matt 10:1 (θεραπεύειν πᾶσαν νόσον καὶ πᾶσαν μαλακίαν), v 8 (ἀσθενοῦντας θεραπεύετε, νεκροὺς ἐγείρετε, λεπροὺς καθαρίζετε, δαιμόνια ἐκβάλλετε) does refer to this therapeutic function. Though the imagery will change by Matt 10:16, where the disciples are sheep (probably occupying the space of persecuted Israel in Ezek 34), Matt 10:6 maps the shepherd figure to them, particularly as in regard to their healing mission.

But how has Matthew gone from the shepherding task of Ezek 34 to the apostles' mission in Matt 10? As with the other uses of this text in the NT, the section applies the material from YHWH as shepherd, not the more narrowly messianic portion. Here we can hardly explain this mapping by seeing the referent as the embodiment of YHWH. Instead, the text has YHWH as the primary agent, but this assumes the execution of this mission requires secondary agency, as we saw was the case in the second set of texts above (the *Animal Apocalypse*, Pss. Sol. 17, Matt 25). Moreover, the Matthean Jesus, at least, feels comfortable in putting the disciples, and not only himself, in that role. This does not elevate the apostles to the same position as Jesus as he is their sender, teacher, and Lord (e.g. Οὐκ ἔστιν μαθητὴς ὑπὲρ τὸν διδάσκαλον οὐδὲ δοῦλος ὑπὲρ τὸν κύριον αὐτοῦ – 10:24),[79] but it does amount to them sharing the same prophesied eschatological function of Ezek 34.

---

76   See pgs. 35–36.
77   However, θεραπεύω is a participle in 9:35 and an infinitive in 10:1.
78   Chae, *Jesus as the Eschatological Shepherd*. See especially "The Davidic Shepherd as the 'Therepeutic Son of David,'" 279–324. This seems much more likely than the Solomon as exorcist explanation.
79   The distance between Jesus and the apostles may also be seen in 10:23 if understood to mean that the disciples' purpose is preliminary to that of Jesus' coming, though this is not directly stated in the text and is far from certain.

10:1 and 10:6 explain how the disciples have come to be in this position. The one who was earlier described as shepherd (9:36) now calls the twelve, whom Matthew explains are ἀπόστολοί (10:1) and whom Jesus sends (ἀπέστειλεν) in v 5. Some connect the position of ἀπόστολος to the Semitic concept of שָׁלִיחַ, in which the one sent bears the authority of and represents the sender, frequently with the illustration of *m. Ber.* 5:5, "a man's sent one [שלוחו] is like to himself."[80] The LXX often uses ἀποστέλλω (over 650 times), and is the favorite choice for interpreting שָׁלַח.[81] However, it only uses ἀπόστολος once, at most.[82] Others have pointed out difficulties with Rengstorf's view.[83] Silva argues the Hellenistic churches would not have been expected to know the Hebrew שָׁלִיחַ and that Greek uses are in contexts which have the gods as senders, concluding that the Gentiles probably would have understood the term in that sense. In a Matthean context, however, both of these arguments do not carry much weight as we have already seen that Matthew was conversant with some form of the Hebrew text and his audience does not seem to be primarily Gentile.

Without entering the larger debate of the background and nature of the office of ἀπόστολος, it is sufficient to consider the immediate context's portrayal of the disciples. Matt 10:40–42 certainly have significant similarities to the Semitic role of שָׁלִיחַ and vv 24–25 similarly depict the close association of the disciple-teacher relationship. How one treats the sent one determines how one responds to the sender. The disciples / apostles have been sent to the lost sheep of the house of Israel, thus are in the same mission as Jesus (cf. 15:24),[84] and thus also become significant eschatological agents to fulfill YHWH's ancient promise of shepherding his people. They are tertiary agents, with YHWH as primary and Jesus as secondary. After all, they only have authority or power to occupy this eschatological role because Jesus has given it to them.

---

80 E.g. Silva, *NIDNTTE*, 1:367; E. J. Schnabel, "Apostle," in *Dictionary of Jesus and the Gospels*, 2d ed., ed. Joel B. Green, Jeannine K. Brown, and Nicholas Perrin (Downers Grove, IL: IVP Academic, 2013), 35. This was thoroughly set forth in K. H. Rengstorf, "ἀποστέλλω" *TDNT*, 1:398–447.
81 E.g. Silva, *NIDNTTE*, 1:366.
82 See textual variants in Ralphs for 1 Kgs 14:6.
83 See history of discussion in Silva, *NIDNTTE*, 1:370–73; J. A. Bühner, "ἀπόστολος," *EDNT*, 1:142–46.
84 15:24 also has the verb ἀποστέλλω and the expression πρόβατα τὰ ἀπολωλότα οἴκου Ἰσραήλ, though it is introduced with εἰς instead of πρός.

2.3 The Contribution of Jer 23:1–6[85]

2.3.1 *Matt 9:36 and 10:6 Do Allude to Jer 23:1–6*

Ezek 34 is a well acknowledged intertext with Matt 9:36 and 10:6, and this passage is strongly tied to Jer 23:1–6. Most scholars see Jer 23 as the fountain head, which has been taken up by Ezekiel (and then again further considered in Deutero-Zechariah).[86] However, this view of the direction of influence has its detractors and differences can depend on competing theories of composition history.[87] It is unnecessary here to argue for one initial text, like Jer 23:1–6, and then consider the others as developments in the history of interpretation, since our interests are in Matthew's use of Scripture, who would not have required one theory of compositional history over another. The fact that Ezek 34 and Jer 23 are connected strongly suggests that the latter text deserves consideration as a possible allusion in Matt 9:36 and 10:6.

Furthermore, Matthew refers to Jeremiah elsewhere (e.g. Matt 2:18, 21:13, and 26:28 allude to Jer 31:15, 7:11, and 31:31 respectively)[88] and the reference to the absence of shepherds in Matt 9:36, though it lacks a verbal parallel, finds a thematic one in Jer 23 since הָרֹעִים הָרֹעִים[89] in v 2 were not actually shepherding, so in no meaningful sense can they be called הָרֹעִים. This is made explicit in Ezek 34:5 where shepherds who do not shepherd mean there are no shepherds,[90] but the seed bed is nonetheless present in Jer 23:1–2. Furthermore, the possibility of Jer 23 as an allusion is confirmed by the history of interpretation. Jerome writes in his commentary on Jer 23,

---

85 Section 2.3 follows my argument in "The Apostles as the Messiah's Kingly and Prophetic Shepherds of Jer 23" *BBR* 29.2 (2019): 154–73.
86 E.g. Block, *The Book of Ezekiel*, 275–6. For a full discussion, see Richard L. Shultz, *The Search for Quotations: Verbal Parallels in the Prophets* (JSOTSup; Sheffield: Sheffield Academic, 1999), 31–34.
87 Rosalie Kuyvenhoven, "Jeremiah 23:1–8: Shepherds in Diachronic Perspective" in *Paratext and Megatext as Channels of Jewish and Christian Tradition: The Textual Markers of Contextualization*, ed. August A. den Hollander, Ulrich B. Schmid, Willem Frederick Smelik (JCPS; Leiden: Brill, 2003), 1–36. The opinion of William H. Brownlee "Ezekiel's Poetic Indictment of the Shepherds" *HTR* 51.4 (1958): 198 is rare in denying any dependence.
88 Cf. the extensive work in Michael Knowles, *Jeremiah in Matthew's Gospel: The Rejected Prophet Motif in Matthean Redaction* (JSNTSup; Sheffield: Sheffield Academic, 1993).
89 This repetition emphasizes that shepherds are to care for the sheep. The expression in English would be something like "shepherds who actually shepherd.". In the LXX they do not receive the title "shepherds," but are called ποιμαίνοντας.
90 The LXX has διὰ τὸ μὴ εἶναι ποιμένας, which could mean "they (the shepherds) were not shepherds."

All hope for Jewish rule was cut off. For this reason, he transitions over to the leaders of the church. Since the synagogue and its 'shepherds' were forsaken and condemned, the message addresses the apostles, about whom it is said, [he then quotes Jer 23:4] ... For boldly and without any fear the apostles will feed the ecclesiastical flock, and the remnant of the people of Israel will be saved from all lands and returned to their fields or pastures and they will be fruitful and multiply. And the Lord will attend to the evil shepherds – that is, the scribes and the Pharisees – for their evil doings.[91]

Whatever one may think of the supersessionism of this interpretation, the key components of equating the scribes and Pharisees with the bad shepherds and the apostles with the good shepherds sits well with Matthew 9:36 and 10:6.

Though Jer 23:1–6 satisfies the criteria of availability, historical interpretation, and thematic coherence, the feature that pushes the passage so that it shares the intertextual spotlight with Ezek 34 is its reference to many (or at least more than one) shepherds in v 4. Ezek 34:23 predicts the coming of "one shepherd" (רֹעֶה אֶחָד; ποιμένα ἕνα[92]). This expression is also found in Ezek 37:24, which follows on the heels of the two sticks being joined as one to show the reunification of Israel and Judah (Ezek 37:15–22). Thus, the fact that there is "one shepherd" emphasizes the reunification of the kingdom. On the one hand, this does not contradict Jeremiah's prediction since the existence of one primary, supreme leader is not negated by other leaders operating in a different capacity. But on the other hand, the difference between the רֹעִים; ποιμένας of Jer 23:4 and רֹעֶה אֶחָד; ποιμένα ἕνα of Ezek 34:23, allows the former to have a much more natural mapping to the context of Matt 10:6 where the twelve disciples occupy the space of "shepherds." This is not to deny that Matt 9:36 and 10:6 allude to Ezek 34, but the difficulties in connecting Ezekiel to Matthew here, compared to the more natural connection in Jeremiah, suggest that both should be strongly considered as intertextual backgrounds. Since Matt 9:36 and 10:6 likely allude to Jer 23:1–6 and send the reader back to that referred text, we now turn our attention there.

---

91 *Ancient Christian Texts: Commentary on Jeremiah: Jerome*, trans. Michael Graves, ed. Christopher A. Hall (Downers Grove, IL: Intervarsity, 2012), 137–38.
92 Codex Alexandrinus has the variant ἕτερον. This variant probably stresses the shepherd figure's difference from the shepherds of 34:1–10.

2.3.2 "Shepherds" Are Royal and Prophetic Figures of the Messiah

Jer 23:1–6 begins with a pronouncement of judgment upon those who were "shepherding" (הָרֹעִים; ποιμαίνοντας) YHWH's pasture. Not only will YHWH remove the evil shepherds and then gather his people, but he will also replace the corrupt shepherds with new ones (וַהֲקִמֹתִי עֲלֵיהֶם רֹעִים וְרָעוּם; καὶ ἀναστήσω αὐτοῖς ποιμένας, οἳ ποιμανοῦσιν αὐτούς – v 4). Furthermore, he will raise up a ruling figure to provide safety for the people (vv 5–6). Two details in this scenario are significant for our understanding of the apostles' description in Matthew: the significance of the designation "shepherds" and their eschatological nature in conjunction with the messiah.

2.3.2.1 "Shepherds" Are General Leaders, including Royal and Prophetic Figures of the Messiah

The shepherd metaphor is a general one, simply denoting leadership. It often occurs in political contexts to depict kings or nobles, such as in ANE texts.[93] It clearly has this sense in passages such as 2 Sam 5:2, 1 Chron 17:6, Ps 78:71–72, Isa 44:28, Mic 5:5, and Nah 3:18.[94] For the passage in question (Jer 23:1–6), the preceding context (ch 22) presents kings as the deficient leaders who must be replaced (e.g. Coniah in 22:24–30). This connection between shepherds and kings is so well-known that it is often assumed that the ideas of "shepherd" and "king" are coterminous.[95]

---

[93] E.g. The Weidner Chronicle; A Hymn to Nanaya with a Blessing for Sargon II. 15–20; An Assurbanipal Hymn for Shamash, reverse line 7; Letter Prayer of King Sin-Iddinam to Nin-Isina line 19; The Birth of Shulgi in the Temple of Nippur, line 1. The above can be seen in *The Context of Scripture: Canonical Compositions from the Biblical World, Vol. 1*, ed. William W. Hallo and K. Lawson Younger Jr. (Leiden: Brill, 2003), 468, 472, 474, 533, 553. For a more complete list, see "Mesopotamian deities with shepherd titles" and "Mesopotamian kings with shepherd titles and epithets" in Laniak, *Shepherds After My Own Heart*, 255–59.

[94] However, this list should not be seen as a small sampling. Though a longer list is possible, this is approximately how many references in the Hebrew Bible which demand reference to the king or noble as רעה.

[95] *HALOT*'s entry for רעה cites the possible reference "of kings or others in power" and lists Jer 23:2 as the only reference (1260). *DCH*, 7:519 only assigns it as "ruler over people as a flock." They are understood to be kings or national leaders by J. A. Thompson, *The Book of Jeremiah* (NICOT; Eerdmans: Grand Rapids, 1980), 169; Allen, *Jeremiah*, 41; Charles L. Feinberg, *Jeremiah: A Commentary* (Grand Rapids: Zondervan, 1982), 32; Carl Friedrich Keil and Franz Delitzsch, *Commentary on the Old Testament* (Peabody, MA: Hendrickson, 1870), 8:37; Peter C. Craigie, *Jeremiah 1–25*, (WBC; Dallas: Word, 1991), 29.

Though this royal sense occurs often, it would be a mistake to view "shepherd" as a metaphor strictly referring to kings.[96] Elsewhere Jeremiah employs the image to depict leaders in general, as in as Jer 10:21, 12:10, 25:34, 50:6, and 44.[97] Though these could be understood as references to political rulers, nothing in the context requires only royal figures to be in view. This general use of the metaphor coheres well with Jeremiah's judgment of leadership as a whole, of which kings are only a part (e.g. Jer 1:18; 2:26; 4:9; 5:31; 6:13; 8:1; 13:13). Furthermore, in light of the general nature of the metaphor, the burden of proof falls on those who claim kings are exclusively in view, which is difficult to maintain.[98] As confirmation, the Targum's translation of רֹעִים in 23:4 as פַּרְנָסִין, "community leaders" or "stewards" attests to the general nature of the image. The general nature of this metaphor allows different kinds of leaders to be in view.

Elsewhere in Jeremiah, the shepherd image is also linked with the prophets (cf. Isa 59:11).[99] Jeremiah, who is preeminently a prophet (1:5),[100] has described himself as a shepherd in Jer 17:16. 3:15, another eschatological text, may also

---

96 Contra J. G. S. S. Thomson, "The Shepherd Ruler Concept in the OT and Its Application in the NT," *SJT* 8.4 (1955): 409–10; Allen, *Jeremiah*, 256–58; Thompson, *Jeremiah*, 486–87 (who also includes nobles). Wayne Baxter argues that non-Christ believing Jews (his term) and Christ-believing Jews use the shepherding imagery differently in both his monograph *Israel's Only Shepherd* and his essay "From Ruler to Teacher: The Extending of the Shepherd Metaphor in Early Jewish and Christian Writings" in *Early Christian Literature and Intertextuality: Volume 1: Thematic Studies*, ed. H. Daniel Zacharias and Craig A. Evans (London: T&T Clark, 2009), 213 in which he states "The restriction of the shepherd metaphor to earthly monarchs and civic rulers disappears in the New Testament. 'Shepherd' ... appears explicitly as a title for leaders." Though he notes that the imagery is applied to prophets and priests ("From Ruler to Teacher," 211–2; *Israel's Only Shepherd*, 46), he does not allow for their inclusion in texts like Jer 23 or Ezek 34. There is no reason to exclude the office of prophet and priest from the metaphor, and passages like Jer 3:15 prohibit concluding "teaching was a later and somewhat unexpected association of the shepherd metaphor" (*Israel's Only Shepherd*, 14).

97 The fact that YHWH functions as a shepherd in v 3 also indicates that this metaphor should not be pressed for too much definition, as his kind of leadership is not limited to that of a king.

98 In agreement with Craigie, *Jeremiah 1–25*, 328; Jack R. Lundbom, *Jeremiah 21–36: A New Translation with Introduction and Commentary* (AB; New York: Doubleday, 1999), 164; Feinberg, *Jeremiah*, 161; Keil and Delitzsch, *Commentary on the Old Testament*, 8:216; Gerard van Groningen, *Messianic Revelation* (Eugene, OR: Wipf and Stock, 1990), 698.

99 So J. Andrew Dearman, *Jeremiah and Lamentations* (NIVAC; Grand Rapids: Zondervan, 2002), 217. Feinberg states "a number of commentators understand the godly shepherds to be Zerubbabel, Ezra, Nehemiah, the Maccabees, and others" but does not list any examples. *Jeremiah*, 162.

100 This is how he is depicted by Matthew (2:17 and 27:9).

explain the nature of shepherding as including dispensing knowledge (וְנָתַתִּי לָכֶם רֹעִים כְּלִבִּי וְרָעוּ אֶתְכֶם דֵּעָה וְהַשְׂכֵּיל; καὶ δώσω ὑμῖν ποιμένας κατὰ τὴν καρδίαν μου, καὶ ποιμανοῦσιν ὑμᾶς ποιμαίνοντες μετ᾽ ἐπιστήμης), though deciding whether knowledge is the purpose of the shepherding (i.e. "the shepherds give the sheep knowledge") or the manner (i.e. "the shepherds shepherd skillfully") is difficult. Jer 2:8 warrants special consideration. The fourfold structure may connect shepherds with prophets. This text features four figures, connected with the repeating conjunction וְ; καί.

הַכֹּהֲנִים לֹא אָמְרוּ אַיֵּה יְהוָה	οἱ ἱερεῖς οὐκ εἶπαν Ποῦ ἐστιν κύριος;
וְתֹפְשֵׂי הַתּוֹרָה לֹא יְדָעוּנִי	καὶ οἱ ἀντεχόμενοι τοῦ νόμου οὐκ ἠπίσταντό με,
וְהָרֹעִים פָּשְׁעוּ בִי	καὶ οἱ ποιμένες ἠσέβουν εἰς ἐμέ,
וְהַנְּבִיאִים נִבְּאוּ בַבַּעַל	καὶ οἱ προφῆται ἐπροφήτευον τῇ Βααλ

In this text, הָרֹעִים; οἱ ποιμένες in the third line should be distinguished from הַכֹּהֲנִים; οἱ ἱερεῖς, תֹפְשֵׂי הַתּוֹרָה; οἱ ἀντεχόμενοι τοῦ νόμου and הַנְּבִיאִים; οἱ προφῆται. On the one hand, this may preclude identifying the shepherds as priests and prophets. On the other hand, the meaning of תֹפְשֵׂי הַתּוֹרָה is debated[101] and there may be some overlap in their role with the priests in line 1 (e.g. Mal 2:7). If lines 1 and 2 are coupled together, 3 and 4 may form a pair as well, linking הָרֹעִים and הַנְּבִיאִים. In any case, הָרֹעִים is here linked with offices that may be categorized as spiritual leaders, though an anachronistic division between "church and state" must be avoided, as if kings or nobles were not spiritual leaders as well. But the categorization is helpful inasmuch as it designates those who were set apart to work with God's law.

As noted earlier, the previous material in Jer 22 strongly suggests the well attested meaning "kings," as does the immediately following reference to the Davidic King. However, the following unit (Jer 23:9–40) faults the spiritual leadership. Both prophets and priests are mentioned in v 11, but the prophets are center stage in vv 9, 13, 15, 16, 21, 25, 28, 30, etc. נביא and נבא, not to mention synonymous expressions, occur 11 times in 23:9–25. This suggests that they too are leaders who must be replaced according to the scenario in vv 1–4.

The appropriateness of including Jer 23:9–40 may also be seen in another Matthean allusion. Matt 7:22 (πολλοὶ ἐροῦσίν μοι ἐν ἐκείνῃ τῇ ἡμέρᾳ, Κύριε κύριε, οὐ τῷ σῷ ὀνόματι ἐπροφητεύσαμεν) may evoke Jer 23:25 (οἱ προφῆται, ἃ προφητεύουσιν ἐπὶ τῷ ὀνόματί μου), which similarly considers false prophets. This would be a quieter echo, but if it exists it would increase the likelihood

---

101   See discussion in William McKane, *Jeremiah 1–25: A Critical and Exegetical Commentary* (ICC; London: T&T Clark, 1986), 32; Craigie, *Jeremiah 1–25*, 29.

that Matthew picks up on the prophetic element of the shepherding imagery in Jer 23 in Matt 9:36 and 10:6, since that source text would have been already activated. In light of the links elsewhere in Jeremiah between this kind of leadership and the shepherd motif, this type of leadership should not be ruled out either. Instead, it is best to conceive of the shepherd metaphor as referring to general leadership, with the surrounding context connecting the image to "political" oversight (before) and "spiritual" oversight (after).

2.3.2.2 "Shepherds" Are Eschatological Figures in Connection with the Messiah

The entirety of Jer 23:1–6 would probably have been understood eschatologically by Matthew and his readers. The passage divides into two sections, vv 1–4 and 5–6, and the latter of these units begin הִנֵּה יָמִים בָּאִים נְאֻם־יְהוָה; Ἰδοὺ ἡμέραι ἔρχονται, λέγει κύριος.[102] This foresees future fulfillment, and commentators who deny the category "eschatology" for vv 5–6 only do so because of a different definition of the term than used here.[103]

Vv 1–4 are not so self-evidently eschatological. Vv 1–2 denounce the shepherds who scatter the flock, typically understood as the then current negligent Jewish leaders.[104] Vv 3–4 promise that YHWH will bring them back from their scattered state and set up (וַהֲקִמֹתִי; ἀναστήσω) new shepherds in their place. Yet, though vv 3–4 are not introduced like vv 5–6, the context is nonetheless future. V 3 locates these events when the flock has been brought back מִכֹּל הָאֲרָצוֹת; ἀπὸ πάσης τῆς γῆς. According to Jeremiah, this return from exile will happen no sooner than seventy years later (25:11–12, 29:10–14). But Matthew would not have seen this as completely accomplished in the Persian restoration. For him, it would have required an eschatological fulfillment. The theme of return

---

102   In the MT, the unit extends from v 1 to v 8 and is in three sections. Verse seven transitions to the third section with the conjunction לָכֵן. The LXX does not include verses 7–8.

103   E.g. Leslie C. Allen, *Jeremiah: A Commentary* (OTL; Louisville, KY: Westminster John Knox Press, 2008), 259 writes "it is not 'eschatological' in the sense that it contains anything that deviates from the course of ongoing human history under Yahweh's providential control."

104   Craigie, *Jeremiah 1–25*, 325; Feinberg, *Jeremiah*, 161; Lundbom, *Jeremiah 21–36*, 164. Other commentaries equate the shepherds with kings but without much discussion besides ANE context (McKane, *Jeremiah*, 1:555; Thompson, *The Book of Jeremiah*, 487; Allen, *Jeremiah*, 257). In discussing the Ezekielian counterpart, Block argues the negligent shepherds must only be the former kings of Judah, not the leadership in general, since the ram and goat imagery (Ezek 34:17–22) applies to the citizens of the nation and since the answer to the dilemma is the establishment of the Davidic ruler in 34:23–24. (Block, *Ezekiel*, 282). However, there is no reason to insist the imagery is used consistently and since our text (Jer 23:4) lies in the background of Ezek 34, others besides the messiah are established in response to the poor leadership of Jeremiah's time.

from exile has received much scholarly attention, with varying approaches, but there is a general consensus that Matthew viewed the restoration from exile in eschatological terms, fulfilled in the events of his narrative.[105] Moreover, since these events are logically connected to vv 1–2, it seems likely that Matthew would have seen the section about the poor leaders as having some element of fulfillment at his time, confirmed by implicit judgment of the religious leaders in Matt 9:36.[106]

Not only are these shepherding kings and prophets placed within the eschaton, but four features of vv 5–6, taken together, suggest those verses are messianic and thus the shepherds should be seen as related to him. First, in contrast to the failing kings decried in previous chapters, the passage foretells in v 5 that וּמָלַךְ מֶלֶךְ וְהִשְׂכִּיל. The double emphasis of the root מלך, as well as the contrast with previous kings, emphasizes the royal nature of this figure, also preserved in the LXX, βασιλεύσει βασιλεύς. Second, this character clarifies the judgment against Coniah in Jer 22:30, who will not have a successor on the throne of David. To clarify this is not the end of the Davidic monarchy, 23:5 states וַהֲקִמֹתִי לְדָוִד צֶמַח צַדִּיק; καὶ ἀναστήσω τῷ Δαυιδ ἀνατολὴν δικαίαν.[107] This figure's description as צַדִּיק very well may have the idea of "legitimate," as attested in other ANE uses.[108] However, the other use of צְדָקָה in this verse, as well as its other uses in Jeremiah has an ethical / moral component (for צַדִּיק, see Jer 12:1 and 20:12; for צְדָקָה see 3:11, 4:2, 9:24, 22:3, and 22:15).[109] But the two are far from exclusive and the strong support for both understandings suggests Jeremiah is making a *double entendre* here, as only the king who does righteousness is the rightful king.[110] Third, the singular מֶלֶךְ; βασιλεύς may indicate one specific figure is in

---

[105] For a succinct overview see J. M. Scott, "Exile and Restoration" in *Dictionary of Jesus and the Gospels*, 2d ed., ed. Joel B. Green, Jeannine K. Brown, and Nicholas Perrin (Downers Grove, IL: IVP Academic, 2013), 251–58. For a fuller exploration, see Jörg Frey, "The Reception of Jeremiah and the Impact of Jeremianic Traditions in the New Testament: A Survey," in *Jeremiah's Scriptures: Production, Reception, Interaction, and Transformation*, ed. Hindy Najman and Konrad Schmid (JSJSup; Leiden: Brill, 2016), 499–543.

[106] Additionally, Jer 23:3 states that when returned, וּפָרוּ וְרָבוּ; καὶ αὐξηθήσονται καὶ πληθυνθήσονται, which might echo Gen 1:28 and thus depict the eschatological "new creation." Lundbom, *Jeremiah 21–26*, 169; Craigie, *Jeremiah 1–25*, 328, who also suggests it evokes exodus terminology from Ex. 1:7.

[107] Terrence E. Fretheim, *Jeremiah* (SHBC; Macon, GA: Smyth & Helwys, 2002), 324.

[108] See discussion and references in Lundom, *Jeremiah 21–36*, 172.

[109] It also includes "legal responsibilities in connection with the machinery of justice" (McKane, *Jeremiah*, 564–5).

[110] Craigie, *Jeremiah 1–25*, 330; McKane, *Jeremiah*, 561.

view, though a generic use is possible.[111] Fourth, the title צֶמַח; ἀνατολή[112] may be a thematic, but not verbal, allusion to Isa 11:1

וְיָצָא חֹטֶר מִגֵּזַע יִשָׁי וְנֵצֶר מִשָּׁרָשָׁיו יִפְרֶה Καὶ ἐξελεύσεται ῥάβδος ἐκ τῆς ῥίζης Ιεσσαι,
καὶ ἄνθος ἐκ τῆς ῥίζης ἀναβήσεται.

This context is as messianic as they come in the Hebrew Scriptures.[113]

These features in Jer 23:5–6 together suggest a messianic understanding and the passage's later use in Jewish literature demonstrates this perspective in varying degrees. Some of these portions are in relatively clear messianic contexts and the fact that they call to mind Jer 23:5–6 is best explained by the writers seeing this text as a messianic oracle. As mentioned earlier, Ezek 34 is well established as having some intertextual link with Jer 23:5–6 and the likelihood that Ezek 34:23–24 has the messiah in view is high. For the sake of space, only a whistle-stop tour of Jer 23's history of interpretation can be offered here.

The Targum is undisputedly messianic, translating v. 5 וַאֲקֵים לְדָוִד מְשִׁיחַ דְצִדְקָא וְיִמְלוֹד מַלְכָּא.[114] Also, the title צמח / ἀνατολή is used in biblical literature as a messianic title in Zech 3:8. Though this text mentions Joshua the high priest and his companions, they are not equated with the צֶמַח / ἀνατολή but are a sign (מוֹפֵת) of it.[115] The messianic nature of this passage in Zechariah is

---

111 For an example of how a seemingly generic use of the singular can be understood messianically, see Richard B. Hays' treatment of Hab 2:4 in "The Righteous One as Eschatological Deliverer" in *Apocalyptic and the New Testament: Essays in Honor of J. Louis Martyn*, ed. J. Marcus and M. L. Soards (JSNTSup; Sheffield: JSOT Press, 1989), 191–225.

112 The LXX translation is typically described either as mistaken or picking up on the "glow" elements of צמח. Gregory Lanier persuasively argues that ἀνατολή can have an agricultural connotation and is used to refer to arising deliverers, making it an accurate translation of צמח. "The Curious Case of צמח and ἀνατολή: An Inquiry into Septuagint Translation Patterns," *JBL* 134.3 (2015): 505–27.

113 Marvin A Sweeney, "Jeremiah's Reflection on the Isaian Royal Promise: Jeremiah 23:1–8 in Context," in *Uprooting and Planting: Essays on Jeremiah for Leslie Allen*, ed. John Goldingay (LHBOTS; New York: T&T Clark, 2007), 317 discusses the relationship (though he argues Isa 11 refers to King Josiah). Gerbern S. Oegma's study of messiah texts from 300 BCE to 200 CE concludes that Isa 11 and Dan 7 were the two most often referred texts when discussing the messiah (*The Anointed and his People: Messianic Expectations from the Maccabees to Bar Kochba* (JSPSup; Sheffield: Sheffield Academic, 1998), 303).

114 A. Sperber, *The Aramaic Bible* (Leiden: Brill, 1974) notes a textual variant of משיחא דצדקא, but this does not affect the argument here. A messianic interpretation is not surprising since in Targum Jeremiah, "the goal and seal [of right interpretation] is the Messiah, the Son of David, who is to restore righteousness in Jerusalem" (Flesher and Chilton, *The Targums*, 211).

115 The LXX translates this with τερατοσκόποι, "observer of τέρατα, soothsayer, divine" (LSJ, 1776).

suggested by the expression עַבְדִּי, and relevant for our study is the witness to a messianic understanding within the Christ movement in Rev 5:6 (ἀρνίον ... ἔχων ... ὀφθαλμοὺς ἑπτά. Cf. Zech 3:9, עַל־אֶבֶן אַחַת שִׁבְעָה עֵינָיִם; ἐπὶ τὸν λίθον τὸν ἕνα ἑπτὰ ὀφθαλμοί εἰσιν). צמח / ἀνατολή also occurs in Zech 6:9–15 which has been understood messianically.[116] Willitts has also argued that Jer 23 stands behind all of Pss. Sol. 17, pointing to the following correspondences: condemnation of current leaders (Jer 23:1–2 / Pss. Sol. 17:5–25); gathering the flock of Israel (Jer 23:3 / Pss. Sol. 17:26, 44); and the installation of a wise and just Davidic king (Jer 23:5–6 / Pss. Sol. 17:26–43).[117] If this allusion exists, which seems likely, then again Jer 23 is connected to a clearly messianic passage (e.g. Pss. Sol. 17:35–6, αὐτὸς βασιλεὺς δίκαιος ... καὶ βασιλεὺς αὐτῶν χριστὸς κύριος). 4Q252 5:3–4 sees Gen 49:10 messianically and supports its interpretation with an allusion to Jer 23:5 when it states Israel and her rulers will continue עד בוא משיח הצדק צמח דויד. 4Q174:10–11 cites 2 Sam 7:13–14 (though not the condition about sinning against YHWH and this decreases the possibility that Solomon is in view, shifting the focus to an ideal king) and then states לבן הואה צמח דויד.

Other texts contain a less likely, though still quite possible, messianic use of Jer 23:5–6. There may be a connection between Jer 23:5 and Ps 132:17, which states שָׁם אַצְמִיחַ קֶרֶן לְדָוִד עָרַכְתִּי נֵר לִמְשִׁיחִי. However, deciding the direction of potential influence depends on the dating of the psalm, which is far from certain.[118] Moreover, the messianic nature of the text is disputed as well.[119] 4Q285 similarly may use צמח דויד messianically in fragment 5:2–3. Though this is not universally acknowledged[120] and there are many lacunae, the relevant portion reads ויצא חוטר מגזע ישי |...| צמח דויד.[121] This connects Isa 11:1 with

---

116 Joyce G. Baldwin, "*Semah* as a Technical Term in the Prophets," *VT* 14 (1964): 93–97.
117 *Matthew's Messianic Shepherd-King*, 83 n138.
118 John Goldingay, *Psalm 90–150* (BCOTWP; Grand Rapids: Baker, 2008), 544 suggests it is so difficult that it should not be pursued. Allen P. Ross, *A Commentary on the Psalms: Volume 3* (Grand Rapids: Kregel, 2016), 728–30 explores different suggestions, but favors the traditional view that it was written by David after receiving the covenant.
119 Some see the verse as describing the kingship of David (e.g. Nancy deClaissé-Walford, "Psalm 132" in *The Book of Psalms*, ed. Nancy deClaissé-Walford, Rolf A. Jacobson, and Beth LaNeel Tanner (NICOT; Grand Rapids: Eerdmans, 2014), 936; Leslie C. Allen, *Psalms 101–150* (WBC; Nashville: Word, Thomas Nelson, 2002), 274–75. Goldingay, *Psalms 90–150*, 557 is more nuanced, but states צמח is a messianic term within the OT. Ross, *A Commentary on the Psalms*, is closer still, but explains "the psalm does not say this is 'the' Messiah, only that there will be a glorious future king who will flourish and put down all their enemies," 741.
120 See discussion in John J. Collins, *The Scepter and the Star: Messianism in light of the Dead Sea Scrolls* (Grand Rapids: Eerdmans, 2010), 67.
121 The translation by F. Garcia Martinez and E. J. C. Tighchelaar has "A shoot will emerge from the stump of Jesse ... the bud of David." *The Dead Sea Scrolls Study Edition* (Leiden: Brill, 2000), 643.

Jer 23:5, though the former is a more exact quotation, וְיָצָא חֹטֶר מִגֵּזַע יִשָׁי, and the latter inverts the word order and omits the preposition ל, (Jer 23:5 reads וַהֲקִמֹתִי לְדָוִד צֶמַח). 4Q161 3:18 may also use צמח in messianic contexts, but lacunae make this a difficult connection.

Though some references have clearer allusions than others and the messianic nature of some of the referring texts are more certain than others, there is nonetheless abundant evidence that ancient Jewish literature evoked Jer 23 when discussing the messiah and this increases the likelihood that Matthew would have seen the text similarly.[122] Though Jer 23:4–6 does not explain the exact relationship between the "shepherds" and the "shoot," by the latter immediately following the former, connected with ו; καί, some kind of close relationship is suggested. It is easy to imagine Matthew seeing Jesus and his apostles embodying this relationship.

2.3.3 Matthew Portrays the Disciples as "Shepherds"

2.3.3.1 Matthew Presents the Disciples as Royal Figures in Connection with the Messiah

If the disciples are to be understood in light of Jer 23:4, what does this say about them? The ruling elements of the source domain find an easy mapping to the apostles.[123] Like the shepherds of Jer 23, Matthew depicts the disciples as political rulers. This is most easily seen in the throne logion (Matt 19:28), which

---

122   Some equate these shepherds with the righteous shoot of v 5, taking the latter as a dynasty as opposed to a singular messianic figure. E.g. Allen, *Jeremiah*, 259; Fretheim, *Jeremiah*, 326. However, not only have we seen arguments for why Matthew would have seen v 5 as messianic, but the arguments for equating the two verses seem doubtful. This "equivocation" viewpoint may be supported by a comparison with 33:14–18, which Jeremiah scholars often see as dependent on 23:1–6. [e.g. Sweeney, "Jeremiah's Reflection," 3109–11]. 33:17 states לֹא־יִכָּרֵת לְדָוִד אִישׁ יֹשֵׁב עַל־כִּסֵּא בֵית־יִשְׂרָאֵל (the LXX does not have this text) which may indicate a succession of kings. However, though 23:5–6 and 33:15–16 are extremely similar, this should not be taken to mean 33:17 redefines צֶמַח צַדִּיק; ἀνατολὴν δικαίαν. Instead, it explains a significance of the figure's installment, namely that it confirms God's word to David (כִּי־כֹה אָמַר יְהוָה). Moreover, 33:17 is sufficiently ambiguous as to not require a succession of kings as the text uses the singular, לֹא־יִכָּרֵת לְדָוִד אִישׁ. Furthermore, the succession view is harder to substantiate in the Ezekiel counterpart.

123   In light of the above defense of the general nature of the shepherd metaphor in Jer 23:4, which also includes priests, the possibility of the apostles fulfilling this role cannot be ruled out. But while the portrayal of the apostles as prophets and as political rulers is present in Matthew, a priestly role is not prominent in Jer 23:4. Still, the disciples as priests is a definite motif in Matthew. See Michael P. Barber, "Jesus as the Davidic Temple Builder and Peter's Priestly Role in Matthew 16:16–19." *JBL* 132.4 (2013): 935–53. Cf. Jarrett van-Tine, "The Restoration of Israel's Priesthood as the Framework for Matthean Ethics." SBL Presentation, Boston, MA, November 21, 2017.

states the twelve will rule over the restored twelve tribes in the παλιγγενεσίᾳ.[124] This should be connected to the expectation of restored twelve phylarchs which was "in the air in the first century."[125] In addition to Willitts' arguments concerning the political nature of these positions, it can be added that the disciples are often associated with being first or great in the kingdom (Matt 18:4, cf. 5:19, 19:30, 20:25–27) which has connotations of political authority in at least some Matthean contexts. Matt 19:30 is extremely close at hand to the throne logion (v 28) and thus the use of πρῶτος likely has ruling implications, as seen in the participial phrase (perhaps telic) κρίνοντες τὰς δώδεκα φυλὰς τοῦ Ἰσραήλ. Though κρίνω may have connotations of "judging" here, aspects of "ruling" seem more likely.[126] In any case, the sense of πρῶτος would be the same and one can agree at a minimum with Nolland's conclusion, "We do not yet know what is to be reversed, but after vv. 27–29 a connection with rewards and status is likely."[127]

Πρῶτος in Matt 20:25–27 is also explicitly about political positions in the kingdom (cf. vv 21–23). In fact, 19:28–20:28 form a unit in response to Peter's question in 19:27. The unit is tied together with statements about the reversal

---

124 Contra UBS5 and NA28 reading, which places the comma after παλιγγενεσίᾳ so that it modifies οἱ ἀκολουθήσαντες.

125 Willitts, *Matthew's Messianic Shepherd-King*, 120; William Horbury, *Messianism Among Jews and Christians*, 2d ed. (London: Bloomsbury, 2016), 186–219. He also observes that the repetition of the phrase "sheep without a shepherd" occurs in Num 27:17, 1 Kgs 22:17, and 2 Chron 18:16, which are all in political contexts (122–125). However, as noted earlier, I doubt these specific texts are being evoked.

126 Warren Carter, *Matthew and the Margins: A Socio-Political and Religious Reading* (JSNTSup; Sheffield: Sheffield Academic, 2000), 392 helpfully comments, "While various traditions envisage Israel judging the Gentiles (Wis 3:8; *T. Abr.* A 13:6) or the elect/righteous judging the nations (1QpHab 5:4; 1QS 5:6–7; 1QM 6:6; 11:13–14), several observations count against the first option here. (1) Judgment of others is not something disciples are permitted to do (cf. 7:1–2; the same verb κρίνω [*krino*]). (2) In the eschatological scenes, the Son of Man and his angels enact judgment (13:39–43; 25:32), not disciples. In support of the second option of ruling as their role are scenarios such as Dan 7 (involving the Son of Man) in which the saints reign in 'an everlasting kingdom' (7:27), and traditions in which the twelve patriarchs rule gathered Israel (1QM 2:1–3)." Cf. Ben Witherington, *Matthew* (SHBC; Malcon, GA: Smyth and Helwys, 2006), 372; Turner, *Matthew*, 475; Matthias Konradt, *Israel, Church, and the Gentiles in the Gospel of Matthew*, transl. Kathleen Ess (Waco: Baylor, 2014), 259–63; Davies and Allison, *Matthew*, 3:55–56. Furthermore, it is important to avoid anachronistically separating ruling from judging.

127 Nolland, *Gospel of Matthew*, 805. Matt 19:30 may form the conclusion of the previous section, similarly to 20:16 (an extremely similar but not verbatim repetition), but the two probably form an inclusio around the parable of the vineyard laborers. If the former, then the δέ introducing Matt 19:30 is simply a coordinating conjunction. But if the latter, it would be contrastive, to qualify the above discussion which stresses merit over grace.

of first and last (with only slight variation) in 19:30 and 20:16 and a discussion about greatness in terms of "sitting" bracket the unit. In 20:21, the "right hand" is an expression referring to high regard and honor (Gen 35:18, 1 Kgs 2:19, Ps 45:9, Zech 3:1).[128] Though the term left hand sometimes refers to the opposite of the right (e.g. Matt 25:33), this can hardly be the mother's request in Matt 20. That this position speaks of ruling authority can be seen by Jesus' comparison with οἱ ἄρχοντες τῶν ἐθνῶν (v 25).[129] Blomberg's statement, "Jesus' point may well be that God has chosen no particular individuals for such roles"[130] is hardly justified by appealing to 20:1–16. To the contrary, Jesus does not deny the disciples' categories of greatness, but affirms them and states these positions do exist οἷς ἡτοίμασται ὑπὸ τοῦ πατρός μου (v 23). It would be wiser to let a clear text like 19:28–30 and 20:20–28, which specify positions of greatness, inform the uninterpreted parable of 20:1–16 rather than the reverse.[131]

The political overtones of greatness or being first in the kingdom can also be seen in the description of Mordecai's political position. The LXX renders Esther 10:3 ὁ δὲ Μαρδοχαῖος διεδέχετο τὸν βασιλέα Ἀρταξέρξην καὶ μέγας ἦν ἐν τῇ βασιλείᾳ. This being "great in the kingdom" at least includes his high rank as second to Ahasuerus. Though certain uses of "great" or "first" in the kingdom do not demand a political interpretation (5:19, 11:11, and 18:1–4), it may be that the other uses should inform them.[132] But if not, they do nothing to detract from the political connotations found elsewhere. Thus, though not all of Matthew's references to the disciples as royal figures are equally clear, there

---

128   Silva, *NIDNTTE*, 1:665. The right hand is often the description of where Jesus has ascended (e.g. Matt. 26:64, Acts 2:33, 5:31, Rom. 8:34, Eph. 1:20, Col. 3:1, Heb. 1:3, 1 Pet. 3:22). *Midr. Ps.* 18 § 29 in discussing Ps. 110:1 says the messiah will sit on God's right hand and Abraham at his left. This shows that the left is not a derogatory place, but still less than the right. See discussion in Walter Grundmann, "Δεξιός" TDNT, 2:40.
129   Contra Witherington, *Matthew*, 378 who sees this as a reference to the messianic banquet.
130   *Matthew*, 307; cf. Craig Blomberg, "Degrees of Reward in the Kingdom of Heaven?" *JETS* 35.2 (June 1992): 167.
131   On the overuse of the laborer parable to the neglect of the wages theme in Matthew, see Nathan Eubank, "What Does Matthew Say about Divine Recompense? On the Misuse of the Parable of the Workers in the Vineyard (20:1–16)" *JSNT* 35.3 (March 2013): 242–63. Cf. John K. Goodrich, "Rule of the Congregation and Mark 10:32–52: Glory and Greatness in Eschatological Israel" in *Reading Mark in Context: Jesus and Second Temple Judaism*, ed. Ben C. Blackwell, John K. Goodrich, and Jaston Maston (Grand Rapids: Zondervan, 2018), 166–73.
132   If Matt 5:19 is about leadership in the future kingdom, then the passage links the two aspects of shepherding discussed here. The result would be the idea that those who shepherd now (doing and teaching the law), will become shepherds in the eschaton (will be called great in the kingdom).

is still enough textual warrant to see how they could function as Jeremiah's shepherding kings.

2.3.3.2 Matthew Presents the Disciples as Prophets in Connection with the Messiah

Though Matthew eventually describes the disciples as rulers, this is not found in the immediate context. Instead, the mission discourse more loudly resonates with the aspect of the shepherds as prophets and therefore forms the primary intertextual connection. The priestly elements of Jer 23 easily map to the disciples' portrait in the Mission Discourse. Matt 10:7 records their first responsibility in mission, πορευόμενοι δὲ κηρύσσετε. Moreover, the following imperatives in v 8 are best understood as subsumed under the command to preach. That is to say, the work of healing, raising, cleansing, and exorcism is confirmation of the message "Ἤγγικεν ἡ βασιλεία τῶν οὐρανῶν.[133] The priority of their speaking ministry is also seen in the imperatives εἴπατε and κηρύξατε in 10:27.

This is not to say that the apostles hold the same office as the prophets as there are differences between the two positions in Matthew (e.g. in the parable of the wicked tenants of Matt 21:33–41 prophets occupy the space of "servants" whereas the apostles are linked with the new "farmers" in charge of the vineyard). Still, seven observations suggest a comparison, though not identification, is natural. First, Jer 23 highlights the prophet's need to proclaim God's message (v 28) and this corresponds to the apostles' task in the mission discourse. Second, the apostles' activity may have more of a charismatic element than simple preaching in light of Matt 10:19–20 (i.e. τὸ πνεῦμα τοῦ πατρὸς ὑμῶν τὸ λαλοῦν ἐν ὑμῖν in v 20). Third, Matt 10:40–41 connects the apostles to prophets and righteous men, though why these descriptions come in a three-part structure is unclear. Fourth, the Sermon on the Mount presents the disciples in continuity with the prophets of old (Matt 5:12) who are πρὸ ὑμῶν. This phrase seems to mean more than "chronologically prior," which would have gone without saying.[134] David Turner rightly describes these verses as "the crucial text on the disciples as rejected prophets."[135] The Sermon on the Mount also seems to assume prophetic activity on the part of Jesus' disciples, though far from being the necessary feature of a genuine follower (Matt 7:21–23). Fifth,

---

133　This is a common explanation for the significance of Jesus' miracles. E.g. Mark Strauss, *Four Portraits, One Jesus: A Survey of Jesus and the Gospels* (Grand Rapids: Zondervan, 2011), 461–66.

134　Contra BDAG, 864.

135　David Turner, *Israel's Last Prophet* (Minneapolis: Fortress Press, 2015), 178. He devotes a chapter in his monograph to this motif, 177–224.

prophetic activity is described in 7:15 as interacting with sheep. Though the image is a negative one and the false prophets are wolves in sheep's clothing,[136] still this provides support for viewing the prophetic work as interacting with sheep. Sixth, Matt 23:34 does envisage a kind of "Christian prophet," along with sages and wise men.[137] Seventh, the message "Ἤγγικεν ἡ βασιλεία τῶν οὐρανῶν[138] connects the function of the apostles with Jesus (Matt 4:17) and John the Baptist (3:2). Though Matthew describes both of these characters as surpassing the role of prophet, this does not eliminate that aspect of their description. For John the Baptist, Matt 14:5 and 21:26 state that the people viewed him as a prophet. That this is correct, though not far enough, is seen from Jesus' appraisal in 11:9 that John is both a prophet (προφήτην; ναί) and "more than a prophet" (περισσότερον προφήτου), as well as John's connection to the prophet Elijah (17:11–13). For Jesus, the crowds are stated as seeing him as a prophet (16:14, 21:11). That this is not an inappropriate title (though, analogously with John, it is insufficient) can be seen from 13:35 where the Matthean narrator connects Jesus as the "fulfillment" of the prophet Isaiah and 13:57 where the Matthean Jesus applies a saying about a prophet being without honor to himself. With these prophetic aspects of the apostles' mission in ch 10, there are sufficient reasons to connect them with Jeremiah's eschatological shepherds (Jer 23:4) who are raised up in conjunction with the messiah.

Though Willitts brings valuable insights into Matthew's political use of the shepherding motif (discussed above), he goes too far in his redactional comparison between Matt 9:36–37a and Mark 6:34 when he states "Rather than teaching Matthew's Jesus *appoints* the Twelve and sends them out on a mission to the 'lost sheep of the house of Israel.'"[139] On the one hand, Mark immediately follows his description of the shepherd-less people with καὶ ἤρξατο διδάσκειν αὐτοὺς πολλά, and based on a view of Markan priority, Matthew has removed the shepherdless sheep saying from *that* teaching context. But on the other hand, *this* context to which Matthew relocates it also has teaching and preaching elements. In Matthew, a significant difference is that the apostles are sent as emissaries of Jesus with his message, but the overall effect is still Jesus' concern to reach Israel with God's message.

---

136   Heil suggests the repetition of this description in 10:16 connects the passages. "Ezekiel 34," 702.
137   Carlston and Evans, *From Synagogue*, 309–313 discuss "prophets" as the first category of "Christian leaders" in Matthew.
138   The statement is identical except 3:2 and 4:17 include the postpositive γάρ since it is preceded with the command to repent.
139   Willitts, *Matthew's Messianic Shepherd-King*, 133, emphasis his.

Thus, Jer 23:1–6 offers intriguing possibilities as an intertextual background for Matt 9:36 and 10:6. It provides specific textual warrant from the Hebrew Scriptures for Matthew's description of the twelve apostles as eschatological shepherds, sharing in the work of restoration with the messiah, the צֶמַח צַדִּיק; ἀνατολὴν δικαίαν. Moreover, this connection highlights the significance of the apostles in their prophetic role during the gathering process, as well as their ruling responsibilities afterward. Jer 23, with its direct mapping of the plural shepherds of v 4 to the apostles (via the Vital Relation of "identity"), demands serious consideration in understanding Matthew's description of the apostles.

Whether Jer 23:1–6 or Ezek 34 is considered as the background, the action attributed to YHWH is executed by the agency of the disciples as those whom Jesus commissions and summons alongside of (and also underneath) him. If one starts with Ezek 34, the mapping to the disciples is best described as via the Vital Relation of "role," in which YHWH uses agents to actualize his blessings. If one starts with Jer 23, the Vital Relation is most likely "identity" and comes through the plural shepherds of v 4. Since both Ezek 34 and Jer 23 contain a section which Matthew and his readers would have likely seen as messianic, the decision to focus on other components of the passage with agency besides Jesus reflects Matthew's wider purposes and his concern for the disciples' eschatological significance. The use of Ezek 34 in Matt 25 (cf. 15:24) firmly places Jesus in the role of eschatological shepherd. But the fact that Matt 10:6 has the disciples occupying that space shows that Matthew does not see the eschatological shepherd as a narrow role in which only Jesus belongs.

We set out to establish that in Matt 9:36 and 10:6, the Matthean Jesus creates a conceptual blend in which he:

(1) maps a messianic figure from a source domain
and (2) maps the disciples from the target domain to that figure.

Regarding (1), we have seen that the blend's most likely source domain is Ezek 34, an allusion which is relatively well accepted. We have also seen that Jer 23 is more than satisfactory in meeting the criteria of an allusion and should also be considered as a source domain for our blend. However, we cannot be entirely certain if Matthew has only Ezek 34 in view or if he also intends Jer 23 to be considered (such a multi-scope blend seems the most likely option). But in either situation, the argumentation works. Both Jer 23 and Ezek 34 are messianic in that they are contexts which include information about the messiah and the general passage was used messianically by later interpreters. However, if Jer 23 is considered as the source domain, the mapping scheme only concerns v 4. This verse is not messianic in the sense that it speaks of the messiah (who is only introduced in vv 5–6). The figures described in v 4 can only be considered "messianic" in that they are associated with the messiah. Thus, this second allusion does not quite fit (1) above. Yet it is still significant for our research since the nearby verses (Jer 23:5–6) were seen as messianic, but when Matthew evokes this passage, he passes on possibility of mapping the צמח to Jesus, but instead maps the רעים to the apostles. On the other hand, with Ezek 34 as the source domain, (1), (2), and (3) are met, though it is not clear how relevant vv 23–24 are to its messianic use. But later interpreters (most significantly Matthew in ch 25) evoke this passage to portray the messiah as fulfilling the shepherding ministry assigned to YHWH in the wider context of the chapter.

Regarding (2), we have seen that the disciples are clearly mapped into the blend to the eschatological figure from Jer 23 and/or Ezek 34. If Jer 23 is the source of information about the eschatological shepherds, this accentuates the disciples' role as both kingly and prophetic leaders of the nation. If Ezek 34 is considered as the source, this results in highlighting the disciples' healing ministry. In either case, messianic imagery is used to non-messianically, such that the disciples fulfill a role traditionally assigned to the messiah.

2.4 The Contribution of Zech 10:2–4

2.4.1 *The Possibility That Matt 9:36 and 10:6 Allude to Zech 10:2–4*

After describing the futility of consulting idols,[140] Zech 10:2 explains the consequence (עַל־כֵּן; διὰ τοῦτο) of this behavior for Judah with the phrase נָסְעוּ כְמוֹ־צֹאן יַעֲנוּ כִּי־אֵין רֹעֶה; ἐξήρθησαν ὡς πρόβατα καὶ ἐκακώθησαν, διότι οὐκ ἦν ἴασις.[141] In response, YHWH's anger leads him to punish (פקד) the shepherds so he can rescue (פקד, paronomasia) his flock with the result that they are no longer oppressed, but become like glorious war horses (וְשָׂם אוֹתָם כְּסוּס הוֹדוֹ בַּמִּלְחָמָה; καὶ

---

[140] This verse has raised questions about the dating of the oracle since the Persian period seems to have lacked idolatry as found earlier in Israel's history. But the expression may be deliberately using archaic language to express unfaithfulness. Mark J. Boda, *The Book of Zechariah* (NICOT: Grand Rapids: Eerdmans, 2016), 602.

[141] BHQ rightly notes that Aquila, Symmachus, and Theodotion have mistakenly read רעה as רפא. Anthony Gelston, *Biblia Hebraica Quinta: The Twelve Minor Prophets: Volume 13* (Stuttgart: Deutsche Bibelgesellschaft, 2010), Zec 10:2. Cf. ἐπὶ τοὺς ποιμένας in v 3. The Vulgate and Syriac also have "shepherd." ἐξήρθησαν, the LXX reading here (Rahlfs), is attested in recension of Lucian and the corrected Sinaiticus. Vaticanus, the original Sinaiticus, Alexendrinus, Marchalianus, Freer, and the recension of Catena Magna in Prophetas Inventa all have εξηρανθησαν – "they were dried up." Neither exactly corresponds to נסע, though ἐξαίρω is closer.

τάξει αὐτοὺς ὡς ἵππον εὐπρεπῆ αὐτοῦ ἐν πολέμῳ, v 3). Unlike Jer 23 and Ezek 34, Zech 10:2–4 makes no mention of a shepherd (or shepherds) whom YHWH uses in this process. This decreases the likelihood that Matt 9:36 and 10:6 allude to the text since there the disciples are shepherds. Without shepherding agency in Zech 10:2–4, the potential allusion stands in a class apart from Jer 23 and Ezek 34.

However, reasons to think Matt 9:36 and 10:6 quietly echo the Zechariah text remain. Like the sources from which it came (Jer 23 and Ezek 34), Zechariah 10:2–4 describes Israel as functionally shepherdless because of deficient leadership (v 2) and states that God will intervene to rescue his flock (v 3). The frequent use of Deutero-Zechariah elsewhere in Matthew, particularly with the shepherd motif (26:31, cf. Zech 13:7) also strengthen the possibility of an allusion to Zech 10.[142] But though these features are important in establishing the possibility of an allusion, by themselves they do not require an intertextual connection. However, the following two observations tip the balances in favor of an allusion:[143] (1) Matthew would have seen Zech 10:2–4 similarly to Jer 23:4–6 (though with considerably less delineation) as combining a description of both the messiah and general eschatological rulers; and (2) Zech 10 uniquely resonates with the complex portrayal of the apostles in the mission discourse as oppressors who execute God's judgment. Nothing in the overall argument of this volume requires there to be an allusion to Zechariah, yet the possibility is worth exploring since, if valid, this proposed allusion would strengthen our argument as well as provide another layer of complexity to the intertextual portrayal of the apostles. The prominence of the allusion to Ezek 34 and Jer 10 makes judging an allusion to Zech 10 difficult. Still, textual features suggest the connection and the resulting picture of the apostles as warriors engaged in conflict fits well with the context of the Mission Discourse.

2.4.2 The Combination of the Messiah and General Eschatological Rulers Suggests the Allusion

Zech 10:4 states מִמֶּנּוּ פִנָּה מִמֶּנּוּ יָתֵד מִמֶּנּוּ קֶשֶׁת מִלְחָמָה מִמֶּנּוּ יֵצֵא כָל־נוֹגֵשׂ יַחְדָּו; καὶ ἐξ αὐτοῦ ἐπέβλεψεν καὶ ἐξ αὐτοῦ ἔταξεν, καὶ ἐξ αὐτοῦ τόξον ἐν θυμῷ· ἐξ αὐτοῦ

---

142   See John Nolland, "The King as Shepherd: The Role of Deutero-Zechariah in Matthew" in *Biblical Interpretation in Early Christian Gospels: Volume 2: The Gospel of Matthew* (London: T&T Clark, 2008), 133–46 for an exploration of this theme. Though Nolland also notes that the resulting compassion for the sheep is present in both texts, this is not as loud of a resonance as the other parallels.

143   Since there are not sufficient references to this passage in later relevant writers (besides the Targum) this section focuses primarily on the actual text of Zech 10:2–4. The Targum translates פנה with מַלְכַיָּא and יתד with מְשִׁיחֵיהּ.

ἐξελεύσεται πᾶς ὁ ἐξελαύνων ἐν τῷ αὐτῷ. Several features demonstrate Zechariah views some kind of leadership, most clearly the use of פִּנָּה and יָתֵד. HALOT describes the semantic range of the former as a corner (whether of a house, street, or wall), a corner stone, a battlement (Zeph 1:16, 2 Chron 26:15, Sir 50:2), or, metaphorically, for a chieftain or leader (Judg 20:2, 1 Sam 14:38, Isa 19:13, Zeph 3:6), which is how they categorize Zech 10:4.[144] Peterson rightly notes that it could be the foundational stone or last stone, but in either case the figurative use is similar since it "designates a crucial stone in the structure from which the building finds its stability" and suggests the translation "keystone."[145] Concerning the latter, major lexica identify the usage here to refer to a leader, whether "'the support' for a ruler of the people,"[146] "ruler as support of state,"[147] or "a *prince*, from whom the care of the whole state hangs as it were."[148] Wolters suggests יָתֵד should be understood as a weapon, pointing to Judg 4:21,22, and 5:26 (cf. 16:14).[149] However, the use of an everyday object as a weapon in another context does not mean that lexicographers should define the object as a weapon. If, for example, someone learning English read a story about someone defending himself with a frying pan, the correct conclusion would hardly be that the English words "frying pan" fall under the category, "weapon!" Given the previous housing imagery in Zech 10:3–4, we should prefer the predominate usage of יָתֵד as tent peg, used metaphorically here for leadership.[150]

Though the text concerns leadership, how does it expect this to function? Some have understood the passage messianically. Unger, for example, states "this verse constitutes one of the most far-reaching and meaningful Messianic prophecies in the Old Testament."[151] However, this is far from incontrovertible. The following discussion demonstrates that on the one hand, the text contains elements which suggest the messiah is in view, but on the other, factors point to general leadership being considered. In light of the strong exegetical support for both referents and the fact that we have already seen Jer 23 combines both elements, we can conclude that Matthew would have seen both in this text.

---

144   944–45. Similarly Boda, *The Book of Zechariah*, 614.
145   Anthony Robert Petterson, *Behold Your King: The Hope for the House of David in the Book of Zechariah* (New York: T&T Clark, 2009), 161.
146   HALOT, 451.
147   BDB, 450.
148   GHCLOT, 376. Italics theirs.
149   Albert M. Wolters, *Zechariah* (HCOT; Leuven: Peeters, 2014), 322. For further evidence, he also states "In contemporary discussions of the history of weaving, this implement is also frequently called a 'weaving sword'" (322).
150   Zechariah 12:7 specifically uses tent imagery with Judah (as does Ps 78:67). Petterson, *Haggai, Zechariah & Malachi*, 232.
151   Merrill F. Unger, *Zechariah: Prophet of Messiah's Glory* (Eugene, OR: Wipf & Stock, 2014), 177.

2.4.2.1   Reasons to See the Leader as the Messiah

While textual features support the view that the envisioned leadership includes the messiah, the strength of these depends on the extent to which Zechariah should be read intertextually.[152] Possible intertextual connections with the key words in v 4 suggest a messianic understanding. The use of פִּנָּה may allude to other OT texts. Zech 4:7 would be the closest at hand.[153] It has already stated that Zerubbabel will bring out the capstone[154] (וְהוֹצִיא אֶת־הָאֶבֶן הָרֹאשָׁה). Both passages use יצא, though the verb is so ubiquitous as to make this insignificant. The concept of the messiah as a temple builder will be discussed later, but the significant point at this stage is that the imagery of a capstone has already been used in a context discussing God's program for Judah using his chosen leadership, with the potential understanding that the messiah in view. The use of פִּנָּה may also allude to Ps 118:22, a text which we explore more fully in a later chapter. At this point, we can note that Ps 118 was understood messianically, arguably by Matthew as well (21:42), and so if Matthew evokes this passage, one can see how an interpreter would take the cornerstone in Zech 10:4 as a reference to the messiah. פִּנָּה also occurs in Isa 28:16, which the temple builder chapter will discuss as having messianic potential. (However, the connotations of leadership, and perhaps intertextual connections to messianic texts, is only relevant to our consideration of Matthew if one assumes the Hebrew text is in view.) The reference in the second line, 4b, to יָתֵד, also occurs in an Isaianic text (22:23) which has been labeled messianic. Though Matthew does not explicitly refer to this text, Rev 3:7 does allude to it in reference to Jesus.

The occurrence of נוֹגֵשׂ connects our passage to Zech 9:8, specifically וְלֹא־יַעֲבֹר עֲלֵיהֶם עוֹד נֹגֵשׂ; καὶ οὐ μὴ ἐπέλθῃ ἐπ' αὐτοὺς οὐκέτι ἐξελαύνων. This word choice is peculiar since נגשׂ usually refers to oppressors, frequently those from Israel's Egyptian bondage (e.g. Ex 3:7, 5:6, 10 13). Zech 9:10 confirms this connection,

---

152   However, since our research has suspended the issue of whether Matthew had something like the LXX or the MT, both must be kept open as an option. The LXX translates the verse καὶ ἐξ αὐτοῦ ἐπέβλεψεν καὶ ἐξ αὐτοῦ ἔταξεν, καὶ ἐξ αὐτοῦ τόξον ἐν θυμῷ· ἐξ αὐτοῦ ἐξελεύσεται πᾶς ὁ ἐξελαύνων ἐν τῷ αὐτῷ. The translation in the first line seems to be a lexical error, ἐπέβλεψεν, in which the vowel pointing פִּנָּה (MT) was misunderstood to be פָּנָה (Gelston, *Biblia Hebraica Quinta: The Twelve Minor Prophets*, Zec 10:4).

   In the second line, the LXX translates יָתֵד with τάσσω. This is the only time יָתֵד is translated this way in the LXX and seems to have been influenced by the earlier use of τάσσω in v 3, and perhaps τόξον in the next line (the text reads καὶ ἐξ αὐτοῦ ἔταξεν, καὶ ἐξ αὐτοῦ τόξον). The use of verbs here instead of nouns removes emphasis from a new figure on the scene and focuses on the result of YHWH's actions.

153   Meyer and Meyer, *Zechariah 9–14*, 200 identify 4:7 as an allusion.

154   The nature of this "capstone" has received much scholarly attention. See Meyers and Meyers, *Zechariah 1–8*, 246–48 for an overview of interpretations.

which denies there will be סוּס; ἵππον and קֶשֶׁת מִלְחָמָה; τόξον πολεμικόν,[155] corresponding to their existence in 10:3 and 4 respectively. The tables will turn so that Judah's enemies will become the powerless ones, "oppressed" by Judah. The connection to 9:8–10 links our text to the activity of the king in 9:9 (applied to Jesus in Matt 21:5).

Though the expression כָּל־נֹגֵשׂ יַחְדָּו; πᾶς ὁ ἐξελαύνων ἐν τῷ αὐτῷ excludes a singular referent, this does not mitigate against a messianic reference in the verse as the four lines may not have the same referent in view. Commentators have handled this in different ways, with some suggesting the first three lines should be separated from the last with only the former lines being seen as messianic,[156] while other commentators have seen 4d as evidence that a singular messiah cannot be in view in v 4a–c.[157] Indeed, if Jer 23:4 stands behind Zech 10:4d, why might not Jer 23:5–6 stand behind Zech 10:4a–c?

2.4.2.2 Reasons to See General Leadership

However, general, non-messianic leadership may be in view. As with the plural "shepherds" in Jer 23:4, so too the plural "oppressors" of Zech 10:4 resists a messianic interpretation. The most likely reconstruction is that the tribe of Judah leads the nation.[158] As Boda writes, "Judah's restoration is the first step in a pro-

---

155 The LXX here more accurately translates מִלְחָמָה than in 10:4.
156 E.g. George L. Klein, *Zechariah* (NAC; Nashville, TN: B&H, 2008), 192; Duguid, "Messianic Themes," 272.
157 E.g. Wolters, *Zechariah*, 318; Suk Yee Lee, *An Intertextual Analysis of Zechariah 9–10: The Early Restoration Expectations of Second Zechariah* (New York: Bloomsbury, 2015), 182 rightly sees the plural shepherds of Jer 23:4 behind כָּל־נֹגֵשׂ in 10:4 (192), and identifies Jer 23:5–6 as messianic (e.g. 190), but does not allow for the possibility that such a conjunction of several leaders along with the messiah occurs in Zech 10:4.
158 This is not to deny that the possibility general leaders over Judah are depicted, which is possible as well. Not only would the parallel to Jer 23:4 suggest this, but so would the possible connection to Jer 30, suggested by Boda, *The Book of Zechariah*, 612–14. Against the possibility that Judah is here envisioned as the leader is the possible antecedent of the fourfold expression מִמֶּנּוּ; ἐξ αὐτοῦ. The antecedent of this pronoun is debated by Zechariah scholars, with some advocating YHWH, (Boda, *The Book of Zechariah*, 613; Iain Duguid, "Messianic Themes in Zechariah 9–14" in *The Lord's Anointed: Interpretation of Old Testament Messianic Texts*, ed. Philip E. Satterthwaite, Richard S. Hess, and Gordon J. Wenham (Grand Rapids: Baker, 1995), 271; Anthony R. Petterson, *Haggai, Zechariah & Malachi*, (APOTC; Downers Grove, IL: InterVarsity, 2015), 232), and others advocating Judah (Meyer and Meyer, *Zechariah 9–14*, 199; Klein, *Zechariah*, 293; Carl Friedrich Keil and Franz Delitzsch, *Commentary on the Old Testament* (Peabody, MA: Hendrickson, 1996), 10:585). If the antecedent of מִמֶּנּוּ; ἐξ αὐτοῦ is Judah, then this sits most comfortably with the terms referring to Judah's leader(s). However, the phrase is probably best understood as meaning "from YHWH" since he is closest at hand (הֹוד is two words earlier in the MT and αὐτοῦ is five words earlier in the LXX, both clearly

gram that will then impact the tribes of the former northern kingdom."[159] This is the simplest way to understand the flow of thought. V 3 establishes the scenario of YHWH coming as a shepherd[160] (picking up the previous imagery of Zech 9:16), to transform his flock from oppressed sheep into war horses. Judah's militaristic description continues in v 5 (and both continue the imagery from 9:13, 15). The simplest analysis of the structure would be for the intervening v 4 to continue the description of Judah, so that the material from the last line of v 3 through v 5 all form one picture of the restored tribe. Also, line three (v 4c) קֶשֶׁת מִלְחָמָה; τόξον ἐν θυμῷ[161] calls to mind 9:13, which has recently stated דָרַכְתִּי לִי יְהוּדָה קֶשֶׁת; ἐνέτεινά σε, Ιουδα, ἐμαυτῷ τόξον. This identification of Judah as a bow, being so close at hand to Zech 10:4, suggests this line does not describe a leader from Judah, but that the tribe itself is in view.[162]

Thus, each of these possibilities has textual support. The reference to the plural כָּל־נוֹגֵשׂ יַחְדָּו; πᾶς ὁ ἐξελαύνων ἐν τῷ αὐτῷ rules out the messiah being in view for the whole text, but this does not mean lines 1–3 do not envision the figure. The possible intertextual connections to texts Matthew elsewhere sees as messianic, the tradition in the Targum, and the close connection to Zech 9 which Matthew certainly sees as messianic (21:5) at the very least suggest the messiah would have been in mind somewhere in the text. The possibility that the text views others as well has strong textual support. The most likely reconstruction is that Matthew would have seen the messiah in Zech 10:2–4, but not to the exclusion of other leaders.

2.4.3 Zech 10:2–4 Uniquely Resonates with the Complex Portrayal of the Apostles as Oppressors Who Execute God's Judgment

Though the combination of a messianic leader and general eschatological leadership suggests something similar to Jer 23 and Ezek 34 occurs in Matt 9:36 and 10:6, Zech 10's unique contribution to the mission discourse is the most persuasive argument for establishing the allusion. Despite the many similarities between Jer 23:1–6, Ezek 34, and Zech 10:2–4, one notable difference is the use of militaristic language in Zech 10. The wider context of Zechariah specifies

---

referring to YHWH) and since the last reference to Judah was with the plural (Duguid, "Messianic Themes," 271).

159   Boda, *Zechariah*, 612.
160   This is implied from the description of flock belonging to him (עֶדְרוֹ; τὸ ποίμνιον αὐτοῦ).
161   BHQ suggests the Greek comes from בחמה. Targum Jonathan characteristically interprets the figure of speech, using תְּקוֹף קְרָבַיָּא, "the strength of war."
162   However, Jer 49:35–38 may provide precedent for understanding bow imagery to denote specific leaders. Similarly, Egyptian literature gives Ramses II the title "He who repels the Nine Bows," in reference to Egypt's enemies.

the purpose of this violence as being agents through whom God executes his judgment (e.g. 9:14–16). The mission discourse portrays the apostles as "oppressors" or as warriors with a "battle bow" in two ways– their combat with the demonic realm and their conflict with those who do not respond properly to the kingdom message.

2.4.3.1 Matt 9:36 and 10:6 Uses Zech 10:4 to Depict the Apostles Executing Judgment on Demons

The first description of Jesus' commission in 10:1, ἔδωκεν αὐτοῖς ἐξουσίαν πνευμάτων ἀκαθάρτων ὥστε ἐκβάλλειν αὐτὰ καὶ θεραπεύειν πᾶσαν νόσον καὶ πᾶσαν μαλακίαν, foregrounds the conflict with the demonic realm as central to the apostles' mission since it is the first purpose phrase listed. Modern discussions of exorcism often utilize the vocabulary of "spiritual battle," but is viewing this image in Matt 10 anachronistic? On the one hand, the reference to πνευμάτων ἀκαθάρτων suggests purification imagery, especially since this is not Matthew's normal way of referring to these beings (he favors the διαμ- root[163]). The Second Temple Period records several accounts of exorcisms,[164] sometimes added to biblical characters whom the canonical text gives no indication were engaged with demons (e.g. Abraham in *Genesis Apocryphon, 1QapGen* 20:28–29). Though exorcism accounts were prevalent, they rarely associate battle imagery with them. For example, *Psalms Scroll* (11Q5) and *Apocryphal Psalms* (11Q11) describe David exorcising demons through music, but employ no fighting imagery.

On the other hand, good reasons exist to understand exorcism in terms of a cosmic battle. Angelic and demonic beings were depicted as battling in the ancient world. For example, they war in texts like Dan 10 (Michael and the Prince of Persia, e.g. לחם in v 20) and Tobit 3 (Raphael and Asmodeus, e.g. δέω in v 17), as well as a whole section in the DSS entitled "The War Scroll" (1QM, similarly "The Book of War," 4Q471) which describes an angelic battle at the end of time. Some in the early Christ movement (i.e. Revelation) held this view, and it has been argued that Jesus' exorcisms are the first in this "two-stage defeat of Satan."[165] Most significantly, this militaristic motif does surface in Matthew

---

163 Nolland, *The Gospel of Matthew*, 410.
164 Amanda Witmer, *Jesus, The Galilean Exorcist: His Exorcisms in Social and Political Context* (LNTS; London: Bloomsbury, 2012) 41–55 discusses several texts, but notes that firsthand accounts of exorcism do not occur until the first century CE.
165 Graham H. Twelftree, *In the Name of Jesus: Exorcism Among Early Christians* (Grand Rapids: Baker Academic, 2007), 169. See also his work "EI ΔE ... ΕΓΩ ... ΕΚΒΑΛΛΩ ΤΑ ΔΑΙΜΟΝΙΑ!... [Luke 11:19]," in *Gospel Perspectives, Vol. 6: The Miracles of Jesus*, ed. David Wenham and Craig Blomberg (Sheffield: JSOT Press, 1986), 391–92.

in connection to Jesus and his disciples' interaction with the demonic realm. For example, Matt 8:29 records two demons exclaiming to Jesus Τί ἡμῖν καὶ σοί,[166] υἱὲ τοῦ θεοῦ; ἦλθες ὧδε πρὸ καιροῦ βασανίσαι ἡμᾶς; It is not clear that the sending of the demons into the pigs can be described as "torture" (βασανίζω), but nonetheless this seems to use militant imagery in connection with Jesus and the demonic realm. More significantly, Matt 12:25–28 describes the work of exorcism as a confrontation between two kingdoms (βασιλεία) and vv 29 depicts it as binding (δέω) a strong man and plundering (διαρπάζω) his goods. Furthermore, the statement concerning Peter (or the church) that πύλαι ᾅδου οὐ κατισχύσουσιν αὐτῆς, regardless if the church is on the offense or defense,[167] presents some sort of cosmic battle. In light of the general usage of fighting imagery in connection to demons in Jewish literature elsewhere and the other uses in Matthew of exorcism in fighting terms, we have sufficient reason to see the apostles, if they are portrayed via the backdrop of Zech 10:4, as engaging in "spiritual battle."

2.4.3.2   Matt 9:36 and 10:6 Uses Zech 10:4 to Depict the Apostles Executing Judgment on Nonbelievers

Not only does the image of a warrior executing God's judgment depict the apostles' interaction with the demonic realm, but we can detect it in their contact with the unworthy hosts of vv 11–15. In this section, Jesus commands the missionaries to ask in a city or town for one who is "worthy" (ἄξιος), and remain there. There are then two possible responses: if the house actually is worthy, they are instructed ἐλθάτω ἡ εἰρήνη ὑμῶν ἐπ' αὐτήν (v 13). Both the Semitic background of שָׁלוֹם as wholeness and the OT connection between peace and the healing in the kingdom of God (i.e. Isa 57:18–21 and *Tg Isa* 57), suggest that this response should be connected to the miracles of v 8.[168] If the household responded properly, they would not only be assured of future blessings in the kingdom, but they would also benefit from the healing ministry of the apostles at that time. The expression εἰρήνη ὑμῶν confirms this; Matthew portrays these potential blessings (peace) as coming from the apostles themselves (thus, a genitive of source).

If, however, the house responds negatively, Jesus instructs the apostles ἡ εἰρήνη ὑμῶν πρὸς ὑμᾶς ἐπιστραφήτω. The exact nature of this action is unclear, but if the above reconstruction is correct, it suggests the apostles should

---

166 Twelftree, "ΕΙ ΔΕ," 374 argues that, based on parallels with 2 Sam 19:16–23 and 1 Kings 17:18, that these words "were most likely defense mechanisms against Jesus the exorcist."
167 Nolland, *Gospel of Matthew*, 675.
168 John K. Ridgway, "A Correlation between Healing and Peace in Matt 10:1–16, Jesus' Commission to the Twelve," *Proceedings*, 11 (1991): 108.

refrain from healing. Jesus may also be calling them to "undo" their earlier healing. Jesus has thus far offered no precedent for this sort of action, though he later tells disciples that they too, with enough faith, can do such things as wither a fig tree (21:18–22). Matthew has little accounts of the disciples' miracles (though 17:16 implies they were exorcising demons), but Acts does describe harmful miracles done by the apostles (e.g. 5:1–11, 13:4–12). Though the enacting of ἡ εἰρήνη ὑμῶν πρὸς ὑμᾶς ἐπιστραφήτω remains unclear, still Jesus portrays them as agents of judgment, removing their peace. Jesus then instructs the apostles to shake the dust from their feet as a testimony against them, probably a symbol of the inhospitable treatment they received.[169] The apostles' action results in condemnation of the city, worse than what was received by Sodom and Gomorrah (v 15). Again, Jesus' portrays the disciples' role as active agents of judgment. Luz rightly comments

> The symbolic action of shaking the dust from the feet ... is neither a symbolic discharge of responsibility, nor a curse, nor a pronouncement of judgment; it is an execution of judgment ... since they are bearers of the saving sphere of the eschatological peace that returns to them, they become instruments of judgment.[170]

Luz's statement probably goes too far – the element of a pronouncement of judgment remains as the punishment still lies in the future (ἀνεκτότερον ἔσται ... ἐν ἡμέρᾳ κρίσεως), but this does not eliminate the role of the apostles as agents of God's judgment, negatively affecting the unworthy house both in the present and the future. With Zech 10:4 in the background, this is another way the apostles may be understood in such militant language as YHWH's "battle-bow" and "oppressors," executing divine judgment on his enemies.

2.5 Conclusion

With its theme of eschatological shepherding, Matt 9:36 and 10:6 allude to Ezek 34, Jer 23:1–6, and Zech 10:2–4 to describe major literary characters. Yet, of all these characters Matthew foregrounds the apostles as God's agents of

---

169 T. J. Rogers, "Shaking the Dust off the Markan Mission Discourse" in *JSNT* 27.2 (2004): 171 rightly connects this to the universal tradition of providing water to wash a guest's feet. Some commentators see this as a reference to the tradition of shaking off the dust from one's feet after being in Gentile territory as unclean (e.g. France, *The Gospel of Matthew*, 387; Morris, *The Gospel according to Matthew*, 250; Osborne, *Matthew*, 381). Cf. *m.'Ohal.* 2:3; *m.Tehar.* 4:5; Acts 13:51.
170 Luz, *Matthew*, 81 and fn. 95.

restoration and judgment. Each intertextual background highlights a significant aspect of the apostles' task in the mission discourse. The allusion to Ezek 34 emphasizes their healing ministry, being used by YHWH to genuinely care for his wounded flock. The allusion to Jer 23:1–6 paints them as prophets and ruling figures, replacing poor leadership of Israel. The allusion to Zech 10:2–4 highlights the opposite feature of their task as those who execute judgment on the demonic realm and unbelievers. Both Jer 23 and Zech 10 contain a direct link to the mission of the apostles with their description of agency in the plural. The connection between Ezek 34 and Matt 9:36 and 10:6 is harder to trace, but as with other uses of Ezek 34, a broad eschatological framework functions in which agency is assumed to perform the tasks ascribed to YHWH alone. The contexts of each of these three intertextual backgrounds contains a component with significant messianic potential. Yet Matthew bypasses these elements and focuses elsewhere, showing that his hermeneutic of fulfillment is not strictly Christocentric. Instead, Matthew's interest as he reads through these eschatological texts concerns how God ushers in the kingdom program in the events of his narrative. Though a predominate motif in Matthew's use of Scripture is how God has chosen Jesus as his central agent, this does not exclude the apostles as fulfilling a significant eschatological role, such as in Ezek 34, Jer 23, and Zech 10.

CHAPTER 3

Matthew's Non-Messianic Use of Isaiah's Vineyard Care-Givers

3.1 Introduction

The first chapter claimed that the predominate theory of Matthew's Christocentric hermeneutic must be nuanced to a broadly eschatological paradigm because it does not include times when the Matthean Jesus creates a conceptual blend in which he:

(1) maps a messianic figure from a source domain
and (2) maps the disciples from the target domain to that figure.[1]

In chapter 2, we saw that Matt 10:6 (1) maps the messianic figure of the eschatological shepherd from Ezek 34 and (2) does not map this image to Jesus (though the narrator implicitly does so in 9:36), but maps the disciples into the blend to this space via the Vital Relation of role. We also discussed the possibility that Matt 10:6 is a multi-scope blend, with Jer 23 and Zech 10 as additional source domains. If so, the above three step procedure needs to be nuanced slightly. The agents, ("shepherds" in Jer 23 and "oppressors" in Zech 10) map into the blend, but these, given their plurality, cannot be *the* messiah. One might conceivably use "messianic," as an adjective to modify them since, though not *the* messiah, they are associated with him. This distinction also means that the Vital Relation is most likely one of "identity," since it seems that Matthew would have seen these figures in connection to the messiah as none other than the disciples.

In chapter 3, we will see that the Matthean version[2] of the Wicked Tenant Parable (hereafter WTP) in 21:33–45 meets the above two steps. Again, certain elements of this claim come much more easily than others. Commentators

---

[1] Another option outlined in the introduction was for Jesus to evoke a potentially messianic text as a source domain, map various elements into the blend, but not explicitly map the messianic figure himself, a possibility which will be explored in chapter 5.
[2] The argument of this chapter will focus on the Matthean version because of our interest in Matthew's hermeneutic. However, though Matthew uses the WTP slightly differently than Mark and Luke, the argument of this chapter also applies to the other Synoptics, though it works the most easily in Matthew.

almost universally acknowledge that the WTP alludes to Isa 5,[3] and clearly the disciples function in some sort of leadership agency as the replacement farmers.[4] Thus, regarding (1), the WTP surely maps an image from an intertextual source domain – but is it messianic? Regarding (2), the WTP clearly maps the disciples from the target domain into the blend – but does this result in them occupying a place traditionally reserved for the messiah? The difficulty lies in seeing how the text Jesus evokes is potentially messianic and how the replacement farmers are being used to fulfill OT eschatological hopes.

At first, this does not seem to be the case for either question. On a cursory reading, nothing eschatological or messianic seems to be operating in Isa 5:1–7, nor is it clear why Jesus would evoke this text to discuss agency/leadership. As will be shown in section 3.7.3, the WTP addresses the leaders' inadequate appreciation of their position as agents who are mere stewards and establishes the disciples' new leadership role. As will be more fully explored in section 3.7.4, the mention of βασιλεία (Matt 21:43) and Jesus' status as the unique υἱός in contrast to other δοῦλοι (vv 34–37) demonstrates Isaiah's song is being used to address eschatological and messianic ideas. Thus, upon a cursory reading of Isa 5:1–7, Jesus' decision to evoke this specific text seems strange since these key issues are of concern in the Matthean passage but do not seem to surface in Isa 5. If Jesus wants to talk about messianic authority and God's kingdom agents, Isa 5:1–7 appears at first to be a peculiar choice.

However, situating Isa 5 in a metaphorical conversation with other interpreters will demonstrate its potential as an eschatological and messianic text. Listening carefully to Isa 5:1–7 in its broader literary context, as well as uses of Isaiah's vineyard by other authors, will show that a first century interpreter easily *could have* used the passage messianically and eschatologically, and that the passage actually is well suited to address problems of leadership and agency. Moreover, the inner logic of Isaiah, as well as the connections to other vine imagery in the book, provides fodder for these kinds of interpretations. All the contributors to this conversation considered here discuss these topics, though

---

3   There is debate, however, as to if the allusion is to the Hebrew text and only secondarily Septuagintized. E.g. Craig A. Evans, "How Septuagintal is Isa 5:1–7 in Mark 12:1–9?" *NovT* 45.2 (2003): 105–10 and T. Schmeller, "Der Erbe des Weinbergs: Zu den Gerichtsgleichnissen Mk 12,1–2 und Jes 5,1–7," *MTZ* 46 (1995): 194 or the LXX (e.g. John S. Kloppenborg, "Egyptian Viticultural Practices and the Citation of Isa 5:1–7 in Mark 12:1–9" *NovT* 44 (2002): 134–59; John S. Kloppenborg, "Isa 5:1–7 LXX and Mark 12:1, 9, Again" *NovT* 46 (2004): 12–19); Weren, *Studies in Matthew's Gospel*, 203. Evans is responding to Kloppenborg's first article, whose second is a surrejoinder. The issue has relevance for historical Jesus scholars in determining the originality of the allusion. Moreover, some see the Aramaic being the source, a view which will be discussed in the next chapter.

4   However, the exact intended identification of the disciples is debated. See section 3.7.3.

some are more "outspoken" about these issues than others. After seeing the latent agency, eschatological, and messianic elements of the text, we will see that the Matthean Jesus avoids mapping potentially messianic motifs to himself, but portrays the disciples as eschatological agents.

Unlike chapter 2, in which specific figures from the source domain are mapped into the blend (the "shepherd" of Ezek 34; the "shepherds" of Jer 23:4; the "oppressors" of Zech 10:4), the text of Isa 5 does not provide the antecedent for the farmers. Instead, we must go beyond the surface meaning of the text and consider the hermeneutical milieu, concepts hanging in the air from other interpretations of Isa 5, to discover the connections to eschatology, messianism, and agency. The WTP will construct a blend in which these entailments are specifically brought into focus (via the governing principle of "Pattern Completion"). But, unlike other interpreters, Matthew maps the role of caring for the vine(yard) gets not to the son figure (Jesus) but to the replacement farmers (the disciples). A broad hermeneutic of fulfillment in which God is actualizing his kingdom blessings through agency which does not consist of Jesus alone best explains this decision to portray the disciples, not Jesus, in this way.

Thus, this chapter listens to six conversation partners regarding the Isaian Vineyard Parable: the original parable itself (5:1–7) particularly in its larger Isaian context; Ezekiel's vineyard parables in chs 15, 17, and 19; the cedar and vine apocalypse of 2 Baruch 36–40; Ps 80; John 15:1–8; and the WTP, especially in its Matthean form in 21:33–45.[5] Each of these sections will normally include the following elements: a brief overview of its contents; the connection to Isa 5:1–7; and the text's adaptation of the Isaian vineyard to address the

---

5   Certainly there are uses of Isaiah's vine which do nothing with its messianic potential. E.g., Jer 2:21 and 12:10–11 clearly allude to Isaiah's vineyard (W. L. Holladay, *Jeremiah 1: A Commentary on the Book of the Prophet Jeremiah Chapters 1–25* (Hermeneia; Philadelphia: Fortress, 1986), 53, 98). In Jer 2:21, not only is נטע from Isa 5:2 repeated, but it and Isa 5:2 contain the only occurrences of שׂרֵק in the MT. Similarly, Jer 12:10–11 alludes to the Isaian vineyard of 3:14 and 5:1–7 by not only symbolizing Israel with כֶּרֶם, but also describing it as "desolate" in v 11 (cf. Isa 5:6, 9) because rulers (cf. Isa 3:14) have "trampled it down" in v 10 (cf. Isa 5:5). Most of these comparisons are thematic, not lexical. Yet the emphasized "desolate" in Jer 12:10–11 does seem to allude to Isa 5:9. However, Jeremiah's vine references do not pick up any element of hope (unless the more literal references to future planting of vineyards are counted – see Jer 5:13 and 51:23 – which has merit since even in Isa 5 the metaphorically ruined vineyard is connected to literal unproductive vineyards in v 10. Furthermore, the reader may wonder why the significant 4Q500 and *Targum Jonathan* are not discussed. These will receive treatment in the next chapter due to their significance for the theme of temple building.

themes of agency, eschatology, and messianism, so as to appreciate the broad hermeneutic of fulfillment at work when the WTP alludes to Isaiah's vineyard.

3.2 Isaiah 5:1–7

Since Isa 5:1–7 is the clearest allusion in the WTP and becomes the fountain head[6] from which the other streams of interpretation considered here flow, we will give this text a prominent voice in our metaphorical conversation. However, as discussed in the section on methodology in chapter 1, we do not want to mistake our exegesis of the text for that of other readers. Instead, while still being concerned with the clear overall thrust of the text, we also have an eye out for the passage's possibilities, especially as it pertains to the themes of agency, eschatology, and messianism. In the same vein, we are concerned with understanding the text so we can appreciate what other readers of it do and we must situate the passage in its larger Isaian setting since these later authors are readers of Scripture, not redaction or source critics.

3.2.1 *Overview of Contents*

Watts rightly says regarding Isa 5:1–7, "the very creative form is unique and has defied analysis which all accept."[7] Perhaps the fact that our passage resists literary expectation suggests the theme of the passage itself.[8] The song begins by calling itself a שִׁירַת דּוֹדִי (5:1),[9] but the readers, like YHWH himself, are disappointed in what follows, which is a complaint or accusation in the form of a juridical parable.[10] The song describes a farmer who has done everything

---

6 This is not to deny that the image is used of Israel in Gen 49:11 and Deut 32:32. Isaiah may have received his metaphor from these places. In fact, a connection to Gen 49 (i.e. v 10) might also explain how Isaiah's vineyard could have been viewed as messianic. But Isa 5 is the "fountainhead" in that it is the first lengthy use of the image on which other interpreters rely.

7 John D. Watts, *Isaiah 1–33*: Revised Edition (Grand Rapids: Zondervan, 2018), 53.

8 For a full exploration of this theme, see Gary R. Williams, "Frustrated Expectations in Isaiah V 1–7: A Literary Interpretation" *VT* 35.4 (1985): 459–65.

9 Hans Wildeberger, *Isaiah 1–12*, transl. Thomas H. Trapp (CC; Minneapolis: Fortress, 1991), 177 argues that the text should be understood as "love song," requiring the reading דּוֹדִי. This is possible, but understanding the text without alteration is preferable. As it stands in the MT, the דּוֹדִי is masculine and must refer to YHWH (v 7). Though the song is addressed to the people of Israel, the song is about (לְ) YHWH and his vineyard (v 1).

10 Watts, *Isaiah 1–33*, 54. Over 40 years ago, John T. Willis, "The Genre of Isaiah 5:1–7," *JBL* 96 (1977): 337–62 gave twelve ways of classification, but "juridical parable" is now widely accepted. Craig Evans writes "it would appear that a consensus has emerged in which

that could be done to produce a profitable vineyard (vv 1–2a) but instead the result is "stinking grapes" (v 2b).[11] Since the farmer has done everything that could have been done (vv 3–4), he can only abandon it and allow the vineyard to be destroyed (vv 5–6). The parable concludes in v 7 with a key to identify the major symbols: the farmer is YHWH (foreshadowed in the judgment of no rain in v 6); the vineyard is Israel and Judah;[12] the expected good grapes are "justice" (מִשְׁפָּט) and "righteousness" (צְדָקָה); the bad grapes are "legal infringement" (מִשְׂפָּח) and a "call for help" (צְעָקָה).[13] The following unit (vv 8–30) explores the meaning of the destruction of the vineyard as the exile (especially v 13).

3.2.2 *Agency Potential*

Since the topics under discussion in our metaphorical conversation include agency, eschatology, and messianism, we must first listen to the original text to see if it says anything about these themes, or if it has the potential to do so. At first, nothing about leadership or agency appear to be of concern. The parable seems only to regard the failure of Israel and Judah. Kloppenborg has argued that the LXX version does imply some sort of agency since attention is given to the vineyard (ἀμπελών) instead of the vine (ἄμπελος) and because the presence of thorns (ἄκανθα in v 2) implies neglect by workers (referencing 7:23–25, 32:13).[14] This has not gained wide acceptance however since it does not fit the logic of the song. Instead, the text challenges the reader with the climax in vv 3–4, asking for the people to judge between YHWH and his vineyard (שִׁפְטוּ־נָא בֵּינִי וּבֵין כַּרְמִי; κρίνατε ἐν ἐμοὶ καὶ ἀνὰ μέσον τοῦ ἀμπελῶνός μου), forcing the audience to either place the blame on God or the people. There is no third option in which hired workers are at fault. The provocative question in v 4 then underscores this feature:

Isaiah's Song of the Vineyard is understood as an instance of the genre of juridical parable." *Jesus and His Contemporaries: Comparative Studies* (AGJU; Leiden: Brill, 2001): 396.
11   From בְּאֻשׁ, a hapax legomenon. See discussion by J. Alec Motyer, *Isaiah: An Introduction and Commentary* (Downers Grove, IL: Intervarsity, 1993), 68.
12   This basic identification continues through the next several centuries. During the first Jewish revolt of 66–70 CE, coins depicted a vine with branches as symbol for Jerusalem (Andreas Köstenberger, *The Gospel of John* (BECNT; Grand Rapids: Baker, 2004), 450). Josephus describes the temple gate as being "all over covered with gold, as was its whole wall about it; it had also golden vines above it, from which clusters of grapes hung as tall as a man's height" (*Wars of the Jews* 5.210, cf. *Antiquities* 15.11.3 (395)). However, as we will see, later users of this image can have a more nuanced understanding.
13   Translations are from *HALOT*. The paranomasia with מִשְׁפָּט and צְדָקָה is lost in the LXX where the contrast is with κρίσις and δικαιοσύνη.
14   Kloppenborg, "Egyptian Viticultural Practices," 150.

מַה־לַּעֲשׂוֹת עוֹד לְכַרְמִי וְלֹא עָשִׂיתִי בּוֹ; τί ποιήσω ἔτι τῷ ἀμπελῶνί μου καὶ οὐκ ἐποίησα αὐτῷ;

But Jesus evokes *this* parable, whose rhetoric depends on the possibility of *only two options* with no intermediary workers, to evoke and adapt to address the issue of agency! Many commentators have seen the lack of a concern with agency in Isa 5 and concluded that the inclusion of this topic in the WTP was a product of Jesus' creativity.[15] For example, Keener states "Thus while Jesus borrows the imagery of Isaiah, he adapts it so that the primary evildoers represent not Israel but her leaders"[16] and Turner writes "Isaiah's song of the vineyard (Isa 5:1–7) is alluded to here, but Matthew adds a crucial new element."[17] Hays describes the use in Mark 12 as "Jesus' improvisational riff on Isaiah's song," explaining that "the shift here in emphasis is striking, for the brunt of accusation falls on the chief priests, scribes, and elders rather than upon the people."[18] Konradt states, "Jesus' parable takes a different path in comparison with the Old Testament point of reference taken up in v. 33: the failure of the vineyard is not under discussion here but rather the failure of the vinedressers, who have no counterpart in Isa 5.1–7."[19]

The above comments rightly notice Jesus' creative use of the Isaian vineyard and his new emphasis. Yet, Jesus' "improvisational riff" is not as entirely new as the above quotations suggest, since the WTP picks up on features already present in Isaiah. In light of the apparently fragmentary character of Isa 3:13–15, its similarities to 5:1–7, and other displacements in Isaiah, Sheppard suggests that Isa 5:1–7 originally was a juridical parable containing 3:13–15 interspersed, and that it was also originally connected to 27:2–6.[20] While our purposes do

---

15 There is some argument as to whether or not Mark added the connection to Isa 5 since the *Gospel of Thomas* 65 does not make the connection. John Nolland, *Luke* (WBC; Nashville, TN: Thomas Nelson, 1994), 3:948–49 argues *Gospel of Thomas* is not independent, but that it, with Luke, is a more original form. See Klyne Snodgrass, "The Parable of the Wicked Husbandmen: Is the *Gospel of Thomas* Version the Original?" *NTS* 21 (1975): 142–44 for an argument that it is not more original.
16 Keener, *The Gospel of Matthew*, 510.
17 Turner, *Matthew*, 513.
18 Hays, *Echoes of Scripture in the Gospels*, 41.
19 Konradt, *Israel, Church, and the Gentiles*, 175–76. However, he notes that "In Old Testament prophecy, the authorities appear not infrequently as the particular addressees of the prophets' words … Isa 3.14 could be of particular interest for Matt 21.28–46" (n 47).
20 Gerald Sheppard, "More on Isaiah 5:1–7 as a Juridical Parable" *CBQ* (1981): 45–46. He reconstructs the parable as follows: "parable, 5:1–2; judgment (implied on part of audience); interpretation, 3:13–14; indictment, 3:15; further interpretation, 5:7; summons to judge in the light of the interpretation, 5:3–4 (cf. 2 Sam 14:15ff.); sentence, 5:5–6."

not require interaction with redaction theories of Isaiah, that enough similarities exist to allow for Sheppard to make his argument alone demonstrates that 3:13–15 and 27:2–6 should be examined in connection with Matthew's use of Isa 5:1–7.[21] Isa 3:14 places the blame for what it presents as the ruined state of the vineyard (כֶּרֶם; ἀμπελῶν) on the leaders (עִם־זִקְנֵי עַמּוֹ וְשָׂרָיו; μετὰ τῶν πρεσβυτέρων τοῦ λαοῦ καὶ μετὰ τῶν ἀρχόντων αὐτοῦ), particularly for their oppression of the poor. Words for leadership like this do not occur in Isa 5:1–7, but the בָּאֻשִׁים; ἄκανθαι (vv 2, 4) symbolize מִשְׂפָּח; ἀνομία and צְעָקָה; κραυγή (v 7). Not only is there thematic similarity with the indictment in 3:15 (תְּדַכְּאוּ עַמִּי וּפְנֵי עֲנִיִּים תִּטְחָנוּ; ἀδικεῖτε τὸν λαόν μου καὶ τὸ πρόσωπον τῶν πτωχῶν καταισχύνετε), but some sort of leaders would be the most likely candidate for those guilty of oppression described in 5:7.[22] Both the nature of the "stinking grapes" and the fact that 5:1–7, in the form Matthew and his readers would have had, contains some sort of connection to 3:13–15 suggests that later interpreters could have used 5:1–7 to address matters of leadership.[23] Moreover, the 'second verse' of Isaiah's vineyard song also emphasizes God's actions against those who would destroy it (27:3–5).

3.2.3 Eschatological Potential

But if Isa 5:1–7 can be understood as directed, at least in part, at the historical leaders of Israel, can it also be seen in an eschatological framework? Isa 5 appears to only be a message of judgment. In the words of Oswalt, "It is a word which is devoid of hope … Here the need is to face the present and its relation to what lies immediately ahead."[24] However, even the previous four chapters have mingled themes of judgment with future restoration, not to mention the situation in the rest of Isaiah. Ch 1 has briefly compared ruined Zion to a "hut in a vineyard," and that passage also contains elements of hope (e.g. vv 18, 23–27). 4:2 has described future renewal in botanical terms. This suggests that though

---

21 Other commentators have noticed this important connection, e.g. Otto Kaiser, *Isaiah 1–12: A Commentary*, trans. John Bowden (OTL; Philadelphia: Westminster, 1983), 90 and Brevard S. Childs, *Isaiah: A Commentary* (OTL; Louisville, KY: Westminster John Knox Press, 2001), 46.

22 Some Isaiah commentators explain this oracle as against rulers, though still leaving room for the song to be against the house of Israel and people of Judah (v 7), e.g. Patricia K. Tull, *Isaiah 1–39* (SHBC; Macon, GA: Smyth & Helwys, 2010), 123. Marvin L. Chaney, "Whose Sour Grapes? The Addressees of Isaiah 5:1–7 in the Light of Political Economy," *Semeia* 87 (1999): 105–18 argues at length that only "the top of the social pyramid in Israel and Judah" (105) are in view.

23 When the expression "The Isaian vineyard" is used in this chapter, it is to emphasize that the vineyard image is found in other places in Isaiah besides 5:1–7.

24 John Oswalt, *The Book of Isaiah: Chapters 1–39* (NICOT; Grand Rapids: Eerdmans, 1986), 151.

the song of Isa 5 is in a minor key, the tune may change later. Such turns out to be the case in 27:2–13.[25] The author of Matthew's Gospel who has shown himself to be so well versed in Scripture would surely have been aware of this "second verse" to Isaiah's "love song" in which restoration is foretold after a time of destruction.

Several elements of Isa 27:2–13 form connections to 5:1–7 that warrant calling it a "second verse." Not only does it repeat the theme of caring for a vineyard in v 2 (כֶּרֶם; ἀμπελών), in the MT it is set as a song (עַנּוּ־לָהּ) which would connect with the use of אָשִׁירָה and שִׁירַת in 5:1. The LXX translates עַנּוּ־לָהּ in 27:2 as ἐπιθύμημα ἐξάρχειν κατ' αὐτῆς. This shares similarities with the address of the song being τῷ ἠγαπημένῳ ᾆσμα τοῦ ἀγαπητοῦ τῷ ἀμπελῶνί μου (5:1).[26] 5:6 says that in the ruined state, וְעָלָה שָׁמִיר וָשָׁיִת and this explains the place of שָׁמִיר שַׁיִת in 27:4.[27] However, the LXX lacks these last two commonalities about being burned and having thorns and weeds.[28] Thus, Isa 27 finishes the story which had seemed to end so bleakly in 5:1–7. But this resolution would have been understood eschatologically. The introduction בַּיּוֹם הַהוּא; τῇ ἡμέρᾳ ἐκείνῃ (v 2) forms a bridge from v 1, where YHWH slays the serpent in the sea. From the perspective of NT authors, this describes the future destruction of Satan (MT: לִוְיָתָן 2×, נָחָשׁ 2×, and תַּנִּין 1×; LXX: δράκων 3× and ὄφις 2×; cf. Rev 20:2).[29] The earlier reference to the dead living in 26:19 also confirms the eschatological

---

25 See further exploration in John T. Willis, "Yahweh Regenerates his Vineyard: Isaiah 27" in *Formation and Intertextuality in Isaiah 24–27*, ed. J. Todd Hibbard and Hyun Chul Paul Kim (AIL; Atlanta: SBL, 2013), 201–08, who says "Isaiah 27:2–6 completely and intentionally counters 5:1–7" (204). Gene M. Tucker thinks "The close parallels to the language indicate that the writer of 27:2–6 has Isa 5 before him" ("The Book of Isaiah" in *The New Interpreter's Bible*, ed. L. E. Keck et al. (Abingdon: Nashville, 2001), 6.226.

26 Planting a vineyard may have been a romantic or erotic metaphor in ancient Israel, as evidenced by the use of the image in the Song of Songs. See Wildeberger, *Isaiah*, 1:182. The "beloved" concept does resurface in the Markan and Lukan accounts of the WTP to describe the son, though the significance of this is difficult to determine with any degree of certainty. See Von Thomas Schmeller, "Der Erbe des Weinbergs," 193 for more on this connection.

27 1QIsᵃ, the Syriac, and the Vulgate witness to a ו before שַׁיִת, which would only strengthen the connection.

28 The LXX is quite different from the MT. It continues the vineyard imagery, but vv 2–5 describe the destruction, not the flourishing, of the vine. V 6 then begins the message of restoration. The argument for an eschatological vineyard due to ch 27 is weaker in the LXX, but not entirely absent.

29 The original context is probably interacting with Ugaritic texts which depict Lotan (Leviathan), Yam, and Tannin as villains of the deities Baal and Anat. See discussion in Willis, "Yahweh Regenerates," 203.

nature of this continuation of the vine image.³⁰ The connections between Isa 5 and 27 suggest that, for one familiar with the book of Isaiah, the destruction of Isa 5 does not bring the vineyard to a final end, but that it somehow survives to flourish in the eschaton. Moreover, even if there were no connections to other horticultural or vineyard imagery in Isaiah, the overall framework of the book suggests that the destruction of 5:5–6 would have been seen as eventually leading to the eschaton. For Isaiah, the answer to the problem of exile can only be the coming kingdom of God.

3.2.4 Messianic Potential

Not only does a consideration of Isaiah's vineyard from the wider context of Isaiah allow it to be seen in an eschatological framework, but there are potential messianic features as well. 4:2 states that for the remnant, יִהְיֶה צֶמַח יְהוָה לִצְבִי וּלְכָבוֹד וּפְרִי הָאָרֶץ לְגָאוֹן וּלְתִפְאֶרֶת.³¹ As noted earlier, the presence of botanical imagery so close at hand to ch 5 suggests there will be an eschatological renewal of the vineyard. But though צֶמַח stands in parallelism to פְּרִי and may not appear initially to have any messianic significance,³² the fact the "shoot" concept reappears in the strongly messianic 11:1 suggests such a component can even come from the standpoint of the canonical text of Isaiah.³³ Perhaps this explains why the Targum translates 4:2 with בְּעִידָנָא הַהוּא יְהֵי מְשִׁיחָא דַיוי לְחֶדְוָא וְלִיקָר ("and at that time the messiah of the Lord will be for rejoicing

---

30   Again, we are concerned with the likely NT understanding of the text. There is debate about the original meaning of 26:19, with some seeing it as metaphorical for the rebirth of the nation (e.g. Wildberger, *Isaiah*, 2:567–68; John Day, "The Development of Belief in Life after Death in Ancient Israel," in *After the Exile: Essays in Honour of Rex Mason*, ed. John Barton and David J. Reimer (Macon, GA: Mercer University Press, 1996), 231–57) and some as literal resurrection (Childs, *Isaiah*, 187–88; Motyer, *Isaiah*, 219).

31   The only element of the botanical imagery which remains in the LXX here is the use of γῆ, but this is extremely slight. The minimizing of the vineyard imagery in ch 27 and in ch 4 illustrates J. Ross Wagner's description of the LXX in Isaiah: "Rather than pass ambiguities and aporias on to the audience, the translator normally attempts to resolve them" (*Reading the Sealed Book: Old Greek Isaiah and the Problem of Septuagint Hermeneutics* (Waco, TX: Baylor, 2013), 235).

32   Even if one insists on the consistency of the parallelism, this could go either way. E.g., H. G. M. Williamson, *Isaiah 1–5: A Critical and Exegetical Commentary* (ICC; London: T&T Clark, 2006), 306–09 argues that since "what qualifies one pair must also qualify the other" (307), so that the non-messianic פְּרִי could demonstrate that צֶמַח is non-messianic. However, the messianic צֶמַח could imply פְּרִי should be understood similarly (e.g. Keil and Delitzsch, *Commentary on the Old Testament*, 7:99).

33   The connection is only thematic, not lexical, since Isa 11:1 has חֹטֶר and נֵצֶר. It has been suggested that the latter is in mind in Matt 2:23 (e.g. Nolland, *The Gospel of Matthew*, 130, but see Turner, *Matthew*, 99–100). The reference is obscure, but if this is the correct allusion, it contributes to the likelihood that Matthew would have seen 4:2 as messianic.

and glory"). Moreover, we have also seen in 2.3.2.2 that Matthew would have understood the צֶמַח of Jer 23 as messianic and this strongly suggests that when he came across Isa 4:2 he would have seen the messiah predicted there too. The proximity of ch 4 and ch 5 and their conceptual overlap makes it easy to imagine how later interpreters could see the messiah as somehow part of YHWH's vineyard who would rise up after the time of destruction during the renewal. However, even if the messiah is found in 4:2 and this is connected to the horticultural imagery of ch 5, the text assigns no role to him in the restoration of the vine. It only asserts that he will prosper in a coming day.

The enigmatic beginning of Isaiah's song may signal messianic possibilities for Isa 5 since it locates the vineyard בְּקֶרֶן בֶּן־שָׁמֶן. קֶרֶן surely means something like "hill" here, though it is the only time the OT employs this metaphorical usage.[34] On the one hand, קֶרֶן is used because it resembles כֶּרֶם and rhymes with בֶּן and שָׁמֶן. But on the other hand, the combination of "horn" and "oil" may have anointing/messianic connotations (1 Sam 16:1, 13, 1 Kgs 1:39, Ps 92:10, cf. Ps 132:17 which joins קֶרֶן, צֶמַח, and מָשִׁיחַ[35]). Though the significance of this should not be pressed too far, this feature of the Hebrew text does provide Isaiah's song with subtle messianic overtones.

3.2.5 *Summary of Isaiah 5:1–7*

Though Isaiah's vineyard parable may not at first seem to address issues of agency, eschatology, and messianism, the text itself as situated within the larger framework of Isaiah, especially in connection to other Isaian horticultural imagery, demonstrates the potential to contribute to these topics. Placing the blame for the ruined state of the vineyard on the shoulders of the elders (זקן) and rulers (שׂר) in 3:14, as well as the nature of oppression in 5:7 suggests some kind of leaders are in view. Moreover, these leaders, in the wider paradigm of the OT, should be understood as called to function as agents of God. Yet the text has eschatological potential too since Isaiah's eschatological "second verse of the vineyard song" (27:2–13) provides further details regarding the vineyard. The presence of messianic features also confirms this eschatological element. Isaiah contains other horticultural images of the messiah (e.g. 11:1, 10), but the nearest at hand is a mere five verses prior (4:2) in its canonical context. The above are possible directions an interpreter of Isa 5:1–7 might take. Eventually we will see that Jesus takes the Isaian vineyard in these directions, though we cannot be sure if his rationale was in line with the above observations. Before

---

34   Watts, *Isaiah 1–33*, 68.
35   See Lanier, *Old Testament Conceptual Metaphors*, 35–78 for an exploration of the messianic use of the horn metaphor.

considering the WTP itself, we will listen to four other conversation partners in order to demonstrate that, though the text is employed and adapted in different ways, the themes of agency, eschatology, and messianism are in the hermeneutical milieu of later interpreters of the Isaian vineyard. This will put us in a position to appreciate the ways Jesus similarly uses Isa 5, as well as the ways he significantly departs.

3.3 Ezekiel 15, 17, 19

After the text of Isa 5 itself, Ezekiel contributes next in our metaphorical conversation. His three vine parables, taken together, pick up the imagery of Isaiah's vineyard and carry it in the general direction described above. He speaks even more loudly than Isaiah in using this imagery to denounce leadership and particularly in the second parable he makes a much more obvious connection to the eschaton and the messiah. However, due to its strong emphasis on the condemnation of the vine, it introduces a competing botanical image – the cedar – to incorporate eschatological and messianic elements.

3.3.1 Overview of Contents

Ezek 15:1–8, 17:1–24, and 19:10–14 each present a parable about a vine in connection with the Babylonian invasion. Both the first and last lack an element of hope and only describe the vine as something that will be burned (15:5–7, 19:12–14). The ominous conclusion to ch 19 – קִינָה הִיא וַתְּהִי לְקִינָה (v 14) capture the despair of these two parables. Ch 15 sarcastically asks about the value of vine "wood" (the multivalency of עֵץ, meaning "wood" in v 2, allows for a direct comparison with other "trees") and states that is not useful as building material or for making pegs. Furthermore, even when burned it profits little.[36] Destruction certainly awaits those who are in Jerusalem because of their unfaithfulness (vv 6–8). Ch 19 differs in that it describes a time when the vine was once fruitful (vv 10–11). But then, without stating a reason, the vine is removed, planted in a wilderness, and destroyed (vv 12–14).

Though it too contains bleak imagery, the parable in ch 17 also provides an element of hope. Here, a large, beautiful eagle takes a twig (יְנִיקָה) from the top of a cedar in Lebanon to a city (vv 3–4; representing Nebuchadnezzar taking Jehoiachin to Babylon, v 12). Afterwards, the eagle plants a flourishing vine

---

36 Margaret S. Odell, *Ezekiel* (SHBC; Macon, GA: Smyth & Helwys, 2005), 175 argues that the purpose of this first parable is not that the vineyard is burned per se, but that it is even useless in being burned.

which turned to it (vv 5–6; representing Zedekiah living in Jerusalem in a treaty with Nebuchadnezzar, vv 13–14). But then the vine turns toward a second eagle, less impressive than the first (v 7; representing the treaty with Apries/Hophra of Egypt, v 15)[37] and is easily destroyed (vv 9–10; representing the destruction of Zedekiah, vv 16–20). Like chs 15 and 19, the vine imagery only has negative connotations. Yet, with the extra element of the cedar, vv 22–24 insert a positive botanical picture. Though this may rightly be considered an "epilogue,"[38] it plays a much more significant role than a mere afterthought. Since the latter two parables describe the ruin of the ruling dynasty, they may be taken to imply that exile is Israel's permanent fate and self-rule in the future was impossible. Instead, by having the eagle (now representing YHWH) place the twig on a mountain which then grows into a majestic cedar (vv 22–23), Ezekiel communicates that Israel will someday have her own king.

3.3.2 *Connection to Isa 5:1–7*

Though vineyards and vines were common in Israel and nothing in the three chapters requires readers to make an intertextual connection to Isa 5 to get the thrust of the pronouncement, Ezekiel nonetheless likely alludes to Isaiah's vineyard song.[39] Ezek 15 echoes Isaiah's use of a vine being burned and devoured by fire (cf. Isa 5:5), as well as repeats "desolate" (שְׁמָמָה) in Ezek 15:8 (cf. Isa 5:9).[40] Moreover, the logic of the first parable aligns nicely with Isa 5.[41]

---

37 Block, *The Book of Ezekiel Chapters 1–24*, 544.

38 Block, *The Book of Ezekiel Chapters 1–24*, 548. His later outline of the chapter as a chiasm is more helpful ("A The Riddle of the Cedar Sprig (vv. 3–4) B The Riddle of the Vine (vv. 5–10) B' The Interpretation of the Riddle of the Vine (vv. 11–21) A' The Interpretation of the Riddle of the Cedar Sprig (vv. 22–24).") *Beyond the River Chebar: Studies in the Kingship and Eschatology in the Book of Ezekiel* (Cambridge: James Clarke & Co, 2013), 53.

39 Most commentators note that Isa 5 also uses similar imagery and claim that Ezekiel picks up well attested biblical imagery, though they do not necessarily categorize Isa 5 as a direct allusion (e.g. Block, *The Book of Ezekiel Chapters 1–24*, 456; Cooper, *Ezekiel*, 166). Duguid, *Ezekiel*, 157 rightly cautions that we do not read Isa 5 too quickly into these parables and so miss their juridical nature. The story appeals to their common knowledge of vines "to establish unpalatable spiritual truth." But then he allows that "the parable invites comparison with other tradition uses," listing Ps 80 and Isa 5. Allen, *Ezekiel 1–19*, 221 calls the link "debatable." Other commentators are more explicit about Ezekiel alluding to Isaiah, though without a thorough conversation (e.g. Joseph Blenkinsopp, *Ezekiel* (Interpretation; Louisville: Westminster John Knox, 1990), 75).

40 Cf also Jer 2:21 and 12:10–11.

41 Since Isa 5 is in the background, this means the interpretation in Block, *The Book of Ezekiel*, 456, "there is no hint of the vine every having been the object of Yahweh's affection, let alone bearing fruit. On the contrary, the vine is inherently worthless, fit only for fuel for the fire" is too harsh. The intertextual connection with Isa 5 still places the blame on Israel.

Ezek 15 centers around the usefulness of a vine. The logic of this story rests on the premise that the vine is not producing good enough grapes. Only then is a vine useless, which is the owner's frustration in Isa 5:4 and explains his punitive actions in v 6. However, though Ezekiel evokes Isa 5, he takes a good deal of liberty in adapting the imagery to his own context. As Block summarizes, "The prophet has a habit of seizing upon traditional images and deliberately distorting them for rhetorical effect."[42] An allusion to Isa 5 does not require all the symbolism to function consistently.

3.3.3 *Agency*

The symbolism changes within Ezekiel, with increasing focus on the agency/leadership role of the vine. In ch 15, this focus is at most minimal. The useless vine which is only destined for burning is said to represent יֹשְׁבֵי יְרוּשָׁלָם (v 6). Though this expression can approximate "citizens of Jerusalem,"[43] the connection to ch 14[44] implies the strict geographical boundary of being inside the city is in view. 14:22–23 describes a remnant which will return from exile and be saved. But those presently dwelling (יֹשְׁבֵי) in Jerusalem will be destroyed because the downfall of the city is certain. Of course, the ruling portion of Judah can be expected to be found in Jerusalem. Though the text includes them in the judgment, the other inhabitants of the city will not be spared. Thus, in the first of Ezekiel's three vine parables, the vine maps to those living in Jerusalem, an expression which includes "average citizens" of the city, but may potentially emphasize the nation's leaders.

Ch 17 similarly uses the vine to symbolize those not exiled but living in Jerusalem, but with increased attention to leaders. This parable clearly separates the exiles (from the cedar in the city) from those living in Jerusalem (the vine in the field). So far, this is a similar but more explicit scenario than the one in ch 15. However, ch 17 says those taken away (the top most twig of the cedar) are Jerusalem's king (מֶלֶךְ) and leaders (שַׂר). The vine which is not taken away and is destroyed mostly applies to Zedekiah since 3ms verbs and 3ms pronouns fill vv 16–20 and the subject of these verbs must be מֶלֶךְ (v 16). Yet the result of Zedekiah's downfall will also include the destruction of "all the refugees and troops" (כָּל־מִבְרָחָו בְּכָל־אֲגַפָּיו) and the scattering of the "remnant" (הַנִּשְׁאָרִים)

---

42   Block, *The Book of Ezekiel Chapters 1–24*, 456.
43   The NIV and NASB regularly translate with "people of Jerusalem" while the ESV, NRSV, and NKJV use "inhabitants of Jerusalem." The expression is sometimes used in parallelism with more generic description of Israelites with little or no emphasis on geographical location, e.g. 2 Chron 20:20, 33:9, 34:40, Jer 4:4, 11:9.
44   Odell, *Ezekiel*, 173.

in v 21. Thus, the second parable uses the vine to describe the Jewish people in Jerusalem, but foregrounds king Zedekiah as the one represented by the vine.

In 19:10–14, the image continues to move in this direction. וְאַתָּה שָׂא קִינָה אֶל־נְשִׂיאֵי יִשְׂרָאֵל in v 1 introduces a set of two parables. In the second parable, Ezekiel describes a planted vine which flourishes with many strong branches, which represents שִׁבְטֵי מֹשְׁלִים, "scepters of rulers." Without specifying the agent, Ezekiel says the vine is plucked up, the east wind dries its fruit, and fire comes from its branches to devour it. V 10 says the vine is "your mother," whom vv 1–9 describe as a lioness which births several lions.[45] Granted, the possibility that the vine itself is only Israel cannot be ruled out as impossible, but most commentators take this as a reference to something like "the entire Davidic royal house"[46] since the ruling element is certainly being emphasized. Thus, Ezekiel's three vine parables evoke Isa 5, but change the symbolism to refer to those who remained in Jerusalem, with increasing emphasis on the ruling element among them. This demonstrates that not only did Ezekiel take some creative license with the image, but he too highlighted the ruling element to varying degrees.

3.3.4 *Eschatology*

As mentioned earlier, only the second vine parable depicts a future hope. By having separate botanic imagery – a vine and a cedar – there can be future restoration while still emphasizing the complete destruction of the vine (the royal line of Zedekiah). After the twig is planted on a mountain, it becomes a great tree that will provide shelter for כֹּל צִפּוֹר כָּל־כָּנָף[47] and כָּל־עֲצֵי הַשָּׂדֶה (Ezek 17:23) will know of YHWH's actions. In light of the previous bird imagery, this surely includes the likes of the kings of Babylon and Egypt. Other use of trees as rulers (e.g. Ezek 31) means the significance of this tree goes beyond Israel to the gentiles. This עֵץ גָּבֹהַ may be a reference to the "cosmic tree" seen in Mesopotamian and Assyrian art, specifically in the Assyrian throne room, which depicted universal rule.[48] If so, this reinforces the point that the current

---

45 Our purposes do not require identifying these figures, but simply observing that they are royal persons. For a thorough investigation of proposals throughout history see Christopher T. Begg, "The Identity of the Princes in Ezekiel 19: some reflections" *ETL* 65.4 (1989): 358–69.

46 Zimmerli, *Ezekiel*, 1:397. So also Block, *The Book of Ezekiel*, 1:591; Allen, *Ezekiel*, 287.

47 Sinaiticus has πᾶν θηρίον, καὶ πᾶν πετεινόν, but Vaticanus agrees with the MT with ὄρνεον instead of θηρίον. Cf. Ezek 31:6, where the image of the "cosmic tree" is also used.

48 Odell, *Ezekiel*, 212; Block, *The Book of Ezekiel*, 1:551; Howard N. Wallace, "Tree of Knowledge and Tree of Life" in *The Anchor Yale Bible Dictionary*, ed. David Noel Freedman (New York: Doubleday, 1992), 6:658. However, equating the Assyrian sacred tree with the cosmic tree is far from the consensus view of scholars studying Assyrian art. Mariana Giovino,

"world rulers" will one day be ruled by the twig/tree. But the argument here does not depend on this identification. Not only does the situation envisioned in 17:22–24 go beyond Israel and encompass the whole world, but the tree provides for those under its care. Whereas Isaiah's restoration involves the vineyard (27:2–6), Ezekiel 17 only predicts destruction for the vine and reserves hope for a separate image in ch 17, that of the future tree. But though this rule has a worldwide scope, the fact that the tree is planted on a mountain clearly evokes Zion.[49] Block rightly compares this to other eschatological visions (Isa 2:2–4, Mic 4:1–3, Ps 78:68–72) and observes

> Although this mountain will become increasingly significant in later oracles, only here in Ezekiel are the motifs of Davidic line and Zion brought together. In so doing the prophet reminds the exiles that YHWH had not forgotten his covenant with David (2 Sam 7). The dynasty would survive the deportation; it would be revived within the context of its original founding, and its protective influence would be felt all around the world.[50]

3.3.5 *Messianism*

Not only do the latter two parables highlight the rulers, but this crosses over into evoking the messiah figure. 17:22–24 provides the clearest occasion of messianic concerns. Lexical similarities with Isa 11:1, Jer 23:5, 33:15, and Zech 3:8 and 6:12 suggest this king is the messiah, and the effect of all "trees" knowing that YHWH exalts and humbles is strong confirmation.[51] Zimmerli explains,

---

The Assyrian Sacred Tree: A History of Interpretations (Fribourg, Switzerland: Academic Press, 2007) explores three main approaches, arguing for seeing it as a cultic object. She states that the cosmic tree interpretation "never attracted much attention and has, for the most part, been discarded" (2). Block suggests that it is just as likely that the tree image in Ezek 17 comes from Isa 11:1–10.

49   On the eschatological use of Zion as a world mountain, see Richard J. Clifford Jr., *The Cosmic Mountain in Canaan and the Old Testament* (Eugene, OR: Wipf & Stock, 2010), 131–60.
50   Block, *Beyond the River*, 32.
51   The LXX does not clearly embellish the messianic element of these verses. This may mean that these translators did not understand the text this way, but not necessarily. Still, there is a hint of an additional messianic element in the LXX, which uses singular masculine pronouns for the feminine κέδρος (Manning, *Echoes of a Prophet*, 143. The Targum does not use משיחא, but it does reference a child (or "suckling," יָנִיק) from David's line as the cedar, who becomes a "might king" (מֶלֶךְ תַּקִּיף). Hummel suggests that the earliest explicit messianic interpretation is the Vulgate, which has 'I will break off from the topmost of its branches a tender one and stretch it out [*tenerum distringam*] and plant it on the most high and prominent mountain,' which he takes as an allusion to Jesus' arms stretched out in crucifixion. (Horace D. Hummel, *Ezekiel 1-20* Concordia Commentary [St. Louis:

> Undoubtedly there is here a word of messianic promise, as is to be found again in 34:23f; 37:24f. Yahweh will again bring to honor in Jerusalem a member of the Davidic royal house, which has been temporarily humbled ... That the allegory does not tell of the restoration of the vine stock, but the exaltation of the cedar shoot points to the fact that the promise of the new beginning was emphatically not seen as applying to the family of those ruling in the land after 597 BC, but through the family of those deported in 597 BC.[52]

In a subtler manner, Ezek 19 also contains a messianic reference. The combination of a lion with a vine, as well as several lexical links convinces many commentators that the text evokes Gen 49:8–12.[53] The allusion in Ezek 21:32 (ET 21:27) to the same text confirms this.[54] Gen 49:8–12, specifically v 10, is famously messianic.[55] But here again Ezekiel "distorts" the traditional image by saying וְלֹא־הָיָה בָהּ מַטֶּה־עֹז שֵׁבֶט לִמְשׁוֹל (19:14). Hummel goes so far as to call this use "de-messianic," not because it outright denies the messianism but because it "seriously qualifi[es] the hope and the confidence Gen 49:8–12 enshrined, at least in the illegitimate form which that hope had assumed in Ezekiel's day" and also states "While the divine wrath is consuming fire, Ezekiel does *not* say that the 'scepter' would indeed depart from the royal house of Judah until God's final judgment came; he does not negate the ancient messianic promise in Gen 49:10."[56] On the assumption that Ezekiel does not contradict what we find in Torah and that he has already referenced the messianic hope in 17:22–24, this interpretation seems on target. Ezekiel's messianic reference is only by way of allusion. Ch 19 promises destruction for the rulers and evokes the messiah of Gen 49 as a foil to contradict the audience's overconfidence in the Davidic line. Though Ezek 19 has playfully adapted Gen 49:8–12, the allusion demonstrates the connectedness of the scriptural vine image and the messiah.

Concordia, 2005], 516). Moreover, the initial description of the "twig" (יוֹנֵק in vv 4 and 22) may allude to the suffering servant of Isa 53:2, which Matthew certainly saw as messianic (Matt 8:17).

52 *Ezekiel*, 368.
53 Block, *The Book of Ezekiel Chapters 1–24*, 603, 608; Odell, *Ezekiel*, 235; Paul M. Joyce, *Ezekiel: A Commentary* (LHBOTS; New York: T&T Clark, 2007), 148, 157.
54 William L. Moran, "Gen 49:10 and its use in Ezek 21:32" *Bib* 39.4 (1958): 405–25.
55 Craig A. Evans, "The Messiah in the Dead Sea Scrolls" in *Israel's Messiah in the Bible and the Dead Sea Scrolls*, ed. Richard S. Hess, M. Daniel Carroll (Eugene, OR: Wipf & Stock, 2003), 91 lists it as one of the "three passages [which] in particular played an important, generative role in the rise of messianism" along with Num 24:17 and Isa 10:34–11:5 and explores such a use in the DSS.
56 Hummel, *Ezekiel*, 593, 565 (emphasis original).

3.3.6 Summary of Ezek 15, 17, 19

Thus, Ezekiel's three vine parables adapt Isaiah's vineyard to address each of the themes in question. Ch 15 contributes the least, with only slight emphasis on the leadership of Judah. Ch 17 specifically has the king in view and ch 19 emphasizes the scepters for ruling, though neither of these necessarily excludes normal citizens. Ch 17 most clearly reveals eschatological and messianic themes, though it accomplishes this by introducing a competing horticultural image, the cedar. Still, the vine is part of a parable in which the messiah establishes a time of eschatological peace. Ch 19 may also have something to say in this conversation about the messiah with its allusion to Gen 49, though this contribution is far subtler than ch 17. While this survey of Ezekiel's vine parables demonstrates how a later interpreter might use Isaiah's vineyard to address the themes in question, it also adds to the hermeneutical milieu surround Isa 5. After all, Matthew is not only a reader of Isaiah, but of Ezekiel as well, and so would be familiar with the direction he took the vine imagery.

3.4 2 Baruch 36–40

The "Vine and Cedar Apocalypse" of 2 Baruch 36–40 contributes next in our metaphorical conversation. This text clearly uses vine imagery to address the themes of agency, eschatology, and messianism. Like Ezek 19, it also adds the image of a cedar in distinction to the vine, but for the opposite effect. It does not allude to Isa 5 as clearly as other contributors, but a connection nonetheless exists, making it a helpful indicator of the hermeneutical milieu surrounding Isaiah's vine in the first century CE.

3.4.1 Overview of Contents

The passage describes a forest surrounded by mountains, "over against"[57] which grows a vine and under which comes a fountain (36:2–3). The fountain becomes a flood which destroys the mountains and the forest except for one cedar tree (vv 4–5). The vine then speaks to the remaining cedar and condemns it, resulting in its destruction and torment (vv 9–11). The destruction of the forest and trees represents the ruin of three kingdoms, and the remaining cedar is

---

[57] This could mean that the vine is either above or opposite the forest. See Liv Ingebord Lied, *The Other Lands of Israel: Imaginations of the Land in 2 Baruch* (JSJSup; Leiden: Brill, 2008), 189.

the fourth kingdom, usually identified with Rome (39:3–5).[58] The destruction of the cedar is described in 40:1–4,

> The last ruler who is left alive at that time will be bound, whereas the entire host will be destroyed. And they will carry him on Mount Zion, and my Anointed One will convict him of all his wicked deeds and will assemble and set before him all the works of his host. And after these things he will kill him and protect the rest of my people who will be found in the place that I have chosen. And his dominion will last forever until the world of corruption has ended and until the times which have been mentioned before have been fulfilled. This is your vision, and this is its explanation.[59]

Our argument does not require knowing the precise date of composition since we are only considering this as an example of how a first century interpreter might interact with vine imagery and not claiming that any of the synoptic writers specifically allude to this passage. Still, it has been argued that the passage may have been written before 70 CE,[60] though the current consensus is that it was written between 70 and 132 CE.[61] Though any direction of influence between 2 Baruch 36–40 and Matthew is unlikely, the two are rough contemporaries.

3.4.2 Connection to Isa 5:1–7

While it does not make as clear of a connection to Isaiah's vineyard as Ezekiel, the "Cedar and Vine Apocalypse" of 2 Baruch 36–40 contains relevance for appreciating the imagery in the WTP since it incorporates vine symbolism in an eschatological context so that those who are ruling wickedly are judged and

---

58 Robert H. Charles, *The Apocrypha and Pseudepigrapha of the Old Testament in English: with introductions and critical and explanatory notes to the several books* (Oxford: Clarendon Press, 1913), 1:501 suggests the first three are Babylon, Persia, and Diadochi respectively. Similarly, see *4 Ezra* 12:11–12.

59 Translation from James J. Charlesworth, *The Old Testament Pseudepigrapha*, vol. 1 (London: Yale University Press, 1983), 633.

60 Charles, *Commentary on the Pseudepigrapha*, 2:500 argues for this position since the text does not mention the Roman destruction of Jerusalem, the restoration of the city under the messiah, or a return from dispersion (in contrast to the material in chs 1–9, 32:2–4, 43–44:7, 45–46, 77–82, 84; 86). But this rests on a now rejected view of 2 Baruch that it was written in several stages.

61 Michael E. Stone and Matthias Henze, *4 Ezra and 2 Baruch: Translations, Introductions, and Notes* (Minneapolis: Fortress, 2013), 10–11; Ken Jones, *Jewish Reactions to the Destruction of Jerusalem in A.D. 70: Apocalypses and Related Pseudepigrapha* (Leiden: Brill, 2011), 88–89. Lied, *Other Lands*, 26.

God's people are restored and cared for through a messianic figure. This apocalyptic vision certainly employs biblical imagery, but which text is not clear. The four kingdoms resonate with Dan 2 and 7[62] and the mention of a vine, a cedar tree, and the messiah strongly suggest it has Ezek 17 in view,[63] though strangely their function has changed. In Ezek 17 the new cedar tree represents the protagonist and the vine the antagonist, but 2 Baruch 36–40 reverses this situation. The positive association in other Scriptures of the vineyard and the messianic branch most likely explain this unexpected reversal. Bauckham has argued that "the whole vision can be explained as resulting from an exegesis of Isa 10:34 in its immediate context and in close connexion with a number of other passages which have been exegetically linked with it."[64] We have already seen reasons to think Ezekiel's vineyard parables pull from Isa 5, though this does not necessarily mean the allusions in 2 Baruch 36–40 go back to this source. Whether 2 Baruch 36–40 goes to Isa 5 directly or only goes via Ezek 17 is not certain, yet Isaiah's vineyard nonetheless lies somewhere in the intertextual background.

3.4.3 *Agency*

Unlike Ezekiel's vineyard parables and the WTP, the apocalypse of the vine and cedar speaks against the Roman empire. Yet the line between the empire and the emperor is blurred. In the interpretation section (chs 39–40), the cedar represents a "kingdom" (39:3–5). Moreover, the passages says the vine will "root out the multitude of its host" (39:7), which does not have only the emperor in view. But the parable directs the rebuke toward the cedar as a person, who is wicked (36:7), does not show compassion (v 8a) and is proud (v 8b). Ch 40 foregrounds the "last leader of that time, representing the final Roman emperor.

3.4.4 *Eschatology and Messianism*

Moreover, 2 Baruch 36–40 employs the messiah in bringing about a reversal of roles with the antagonist. Though 2 Baruch focuses more on the nature of the eschaton than the messiah himself, this is one of the few times he plays a

---

62 Richard Bauckham, "The Messianic Interpretation of Isa 10:34 in the Dead Sea Scrolls, 2 Baruch and the Preaching of John the Baptist" *DSD* 2.2 (1995): 208.
63 So Charles, *Commentary on the Pseudepigrapha*, 500.
64 Bauckham, "The Messianic Interpretation," 208. The article explores how this messianic interpretation of Isa 10:34 is also seen in 4Q285, 4QpIsa[a], and the judgment pronounced by John the Baptist. Bauckham thinks the vine in 2 Baruch comes from "association with Ezek 17:6–8, where the twig which symbolizes a scion of the royal house of Judah is said to have sprouted ... and become a vine" (209). However, this would require the author of the "Cedar and Vine Apocalypse" to be unaware that the messianic imagery of vv 22–24 is distinctly separate from the vine, which seems unlikely.

significant role. The vine and the fountain both represent the messiah (39:7, "then the principate of My Messiah will be revealed, which is like the fountain and the vine,").[65] How the author has made this identification is uncertain. It is tempting to say that the messianic figure acts as the embodiment of Israel, given Isa 5:7. Alternatively, the author may have made the connection to other branch imagery, like Isa 4:2, or even Ps 80 (discussed below). But whatever the case, the Cedar and Vine Apocalypse portrays the messiah as victorious over the antagonists, bringing about their destruction, and actively providing protection for God's people (40:2).[66] 40:1 mysteriously states that "they will bring him [the last Roman leader] up to Mount Zion." The antecedent of "they" is not clear, but Lied suggests they are the "protagonists of the Messiah," who are also "the remnant."[67] Since the vine is the messiah, the text certainly views the eschaton, supported by the possible allusions mentioned earlier, especially to Dan 7. Granted, 2 Baruch 40:3 says that the messianic reign will only last "until the world of corruption is at an end, and until the times aforesaid are fulfilled." But this end cap does not imply a non-eschatological period. For our purposes, the significant observation from this passage is the substitution of rule (the vine instead of the cedar) results in the messiah protecting God's people, doing what the previous ruler ought to have done (36:7–8).

3.4.5 *Summary of 2 Baruch 36–40*

The influence of 2 Baruch 36–40 on the Matthean WTP seems unlikely. Yet the text helpfully illustrates how a first century writer uses the famous symbol of the vine to address the themes of leadership, eschatology, and messianism. The earlier leaders in this vision are Gentile world powers. One may wonder

---

65 Charles' translation, taking ܡܕܒܪܢܘܬܐ ("principate") for ܡܕܒܪܢܘܬܐ ("beginning"). Cf. Charles, *Commentary on the Pseudepigrapha*, 500. Bruno Violet, *Die Apokalypsen des Esra und des Baruch in deutscher Gestalt, II* (Leipzig: J. C. Hinrichs, 1924), 256 suggests ("vielleicht") that the underlying Greek was originally ἀρχή. In that case the meaning "ruler" or "beginning" would still be possible in the first century CE (LSJ, 252). However, Matthias Henze, *Jewish Apocalypticism in Late First Century Israel: Reading 'Second Baruch'* (TSAJ; Tübingen: Mohr Siebeck, 2011), 300 insists that "beginning" is the correct reading and that emendations "miss the point of the text: the first visitation of the Messiah merely marks the initial phase of his sovereignty, a period that is still part of this world."

66 This theme of protection is also found in the apocalyptic section in 2 Baruch 29–30, 53, and 74. Lied, *Other Lands*, 194; Lutz Doering, "The Epistle of Baruch and Its Role in 2 Baruch," in *Fourth Ezra and Second Baruch: Reconstruction after the Fall*, ed. Matthias Henze and Gabriele Boccaccini (Leiden: Brill, 2014), 156. This is especially stressed in connection to being in the land (see Lied's discussion on 197–203, who argues at length that the recipients of this protection are a righteous Jewish remnant who have returned to the land).

67 Lied, *Other Lands*, 201.

if these can be seen as "agents of God," but in light of passages like Dan 4:17, it seems likely that the understanding of kings as agents would include even Gentiles. The apocalypse clearly describes the eschaton and the role the messiah has in not only destroying wicked rulers who oppress God's people but also establishing a new age in which they will flourish.

3.5   Ps 80

We can consider Ps 80, particularly vv 9–20, as the next conversation partner. Besides the WTP, this passage echoes Isa 5:1–7 more loudly than any of those considered here. A good case can be made that it includes eschatological elements. The most significant contribution this conversation partner makes regard the statements about the "son of man" whom God establishes so the vine can flourish again. Especially in later understandings and forms of the psalm, this is a messianic figure who secures the wellbeing of God's people. Like all the other contributors, the psalm demonstrates the sorts of things a later writer can do with Isa 5, and like Ezekiel's parables, they are significant because of their place in the canon, with which Matthew has shown himself to be so thoroughly familiar. But more than that, this text may be more than a conversation partner since there are strong reasons to think that the WTP specifically alludes to this psalm. If so, this means the WTP's use of a vineyard must be seen through the lens of both Ps 80 and Isa 5.

3.5.1   Overview of Contents

Ps 80 contains a common refrain in vv 4, 8, and 20, אֱלֹהִים הֲשִׁיבֵנוּ וְהָאֵר פָּנֶיךָ וְנִוָּשֵׁעָה. This repetition reinforces the overall thrust of the psalm as a prayer for God's[68] help and deliverance amidst national calamity. The refrain divides the psalm into sections, though it is unclear if we should consider v 15 as an instance of the refrain.[69] The first petitions God for salvation and the second describes the people's misery before the surrounding nations. The third and fourth both utilize the vine motif, with the planting of the vine, and its prosperity among the nations. This forms a basic chiasm (assuming v 15 is another occurrence of the refrain):

---

[68] In the MT, the occurrences are identical except the references to God are continually expanded. This pattern is obscured in other translations though (e.g. Syriac, Vulgate, and LXX). ET verse numbers are one verse higher than the MT and LXX.

[69] This explains why some scholars have three sections and others four. See discussion by Allen Ross, *A Commentary on the Psalms: 42–89* (Grand Rapids: Kregel, 2013), 693 who lists corresponding adherents.

A	Request for God's salvation (vv 1–3) and refrain (v 4)
B	Misery among the nations (vv 5–7) and refrain (v 8)
B'	Misery among the nations using vine image (vv 9–14) and refrain (v 15)
A'	Request for God's salvation using the vine image (vv 16–19) and refrain (v 20)[70]

3.5.2 *Connection to Isa 5:1–7*

Though no clue remains why the psalm only specifies the tribes descending from Rachel – Ephraim, Benjamin, and Manasseh (v 3), many have deduced from this reference to northern tribes that the calamity is the Assyrian invasion, placing the composition of the psalm around 722 BCE.[71] The LXX[72] views it this way, containing ψαλμὸς ὑπὲρ τοῦ Ἀσσυρίου in its heading (79:1). However, commentators often detect another layer of composition, with redactors adding the second half of the psalm later.[73] This means it is not clear if later prophetic uses of the vine (Jeremiah and Ezekiel) should be considered as possible sources for allusions.[74] But Isa 5 seems to have been an option for allusions, even if the early date of 722 BCE is adopted.

Many commentators note this connection.[75] In particular, the following similarities suggest that Ps 80 alludes to Isa 5. First, Isa 5 compares Israel to a

---

70 The first section (vv 1–4) petitions God to "shine before Ephraim, Benjamin, and Manasseh" (v 3). Some Hebrew mss have לבני instead of לפני. If so, this might anticipate the use of בן in the corresponding A' (specifically vv 15 and 17). בִּנְיָמִין may also correlate to the expression עַל־אִישׁ יְמִינֶךָ.

71 E.g. Keil and Delitzsch, *Commentary on the Old Testament*, 5:536. However, Peter D. Akpunonu, *The Vine, Israel, and the Church* (New York: Peter Lang, 2004), 45, states "I have rarely studied a biblical problem that has such a variety of opinions as the historical setting of this psalm."

72 Except for Sinaiticus.

73 Frank Lothat Hossfeld, Erich Zenger, and Linda M Maloney, *A Commentary on Psalms 51–100* (Hermeneia; Minneapolis: Fortress, 2005), 311; deClaisse-Walford, *The Book of Psalms*, 311. Furthermore, Thomas Hieke rightly notes "Psalm 79 almost certainly bewails the catastrophe in 586 BCE. So the collectors that place Psalm 80 after Psalm 79 conceived and used the psalm as an appropriate reaction to the destruction of Jerusalem and the Exile" ("Psalm 80 and Its Neighbors," *BN* 86 [1997]: 39).

74 Though it less certain than Isa 5, it may be that Ezek 17 is in the background, as argued by Bernard Gosse, "Le Psaume 80 Dans Le Cadre Du Psautier Et Ezechiel 17," Scandinavian Journal of the Old Testament, 19.1 (2005): 52. However, the direction of influence could the reverse, as suggested by Marvin E. Tate, *Psalms 51–100* (WBC; Nashville: Thomas Nelson, 1990), 309.

75 E.g. Water Brueggemann, *Psalms* (NCBC; Cambridge: Cambridge University Press, 2014), 349; John Goldingay, *Psalms: Psalms 42–89* (BCOTWP; Grand Rapids: Baker, 2007), 539–40; Tate, *Psalms 50–100*, 314.

vineyard (כֶּרֶם) and Ps 80 compares it to a vine (גֶּפֶן).[76] Not only do the semantic ranges of these words overlap, but Ps 80 portrays the single plant as growing to mammoth proportions, filling the land, covering cedars, and extending to the sea (vv 9–11). Thus, the picture in Ps 80 extends beyond a simple plant and, conceptually, represents a large vineyard. Depending on the time of composition, this could possibly explain other occurrences we have seen in which the vine is unusually large. Second, יְהוָה צְבָאוֹת is the farmer in Isa 5 (v 7) and though the divine farmer in Ps 80 receives many titles, they include יְהוָה (vv 5 and 20) and צְבָאוֹת (vv 5, 7, 15, and 20). Third, both texts describe at length the establishment of the vine, specifically its planting (נטע in Isa 5:2, Ps 80:8, 15). Fourth, the farmer destroys the vineyard by breaking (פרץ) the surrounding wall (גָּדֵר) in Isa 5:6 and Ps 80:13.

Certainly the two contains other significant differences, but these are best understood as a rhetorical device to reinforce the purpose of the psalm as a cry for God's deliverance. Unlike Isa 5, Ps 80 records the initial growth and prosperity of the vine (vv 10–11), reminding YHWH of his former pleasure in the vine that he might repeat the same blessing. Isa 5:4 dramatically asks what else YHWH could have done, but Ps 80:13 asks why he has broken down the wall of protection. On the one hand, the allusion to Isa 5 provides the answer and toward the end, the psalm implicitly acknowledges the sin of Israel (v 19). But on the other hand, this question suggests that the time of punishment should be over. Goldingay's explanation seems on target, "The psalm implicitly recognizes the guilt of the past but wants YHWH to reckon that enough is now enough. The 'Why?' then asks not so much why YHWH acted in chastisement at all but why YHWH acted in a way that brought such far-reaching destruction."[77] Ps 80 does not contradict Isa 5's description of judgment in placing the blame on Israel, but acknowledging that the punishment has already come (Isa 5 looks forward to destruction and Ps 80, probably, backward), it pleads for restoration. Thus, the similarities between the passages and the rhetorical sense that can be made of their differences strongly suggest Ps 80 alludes to Isa 5.[78]

3.5.3 *Agency*

Unlike the previous contributors to our conversation, Ps 80 adds nothing to the topics of agents and leadership. The psalm's essential bypassing of the causes for the vine's destruction probably accounts for this lack. Instead, it

---

76 KJV and NKJV have "vineyard" in v 15 (MT v 16), but this translation of כַּנָּה is almost certainly incorrect, as will be discussed below.
77 Goldingay, *Psalms 42–89*, 540.
78 Cf. "Inverted Use of the Old Testament" from fn. 44 in chapter 1.

emphasizes the prayer for restoration. However, that section (vv 14, 16, and 17) a potentially messianic figure emerges who functions as God's agent to protect and care for the vine (see 3.5.5).

3.5.4 *Eschatology*

Questions about messianism and the identity of the mysterious figure connected to the vine warrant most of our attention, and the extent to which one sees the eschaton as being in view will largely depend on how the branch / son figure is understood. However, the eschatological nature of Ps 80 may be suggested without engaging this issue. The very fact that Ps 80 adapts Isa 5 implies that the psalmist has the larger picture of Isaiah in view. It seems likely to me that either Isa 4 or 27 lurks somewhere in the background of Ps 80 since this explains the logic of the text in presuming that YHWH will not ultimately allow the vine to remain ruined. But even if those specific passages are not in view, according to the overall theology of Isaiah (even if Deutero and Trito Isaiah are excluded), the answer to the crisis of exile is the eschaton (e.g. 4:1–6). If Ps 80 describes the current ruin as what was predicted in Isa 5, then only the coming kingdom depicted in Isaiah ushers in the longed-for restoration.[79] Moreover, there is no reason to think that Matthew would have parted ways with the predominate first century perspective of viewing the psalms as eschatological.[80]

3.5.5 *Messianism*

Though Ps 80 discusses themes of judgment and the eschaton, the role of messianism is particularly significant for our purposes. V 15 records the petition וּפְקֹד גֶּפֶן זֹאת, which certainly refers to Israel given the symbolism provided earlier. But the objects of פקד continue in v 16, וְכַנָּה אֲשֶׁר־נָטְעָה יְמִינֶךָ וְעַל־בֵּן אִמַּצְתָּה לָּךְ. Both terms continue the horticultural imagery, and yet they do not function as synonyms for גֶּפֶן. The hapax legomenon כַּנָּה is difficult to define with certainty. BDB argues that it comes from כנן, "base, pedestal," and that similarities

---

[79] Andrew Streett provides further reasons for seeing the eschaton in Ps 80: its exodus/new exodus motif, its creation/re-creation motif, resonances of the Davidic covenant, and חיה referring to national resurrection (*The Vine and the Son of Man: Eschatological Interpretation of Psalm 80 in Early Judaism* (Philadelphia: Fortress Press, 2014), 26–42).

[80] Cf. Docherty, "New Testament Scriptural Interpretation," 7, "The fact that three fragmentary *pesharim* on the Psalms (1Q16, 4Q171, 4Q173) have survived is therefore significant as an indicator that it was also regarded as a prophetic book by the members of the community. The Qumran *Psalms Scroll*, for instance, includes the claim that: 'All these (songs) he (David) spoke through prophecy which was given from before the Most High …' (11QPs\[a\], XXVII, 11–12). This Understanding of the Psalms was not confined to the Dead Sea sect, as it is reflected also in the New Testament."

with the Syriac ܥܩܪܐ imply it should be understood as "root, stock."[81] The Targum is roughly similar, using "branch" (עוברא) and BHS suggests the LXX understood it as וְכוֹנְנָהּ, translating καὶ κατάρτισαι αὐτήν. The original meaning is difficult to ascertain, but if we take the idea of "root" or "stock," as with most modern translations,[82] then this suggests a parallel to the messianic שֹׁרֶשׁ of Isa 11:10. But whatever the meaning of כַּנָּה, we should not miss the immediately following connection to God's right hand, also occurring in v 18. The right hand of God stands for his power (e.g. Ps 17:7, 18:35, 44:3) and connections to the messianic Ps 110:1, not to mention Pss 116:8, 11, and 118:16 imply a messianic connotation.

The second object of פקד, בֵּן, as a purposefully ambiguous double entendre denotes both a "branch" of the vine (e.g. בֵּן means "branch" in Gen 49:22) and a "son" (Ps 80:18).[83] But though the text does not use צמח, a thematic connection to this messianic concept which we have already explored remains. This may explain the Targum's gloss מלכא משיחא. V 18 then repeats בֵּן in the expression בֶּן־אָדָם. The LXX, also includes ἀνθρώπου after υἱόν in v 16. The term by itself simply means "human one," but intertextual connections strongly suggest a meaning like that of Dan 7:13–14 is in view.[84] Much has been written about the identity of this figure in Ps 80 and not all scholars agree that the original psalm had a messianic figure in view, or even a king, but most of this objection concerns a reconstructed original form of the psalm. There is a general consensus however that the passage in at least its later forms, and obviously by the time of the Targum translation, viewed it as messianic.[85] The argument of this chapter does not require establishing the messianic nature of the early version

---

81   BDB, 488.
82   ESV and NRSV "stock;" NASB "shoot;" NIV and HCSB "root."
83   There is a good possibility that this line was added later to connect the vine image to the son language later. See Streett, *The Vine*, 43.
84   For more, see Streett, *The Vine*, 39; A. Gelston, "A Sidelight on the 'Son of Man'" *SJT* 22 (1969): 189–96; David Hill "Son of Man' in Psalm 80 v 17," *NovT* (1973) 261–9; Ross, *Psalms*, 704; Samuel Terrien, *The Psalms: Strophic Structure and Theological Commentary* (Eerdmans' Critical Commentary; Grand Rapids: Eerdmans, 2003), 580. For the intertextual connections with Ps 89 so that Ps 80 is messianic, see Gosse, "Le Psaume 80 Dans Le Cadre Du Psautier Et Ezechiel 17," 52. For intertextual connections to Gen 1–3, Ps 8, 72, 110 and Dan 7, see Andrew Streett, "From Marginal to Mainstream: The Adamic Son of Man and the Potential of Psalm 80" *CTR* 13.2 (2016): 77–98.
85   Walter C. Kaiser Jr., "The Messiah of Psalm 80" *BSac* 174 (Oct–Dec 2017): 287–93 argues that "the psalm is not primarily about a Davidic Messiah, yet the individual mentioned here [vv 16–19] seems to be messianic … What was needed was a royal image of a Davidic king who was sovereign over all, along with an image of a suffering Joseph figure who goes down into a pit, down into Egypt, down into prison, and then ascends to the ruling position alongside Pharaoh" (392).

of the passage (though I find Streett's discussion compelling) since we are only concerned with establishing what a "wider" view of Isa 5 – including themes of eschatology and messianism – would have been during the first century.

Beyond the son's messianic identity, we are particularly interested in the role he plays. The psalm intimately connects the branch/son to the wellbeing of the vine. The psalmist is clearly concerned with the state of the vine, and yet there are requests for YHWH to establish the branch/son figure. If God establishes it/him, then Israel will prosper. One can easily imagine either the בֵּן protecting the vine from the wild beasts of v 14 or being a farmer, working on the vine. Alternatively, if "root" is the intended concept in v 16, then the בֵּן affects the prosperity of the vine by supplying it with nutrients. The text does not provide these details. But the significant observation for our purposes is that the vine's flourishing depends on the establishment of the messianic branch/son. Somehow or other, he/it takes care of and provides for the vine so that it prospers according to the farmer's original intention.

3.5.6 *Excursus: What If the WTP Alludes to Ps 80?*

The earlier consideration of Ezekiel's vineyard parables and 2 Baruch 36–40 (and later John 15) illustrate how later writers could adapt the vine/vineyard image found in Isa 5 to address issues of agency, eschatology, and messianism. We have been exploring these texts in order that the use of Isaiah's vineyard in the WTP could be properly placed in its hermeneutical milieu. Psalm 80 serves that purpose as well. But it very well may do more than that. Streett argues at length in his recent monograph on Ps 80 that the WTP directly alludes to this passage,[86] and he is not alone in this suggestion. Carson suggests the verses, "clearly allude to Isaiah 5:1–7 and Psalm 80:6–16: Jesus' parable is an old theme with new variations."[87] Black similarly writes, "the allegory of the desolated vineyard of Psalm lxxx may be even more important than the imagery of the deserted and doomed vineyard of Isaiah v."[88] If so, this requires interpreters to understand not only Isa 5 as the intertextual background, but specifically Isa 5 as employed in Ps 80, and this would greatly strengthen the argument here that a "wider conception" of Isa 5 is being evoked in the WTP and would make the

---

86 Streett, *The Vine*, esp. 193–208.

87 Carson, "Matthew," 452.

88 Black, "Christological," 13 n3. Hill, "'Son of Man'," 261–62; Gelston, "Sidelight," 196; Klyne Snodgrass, *The Parable of the Wicked Tenants: An Inquiry into Parable Interpretation* (WUNT; Eugene, OR: Wipf and Stock, 2011), 75 n. 14 (hesitatingly); Robert D. Rowe, *God's Kingdom and God's Son: The Background to Mark's Christology from Concepts of Kingship in the Psalms*, (AGJU; Leiden: Brill, 2002): 193; N. T. Wright, *Jesus and the Victory of God* (London: SPCK, 1996), 493.

conclusions about the surprising use of agency and messianism in the WTP all the more certain. To that end, Streett's argument is summarized in the following paragraph. However, if this argument fails to convince, Ps 80 still remains in the same category of 'conversation partner' as Ezekiel's vineyard parables and 2 Baruch 36–40 in illustrating the hermeneutical milieu of the WTP.

According to Streett, "four points argue for an allusion to Psalm 80 in Mark 12:1–12: (1) the juxtaposition of the vineyard and the son; (2) broad thematic consistencies; (3) lexical, thematic, and sequential similarities between Psalm 80:9–19 and Mark 12:1–11; and (4) connections between Psalm 80 and Isaiah 5, on the one hand, and Psalm 118, on the other."[89] He elaborates (1) by observing that the son is central to the WTP, but Isa 5 alone cannot account for his presence. Yet Ps 80 has at least the potential of presenting the branch/son as a messianic figure somehow connected to the vine. He explains (2), "thematic consistencies," by pointing to Ps 80's similarities with the WTP: in both the vineyard is treated positively and not condemned, in both the owner restores the vineyard, in both there are enemies of the vineyard (beasts in Ps 80 and selfish farmers in the WTP), and both have "undercurrents" of temple destruction. For (3), he outlines the common progression as "The vineyard established" (Ps 80:9–12; Mark 12:1); "The culprits' misdeeds" (Ps 80:13–14; Mark 12:1–5); "The death of the branch/son" (Ps 80:16b–17b; Mark 12:6–8); "The culprits destroyed" (Ps 80:17c; Mark 12:9); and "The son's reversal" (Ps 80:18–19; Mark 12:10–11).[90] For (4), he notes that the use of Ps 118 in the WTP rests on the אבן/בן wordplay and Ps 80 also plays with the use of בן, and that both psalms have the themes of salvation, God's right hand, and salvation from death to life.[91]

To be sure, some of these points are stronger than others. Ps 80 would present a clearer reason for seeing agency stressed in the WTP, but we have also seen that other interpreters took this route and that Isaiah itself at least has the potential for doing so. Similarly, seeing Isa 5 in light of other Isaian references to a vineyard would explain why the vineyard does not finally end in a state of destruction. The presence of particularly a son figure, however, is the strongest argument for seeing a direct allusion. Moreover, the enemies being animals, representing gentile nations in Ps 80 and the enemies being farmers, representing Israel's leaders in the WTP[92] does not seem to be strong enough to be a

---

89   Streett, *The Vineyard*, 200.
90   Streett, *The Vine*, 205.
91   He rightly notes that these are common in Psalms, but adds "nevertheless, the combination of the three in close proximity in both psalms makes it more likely that the author of the parable saw the two texts as going together" (206).
92   Streett, *The Vine*, 204 observes that this is problematic. Unfortunately, this section does not describe any lexical similarities as claimed on p. 200.

confirming correspondence to demonstrate an allusion. If the allusion exists, this may be an example of target domain override. This may be an entailment, an implied mapping by the Vital Relation of disanalogy. The rhetorical thrust of this juxtaposition would be to ironically put Israel's leaders in the position of gentile oppressors.[93] Something similar is to be at work in the use of the rejected-stone logion (discussed in the next chapter) in which the builders represented gentile oppressors in Ps 118 but are the religious leaders of Israel in the WTP. Moreover, the fact that this correspondence occurs within a citation means that the connection is certain. Thus, the contrast cannot be used to disprove the allusion to Ps 80. Streett's third point concerning common progression is, over all, valid but not powerful. Both follow the normal contours of a standard plot structure (e.g. Freytag's pyramid) and are not exceptional. Similarly, the common themes of salvation are unremarkable. The death of the branch/son in Ps 80 is far from certain. But the weaker points must not be allowed to "cross contaminate" the weightier points. This proposed allusion has the advantage of demonstrating how a messianic son gets to be associated with the story of the vineyard, which Isa 5 alone cannot do.

If the WTP alludes to both Isa 5 and Ps 80, how does this impact our query into Matthew's hermeneutic of fulfillment? It may be that 80:17 describes the destruction of the branch/son, and this would map to the murder of the owner's son in the WTP. However, as noted earlier, the messianic branch/son in Ps 80 somehow (the text is silent on the details) provides for the wellbeing of the vine so that the psalmist prays for the vine's restoration by praying for the branch/son's establishment. Thus, as will be discussed in greater detail later, here we are at a contrast with the WTP, in which the son's death, not establishment, ends up being the turning point for the proper function of the vine/vineyard (though in the WTP the vineyard is never said to be ruined). Instead, the responsibility of caring for the vineyard falls on the shoulders of the replacement farmers in the WTP. If Ps 80 lies in the background, this important role maps back to the messianic branch/son. In this case, the branch/son of Ps 80 maps in two ways to the WTP. The messianic nature of the figure in Ps 80:16 suggests he should be connected to the son, but the function of caring for the vine suggests that he also maps to the replacement farmers. The above observation does not mean that Matthew is depicting the new farmers as the messiah. For Matthew, Jesus alone bears that title. The mapping would be via the Vital Relation of role, not identity. As will be discussed in the next chapter, the following citation of Ps 118 includes Jesus as crucial element to

---

93 As in the use of Ps 2 in Acts 4:25.

the picture of restoration, so it is not as though Jesus plays no restorative all in this section. But if Matthew intends us to read the WTP in light of Ps 80 and its messianic features, the replacement farmers take up this messianic mission, a point which will be explored more fully in section 3.7.

3.5.7 Summary of Ps 80

Besides Isa 5:1–7, Ps 80 is the most important intertextual background for the WTP. Sufficient indications exist in the WTP to think that, at the least, the Matthean Jesus adapts Isa 5 in a way similar to the author of Ps 80, if not making a direct allusion to this text. Though this text does not contribute much to the conversation about agency or the eschaton, it significantly describes the messiah as the son of man who ensures the future flourishing of the vine. This clearly captures the messianic ideas present in Ezek 17, and 2 Baruch 36–40. As we will be seen, the WTP use of Isa 5 shares similarities with these texts, but also departs in significant ways.

3.6 John 15:1–8

The fifth contributor in our conversation is the Johannine Jesus in John 15:1–8. Similarly to 2 Baruch 36–40, we consider this text since it represents a way of adapting Isaiah's vineyard in the first century to discuss the themes of agency, eschatology, and particularly messianism. Like 2 Baruch, it equates the vine with the messiah, and like Ezek 19, the vine and its branches have different mappings. As with the other contributors, the messiah's role in this vine parable is a victorious one who ensures the eschatological wellbeing of God's people.

3.6.1 Overview of Contents

John 13–17 contains Jesus' "farewell discourse"[94] in which he prepares his disciples (after 13:30 the eleven without Judas) for what to expect after his departure. In approximately the center, 15:1–16 contains a parable (loosely defined) centered around Jesus' seventh "I am" saying – Ἐγώ εἰμι ἡ ἄμπελος (vv 1, 5). The bulk of the vine imagery can be found in vv 1–8, but v 16 contains a final mention of "fruit" and "abide" (ὑμεῖς ὑπάγητε καὶ καρπὸν φέρητε καὶ ὁ καρπὸς ὑμῶν

---

94   Emphasizing the last words of an important figure was often done in antiquity. See L. S. Kellum, "Farewell Discourse," *Dictionary of Jesus and the Gospels*, 2d ed., ed. Joel B. Green, Jeannine K. Brown, and Nicholas Perrin (Downers Grove: IVP Academic, 2013), 267–269.

μένῃ).⁹⁵ In this metaphor, Jesus explains how the disciples can be productive even in his physical absence. Through the work of the Holy Spirit (e.g. 14:16), the disciples can still be "connected" to Jesus. In fact, they must do so to "bear fruit" (15:5) and if they do not, they will be burned in the fire of judgment (v 6).

3.6.2 *Connection to Isa 5:1–7*

Several backgrounds for Jesus' parable have been suggested,⁹⁶ but an OT one seems the most likely, given John's other use of OT imagery (e.g. 1:29, 2:21, 3:14, 6:32, 10:14). Many commentators recognized this, though they disagree as to which text(s) John intends, with most suggestions being Isa 5 and 27, Jer 2:21, Ezekiel 15, 17, and 19, Ps 80, and *Sirach* 24:17–21. More than 50 years ago, Borig thoroughly explored proposals,⁹⁷ and today a wide divergence of opinion remains.⁹⁸ Some proposed allusions can claim more volume than others,⁹⁹ but the lack of consensus demonstrates that more than one passage is probably in view. Moreover, Isa 5 is the fountainhead for the other proposals (except for perhaps *Sirach* 24) and so John 15 likely interacts with this passage, whether directly or indirectly.

3.6.3 *Agency*

The placement of this metaphor in the farewell discourse, preparing Jesus' followers for ministry in his absence, suggests themes of agency are present. The thought clearly differs from Ezekiel's ruling branches (19:14), but John still presents them as agents, sent by God who share in Jesus' mission (cf. John 20:21) so others may believe (17:20). In his thorough study of John 17,

---

95   Donald A. Carson, *The Gospel According to John* (PNTC; Grand Rapids: Eerdmans, 1991), 520 suggests the section from vv 9–16 play an important role in clarifying the inherent limitations to the vine metaphor.

96   John C. Hutchison, "The Vine in John 15 and Old Testament Imagery in the 'I am' Statements," *BSac* 168 (Jan–March, 2011): 65–66 outlines several suggestions, including the wine of the Last Supper, the vine of the temple gate, the pruning fires of Kidron, and Gnosticism.

97   Rainer Borig, *Der wahre Weinstock: Untersuchungen zu Jo 15, 1–10* (SANT; München: Kösel, 1967), 94–194.

98   E.g. George R. Beasley-Murray, *John* (WBC; Nashville: Thomas Nelson, 1999), 272; Carson, *John*, 513; Akpunonu, *The Vine*, 134; Andreas J. Köstenberger, *John* (BECNT; Grand Rapids: Baker, 2004), 449–50; Ben Witherington III, *John's Wisdom: A Commentary on the Fourth Gospel* (Louisville: Westminster John Knox, 1995), 255; Thomas L. Brodie, *The Gospel according to John: A Literary and Theological Commentary* (Oxford: Oxford University, 1995), 255; Street, *The Vine*, 210–21; Manning, *Echoes of a Prophet*, 135–46.

99   Manning, *Echoes of a Prophet*, 140 has a helpful chart to show the primacy of Ezekiel's parables.

Ferreira demonstrates that this climactic prayer "serves as the Gospel's mature and final description of the Johannine community's ecclesiology ... [it] emphasizes the purpose of the community which is to continue the sending of the Son into the world."[100] John's vine parable must be seen in this connection. Ferriera suggests "The parable of the vine deals with the relationship between the community and Christ and also with the missiological function of the community."[101] Köstenberger concludes in discussing the vine imagery of John 15, "Jesus' followers are taken into the mission of the triune God and serve as his divinely commissioned representatives," calling them "Jesus' new messianic community."[102] Thus, though John 15:1–8 does not specifically emphasize agency, the broader context of John, specifically the farewell discourse, provides this perspective.

3.6.4 Eschatology

Nothing in the text of John 15:1–16 points to an eschatological function of Isaiah's vineyard, and thus, in our reconstructed conversation, John 15 may have nothing to contribute to this topic.[103] However, we should see the text in light of John's larger theological use of inaugurated eschatology, in which he presents believers as presently having eternal life (e.g. 3:15–16, 36, 5:24, 6:47, 10:28), and after his death and resurrection, Satan is defeated (John 12:31–33), Jesus is glorified (e.g. 3:14, 8:28, 12:32, 34), and the Spirit is given (7:38).[104] Again, the setting of the parable in the farewell discourse indicates that this paradigm describes the situation after Jesus' departure.

3.6.5 Messianism

Similarly to Isa 5 (and dissimilarly to the WTP), God is the farmer (ὁ πατήρ μου ὁ γεωργός ἐστιν, John 15:1). John 15:1–8 also continues the trend of employing the vine image to address the topic of messianism. The parable begins with Jesus saying Ἐγώ εἰμι ἡ ἄμπελος ἡ ἀληθινή (probably in juxtaposition with

---

100 Johan Ferreira, *Johannine Ecclesiology* (JSNTSup; Sheffield: Sheffield Academic, 1998), 201, 203.
101 *Johannine Ecclesiology* 204.
102 Andreas Köstenberger, *A Theology of John's Gospel and Letters: The Word, the Christ, the Son of God* (Grand Rapids: Zondervan, 2015), 508, 457.
103 The fire in v 6 likely refers to eschatological judgment, but this is done to the vine and does not require the vine itself to be an eschatological entity.
104 For more on this commonly accepted characteristic of the gospel of John, as well as a brief history, see R. S. Schellenberg, "Eschatology," *Dictionary of Jesus and the Gospels*, 2d ed., ed. Joel B. Green, Jeannine K. Brown, and Nicholas Perrin (Downers Grove, IL: IVP Academic, 2013), 238.

Jer 2:21 – ἐγὼ δὲ ἐφύτευσά σε ἄμπελον καρποφόρον πᾶσαν ἀληθινήν· πῶς ἐστράφης εἰς πικρίαν, ἡ ἄμπελος ἡ ἀλλοτρία;). We had noted before that Isa 5, in its literary context, contained the potential for a messianic interpretation due to the eschatological צֶמַח in 4:2. This does not seem to be in view since John 15 separates the vine image from the branches (as did Ezek 17), but equates the disciples and not the messiah with the branches (κλῆμα, v 15).[105] Alternatively, Kee argues this switch may be purposeful to show the close relationship and shared function of Jesus and the disciples.[106] However, this emphasizes a contrast not seen in the Hebrew or Greek – in English translations, comparing the "branches" of John 15:1–8 with the "branch" of Isa 4:2 comes easily, but we have already seen that "branch" is a poor translation of צֶמַח[107] and thus has little semantic overlap with κλῆμα. The function of the messianic vine in John 15 is to provide the nutrients and sustenance for the branches so that they will ultimately bear much fruit.

3.6.6 Summary of John 15:1–8

Thus, though John 15 applies Isaiah's vineyard in quite a different way than the WTP, it nonetheless offers another example of how the image could be used to answer questions about agency, eschatology, and particularly messianism. An intimate connection (represented by μένω, 12× in John 15:1–16) with Jesus resolves the problem of fruitlessness from Isa 5. But if the disciples lose this connection, the judgment of Isa 5 and/or other vineyard uses (e.g. Ezek 15) maps to them. Though Jesus' function in this parable serves to protect from judgment, this happens because he energizes the branches so as to produce fruit. The messianic function in John's use of the vineyard motif involves some sort of care for the vine. Both the Father and Jesus have a role to play in seeing to the productivity of the field. The symbolism certainly differs from what we have seen so far, but it points to a significantly similar reality. In John 15, the messiah's function is to enable God's people to do works for his glory (cf. v 8).

---

105 Streett, *The Vine*, 216–17 argues this resonates with *Tg Ps* 80:12, which equates the sent-out branches with disciples (though because of the uncertainty in dating the Targum, this may only represent "awareness of a traditional understanding of Ps 80:12 already circulating in the first century").

106 Howard C. Kee, "Messiah and the People of God" in *Understanding the Word: Essays in Honor of Bernhard W. Anderson*, ed. James T. Butler, Edgar W. Conrad, and Ben C. Ollenburger (JSOTSup; Sheffield: JSOT Press, 1985), 355.

107 The LXX's ἀνατολή gets us no further.

As with Ps 80, the messiah is the one upon whom the wellbeing of the whole plant depends.[108]

3.7 Matt 21:33–45

To recap our findings so far in this chapter, we have been investigating the hermeneutical milieu surrounding the Isaian vineyard to prepare us for understanding why Jesus would select this particular intertextual backdrop and manipulate it in order to address the prominent themes in the WTP, namely agency, eschatology, and messianism. At first blush, his choice appears strange because none of these issues seem to have a place in Isa 5:1–7. Yet these topics were seen to be 'hanging in the air' regarding this image. We started by looking at interpretive seedbeds within the Isaian context – small potential hints within the immediate text that later users might give attention to and take in particular directions – and found that the topics of agency, eschatology, and messianism have semantic potential in Isa 5:1–7. We then considered Isaiah's other uses of this vine image, as well as other occurrences in the history of interpretation (Ezekiel 15, 17, 19; 2 Baruch 36–40; Ps 80; John 15) to see how the hermeneutical milieu of Isaiah's vineyard did lead to the topics described above.

This provides a helpful backdrop to the WTP and allows us to see clearly ways in which Jesus agrees with other interpreters and yet significantly departs. On the one hand, the WTP agrees with other uses of the vineyard in using it to zero in on corrupt leadership/agency and pronounce their downfall. Moreover, the WTP agrees with other interpretations in depicting God as the ultimate owner of the vineyard, who establishes replacement leadership, and describes this in eschatological categories. But on the other hand, whereas other usages attribute this eschatological replacement agency to the messiah, the WTP speaks up in our metaphorical conversation and voices disagreement. We will

---

108   As with 2 Baruch 36–40, it is unclear as to how Jesus becomes equated with the vine. But dissimilarly, John 15 does include the disciples as branches, making them part of the "vine plant" as well. This does not require the image to mean Jesus has replaced the nation of Israel. Contra, e.g., Beasley-Murray, *John*, 272. Space does not allow for a defense of a post-supersessionist reading of John 15, but it should be observed that nothing here excludes the nation of Israel, but only that Jesus presents himself as central for the wellbeing of God's eschatological people. Streett suggests the significance is that "John may be interpreting Psalm 80 as a Messianic prophecy fulfilled in Jesus: God is doing in Jesus exactly what the psalmist asked him to do" (*The Vine*, 216).

see that the WTP does have a messianism of sorts with its uses of υἱός. But the logic of the parable does not allow for him to be the eschatological replacement leadership as was the case for the other conversation partners. Instead, this role, traditionally assigned to the messiah, maps to the disciples. We have made a heavy investment in listening to other conversation partners so we can appreciate that, though no specific messianic figure or eschatological agent is described in Isa 5:1–7, nonetheless these concepts are being mapped into the blend, not so much from the source domain of the text of Isa 5:1–7, but from the hermeneutical milieu surrounding it in the first century. Matthew maps certain messianic ideas into the blend, but when we consider the WTP as the target domain, we will discover that again Matthew demonstrates a non-messianic mapping of messianic figures. While no other case study examined in this research project quite functions this way, the WTP nonetheless serves as a fascinating example of Matthew's non-messianic use of OT messianic imagery.

3.7.1   *Overview of Contents*

We now turn to consider the position of the Matthean WTP in its broader literary context. The parable proper begins by introducing a landowner (οἰκοδεσπότης) who sets up a vineyard and hires tenant farmers to care for it (v 33).[109] The parable assumes, in contrast to Isa 5, that the vineyard produces desirable grapes. But when the harvest time approaches, the tenant farmers refuse to give the fruit, killing the owner's servants and even his son (vv 34–39). The parable concludes by stating that the tenant farmers will be destroyed and replaced by those who will produce (ποιέω) the desired fruit (vv 41, 43). The parable's conclusion also includes a citation and application of Ps 118:22–23, to be discussed in the next chapter.

3.7.2   *Connection to Isa 5:1–7*

The majority of commentators identify Isa 5:1–7 as the chief allusion made in the WTP.[110] This is primarily established by v 33. The fact that the setting up of the vineyard contributes little to the plot line and has so many lexical similarities with Isa 5:2 strongly suggests its function is to establish the allusion. The similarities are demonstrated in the following table (similarities in bold):

---

109 Herbert W. Basser, *The Gospel of Matthew and Judaic Traditions: A Relevance-based Commentary* (Leiden, Brill, 2015), 553 argues that the reference is to an *aris*, sharecropper, who worked a landowners' property, with the expectation that that he would turn over two-thirds of the crop and keep a third (or other proportions).

110 Weren, *Studies in Matthew's Gospel*, 205 argues that the Matthean version "obviously greatly strengthened the relation between the parable and Isa 5:1–7."

TABLE 2   Similarities between the Wicked Tenant Parable and Isaiah's Vineyard Song

Isa 5:2 (MT)	Isa 5:2 (LXX)	Matt 21:33
וַֽיְעַזְּקֵ֖הוּ	καὶ φραγμὸν περιέθηκα	ἐφύτευσεν ἀμπελῶνα
וַֽיְסַקְּלֵ֔הוּ	καὶ ἐχαράκωσα	καὶ φραγμὸν αὐτῷ περιέθηκεν
וַיִּטָּעֵ֣הוּ שֹׂרֵ֔ק	καὶ ἐφύτευσα ἄμπελον σωρηχ	καὶ ὤρυξεν ἐν αὐτῷ ληνὸν
וַיִּ֤בֶן מִגְדָּל֙ בְּתוֹכ֔וֹ	καὶ ᾠκοδόμησα πύργον ἐν μέσῳ αὐτοῦ	καὶ ᾠκοδόμησεν πύργον
וְגַם־יֶ֖קֶב חָצֵ֣ב בּ֑וֹ	καὶ προλήνιον ὤρυξα ἐν αὐτῷ	
וַיְקַ֖ו לַעֲשׂ֥וֹת עֲנָבִ֖ים	καὶ ἔμεινα τοῦ ποιῆσαι σταφυλήν	

3.7.3   Agency

The central theme of the WTP is agency. Each of the parable's characters relate to the owner as his agents. Whereas most, if not all, the other texts considered in this chapter have used Isaiah's vineyard to address the issue of agency, the WTP does even more so by creating new positions of servants, the son, and the farmers. The servants, and then son, are certainly to be understood as agents, who are sent (ἀποστέλλω in vv 34, 36, and 37[111]) on the owner's behalf to collect his fruit. The servants represent the prophets (cf. 2 Kgs 17:13, 14, 2 Chron 36:15, 16) and Jesus is the son.[112] The messianic nature of the son figure is discussed below, but the surrounding context emphasizes his status as agent. Earlier, the religious leaders questioned Jesus, Ἐν ποίᾳ ἐξουσίᾳ ταῦτα ποιεῖς; καὶ τίς σοι ἔδωκεν τὴν ἐξουσίαν ταύτην; (Matt 21:23, cf. Mark 11:28, Luke 20:2).[113] In each of the Synoptics, Jesus responds with a counter-question about the origin of John's ministry (Matt 21:24–27, cf. Mark 11:29–33, Luke 20:3–8). This not only allows

---

111   The significance of this word regarding agency was discussed in 2.2.4.2.
112   Arthur Gray, "The Parable of the Wicked Husbandmen," *HibJ*, 19 (1920–21): 42–52 and Merrill Miller, *Scripture and Parable: A Study of the Biblical Features in the Parable of the Wicked Husbandmen and Their Place in the History of Tradition* (Unpublished Ph. D. Dissertation, Columbia University 1974) argue that the son is meant to represent John the Baptist, but this has not gained much acceptance, particularly given Matthew's use of υἱός elsewhere in reference to Jesus (esp. 2:15, 3:17, 4:3, 6, 8:29, 14:33, 16:16, 17:5, 26:63–64, 27:40, 43, 54). However, in light of 11:13–14 and 21:25, John the Baptist is probably in view as one of the servants in light of 11:13–14 and 21:25.
113   The first clause in all three are identical. For the second, Matthew has omitted Mark's longer ending – ἵνα ταῦτα ποιῇς, and has changed ἤ for καί. The second clause in Luke is more different from Matthew and Mark, but communicates the same idea – ἤ τίς ἐστιν ὁ δούς σοι τὴν ἐξουσίαν ταύτην;

him to escape a potential trap,[114] but also reveals the reason for their ignorance. Their fear of negative public perception (Matt 21:46) ironically demonstrates that their later statement about Jesus could not be said of them, "you are true and teach the way of God in truth and no one is a concern to you, for you do not look on the appearance of a person" (22:16). Jesus' refusal to answer here embodies the secrecy motif found elsewhere (e.g. 13:10–15). But though Jesus has pronounced that he will not tell them the source of his authority (Matt 21:27, Mark 11:33, Luke 20:8), the WTP provides a thinly veiled answer to their question. Mark, followed by Luke, places the WTP immediately after the above pericope.[115] Matthew inserts the parable of the two sons between the John the Baptist question and the WTP, but the introduction to the WTP as ἄλλην παραβολήν (21:33) links the two parables together. Thus, in all three Synoptics, the proximity of the WTP and the fact that nothing suggests a new topic means the WTP is also a response to the leaders' question about who gave Jesus his authority.[116] Jesus' answer is that he is the son who has come from the Father who sent him on a mission. As the son, he has a closer connection to the Father than anyone else in the story. However, though the WTP does answer the religious leaders' question, the bulk of the three answering parables (the two children sent to work in 21:28–32; the WTP in 21:33–46; the wedding feast in 22:1–14) does not focus so much on the legitimacy of Jesus' agency but on the illegitimacy of the current leaders and on their replacement.

Not only are the servants and the son presented as agents of God, so are the farmers, to whom the vineyard is "leased" (ἐκδίδωμι) in v 33. The earlier, wicked

---

[114] Davies and Allison, *Matthew*, 3:159 suggest that if Jesus' answer was "by human authority," this would "contradict his own bold behaviour," and that if his answer was "by divine authority" he would be claiming to be the messiah. So also Osborne, *Matthew*, 776 and Craig Blomberg, *Matthew* (NAC; Nashville: Broadman & Holman, 1992), 319. However, this explanation falters since John the Baptist is "from heaven." Admitting he was by divine authority would not require seeing him as the messiah. As will be explored below, it also does not account for the owner of vineyard sending many servants. The crowds' earlier perception of Jesus in his entry as a prophet means they would have seen him as operating on God's authority, but this does not necessarily add up to viewing him as the messiah.

[115] Luke states that the parable was spoken to the people (20:9), but v 19 shows that it was nonetheless directed as an attack on the leadership.

[116] Jack D. Kingsbury, "The Parable of the Wicked Husbandmen and the Secret of Jesus' Divine Sonship in Matthew: Some Literary-Critical Observation" in *JBL* 105.4 (1986): 643–55 argues that the WTP is the first time the veil is publicly lifted to show Jesus' true identity in Matthew. That all three parables form a trilogy and are in response to the Jewish leaders has been much explored, e.g. Rowland Onyenali, *The Trilogy of Parables in Mt 21:28–22:14: From a Matthean Perspective* (ATS; Frankfurt am Main: Peter Lang, 2013) and Wesley G. Olmstead, *Matthew's Trilogy of Parables: The Nation, the Nations, and the Reader in Matthew 21:28–22:14* (SNTSMS; Cambridge: Cambridge University, 2003).

group of farmers clearly stand for the current religious leaders (v 45). V 45 records the listeners, who realize they stand for the wicked farmers, as "the chief priests and the Pharisees." These literary characters are distinguished from "the crowds" in v 46. Moreover, the interaction begins in v 23 with those who approach Jesus as "the chief priests and elders of the people" (who also are distinguished from "the crowd" in v 26). The trilogy of parables (of which the WTP is the second), ends with the anger of the Pharisees, but the chief priests, scribes, and elders are not mentioned. Each of these groups have differing levels of formal leadership within Israel, with Pharisees being the most unofficial. Yet Matthew portrays them as having authority as teachers (e.g. 23:2–3). Whether they have been officially invested with power or their position arises from the general respect of the people of the land, the result is the same – all these figures have positions of leadership. Yet the WTP rebukes them for not realizing their simultaneous position as agents. Though they are in charge of the vineyard,[117] they have forgotten one higher up the chain is in charge of them – the owner. The logic of the parable is such that the heinous act of the farmers stems from their refusal to function as mere agents. Instead of seeing themselves as accountable to the owner, they think they should be in charge of the vineyard (21:38). The significance of this observation suggests that if the current leaders knew their true place as accountable to God as his agents, they would not have acted negatively[118] when other agents arrive on the scene. The leaders fail because they do not appreciate their own agency, nor the agency of others, particularly Jesus.

Thus, the theme of agency is paramount in the WTP. We have seen that, on the surface, Isa 5:1–7 does not address this topic (in fact, the rhetoric of vv 3–4 requires there to be only two options – either YHWH is to blame or the vineyard is). We have also seen that a wider view of the Isaian vineyard, including 3:14 and 27:2–6 hints at the presence of this theme and that later interpreters, used Isaiah's vineyard to address issues of agency. From a cognitive linguistics perspective, Jesus has used Isaiah's vineyard as a source domain, mapped in

117 The γεωργοί of the WTP function differently than the ἐργάται of the Vineyard Laborers Parable (20:1–16), in that the latter are simply hired workers but the former seem to have a measurable amount of authority and responsibility.
118 When asking about Jesus' authority to do these things, the "temple cleansing" incident is primarily in view. One would expect this to gain the attention of those in charge of the temple (v 15 describes them as οἱ ἀρχιερεῖς καὶ οἱ γραμματεῖς). Matthew differs from Mark and Luke in describing an interaction between Jesus and the leaders immediately after the temple incident in which he heals the blind and lame in the temple and he defends their praise by citing Ps 8:3 (ET 8:2, cf. Matt 21:14–16). Matthew's text weakens the link between the question about Jesus' authority and the overthrowing of the money changers' tables in Mark, but does not erase it.

key elements into a blend which has an emergent structure, via the governing principle of Pattern Completion, and has run the blend, so much so that the workers are made explicit in Jesus' parable. In doing so, he is explicating what has been in the hermeneutical milieu surrounding the understanding of the Isaian vineyard.[119]

There is some debate, however, as to whether or not this fades into the background by the end of the pericope so that judgment falls on Israel as a whole. Basser, e.g. cites the counter vineyard parable in *Sip. Deut piska* 312, in which the destroyed wicked farmers are "the dregs of Ishmael ... Keturah ... Esau and all the chiefs of Edom," and argues that "Matthew subscribes to the same supersessionist theology found in Acts. This 'replacement theology' was likely the normative perspective of the Christ followers in Matthew's day."[120] However, Olmstead describes the view that 21:43 talks about a replacement of leadership as "an emerging consensus."[121] Konradt persuasively argues that the emphasis falls on the following participial phrase and not on ἔθνος (cf. Prov 26:3, 28:7, Tob 13:8), allowing for the contrast to simply be on two different kinds of people – those who produce the fruit and those who do not.[122] The overall

---

119 The other governing principles discussed in 1.3.2.2 are at work in creating the emergent structure of the blend too. As noted previously in the introduction, the topology principle and the integration principle can conflict, which is the case here. On the one hand, an emerging structure should attempt to preserve relationships between outer relations. But on the other hand, the result must be integrated so that the different domains map coherently. In the WTP, this conflict is seen in the strange turn of events in which hired farmers decide to kill the owner's messengers and the owner then sends his son. Priority has been given to the governing principle of integration, rather than topology. It is more important that the story accurately states the condition of the chief priests and the Pharisees and their murder of Jesus than for the topology of what hired workers could normally be expected to behave be mapped into the blend.

120 Basser, *Matthew and Judaic Traditions*, 557.

121 Wesley G. Olmstead, "A Gospel for a New *Nation*: Once More, the ἔθνος of Matt 21.43" in *Jesus, Matthew's Gospel and Early Christianity: Studies in the Memory of Graham Stanton*, ed. Daniel M. Gurtner, Joel Willitts, and Richard A. Burridge (LNTS; London: T&T Clark, 2011), 115. However, he, consistent with Stanton, argues against it. Examples of this emerging consensus include J. Andrew Overman, *Church and Community in Crisis; The Gospel According to Matthew* (Valley Forge: Trinity Press, 1996), 299–304; Sim, *The Gospel of Matthew and Christian Judaism*, 148–49; Carter, *Matthew and the Margins*, 429–30; Charles H. Talbert, *Matthew* (Paideia Commentary on the New Testament, Grand Rapids: Baker Academic, 2010), 252; Turner, *Matthew*, 516–19; Keener, *The Gospel of Matthew*, 511; Turner, *Israel's Last Prophet*, 225–251.

122 Konradt, *Israel, Church, and the Gentiles*, 174–193. However, this seems to discredit his argument about Matthew using λαός had he wanted to reference the ἐκκλησία – along with Andrew Saldarini, *Matthew's Christian-Jewish Community* (Chicago: University of Chicago Press, 1994), 59–61, he demonstrates ἔθνος can simply refer to a group of people and thus function similarly to λαός.

context suggests a contrast is being made concerning leadership. The suggestion that the rulers stand for the people[123] neglects Matthew's clear delineation of these literary characters, as reinforced in the immediate context – 21:45–46.[124] While I am convinced of this position, our purposes do not require precisely defining the ἔθνος of v 43. Even if the leaders are not exclusively in view, they are nonetheless in the foreground as the primary objects of Jesus' attack.

This seems to especially be the case since the Matthean version is being considered. For example, Marcus concludes concerning the Markan version,

> The question of the identity of 'you' is inextricable from that of the identity of the 'others.' If 'you' were the leaders of Israel, then the 'others' to whom their privileges were given should logically be the apostles, the new leaders of Israel ... In view of the lack of other support for such a view of the apostles in Mark and the constant Markan emphasis on the Gentile mission ... it is better to take the 'others' as the members of the church, especially its Gentile component. This in turn makes it more likely that the 'you' from whom the 'others' are distinguished are the Jewish people as a whole, though 11:27; 12:10–12 are still strong witnesses for identifying 'you' as the leaders.[125]

Whether or not the leadership interpretation should be taken in Mark is not of concern to our argument,[126] but the two factors which dissuade Marcus – a lack of a higher leadership role of the apostles and gentile focus – cannot be said of the gospel of Matthew. Not only are there significant direct statements regarding the importance of the apostles (e.g. 19:28), but the overall argument of chapters 2–5 of this research demonstrates that the Matthean Jesus depicts them as fulfilling significant eschatological roles foretold in the First Testament. Furthermore, though there is a thread of gentile inclusion throughout Matthew culminating in 28:18–20, the mission to Israel is still a central theme and not replaced.

If the parable only intends to explain Jesus' authority and to predict the coming judgement of the Jewish people and Jesus' passion, it could have stopped with the destruction of the wicked farmers. Instead, it introduces other agency with the mention of the replacement farmers in 21:41. Matthew's

---

123 E.g. Osborne, *Matthew*, 790–791.
124 Konradt, *Israel, Church, and the Gentiles*, 183; Snodgrass, *The Parable*, 91.
125 Marcus, *The Way of the Lord*, 128–129.
126 For an excellent defense of Matthew clarifying, not changing this same theme in Mark, see Turner, *Israel's Last Prophet*, 238–39.

redaction emphasizes that the new group's function has continuity with the old. Instead of the vineyard simply being given ἄλλοις (Mark 12:9), Matthew has it given ἄλλοις γεωργοῖς (21:41). Though Matthew places this on the lips of the opponents, it is still presented as true (Mark 12:9 and Luke 20:16[127] ascribe it to Jesus). Moreover, Matthew's redaction emphasizes these characters by including the previous parable of the two children.[128] There too Jesus describes a figure in charge of a vineyard commissioning children to work in some capacity with it. This parable's presentation of two workers/children, one good and one bad, reinforces the dichotomy between the two sets of workers in the WTP. Moreover, these replacement farmers fulfill a significant role. They are in some sort of leadership position, responsible for maintaining and caring for the vineyard. Clearly they are expected to "hand over the crop" to the rightful owner.[129]

Furthermore, due to the internal logic of the story's progression, this position of tending the vineyard must exclude the involvement of the son. After the story's climax and the vineyard starts operating correctly, this parable has no place for the son since he has been murdered and thrown out of the vineyard. As far as the WTP itself is concerned, the agency whom God uses to care for his vineyard cannot include the son.[130] The immediately following discussion about the rejected stone being of primary importance for the new building project corrects the WTP's deficiency in this regard. V 43, which essentially

---

[127] The Lukan account differs considerably in having the opponents object to the new farmers in 20:16.

[128] The offspring parallel is only thematic, not lexical, since τέκνον is used in the first parable, while υἱός is in the second. The third parable also continues discussing how one responds to the son (υἱός).

[129] Craig A. Evans, "Jesus' Parable of the Tenant Farmers in Light of Lease Agreements in Antiquity," JSP 14 (1996): 65–83 discusses the Zenon Papyri to suggest what this care might look like, building off the work of Martin Hengel, "Das Gleichnis von den Weingärtnern Mic 12.1–12 im Lichte der Zenonpapyri und der rabbinischen Gleichnisse," ZNW 59 (1968): 1–39. The expression ποιοῦντι τοὺς καρποὺς αὐτῆς (21:43) does not imply that the imagery is changing so that the vineyard in its earlier state was not producing fruit (contra Weren, *Studies in Matthew's Gospel*, 205). Though ποιέω, when used in conjunction with καρπός, often means "bear" a meaning like "produce" (as in "hand over") is most likely here, given the logic of the parable and the parallel statement in v 41 – ἀποδώσουσιν αὐτῷ τοὺς καρποὺς ἐν τοῖς καιροῖς αὐτῶν. Other occurrences of the expression in Matthew suggest ethical behavior is in view (e.g. 3:8-10, 7:16-20). However, the leadership motif and the parallel to 9:37 suggest the result of missionary endeavors may be in view.

[130] Hays, *Echoes of Scripture in the Gospels*, 41–43 argues that Mark 12:7 alludes to Joseph in Gen 37:20 LXX, who then is raised to rule over Egypt. He argues this transitions to the citation of Ps 118:22–23. However, this would be an extremely quiet echo. While difficult to disprove, it seems unlikely.

rephrases the correct verdict of the leaders in v 41 in Jesus' words, continues the imagery of the vineyard parable, has been placed in the middle of the subsequent image of the stone. This forms an interlocking structure (v 42 stone, v 43 vineyard) which forces the conclusion of the WTP to be seen in light of the rejected stone discussion. As will be explored in the next chapter, this reintroduces the rejected messianic figure as crucially significant for God's future purposes. Thus, Matthew refuses to allow his audience to conclude that Jesus is of no importance in the future state of the vineyard. And yet, the remarkable feature of the WTP is that the agency which ensures the future flourishing of the vineyard maps only to the disciples and, due to the storyline of the parable, cannot map to Jesus.

3.7.4 Eschatology

As with Isaiah's vineyard, the initial image here depicts Israel's existence under its current corrupt leaders. The vineyard before the climactic sending of the son represents a situation when the earlier prophets ministered to Israel, including the work of the current religious leaders (see previous section). As the chief priests and Pharisees realized (v 45), this part of the parable spoke about a historical situation (anticipating the crucifixion of Jesus). Like Isaiah's wider use of YHWH's vineyard (including 27:2–7) and later users of Isaiah's vineyard (Ezek 15, 17, 19; 2 Baruch 36–40; Ps 80; John 15:1–8), the vine also speaks of eschatological realities in its state while under the care of the replacement farmers after the wicked ones have been disposed.

Before exploring reasons for thinking the vineyard of the WTP is eschatological, noting the blurred line between the "already" and "not yet" aspects of the eschatological age may help make this claim seem more plausible. Though there are eschatological dimensions to the vineyard under the replacement farmers' care, this does not mean historical activity such as the apostles with the church in the first century is out of view (or as we may imagine occurred with Matthew and his community). As evidenced by the allusion in the great commission (28:18–20), the eschatological age of Dan 7:13–14 is in some sense operative in the historical work of the apostles. Matthew does not always make neat distinctions between the present and future form of the kingdom.[131] So the claim that the vineyard under the care of the replacement farmers is eschatological does not mean it will only be fulfilled after Jesus' second advent. Instead, it means the new phase of the vineyard is couched in eschatological language and portrayed as an aspect of the reign of God.[132]

---

131 This is not to deny that sometimes the differentiation is quite explicit, e.g. Matt 13:39.
132 A similar concept is at work in the use of the vine image in John 15 (see 3.6.4).

But what are these kingdom elements? First, the expression ὅτε δὲ ἤγγισεν ὁ καιρὸς τῶν καρπῶν (v 34) is reminiscent of the eschatologically charged announcement ἤγγικεν ἡ βασιλεία τῶν οὐρανῶν in 3:2, 4:17, 10:4[133] and of the other references to fruit bearing in 16:3, 21:18–22, and 24:32 which are in eschatological contexts. Making these connections may be behind Matthew's decision here to amplify Mark's simpler τῷ καιρῷ (Mark 12:2). Second, a comparison with the leaders' apparently correct statement in v 41 and Jesus' restatement in v 43 shows that he somehow connects, if not equates, ὁ ἀμπελών with ἡ βασιλεία τοῦ θεοῦ. Especially given the links noted earlier, the mention of the kingdom must be connected to the arriving one announced by John, Jesus, and the apostles. Most importantly, the replacement farmers are established after the death of the son, which for Matthew begins a new eschatological era in some sense (e.g. 27:51–53). Thus, although he sees the earlier state of the vineyard pointing to historical realities, Talbert states concerning the final phase of the vineyard, "a people producing the fruits of God's rule refers to the twelve disciples of Jesus who will rule/judge the twelve tribes in the end time."[134] Whether the fulfillment of the new farmers only includes the twelve disciples or not is not our concern, nor does the argument of this chapter depend on the final state of the vineyard in the WTP only being "in the end of time."[135] But the nature of the vineyard / kingdom as both already existing in connection with the corrupt farmers and as eschatological in connection with the replacement farmers accounts for all elements of the parable.[136]

---

133   3:2 and 4:17 include the postpositive γάρ, since the command to repent is explicated. This connection is stronger in Mark 1:15 which begins, Πεπλήρωται ὁ καιρός.

134   Talbert, *Matthew*, 429.

135   Space does not permit an exploration into 1 Cor 3:5–17, but it seems to me that Paul alludes to a pre-canonical or oral form of the WTP there since he compares God's people to a horticultural field (v 9) and then the temple (vv 9, 16), and himself and Apollos as farmers and builders (v 6). The Corinthians are not explicitly stated to be farmers, but 3:12–15 depicts them as builders. This would demonstrate the adjustable nature of the imagery (as was seen in the sheep and shepherds of Matt 10). Those who are part of the building are also builders. If the identification of this allusion is correct, then Paul portrays himself and Apollos as the new farmers, and by comparison with the temple builder motif, this potentially puts Christ followers in the same category. For brief comments along the same lines, see Harald Riesenfeld, *The Gospel Tradition*. Trans. E. M. Rowley and R. A. Kraft (Fortress: Philadelphia, 1970), 197–200; Hans Conzelmann, *1 Corinthians: A Commentary on the First Epistle to the Corinthians*, trans. James W. Leitch (Hermenia; Philadelphia: Fortress, 1975), 74–75.

136   Donald A. Hagner, *Matthew* (WBC; Nashville: Thomas Nelson, 1995), 617 argues that the coming of the vineyard owner (v 40) refers to the parousia. Though this would increase the eschatological component of the parable, that the owner cannot possibly be the son makes this unlikely.

3.7.5 Messianism

The other contributors to our conversation have all, to varying degrees, included the messiah in their discussion of the vine, the problem of judgment, and the establishment of the eschaton. So too in the WTP a messianic figure is present. The parable portrays Jesus as the υἱός of the owner, clearly in a class apart from the earlier δοῦλοι. Since the owner is certainly God (as with the other uses of Isaiah's vineyard), this means the figure in consideration is portrayed as the son of God. Of course, "son" imagery need not have messianic connotations (e.g. Matt 5:9, 45). Yet, the concept of Jesus being the "son of God" occurs frequently in Matthew (2:15, 3:17, 4:3, 6, 8:29, 14:33, 16:16, 17:5, 26:64, 27:40, 43, 54).[137] Both 16:16[138] and 26:64 place ὁ υἱὸς τοῦ θεοῦ in apposition to ὁ Χριστός, demonstrating that, at the least, it contains messianic connotations.[139] The wicked tenants' statement Οὗτός ἐστιν ὁ κληρονόμος (v 38; Ps 2:8 LXX) emphasizes the messianic identity of the son figure.

In our consideration of the other contributors to this conversation, we have often seen two "scenes" in the story surrounding the vine(yard). Each of the contributors in our metaphorical conversation has used the imagery differently and provided their own details, sometimes with even contradictory features (e.g. the role of the vine and cedar in Ezek 17 and 2 Baruch 36–40). Still, the realities to which the imagery points have basic similarities. To paint with broad strokes, corruption and ruin characterize the first scene, a state contrary to the owner's intention. God, the owner, then acts and brings about the second scene, in which the vine flourishes and prospers. In Isaiah, ch 5 acts out scene 1 and ch 27 (and perhaps 4:2 as well) acts out scene 2. In Ezekiel, the vine image belongs exclusively to scene 1. Scene 2 begins when the twig of the cedar grows. In 2 Baruch, a forest of trees, representing Gentile oppression, acts as scene 1. Then the vine and fountain (the messiah) destroys the forest, including the cedar, and provides shelter. This corresponds to scene 2. In Ps 80, the psalmist portrays Israel as having already received the punishment that describes the end of scene 1 and prays that the branch/son would be established so that they may be revived (scene 2). John 15 does not address a time of failure, but with its inaugurated eschatology, the branches producing much fruit because they abide in the vine represents one aspect of the flourishing in the messianic age

---

137 Reference simply to "the son" occurs in 11:27, 24:36 and 28:19. 22:42 and 45 describe Jesus' question about who the father of the son in light of Ps 110:1 and may describe him as the son of God.

138 Matthew has added ὁ υἱὸς τοῦ θεοῦ to Mark's account (8:29).

139 For more on Matthew's use of this expression, see Robert L. Mowery, "Subtle Differences: The Matthean 'Son of God' References," *NovT* 32 (1990): 193–200 and "Son of God in Roman Imperial Titles and Matthew" *Bib* 83 (2002): 100–110.

(scene 2). In all of these texts, when the messiah appears, he arrives in scene 2 as the necessary guarantor of success for the vine.[140]

From this perspective, the WTP departs from its fellow conversation partners in intriguing and significant ways. It also has two scenes. Like the overall picture above, the owner is not content to leave his vine in scene 1. He attempts for a peaceful resolution to transition to stage 2 by sending his servants – the prophets – and finally his son – the messiah. But in contrast to the hermeneutical milieu described above, the messiah in the WTP *only* appears in scene 1 and there he is murdered! His death marks the zenith of the old leadership's corruption. Unlike the other contributors to the discussion, the Matthean Jesus does not describe the messiah's relationship to the eschaton as the one who victoriously establishes it or who executes judgment. Instead, his murder marks the final heinous act which pushes the owner to then respond in judgment. Because he is murdered, as far as this particular story goes, he does not occupy a place in the second scene.

Instead, the replacement farmers, not the son, carry out the traditional functions of the messiah in connection to the vine which the other conversation partners have described. In this parable, God uses them, not the messiah to replace the corrupt leadership as he establishes the vineyard of the new age. As will be more fully explored in the next chapter, the interlocking structure of vv 41–43 ensures that the rejected son image is nuanced with the rejected-yet-chosen stone image. But though the Matthean Jesus ensures his audience knows he is crucial to the eschaton, his adaptation of Isaiah's vineyard ends up placing the disciples in a remarkably significant role as eschatological agents, which in the hermeneutical milieu surrounding the vineyard metaphor, was accomplished by the messiah. With the possible exception of Ps 80, each of the conversation partners in our metaphorical conversation discusses the issue of leadership. Ezek 17 and 2 Baruch 36–40 particularly describe corrupt leadership in scene 1 being replaced by proper leadership in scene 2. In these texts, the messiah replaces this leadership; in the WTP, the disciples fulfill this role.

3.8 Conclusion

To demonstrate Matthew's broad hermeneutic of fulfillment, the project of this research points to case studies where the Matthean Jesus does the following:

---

140 "The Vine and Cedar Apocalypse" is the only passage which has the messiah interacting with scene 1, and there he condemns the cedar and is a victorious instrument of judgment.

(1) maps a messianic figure from a source domain
and (2) maps the disciples from the target domain to that figure.

That Jesus evokes Isa 5:1–7 in Matt 21:33–45 and places the disciples in a position of care for the Isaian vineyard is clear. But we have also seen that Matthew would have likely seen Isaiah's vineyard as messianic and eschatological. Not only does Isa 5 in its larger context with its connections to other vineyard imagery suggest this, but the later history of interpretation demonstrates how easily later users of the image allude to and adapt the vineyard to talk about God's future kingdom and how it will be established. Moreover, features from within the WTP suggest Jesus had such a view of Isaiah's vineyard in mind. However, the messianic figure so often associated with the vineyard and its restoration overcomes, prospers, and secures the flourishing of the "future vine." This concept is not apparent if one only considers the text of Isa 5:1–7 as the source domain. However, we invested some time in listening carefully to other conversation partners to establish that another source domain is operative – the hermeneutical milieu surrounding the image of the Isaiah's vine. When a multi-scope blend is created in which this too maps in features, one can see how both messianic and eschatological agents map into the blend. However, though the WTP has a place for the messiah, it is part of a failed attempt for the vineyard's restoration. The messiah does not map to the expected images. Instead, the disciples map to the eschatological agents, a role traditionally fulfilled by the messiah. The disciples, not Jesus, become the replacement farmers.

In chapter 2, we saw that Matthew maps the shepherds of Jer 23:4 directly to the disciples. This does not happen in the use of Isa 5:1–7 in the WTP. In chapter 2, we had also seen that an alluded text (Ezek 34) spoke of YHWH's actions in establishing the eschaton, and that the disciples' performance of these actions is best understood by assuming God uses them as his agents, though nothing of the sort can be found in the source text. But this is not quite what is happening in the WTP either. The issue of agency was hanging in the air surrounding the use of YHWH's vineyard. Unlike Ezek 34, the disciples meet a need anticipated and implied by the source text. The source domain does not predict there will be a group of new farmers who will be used by God to ultimately see to the vineyard's proper maintenance, but then Jesus puts the disciples in that slot. However, as Matthew would have likely seen it, there is something about leadership and agency implied by the Isaian vineyard. Destruction comes on the current leadership because of their corruption. But this implies that restoration comes through proper leadership, which, according to Matthew, is accomplished by Jesus' band of disciples. In other words, Jer 23:4 maps the eschatological agents into the blend via the Vital Relation of identity. The text describes "shepherds"; the disciples occupy this space. In Ezek 34, the mapping to the disciples is best seen as "role." The text talks about YHWH acting like a shepherd, and when Matt 10:6 says the disciples are to do so we assume they function as those who are sent by God to do his work. So too with the WTP's use of Isaiah's vineyard in its hermeneutical milieu, the Vital Relation of "role" best describes the mapping of the disciples of Matt 21:41. The passage talks about the judgment of corrupt leadership and suggests this will be replaced during the eschaton. The disciples form a crucial part of this replacement project. We will not quite see this pattern in any of our other case studies, but it nonetheless demonstrates another instance of Matthew's non-messianic mapping of a messianic concept. Unlike other instances, in which one can definitively point to a messianic figure (e.g. the eschatological shepherd), the case here is much more subtle and comes from the hermeneutical milieu surrounding Isaiah's vineyard. But Matthew maps messianic concepts into the blend which surprisingly do not land on Jesus.

CHAPTER 4

Matthew's Non-Messianic Use of Temple-Construction Imagery

4.1 Introduction

Before venturing into new territory, a summary of our findings thus far will help situate us for the upcoming chapter. In our examination of the Matthean Jesus' non-messianic use of potentially messianic texts, we have encountered varying ways that passages which could easily have been used to speak of Jesus as the messiah, instead inform the reader of the disciples' role. This has shown that, as far as Matthew's hermeneutic is concerned, allusions can blur the lines between the boundaries of what might be classified as a "messianic text," since images that might be expected only to apply to Jesus are used of others. We can organize the findings of the previous two chapters into three different categories based on the way Matthew maps the possibly messianic figure into the blend.[1] First, we could label a use of Scripture as "messianic" because, though it does not mention a human figure, the Second Temple Period saw the eschatological mission being accomplished through the means of an agent sent on God's behalf. Matthew maps God from the source domain and the disciples from the target domain into the blend and connects them via the Vital Relation of "role."[2] Second, we have labeled some uses of Scripture "messianic" when they refer to a figure, traditionally understood as the messiah, but the mapping of this figure is not narrowly one-to-one from the OT figure to Jesus. Here, Matthew maps *the* messiah from the source domain and the disciples from the target domain into the blend and connects them via the Vital Relation of "role." Third, we could cautiously label a use of Scripture

---

1 In addition of course to the times when Matthew maps a potentially messianic figure to Jesus via the Vital Relation of identity.
2 William Horbury, *Jewish Messianism and the Cult of Christ* (London: SCM, 1998) surveys major figures of the view that an emphasis on God's activity in salvation excludes messianism in the Persian period through the Second Temple period ("the messianic vacuum"), but he convincingly argues that messianism was still prominent. For example, he states, "Silence, then, need not always be non-messianic, for a heavy emphasis on God's own action was fully compatible with recognition of the activity of a king or messiah … The expectation of future deliverance would normally include expectation of leadership by a divinely appointed king" (83). To use the categories presented here, this situation is category one, "YHWH → (agency) disciples."

"messianic" if it refers to figures (plural) who are not precisely *the* messiah, but still function as significant rulers in the eschaton. In these cases, there is a direct mapping of the figures in the source text to the figures in the target text. Messianic figures (i.e. "messiah-like" in being significant eschatological agents) from the source domain and the disciples from the target domain are mapped into the blend and are connected via the Vital Relation of "identity."

In chapter 2, we saw that Jesus applies the messianic mission of eschatological shepherding to the disciples in Matt 10:6. Ezek 34 as the source text (with no particular emphasis on vv 23–24) falls into category one, since the actions ascribed to YHWH are accomplished by the agency of the apostles. If particularly Ezek 34:23–24 is in view, which specifically depicts a Davidic king, then the situation falls into category two since the text bundles disciples together with the messiah as the target of a broad mapping of incorporation. With Jer 23:4 as the source text, there is a more direct mapping as the passages speak directly of several figures ("shepherds") who serve an eschatological function similar to the messiah, yet Matthew would have not have seen these texts as predicting "*the* messiah" since they speak of several individuals – category three. Something similar happens if Zech 10:2–4 is in view.

In chapter 3, we saw that Jesus assigns the messianic role of caring for the eschatological vine to the disciples as the new farmers. With Isaiah's vineyard (in its larger Isaian framework) in the background, we are in category one, similar to Ezek 34. We observed several texts which demonstrated that a messianic figure connected to the restoration of the vine was in the milieu in the later Second Temple Period, but the only explicit figure of restoration of the Isaian vineyard is YHWH. With Psalm 80 in view, we are in category two, with the role of the caretaking בן ("branch" / "son") being taken over by the disciples, so that, like Ezek 34:23–24, the disciples are in the messiah's space. The results of our findings so far can be organized as follows:

TABLE 3   Vital Relations in Matt 10:6 and 21:33–41

Category One	Category Two	Category Three
YHWH → (role) disciples	Messiah → (role) disciples	Eschatological/messianic figures → (identity) disciples
Ezek 34 → Matt 10:6 YHWH said he would shepherd his sheep and the apostles are sent to accomplish this task on his behalf.	Ezek 34:23–24 Matt 10:6 The messiah as the Davidic King will shepherd God's people, and this figure is mapped to the disciples.	Jer 23:4 → Matt 10:6 YHWH sets up several shepherds in connection to the messiah, all of whom replace the corrupt shepherds of Israel, and the disciples are the new leaders.

TABLE 3 *(cont.)*

Isa 5 (and 27) → Matt 21:33–41 YHWH said he would restore his vine/vineyard and the apostles accomplish this task on his behalf.	Ps 80:14–19 → Matt 21:33–41 The messiah as the branch/son of man will nourish God's vine/vineyard, and this figure's role is mapped to the disciples.	Zech 10:4→ Matt 10:6 Several warriors fight for YHWH, fulfilled in the apostles' exorcisms and judgment on those who reject the gospel.

In this chapter we will again encounter a potentially messianic text / motif – this time centered around temple construction imagery – and explore several Matthean texts to see how Jesus applies it to the disciples. In each occurrence where Matthew connects messianic/eschatological temple construction imagery to the disciples, the mapping is best placed in the second column, "messiah →$_{(role)}$ disciples."[3] In each intertextual reference examined in this chapter, the disciples are portrayed with imagery traditionally reserved for the messiah, and we will see this includes the disciples both as temple builders and as the temple foundation. But in this respect, the cases studies of this chapter differ from the previous ones. In the previous studies, the imagery was relatively simple in that the messiah was represented by the shepherd / vineyard caregiver and God's people were represented by the sheep / vineyard. The cases studied here are more complex in that the evoked scheme involves *two* messianic images. Both the cornerstone and the builder represent the messiah, and the building represents God's people. In Matt 21:42–43 and 16:18, Jesus occupies the space of one of the images and the disciples the other. In the first, Jesus is the cornerstone and the disciples are the builders, but in 16:18 the disciple(s) are the cornerstone and Jesus is the builder.

We will examine three places where eschatological temple construction portrays the disciples in a messianic light: Matt 21:42–43, 16:18, and 7:24–27. The introduction (1.3.2.1) explained that we are considering times when Jesus:

(1) maps various elements into the blend, but does not explicitly map the messianic figure himself.

OR

(2) maps a messianic figure from a source domain
(3) but maps the disciples from the target domain to that figure.

---

3 However, we will see that Matt 21:42–43 does not directly map the messianic figure into the blend. Instead, he emerges as a result of running the blend according to the "Pattern Completion Principle."

Steps (2) and (3) are relevant for the discussions in this chapter. However, the flow of this chapter will be easier to follow if the argument of each section generally proceeds in the following stages:
- Stage one: The passage evokes imagery of eschatological temple construction.
- Stage two: The passage portrays the disciples as involved in this construction (temple builders for Matt 21:42–43 and 7:24–27; temple foundation in 16:18).
- Stage three: The role discussed in stage two was a traditionally messianic image.

Thus, stages one and three will establish step (2) above and stage two will establish step (3).

Moreover, though each section of this chapter has sufficient substantiation to stand on its own, this does not mean all cases are equally strong. The certainty with which Matt 21:41–43 and 16:18 allude to First Testament messianic categories to describe the disciples is roughly equivalent and seems clear. But 7:24–27 is far less certain. As will be discussed later, we can easily establish stages two and three for this text, but the weak link is stage one since the allusion to eschatological temple construction is far opaquer. In the end, I think the evidence does point in this direction. However, at this point, it is worth keeping in mind that the current chapter's investigation of several occurrences of the same images means the total will be greater than the sum of its parts so that the three sections confirm the findings of the others. This means we have a cumulative case that Matthew regularly uses the messianically charged imagery surrounding the temple but applies it to the disciples. Since the previous chapter explored Matt 21:33–41, we turn to the imagery of 21:42–43 first.

4.2   Matt 21:42–43

Matt 21:42–43 clearly maps the rejected stone to Jesus. The argument here is not that in this account the disciples are also the target of this mapping scheme. We will later examine an instance where the image of the messianic temple stone (particularly the foundation) does map to the disciples. But such is not the case in 21:41–43. Instead, the argument runs as follows: (1) the reference to Ps 118:22–23 evokes the concept of the building of an eschatological temple; (2) the disciples' role in this scene is that of builders; (3) though the once-rejected-now-chosen stone was a messianic trope in the first century CE, the different roles are imprecise and the image of an eschatological temple builder was also messianic.

4.2.1 Matt 21:42–43 Evokes Imagery of Eschatological Temple Construction

Unlike the other references which are considered in this research, Matt 21:42 presents a reference more direct than an allusion. Jesus' introduction Οὐδέποτε ἀνέγνωτε ἐν ταῖς γραφαῖς, clearly prepares the reader for the citation of Ps 118:22–23. Moreover, the phrasing not only chides the leaders for their ignorance, but also exhorts the audience to return to the passage and read it. Köstenberger rightly observes, "Jesus' pointed way of wording his argument personally engages his hearers and challenges them to go back to Scripture to see whether or not Jesus' interpretation is correct."[4] That the original context of Ps 118 is in view is also supported by the crowd's cheer in Matt 21:9, Ὡσαννὰ τῷ υἱῷ Δαυίδ. Εὐλογημένος ὁ ἐρχόμενος ἐν ὀνόματι κυρίου· Ὡσαννὰ ἐν τοῖς ὑψίστοις, which clearly echoes Ps 118:25–26 (LXX 117:25–26) הוֹשִׁיעָה נָּא ... בָּרוּךְ הַבָּא בְּשֵׁם יְהוָה; σῶσον δή ... εὐλογημένος ὁ ἐρχόμενος ἐν ὀνόματι κυρίου. This double reference to the same psalm, though different portions, within the span of 33 verses in Matthew strongly suggests the psalm as a whole has significance for understanding the events of Matt 21. Watts' suggestion that these two references form the first and last element of a chiasm in Mark cannot be carried over into Matthew, but it does demonstrate that the repetition of the same quoted source is more than coincidence.[5] The icing on the cake for the original context is the strong likelihood that this psalm was sung at Passover and so could have been expected to have been on the audience's mind.[6] *M. Pesahim* 5:7 describes the Hallel being sung repetitively (קָרְאוּ אֶת הַהַלֵּל) by different groups of priests after the Passover lamb had been sacrificed and blood was being transferred to the altar. Later, the Talmud describes further singing of the Hallel on various days of the Passover (based on Isa 30:29) in *t. Pesahim* 95b. Exactly who was singing this song and when is not certain during the first century CE, but it seems highly likely that the context of the Hallel would have been in the general milieu, especially for Jesus' audience – the religious leaders of Israel.

---

4   Andreas Köstenberger, "Hearing the Old Testament in the New: A Response" in *Hearing the Old Testament in the New Testament*, ed. Stanley E. Porter (Grand Rapids: Eerdmans, 2006), 266. Matthew's redaction of Mark's οὐδέ to οὐδέποτε emphasizes "the religious leaders' failure to note the relevance of the scriptural text" (J. Samuel Subramanian, *The Synoptic Gospels and the Psalms as Prophecy* (LNTS; London: T&T Clark, 2007), 110).

5   Rikki E. Watts, "Mark," in *Commentary on the New Testament Use of the Old Testament*, ed. D. A. Carson and G. K. Beale (Grand Rapids: Baker Academic, 2007), 209.

6   Cf. Richard H. Flashman, "Passover in the Writings" in *Messiah in the Passover*, ed. Darrell L. Block and Mitch Glaser (Grand Rapids: Kregel, 2017), 55. This would be most relevant if one considers the *Sitz im Leben Jesu*, but the Jewish nature of Matthew's audience suggests that this argument has merit even if our concern is with the *Sitz im Leben der Alten Kirche*.

When we turn to the psalm itself, several features demonstrate the ease with which it would have been understood messianically and eschatologically. After a brief introduction (Ps 118:1–3), the psalm focuses on a figure in distress (v 4) among his enemies (v 7), namely the surrounding nations (vv 10–12) that violently push him so that he falls (v 13). However, the figure calls on YHWH (v 5), whom he knows is on his side (v 6) and therefore will be victorious (v 17), though at one point YHWH had "severely chastised" him (יַסֹּר יִסְּרַנִּי; παιδεύων ἐπαίδευσέν, v 18).[7] The salvation which YHWH gives him causes him to go to the temple to worship (vv 19–28). The people's warm reception of him into the temple (v 26) strongly suggests this is a warrior who has fought on Israel's behalf and returned victorious.

It does not take much ingenuity to see how these features of a triumphant warrior fighting Israel's battle would lead to a messianic interpretation.[8] Though the psalm lacks a historical situation in both the MT and LXX,[9] it can easily be compared to the story of David which would have only increased the messianic connection.[10] The precise place of v 22, the verse in question, in the flow of context is difficult to ascertain. The warrior has come to the temple, so the building activity might suggest a sort of temple construction is in view.[11] But the figure does not come to the temple to build it – he is coming to worship (i.e. v 27).[12] Instead, the warrior's own experience of difficulty then triumph is figuratively described as a stone once rejected but then chosen.[13] Since the

---

[7] That "rebuke" or "chastise" is the meaning and not "teach," can be seen in the following explanation, וְלַמָּוֶת לֹא נְתָנָנִי.

[8] Marcus, *The Way of the Lord*, 115 rightly notes the eschatological setting of the psalm (for a more thorough investigation see David C. Mitchell, *The Message of the Psalter: An Eschatological Programme in the Book of Psalms* (JSOTSup; Sheffield: Sheffield Academic, 1997), 65) but incorrectly identifies the speaker as the nation because of vv 1–4, which are better understood as a call to worship YHWH for what he has done for the nation through the warrior figure.

[9] LXX only has Ἀλληλουια (as with Pss 110–118).

[10] Kenneth E. Guenter, "'Blessed is He Who Comes': Psalm 118 and Jesus's Triumphal Entry" *BSac* 173 (Oct–Dec 2016): 425–47 argues that allusions in the first half of the psalm "reveal why a first-century Jewish audience would attribute this psalm to David" (430). His argument that it reflects Absalom's betrayal deserves consideration, but does not affect the argument here.

[11] The building being the temple is suggested by the context of approaching the temple to offer sacrifices. This connection is also demonstrated in later texts like T. Sol. 23:1–4.

[12] The MT has a textual variant (𝔊, in agreement with LXX's ἕως, has עַל instead of עַד), which would make the image of a procession to the altar instead of a sacrifice on it. But in either case, some sort of temple worship is in view.

[13] Nicholas G. Piotrowski, "'Whatever You Ask' for the Missionary Purposes of the Eschatological Temple: Quotation Typology in Mark 11–12" *SBJT* 21.1 (2017): 106 suggests that the "psalmist sees his own deliverance from death as a type of the (future?) temple."

main figure is so easily viewed as the messiah, whatever his connection to the rejected stone of v 22, one can see how the same messianic connotations might carry over to it.[14]

Later interpretation demonstrates the possibility of reading Ps 118:22 messianically and eschatologically. Jeremias argued this song had an eschatological and messianic interpretation by the first century CE and that "the day" (118:24) referred to "the day of redemption which ends all enslavement for ever [sic], i.e. to the Messianic redemption."[15] However, his argument only has limited value since it relies on rabbinic sources which date later.[16]

The earliest attestation to a clear messianic use of Ps 118 (outside of Christian literature) belongs to Rashi (ca. 1100 CE) in his commentary on Mic 5:1. However, some relevant ancient translations date before or at least closer to the time of the NT. The LXX may hint at a messianic interpretation in v 16. The MT reads יְמִין יְהוָה רוֹמֵמָה and the LXX has δεξιὰ κυρίου ὕψωσέν με.[17] Adding the direct object με brings more attention to the central warrior. However, the impact this has on the psalm is minor. The specification of the exalted one focuses on the central warrior, but he is nonetheless present in the MT too and the LXX does not greatly change the tone of the psalm.

The Targum may be understood messianically or speaking of Israel's past history. The "translation" starting in v 22 reads

> The child [טליא] the builders abandoned, he was among the sons of Jesse; and he was worthy to be appointed as king and ruler. 'This has come from before the Lord,' **said the builders** ... 'it is wonderful before' said the sons of Jesse. 'This day the Lord has made,' **said the builders**, 'Let rejoice and

---

While possible, the explanation that the stone is a metaphor for the righteous sufferer is more likely (G. K. Beale, *The Temple and the Church's Mission: A biblical theology of the dwelling place of God* (NSBT; Downers Grove, IVP Academic, 2004), 184.

14   For more on the royal elements of Ps 118, see Andrew C. Brunson, *Psalm 118 in the Gospel of John: An Intertextual Study on the New Exodus* (WUNT; Tübingen: Mohr Siebeck, 2003), 34–37.

15   Joachim Jeremias, *The Eucharistic Words of Jesus* (London: SCM Press, 1966), 255–61; similarly Lindars, *New Testament Apologetic*, 169–74.

16   J. Ross Wagner, "Psalm 118 in Luke-Acts: Tracing a Narrative Thread" in *Early Christian Interpretation of the Scriptures of Israel: Investigations and Proposals*, ed. Craig A. Evans and James A. Sanders (JSNTSup; Sheffield: Sheffield Academic, 1997), 158. Jeremias does acknowledge the difficulty of dating the Midrash, but argues that though the time of their composition is unknown, "the New Testament shows that it certainly *goes back to the days of Jesus*, and that it was the common property of the people" (Jeremias, *Eucharistic Words*, 258, emphasis mine).

17   The Syriac agrees with the LXX. 11Q5 and 11Q6 agree with the MT.

be glad in it,' said the sons of Jesse ... God, the Lord, has given light,' **said the tribes of the house of Judah**, 'bind the child[18] [טליא] for a festal sacrifice with chains until you sacrifice him, and sprinkle his blood on the horns of the altar,' **said the prophet Samuel**. 'You are my God, and I will give thanks in your presence; my God, I will praise you,' **said David**. **Samuel answered and said**, 'Sing praise, assembly of Israel, give thanks in the presence of the Lord, for he is good, for his goodness is everlasting.'

The play between the Hebrew בן and אבן is evidently at work here, though it is under the surface since the Aramaic has טליא.[19] The repetition of "sons of Jesse" alone could allow for any Davidic king to be in view, including the messiah. However, the later references to Samuel and David (in bold) suggest that the abandoning in v 22 has in view the initial rejection of David by Saul.[20] The Targum's translation has been referenced as proof of a messianic interpretation,[21] but this perspective fails to account for the historical references. The stone being David also entails the result of the "new builders" including the company of "the tribes of the house of Judah," and "the prophet Samuel." This appears to be quite different from the interpretation in the WTP. Moreover, the likelihood that this is a reaction against a Christian use of Ps 118 seems highly unlikely since the same word for "child," טליא, is repeated as being used for a sacrifice. If this were meant to be a counter interpretation to the Christian one, portraying the king and ruler as also a sacrifice would be a strange allowance!

A fragment from the apocryphal *Songs of David* (A.18) from Cairo Geniza states פינה ממואסה אשרמאסו הבונים העלת לראש מעל כל דמלכים, "the rejected corner stone which the builders rejected you raised to be the head over all kings."[22] This may confirm the historical interpretation found in the Targum. Though de Moor notes that Flusser and Safrai, who republished the fragment, did not detect any messianism in the text, he argues that a figure beyond the historical David must be in view since the passage also describes him as one who is the

---

18   Or perhaps "animal."
19   Matthew Black, "The Christological Use of the Old Testament in the New Testament" *NTS* 18.1 (1971): 12–13 and especially George J. Brooke "4Q500 1 and the Use of Scripture in the Parable of the Vineyard," *DSD* 2.3 (1995): 287–88.
20   E.g. Strack, H. P. and P. Billerbeck, *Kommentar zum Neuen Testament aus Talmud und Midrash*. (Munchen: 1926), 876; Jeremias, *Eucharistic Words*, 259 n1; Joachim Jeremias, "Λίθος, Λίθινος," *TDNT* 4:273. Klyne R. Snodgrass, "The Christological Stone Testimonia in the New Testament" (PhD Dissertation, University of St. Andrews, 1973), 84.
21   E.g. Craig L. Blomberg, "Reflections on Jesus' View of the Old Testament," in *The Enduring Authority of the Christian Scriptures*, ed. D. A. Carson (Grand Rapids: Eerdmans, 2016), 677.
22   Translation mine.

greatest king, eternal, and a "light for the nations" (cf. Isa 42:6, 49:6) who works "because the end is near."[23] We have already seen from Ezek 34 how easily the person of David and the messiah coalesce. If so, then it is possible that A.18 and perhaps even Tg. Psalm 118 represent messianic interpretations. Thus, there is evidence on both sides[24] though the historical interpretation seems to have the upper hand. But even then, if Ps 118 were connected to David, one can easily imagine how Jesus in the gospels would take the next step and make a messianic self-reference. It is best to conclude cautiously with Nolland, that the Targum (and by extension A.18 also) "would certainly open the way for a messianic understanding."[25]

In the NT, both Acts 4:11 and 1 Pet 2:7 cite Ps 118:22 and attach messianic significance to it. The former specifically applies this to "Jesus, the messiah from Nazareth" (Ἰησοῦ Χριστοῦ τοῦ Ναζωραίου, v 10) in a polemic regarding the messianic identity of Jesus (e.g. 3:18).[26] This use is probably either due to the gospels' use of the passage or an earlier oral tradition. For the latter, Schutter observes that the citation of Ps 118:22 was "primarily to evoke the builder's shame over their mistake and only secondarily to refer to Christ's exaltation."[27] The opponents 1 Peter has in mind surely have similarities with those in Matt 21, but there are nonetheless major differences as well. But though the identity of the builders changes in 1 Peter, the rejected stone does not. Like Matt 21, the rejected stone is a messianic image in Acts 4:11 and 1 Pet 2:7.

The other gospel accounts themselves do not significantly add to our understanding of the use in Matthew, except for perhaps their more focused attention on the person of Jesus. In Mark 12:10–11 and Luke 20:17 the messiah occupies a more central place. Moreover, a good case can be made that the NT alludes to the psalm often and these too confirm an eschatological and

---

23   Johannes C. de Moor, "The Targumic Background of Mark 12:1–12: The Parable of the Wicked Tenants" in *JSJ* (1998): 77, who points to D. Flusser, S. Safrai שירי דוד החיצוניים in עיונים במקרא, ed. B. Uffenheimer (Studies in Memoriam of Joshua Grintz; Tel Aviv: 1970), 83–105.

24   Contra de Moor, who does not mention the use of the historical figure Samuel in arguing for a messianic interpretation of *Tg. Ps. 118*.

25   Nolland, *The Gospel of Matthew*, 878. Rikki E. Watts observes that later Rabbinic writings take this trajectory, as in *Pes. R.* 36.1; *Midr. Ps.* 118.22; cf. 118.24; and *y. Ber.* 2.3 (V.C); *Lev. R.* 37.4 ("The Lord's House and David's Lord: The Psalms and Mark's Perspective on Jesus and the Temple" *BibInt* (2007): 307–322).

26   1 Pet 2:5 has the referent being "Jesus Christ," but this does not seem to foreground the office of the messiah as Acts 4.

27   William L. Schutter, *Hermeneutic and Composition in 1 Peter* (WUNT; Tübingen: Mohr Siebeck, 1989), 136.

messianic understanding of the passage.[28] Furthermore, the NT often uses the rock/stone motif in reference to the messiah.[29] Thus, whether we direct attention to the original psalm or its later use by interpreters, a messianic interpretation is highly likely.

Moreover, the context of the Matthean WTP surely connects the rejected stone with Jesus.[30] In addition to the בֵן / אֶבֶן connection noted earlier, the feature of being rejected clearly links the images. As discussed in the previous chapter, the WTP ends with the son having no place in the future and the reference to Ps 118:22–23 clarifies this potential misunderstanding.

However, though the above discussion of both the potential of the psalm itself and its later usage (particularly in the NT) strongly demonstrates that a couple different figures or images were seen as messianic (the stone and the victorious warrior coming to the temple), this part of our argument is not interested in those images per se since Matt 21:41–43 does not portray the disciples in those terms. Instead, *the significance of these observations lies in their demonstration of the way this psalm was understood eschatologically.* Though Matt 21 does not map the disciples back to the victorious warrior or the rejected stone, we will see that he nonetheless incorporates them into the larger scheme, and since the psalm was understood eschatologically this means the disciples are depicted as significant eschatological agents.

In the above discussion, we have seen good reasons for thinking the quotation of Ps 118:22–23 would have evoked images of constructing an eschatological building. Moreover, this building is most likely the temple in particular. There are at least four significant reasons for thinking this. First, the context of Psalm 118:22 portrays the victorious warrior entering the temple. V 26 specifies that those who bless the figure do so מִבֵּית יְהוָה; ἐξ οἴκου κυρίου. V 27 describes a sacrifice on הַמִּזְבֵּחַ; θυσιαστήριον. Since the figure approaches the temple, this is probably also the building in mind in v 22. Second, the saying's context in Matthew also confirms this identification. The pericope is placed within Jesus' actions in the temple (Matt 21:23), which is far from an incidental location, as Jesus has dramatically entered as one with authority there (21:1–11, 23) and then predicted its destruction (21:12–13, 23:28, 24:1–2). The logion itself contributes to the conclusion to the WTP, which references Isa 5, which in turn may evoke the temple (cf. Tg Isa, 4Q500). Other statements in Matthew about the building of a new temple reinforce this overall motif in Matthew (26:61, 27:40,

---

28 See Brunson, *Psalm 118 in the Gospel of John*, 102–263.
29 See esp. Snodgrass, "Christological Stone Testimonia." This will be explored in more detail in 4.3.3.
30 This is almost universally accepted by commentators, but exceptions are discussed below.

and 16:18 – to be discussed later). Since the temple predominates this portion of Matthew, especially during the Passion Week, a reference to constructing a new building out of stones easily fits this motif. Third, as we have seen, Ps 118:22 had a history of being linked to the temple and its cult with the singing of the Hallel. Fourth, later Christian literature (e.g. T. Sol. 22:7–23:4) specifically connects Ps 118:22–23 with the temple. The most significant use in this regard is 1 Pet 2:7 which clearly uses temple imagery and dates roughly to the time of Matthew's composition. Aside from actually using ἱερόν in Matt 21:42, the case for identifying the building as the temple is as about as strong as one could hope.[31] Thus, when Jesus cites Ps 118:22–23 to talk about builders using (or not using) a stone to construct an edifice, we are to think of the building of a temple, and the messianic factors discussed earlier mean this temple is eschatological.

4.2.2 Matt 21:42–43 Portrays the Disciples as Eschatological Temple Builders

Though the citation of Ps 118:22–23 provides information about God's future vindication of Jesus, and thus does not contradict the Markan version, Matthew's redaction is nonetheless surprising. The significant differences are bolded below:

⁴⁰ ὅταν οὖν ἔλθῃ ὁ κύριος τοῦ ἀμπελῶνος, τί ποιήσει τοῖς γεωργοῖς ἐκείνοις; ⁴¹ λέγουσιν αὐτῷ, Κακοὺς κακῶς ἀπολέσει αὐτοὺς καὶ τὸν ἀμπελῶνα ἐκδώσεται ἄλλοις γεωργοῖς, οἵτινες ἀποδώσουσιν αὐτῷ τοὺς καρποὺς ἐν τοῖς καιροῖς αὐτῶν. ⁴² λέγει αὐτοῖς ὁ Ἰησοῦς, Οὐδέποτε ἀνέγνωτε ἐν ταῖς γραφαῖς, Λίθον ὃν ἀπεδοκίμασαν οἱ οἰκοδομοῦντες, οὗτος ἐγενήθη εἰς κεφαλὴν γωνίας· παρὰ κυρίου ἐγένετο αὕτη καὶ ἔστιν θαυμαστὴ ἐν ὀφθαλμοῖς ἡμῶν; ⁴³ διὰ τοῦτο λέγω ὑμῖν ὅτι ἀρθήσεται ἀφ' ὑμῶν ἡ βασιλεία τοῦ θεοῦ καὶ δοθήσεται ἔθνει ποιοῦντι τοὺς καρποὺς αὐτῆς. [⁴⁴ Καὶ ὁ πεσὼν ἐπὶ τὸν λίθον τοῦτον συνθλασθήσεται· ἐφ' ὃν δ' ἂν πέσῃ λικμήσει αὐτόν.] ⁴⁵ Καὶ ἀκούσαντες οἱ ἀρχιερεῖς καὶ οἱ Φαρισαῖοι τὰς παραβολὰς αὐτοῦ ἔγνωσαν ὅτι περὶ αὐτῶν λέγει.

Matthew's version foregrounds Mark's simple ἄλλοις by not only specifying that they too are γεωργοί, but also with the phrase about producing fruit. Moreover, Matthew's elaboration in v 41 highly correlates to verse 43, which also finds no counterpart in Mark. Τὸν ἀμπελῶνα parallels ἡ βασιλεία τοῦ θεοῦ; ἐκδώσεται parallels δοθήσεται; ἄλλοις γεωργοῖς parallels ἔθνει; οἵτινες ἀποδώσουσιν αὐτῷ τοὺς

---

31 For a fuller defense of the temple in Matt 21:42, see Marcus, *Way of the Lord*, 119–24, whose arguments for Mark easily work for Matthew.

καρποὺς parallels ποιοῦντι τοὺς καρποὺς αὐτῆς. V 43 thus amplifies, or at least explains the extra material in v 41 in its description of the replacement farmers. However, instead of directly following the statement of the religious leaders, as would be expected, this addition surprisingly follows the rejected stone citation. Instead of collecting the different texts about the new farmers producing the fruit together, the imagery bounces from the farmers to temple construction and then back to the farmers. This creates a "clamping structure" around v 42, so that the reference to Ps 118:22–23 is seen to have significance for the new farmers / ἔθνος.[32]

There is some debate as to whether or not v 44 is original.[33] Though its inclusion would complicate the clamping structure described above, it would not significantly affect the observation here that Matthew situates the quotation of Ps 118:22–23 so as to emphasize the significance for the disciples. The inclusion of v 44 would result in the following alternating structure:

A   Producing fruit determines having the vineyard lease (v 41)
B   Those who reject the stone will have their decision overturned (v 42)
A' Producing fruit determines having the kingdom (v 43)
B' Those who reject the stone will be destroyed by it (v 44)

If v 44 is original, then its function is to emphasize the judgment connotations of v 42. It would likely allude to Dan 2:44 and thus reinforce the portrayal of Jesus as the messianic stone. V 44 momentarily takes attention away from the theme of replacement and focuses on judgment since only the messiah and his adversaries are in view in v 44, not the replacement leaders. Yet, even then, the destruction of existing leaders implies new ones will be raised. Thus, if v 44 is an early assimilation, as seems slightly more likely, then the replacement theme is more prominent. But if v 44 is original and the judgment of the

---

32   See 4.7.3 for a discussion of the significance of this word.
33   V 44 is missing in some mss, most notably P104, D, and old Latin mss. Though it may have been inserted due to Luke 20:18, this would have to have been quite early since the verse occurs in so many early mss. The internal evidence suggests its originality since "a more appropriate place for its insertion would have been after ver. 42" (Metzger, *A Textual Commentary*, 47 – though UBS5 considers it an accretion and includes it with a "C" rating). For a defense of its originality, see Kynes, *Christology of Solidarity*, 141–42. For a detailed and convincing argument for it as an early assimilation, see Gregory R. Lanier, "A Case for the Assimilation of Matthew 21:44 to the Lukan 'Crushing Stone' (20:18), with Special Reference to P104" in *TC* 16 (2016): 1–22.

corrupt leaders gets the final word, the strange clamping around v 42 which connects the new leaders to Ps 118:22–23 must still be considered.

Thus, the Mathean Jesus refers to Ps 118:22–23 to demonstrate that Israel will receive new leadership. But how? Matt 21:43 begins with διὰ τοῦτο, but what about Ps 118:22–23 commends it as proof for the future installment of the disciples? The significance of the unexpected direction Matthew takes the stone saying has been observed before, most noticeably by Stanton, who argues "Matthew sees the new ἔθνος (his own community rather than Jesus) as the stone rejected at first by the Jewish leaders but accepted by God."[34] This is unlikely given the reasons above regarding the significance of this statement in connection to the WTP. Since Jesus is the rejected son in Matt 21:33–41, he must be in view in v 42 since that text is presented as a scriptural explanation for the events of the WTP. However, Stanton is correct in observing that Matthew takes this statement in a non-Christological direction.

Trilling has also noticed this feature and concluded that Matthew overlays his ecclesiology on Mark's Christology. For him, Matthew has replaced Mark's emphasis that Jesus is the once rejected stone to highlight the disciples' role. He asserts, "Die christologische Ausweitung bei Markus wird von einer **überdeckt. An de Stelle** des Bekkenntiness zum erhöhten Christus tritt jenes zur Wirklichkeit des neuen Gottesvolkes."[35] Trilling's observation that Matthew has a different interest than Mark is well taken, but there is nothing to suggest that the theme of the new position of the people of God has swallowed up Matthew's Christology. Modern redaction criticism rightly corrects perspectives like Trilling's, so that emphasis is not exclusively given to Matthew's unique additions. After all, the WTP allows for the role of several characters, each of whom takes center stage at different points. Similarly, vv 42–43 speaks to the role of both Jesus and the disciples.

Kynes explains the transition to the disciples by focusing on the solidarity Jesus has with his disciples,

> But if v 42 is allowed to have its natural Christological significance, and if one recognizes the parallel between the rejection and reversal of fortune experience by Jesus and that experiences by his people, then the relationship between v. 42 and v. 43 can be described as one in which Matthew's

---

34   Stanton, *Gospel for a New Nation*, 152, parenthesis his.
35   Wolfgang Trilling, *Das Wahre Israel: Studien zur Theologie des Matthäus-Evangeliums* (SANT; München: Kösel, 1964), 58, emphasis mine. Thus, Trilling's argument requires the textual variant discussed above (Matt 21:44) to be an assimilation. Though it may not be original, his statement "Der an sich gut bezeugte Vers 44 hat jedoch sicher nicht zum ursprünglichen Text gehört" (57) is far from certain.

> ecclesiology is built upon his Christology ... The stone logion in v. 42 gives this transfer a Christological foundation: those once excluded from the kingdom are linked to their rejected Messiah, and the fortunes of both are unexpectedly reversed by God. The people of the Messiah are those who follow him and share in his fate.[36]

This approach has the appeal of allowing Christological significance in the stone saying and yet appreciating the thrust of the citation as meant for the disciples. Moreover, Kynes rightly notes the Matthean theme of reversal. His work successfully argues that for Matthew, "Christian identity is found in Christ: like Master, like disciple, with the former serving not simply as the model but as the enabling source."[37] Kynes' position fits comfortably in my research, as much of this examines how the connection between Ecclesiology and Christology functions in the hermeneutics of eschatological texts.

Though Kynes helpfully points out the fluidity between Christology and Ecclesiology, an explanation beyond "like Master, like disciple" seems to be at play. Kynes' position does not well account for the surrounding context. Though opposition has been predicted for the disciples (e.g. Matt 10:16–39, 16:24–26), this is not in view in the surrounding context of the WTP. Moreover, in the immediate context of the WTP, the disciples (as represented by the new farmers) are in a class apart from the persecuted prophets (represented by the servants) and the son. In fact, the WTP's plotline places Jesus in closer proximity to the servants than to the farmers due to having the same task.

A likelier explanation of how Jesus gleans information about the disciples from Ps 118:22–23 comes from the logic of this miniature parable. Blending Theory observes that the function of a metaphor does not only include the elements which are directly mapped in from the source and target domains, but that attention must also be given to the new world created by the joining of the two domains, the emergent structure which develops from "governing principles" as interpreters often "run the blend." In our situation, we have the new ἔθνος clearly in the blend, mapped from the target domain, but nothing has been mapped in from the source domain. But when one attends to the "governing principles," especially Pattern Completion, that "run the blend," one can imagine how these characters come to have a role in emergent structure. The scene from the psalm is one of builders considering using a stone to construct an edifice, but then setting it aside as unfit for the project. If the רֹאשׁ פִּנָּה; κεφαλὴν γωνίας refers to the foundation stone, then the image is one of a new

---

36 Kynes, *A Christology of Solidarity*, 141, 144. So also Marcus, *The Way*, 123–24.
37 Kynes, *Christology of Solidarity*, 3.

building, starting with the once rejected stone.[38] But if the reference is to a capstone, then there is not necessarily a new building implied, though this too is possible.[39] In either case, the once rejected stone turns out to be of great significance to the project. The assumption in this short story is that, whether or not the old building itself has been abandoned, *the builders have been replaced by those who see the true value of the stone* (whether it is used on the top or the bottom of the structure does not particularly matter, though the latter seems more likely). Granted, v 22 attributes all of this action to God, but the text itself does describe the intermediary use of builders to construct the edifice. In other words, thinking through the situation envisioned in Ps 118:22–23 allows for three "characters" – the old builders, the stone, and the new builders. This allows for the disciples to have their own space and not simply be an extension of the stone.

Three further observations further support seeing the disciples as new builders. First, this fits remarkably well with the stone saying's parallelism with the WTP. In the previous parable, we have seen that the owner displaces the old farmers because they did not respond properly to the son and so he transfers the care of the vineyard to new farmers. The citation of Ps 118:22–23 similarly implies the old builders are replaced because they did not respond properly to the stone, and since it directly states the project does go on to include the stone, it can only do so at the hands of those who see its true value. This connection is especially likely if a tradition like the one in the Targum and 4Q500 is to be in view, in which Isa 5 is linked to the temple. If so, those taking care of the vineyard are easily seen as those who build the temple. But even if the proposed parallels to the Targum and 4Q500 are irrelevant, the nearness of the vineyard parable to the rejected stone saying suggests that as the imagery shifted from old farmers to old builders, so too the imagery shifts from new farmers to new builders.

---

38 As argued by H. Krämer, "γωνία" in *EDNT* 1:268; *NIDNTTE* 1:627; R. J. McKelvey, *The New Temple: The Church in the New Testament* (Oxford Theological Monographs; London: Oxford University, 1969), 195–204. Blomberg rightly observes that ראש; κεφαλή does not require the stone to be on top, but could indicate primacy (*Matthew*, 73). The explanation by Krämer, "γωνία," 1:268 is helpful in the discussion of ראש and κεφαλή, that they "refer not only to the vertical ('head') but also to the horizontal ... the place where a street beings in Ezek 16:25, 31 and elsewhere ... κεφαλή γωνία thus refers to the *most distant corner at the horizontal level*." See further discussion in section 4.2.3.

39 As argued by M. Cahill, "Not a Cornerstone! Translating Ps 118, 22 in the Jewish and Christian Scriptures" *RB* 106 (1999): 345–57; Silva, *NIDNTTE* 3:389–90; France, *Gospel of Matthew*, 815–16. Others do not think the exact reference particularly matters (e.g. Michael J. Wilkins, *Matthew* (NIVAC; Grand Rapids: Zondervan, 2009), 698; Nolland, *Luke*, 3:953; Keener, *Gospel of Matthew*, 515).

Second, like the image of farmers,[40] the image of builders easily lent itself to leadership connotations.[41] For example, Midr. Cant. 1:5 states, "do not read 'daughters' (בנות) but 'builders' (בונות) of Jerusalem; the great Sanhedrin of Israel is meant, who sit and build her through every question and answer."[42] Similarly, CD 4:19–20 and 8:18 predict judgment for "Wall-Builders" (בוני החיץ) who are corrupt leaders in Israel. 1 Cor 3:10 may also reflect the tradition of depicting leaders as builders and this may stem from the WTP itself.[43] Inasmuch as the thrust of Matt 21:33–46 is the judgment of the existing religious leadership and the future installment of another, we can easily envision these new leaders as "builders."

Third, the suggestion that "this mountain" which the disciples are to remove and cast into the sea (21:21) refers to Mt. Zion (and by synecdoche the temple) furthers this description of the disciples, since a portrayal of the disciples as those who "destroy" the temple would follow on the heels of their description as those who "build" it.[44] "This mountain" being Mt. Zion seems likely for at least three reasons. First, the majority of commentators agree that the cursing of the fig tree (21:18–22) represents judgment to come upon Israel. Jesus' statement that the disciples too could pronounce a similar judgment would then occur in the same immediate pericope. Second, the theme of the destruction of the temple itself is of central concern in this part of Matthew (e.g. 21:12–17; 23:38, 24:2). Third, the singular demonstrative pronoun οὗτος suggests (though does not necessarily require) a specific mountain is in mind. For those travelling from Bethany to Jerusalem, Mt. Zion seems the most likely referent.[45]

40 See 4.7.3.
41 J. D. M. Derrett, "The Stone that the Builders Rejected," in *Studies in the New Testament*, 5 vols. (Leiden: E. J. Brill, 1977), 2:64–65. The medieval Tikkunei Zohar 146b discusses Ps 118:22 thus,

מַאי הַבּוֹנִים אִלֵּין אִינּוּן מָארֵי מַתְנִיתִיןדְּאִינּוּן בָּנָאן בִּנְיָינִין דְּעָלְמָא, וּפוֹסְקֵי הֲלָכוֹת "Who are these 'builders'? They are masters of the Mishnah who built buildings in the world and deciders of Halakah" (translation mine).
42 Marcus, *Way of the Lord*, 124. For other Rabbinic parallels, see *b. Shabb.* 114a; *b. Ber.* 64a.
43 See pg. 134, n136.
44 For a recent overview of the arguments for and against, see Watts, *Isaiah's New Exodus in Mark*, 332–337 who argues that both a general call to faith and eschatological symbolism are in view. For a more recent argument, see Piotrowski, "Whatever You Ask." The most thorough investigation is W. R. Telford, *The Barren Temple and the Withered Tree* (JSNTSup; Sheffield: JSOT, 1980).
45 A strong case can also be made for the Mt. of Olives, depending on how much one sees an undercurrent of Zechariah in Matthew's passion week (Robert M. Grant, "The Coming of the Kingdom" *JBL* 67 (1948): 301–302; cf. Paul B. Duff, "The March of the Divine Warrior and the Advent of the Greco-Roman King: Mark's Account of Jesus' Entry into Jerusalem" *JBL* 111.1 (1992): 55–71). Zech 14:4 describes this mountain splitting in two when YHWH

If this is the case, and the reader has just been prepared to see the disciples as participating in the destruction of the temple, the image of them participating in the rebuilding of a new temple is all the more likely.

To summarize, Matthew's redaction of Mark pushes the disciples forward as a relevant component of the rejected stone saying. Various proposals for how Ps 118:22–23 shed light on the role of the disciples have been offered. The views of Stanton and Trilling, that Matthew is replacing Mark's emphasis on Christology does not do justice to the presence of Jesus within the WTP or his audience's antagonism against him. Kynes' view, that the disciples are incorporated because Matthew incorporates the disciples in with Jesus and thus the stone indirectly maps to them, is possible but unlikely given the surrounding context. The most likely explanation as to where Jesus sees the disciples in Ps 118:22–23 is that he sees them as the replacement leaders / builders. Though Matthew does not specifically map these builders from the source domain, this presents no problem according to Blending Theory in which interpreters are expected to "run the blend" and so would fill in the gap – the logic of the story implies a new set of builders who recognize the true value of the stone. From the first section, we have seen that the picture is that of constructing an eschatological temple. But what is the significance of Jesus portraying his disciples as eschatological temple builders?

4.2.3 *The Image of an Eschatological Temple Builder Was a Messianic Concept*

The messianic connotations of building an eschatological temple have recently received attention from a number of scholars[46] and though it is too soon to say this is generally accepted as scholarly consensus, it has much in its favor. We can trace the idea back to one of the most significant messianic texts in

---

comes in order to make easier access to Jerusalem, which will be restored to a state of peace (e.g. v 11). This would fit the motif suggested here of the disciples being portrayed as those involved in building Jerusalem. However, the larger emphasis in Matthew on the destruction of the temple makes the Mt. Zion interpretation more likely.

46   E.g. Ben Meyer, *The Aims of Jesus* (London: SCM, 1979); Donald Juel, *Messiah and Temple: The Trial of Jesus in the Gospel of Mark* (SBLDS; Missoula: Scholars Press, 1977), 198–89; N. T. Wright, *Jesus and the Victory of God*, 411; J. Adna, *Jesu Stellung zum Tempel: Die Tempelaktion und das Tempelwort als Ausdruck seiner messianischen Sendung* (WUNT; Tübingen: Mohr Siebeck, 2000), 50–53; Andrew J. Chester, *Messiah and Exaltation: Jewish Messianic and Visionary Traditions and New Testament Christology* (WUNT; Tübingen: Mohr Siebeck, 2007), 471–96; Joseph A. Fitzmyer, *The One Who is To Come* (Grand Rapids: Eerdmans, 2008), 172; Nicholas Perrin, *Jesus and the Temple* (Grand Rapids: Baker, 2010), 80–113; Grant Macaskill, *Union with Christ in the New Testament* (Oxford: Oxford University Press, 2013), 100–27, 147–71.

the Hebrew Bible – 2 Sam 7. Playing on the ambiguity of בַּיִת, YHWH promises that though David will not build a בַּיִת for him (vv 5–7), YHWH himself will build a בַּיִת (dynasty) for David (v 11). However, YHWH promises that one of David's descendants יִבְנֶה־בַּיִת לִשְׁמִי (v 13), which is then connected to (וְ) the promise that his throne would be established עַד־עוֹלָם. Especially given the predicted consequences of iniquity (vv 14–15) and the rest of the flow through 2 Kgs (e.g. 1 Kgs 5–6), this seems to have Solomon (at least primarily) in view. However, later interpreters make a messianic connection more explicit. 2 Sam 7 is extremely significant for understanding messianism in the first century. Adna writes,

> Wurde 2 Sam 7, die sogenannte Nathanweissagung, mit der festen Zusage Jahwes über den ewigen Bestand des Davidshauses zu einer Kernstelle für die Entwicklung der messianischen Erwartung. Aufgrund der nahen Verbindung zwischen der davidischen Königsherrschaft und dem Tempelbau durch den davidischen "Samen" die 2 Sam 7 vorgibt, mußte sich bei der messianischen Rezeption der Nathanweissagung auch die Erwartung nahelegen, daß der Messias den Tempel baut.[47]

Evidences of a messianic understanding of the temple builder of 2 Sam 7 occur between the time of 2 Samuel and Matthew. The account in 1 Chron 17 omits any reference to discipline for sinning, and thus shows signs that a more messianic interpretation was underway.[48] Zech 6:12–13, which was understood as messianic, likely builds on the Davidic covenant, and describes a "branch/sprout" (צֶמַח) who will build YHWH's temple.[49] Similarly, Isa 44:28–45:1 refers to Cyrus

---

[47] Adna, *Jesu Stellung zum Tempel*, 53.

[48] Surely by the first century the one who was to sit on David's throne was seen as the messiah (e.g. Heb 1:5). But citations or allusions connecting Jesus with 2 Sam 7 do not necessarily require the temple building function to map to the messiah. The proposed allusions to 2 Sam 7 in the NT are legion. Seyoon Kim even argues that the temple incident builds on 2 Sam 7, and further argues that a series of links in Zechariah connect 2 Sam 7 and Ps 118 in Jesus' thinking ("Jesus-The Son of God, the Stone, the Son of Man, and the Servant: The Role of Zechariah in the Self-Identification of Jesus," in *Tradition and Interpretation in the New Testament: Essays in Honor of E. Earle Ellis*, ed. Gerald F. Hawthorne and Otto Betz (Tübingen: Mohr Siebeck, 1987), 138–42).

[49] This is connected to the Davidic covenant and the referent is not Joshua or Zerubbabel but the messiah (Anthony R. Petterson, *Haggai, Zechariah & Malachi* (ApOTC; Downers Grove, IL: InterVarsity, 2015), 186; Mark J. Boda, *The Book of Zechariah* (NICOT; Grand Rapids: Eerdmans, 2016), 397–403). Interestingly, v 15 describes those who will come from afar and will build (in?) the temple of YHWH (וּבָנוּ בְּהֵיכַל יְהוָה; καὶ οἰκοδομήσουσιν ἐν τῷ οἴκῳ κυρίου). בְּ is not normally used with בנה to identify the object (as with אֵת for example), so it seems these returned exiles are building something inside the temple.

as רֵעִי and מְשִׁיחוֹ who will lay the foundation of the temple. The Targums confirm a messianic interpretation of temple builder texts (Zech 4:7–9, 6:12–13)[50] and render Isa 53:5, "and he will build a holy temple (וְהוּא יִבְנֵי בֵית מַקְדְּשָׁא), which will be cleansed of its guilt." 4Q174, also called *The Eschatological Midrashim* or *4QFlorilegium*, too connects the messiah ("the Branch/Sprout") with the work of rebuilding the temple in its midrash of 2 Sam 7:11–14. After citing portions of that Scripture, the text explains "This is the Sprout of David [הואה צמח דויד], who will arise with the interpreter of Torah, who will [arise] in Zi[on in the lat]ter days, as it is written, 'And I shall raise up the hut of David [סוכת דויד] that is fallen.' This is the fallen hut of David [סוכת דויד], [w]hom He shall raise up to save Israel" (3:11–13).[51] This "hut" has the temple in view since the earlier discussion centers around the building of a new temple (esp. 3:3, 6). Other evidences of the messiah as temple builder around the time of Jesus, though with varying degrees of clarity, include Sirach 5:1–2, 5–6; T. Dan 5:10–12; 1 Enoch 53:6; 90:29; Pss. Sol. 17:21–23, 30; Sib. Or. 5:414–27, 432–33.[52] This paradigm may even underly Herod's desire to refurbish the temple so lavishly.[53]

Matthew's scriptural roots and his contemporary fellow interpreters demonstrate that scholarship's understanding of the messiah as temple builder has much in its favor. The claim here is not that every strand of Judaism in the first

---

Either way, this still describes an eschatological temple building by someone besides the messiah. However, the text does not seem to have had much significance during the first century.

50   However, it is possible that the "messiah" in *TgJon* only refers to a postexilic character. Besides the identification of the צֶמַח (Zech 6:12) and הָאֶבֶן הָרֹאשָׁה (4:7) as משיחיה, there are no substantial differences to require an eschatological orientation if one was not there already. See David Shepherd, "When He Comes, Will He Build It? Temple, Messiah and Targum Jonathan," *AS* 12 (2014): 89–107.

51   Translation mine. Contra Michael O. Wise, Martin G. Abegg Jr., and Edward M. Cook. *The Dead Sea Scrolls: A New Translation* (New York: HarperOne, 2005) which translates "this describes the fallen Branch of David." 4Q174's citation of portions from 2 Sam 7:11–14 is connected with Amos 9:11. Too much emphasis must not be placed on 4Q174, however, since the messiah may be understood as the hut itself which will be raised up.

52   Perrin, *Jesus the Temple*, 102 also lists *b. Meg.* 18a, *Lev. Rab.* 9.6, and *Amidah* 14 as later support for this view of the messiah. However, the closest *b. Meg* 18a comes to demonstrating this concept is to say that the kingdom of David will follow the building of Jerusalem. *Amidah* 14 prays that God would rebuild Jerusalem and establish the throne of David. It describes YHWH as builder (בָּרוּךְ אַתָּה יְהוָה בּוֹנֵה יְרוּשָׁלָיִם), but without an intermediary. I have not been able to identify any connection between the messiah and building the temple in *Lev. Rab.* 9.6, except the mention of only thanksgiving sacrifices continuing in the time to come.

53   Michael F. Bird, "Jesus and the 'Parting of the Ways,'" in *Handbook for the Study of the Historical Jesus: How to Study the Historical Jesus*, ed. Tom Holmén and Stanley E. Porter (Leiden: Brill, 2011), 1:1199; Wright, *Jesus and the Victory*, 411.

century held to this paradigm. Perrin explains, "Notwithstanding Judaism's intramural disagreement as to what shape the future temple might take, notwithstanding too those texts which may yield the impression that God would rebuild the temple alone, there remained a vibrant tradition which closely identified the expected messianic figure with the task of temple-building."[54] Besides the evidence that has just been surveyed, Matt 16:18 is of particular interest since it reveals that Matthew adheres to the stripe of Judaism that viewed the messiah as temple builder. This text will be examined shortly, but at this stage of the argument, noting that the text is highly charged with the question of messianism and portrays Jesus as a builder will suffice. Moreover, that Matt 16:18 and 21:41–43 employ similar imagery means the latter should be seen in light of the former.

This connection is especially strengthened if the κεφαλή γωνία is a cornerstone as opposed to a top stone since the rock in Matt 16:18 is clearly being built upon. The most thorough and often cited work against this identification is by Cahill's "Not a Cornerstone!"[55] However, Cahill's argument only concerns "what the psalm-text means" since "how biblical writers subsequently understood and applied it is another question."[56] In fact, he allows "it is possible that such usage [the influence of Isa 28:16, in which a פִּנָּה must be a cornerstone] has influenced, and possibly perverted, the understanding (and translation) of similar stone texts. After all, in 1 Pet 2,6–7, both Is 28,16 and Ps 118,22 are quoted successively."[57]

This observation alone is enough for our argument since we are only concerned with how the Matthean Jesus understood the text. However, we can go farther than this since Cahill's case for the רֹאשׁ פִּנָּה not being a capstone in Ps 118:22 fails to convince for four reasons. First, the strongest of Cahill's arguments is that "cornerstone" would contradict the thrust of the parable, since

> Builders need a pile of stones or bricks to draw on when starting to build ... The cornerstone was chosen and laid with great care ... It is obvious that this was the first stone the builders were especially concerned with. Other stones were rejected at this stage. A stone rejected at this stage could not be the cornerstone for this particular building.[58]

---

54   Perrin, *Jesus the Temple*, 102.
55   Michael Cahill, "Not a Cornerstone! Translating Ps 118,22 in the Jewish and Christian Scriptures," *RB* 106 (1999): 345–57.
56   Cahill, "Not a Cornerstone!" 348.
57   Cahill, "Not a Cornerstone!" 351.
58   Cahill, "Not a Cornerstone!" 349.

On the one hand, it is not clear that Ps 118:22a ("the stone which the builders rejected") only refers to sorting out acceptable vs. unacceptable stones after the foundation was laid. After all, the foundation stone itself must have been selected at one point too. If this were done with great care, their failure in this regard makes them all the more culpable. But on the other hand, even if Ps 118:22a refers to this part of the process, this does not mean Ps 118:22b ("has become the 'head of the corner'") does. The purpose of the stone once approved may differ from the purpose of the stone when it was rejected. There is no reason to eliminate this possibility.

Second, Cahill also argues that the notion of cornerstone "nullifies the force of the argument of the Gospel writers at least, because they wished to express ... climax and completion. The resurrection of Christ crowns his ministry of salvation."[59] However the WTP (at least in its Matthean version) focuses on the future work of the disciples (cf. 21:41–43), who take over the responsibility of the farmers and continue building. Though the work of Jesus does have elements of "climax and completion," it also represents a new beginning.

Third, Cahill argues that "'*Rosh* immediately suggests physical height, and top rather than bottom."[60] But this neglects the possibility for ראש to mean "beginning" or refer to value.[61] Cahill also argues that the parallel to Zech 4:8, which is the only other occurrence of ראש and a stone (there it is אֶבֶן)[62] may also allow for a meaning of "topstone" since Zerubbabel will also finish the temple in v 9.[63] Moreover, he will bring out the stone in the future (וְהוֹצִיא), the laying of the foundation has already happened (יִסְּדוּ), and the finishing of the temple is also future (תְּבַצַּעְנָה). This may suggest the first action should be compared with the third, not the second. However, this seems to read too much significance into the tenses. Moreover, the possibility that the text alludes to Mesopotamian temple building suggests the stone should be connected to the foundation.[64]

Thus, there are insufficient reasons for dismissing "cornerstone" as a possibility. Matt 21:44 is of little help since, even if original, it suggests a stone that

---

[59] Cahill, "Not a Cornerstone!" 347. The distinction with a change in later usage makes this argument unexpected.
[60] Cahill, "Not a Cornerstone!" 352–53.
[61] *HALOT*, 1166; *DCH*, 7:375. For a further discussion, see R. J. McKelvey, "Christ the Cornerstone" *NTS* 8.4 (1964): 354–55.
[62] LXX has ἐξοίσω τὸν λίθον τῆς κληρονομίας.
[63] Cahill, "Not a Cornerstone!" 352.
[64] Cahill, "Not a Cornerstone!" 352 acknowledges the background. See Carol L. Meyers and Eric M. Meyers, *Haggai, Zechariah 1–8: A New Translation with Introduction and Commentary* (AB; Garden City: Doubleday, 1995), 246–68.

is both on the ground and one that is elevated. However, Cahill's observation that Isa 28:16 may have affected the understanding of Ps 118:22 deserves consideration, though one could easily argue that Isa 28:16 sheds light on the ambiguity of the psalm. 1 Pet 2:6–7 does give precedent for thinking the two passages were connected in the Christ movement.[65] Since the stone in the former is clearly a foundation, this suggests a similar image in Ps 118. Granted, the imagery in 1 Pet 2 could shift from a top stone to a foundation stone, but the simpler explanation would be to take them as the same. Moreover, if the suggestion discussed below is correct and Matt 16:18 alludes to Isa 28, this intertextual background would make it all the likelier that Matthew expects his readers to connect 21:42 to 16:18. The common allusion to Isa 28 in both passages, as well as their use of temple construction imagery in a context that stresses both the messianic identity of Jesus and the eschatological role of the disciples strongly suggests that these two passages are linked and invite comparison.

The argument at this point, that readers of Matthew are to connect 16:18 and 21:42, does not require that the stone is a foundation in the latter, but if it is (which seems particularly likely given the way Ps 118:22 is used elsewhere in the NT) then the link is all the stronger. In any case, at least one strand of Judaism viewed the messiah as temple builder and Matthew shows indications of being a part of this tradition. Moreover, we have seen reasons for thinking that Matt 21:42 portrays the disciples as building an eschatological temple, which means they participate in a task traditionally seen as messianic.

4.3 Matt 16:18 Portrays the Disciples as the Messianic Temple Foundation

This section argues that Matt 16:18 utilizes the same imagery discussed above in depicting the construction of an eschatological temple. However, though both chapters 16 and 21 have the same set of actors – Jesus and his disciples – the parts they play in chapter 16 are swapped from chapter 21. The argument of this section comes in three stages. First, we will see that Matt 16:18 is to be understood against the backdrop of eschatological temple construction. Second, we will see that the disciples' role in this imagery is that of the foundation stone. Third, though this has been hinted at in the treatment of 21:42, the final stage formally explores the messianic significance that would have been attached to being the foundation of the eschatological temple.

65　F. F. Bruce, "New Wine in Old Wine Skins: III. The Corner Stone" *ExpTim* (1973): 231–35 argues that Ps 118:22, Isa 28:16 and Isa 8:14 formed an early Christian testimonium.

4.3.1 Matt 16:18 Evokes Imagery of Eschatological Temple Construction

Scholarship has not reached a consensus that temple imagery stands behind Jesus' declaration to Peter,[66] but five factors, taken together, strongly suggest this is the case.[67] First, other texts in Matthew suggest that new temple imagery is significant for Matthew. 12:6 has prepared the reader that a τοῦ ἱεροῦ μεῖζόν ἐστιν ὧδε, "some*thing* (not necessarily some*one*) greater than the temple is here."[68] Temple language and related ideas occur significantly during the Passion Week. Jesus' dramatic entry to the temple (21:1–11), his "cleansing" (or pronouncement of destruction; 21:12–13), his healing in the temple (21:14–16), his allusion to Isa 5 with its temple background (21:31–41), his citation of the rejected cornerstone text (21:42), his eschatological discourse regarding its destruction (24:1–31, cf. 23:38, "your house is left to you desolate"), and the accusations against Jesus that he would destroy and rebuild a temple (25:61, 27:40) all point to a significant temple interest. This theme is so prominent that Piotrowski states, "Once Jesus reaches Jerusalem ... all of his actions and

---

[66] Examples of those who see a temple allusion in Matt 16:18 include Davies and Allison, *Matthew*, 2:624–30; C. N. Hillyer, "'Rock-Stone' Imagery in I Peter," *TynBul* 22 (1971): 58–81; Barber, "Jesus as the Davidic Temple Builder," 935–53; Beale, *The Temple and the Church's Mission*, 187; Meyer, *The Aims of Jesus*, 185–202; N. T. Wright, "Jerusalem in the New Testament" in *Jerusalem, Past and Present in the Purposes of God*, ed. Peter W. L. Walker (Grand Rapids: Baker, 1994), 57; Peter Shäfer, "Tempel und Schopfung: Zur Interpretation einiger Heiligtumstraditionen in der rabbischen Literatur," in *Studien zur geschichte und Theologie des rabbinischen Judentums* (AGJU; Leiden: Brill, 1978), 126. Examples of those who are less convinced or argue against it include Nolland, *The Gospel of Matthew*, 672; Robert H. Gundry, *Peter-False Disciple and Apostate according to St. Matthew* (Grand Rapids: Eerdmans, 2015), 20–22; and Witherington, *Matthew*, 317 (though he advocates it in *Jesus, Paul and the End of the World: A Comparative Study in New Testament Eschatology* (Downers Grove, IL: InterVarsity, 1999), 89). A major competing model argues that 16:18 alludes to Isa 51:1–5, paralleling Peter with Abraham, צוּר חֲצַבְתֶּם (Davies and Allison, *Matthew*, 2:624). But there are sufficient discrepancies to exclude this possibility – see Markus Bockmuehl, *The Remembered Peter* (WUNT; Tübingen: Mohr Siebeck, 2010), 152.

[67] Patrick Schreiner, "Peter, the Rock: Matthew 16 in light of Daniel 2" *CTR* 13.2 (2016): 99–117 argues that Dan 2 stands behind Matt 21 and 16. The textual difficulty of 21:44 is not discussed, but if the allusion exists in the WTP, then Schreiner's argument that both texts have Dan 2 in view may be valid. This would only reinforce what we have been seeing. It would provide another example of a non-messianic hermeneutic since it results in Peter being mapped to the messianic stone of Dan 2. Schreiner explains this as a function of the corporate nature of the Son of Man (Dan 7:25). This important text may lie behind Matthew's non-messianic hermeneutic, but the variety of case studies examined here reveal that this is a general phenomenon which do not require a corporate element in the context of the source domain.

[68] France, *The Gospel of Matthew*, 623.

words in the rest of the gospel bear directly on the temple."[69] Though surely an overstatement, this nonetheless rightly stresses the strong presence of this interest. Certainly these do not all contain "construction" imagery, but they do demonstrate the temple is a significant Matthean motif. Though this does not require every building in Matthew to be the temple, it does show that the possibility in 16:18 warrants serious consideration.

Second, the seemingly disparate images of building on a rock (v 18a) and conflict with πύλαι ᾅδου (v 18b) point to the need for an underlying scheme to unite them. The Targums and later Rabbinic writings portray the temple as resting on a cosmic stone which covered the underworld. For example, *Tg Exod* 28:30 (in the cultic context describing Aaron's garments) describes the "foundation stone with which the Lord of the world sealed up the mouth of the great deep/abyss (תהומא רבא) at the beginning."[70] This matches nicely with the following description in v 18, πύλαι ᾅδου οὐ κατισχύσουσιν αὐτῆς, which suggests the stone and the underworld are in some kind of proximity. Moreover, the cosmic rock was not only seen as something that covers the abyss; it was also seen as the foundation of the temple. The Mishna describes it as the stone upon which the ark rested, three finger lengths above ground: "a stone was there from the days of the earlier prophets, it was called 'Foundation'" (m. Yoma 5:2).[71]

Data concerning the cosmic stone comes later, but the idea here fits quite well with the presence of a rock that is the foundation of a significant structure, as well as being in contact and conflict with the underworld, and this would entail the significant structure being the temple. This coheres well with the common tradition of cultic sites being connected to a special stone, as in Gen 28:10–22; Zech 4:7–9; m. Yoma 5:2; b. Yoma 53b, 54b; T. Sol. 23:6–8. In other words, the concepts of building on a rock and conflict with πύλαι ᾅδου at first seem to be unrelated. If the underlying image is that of a temple, then these formerly disparate ideas are properly linked if the Rabbinic tradition extends back to the time of our text.

Third, several scholars have proposed an allusion to Isa 28:16 in Matt 16:18, which depicts YHWH laying a foundation stone.[72] The original passage indicates

---

69   Piotrowski, "'Whatever You Ask,'" 99. His argument focuses on Mark, but easily applies to Matthew.
70   Translation mine. See Hillyer, "Rock-Stone Imagery," 79; Meyer, *Aims of Jesus*, 185.
71   Translation mine. Rabbi Yose in the *Tosefta* takes this to mean "from it the world was carved," playing on שתיה. See Yaron A. Eliav, "The Temple Mount in Jewish and Early Christian Traditions: A New Look" in *Jerusalem: Idea and Reality*, ed. Tamar Mayer and Suleiman A. Mourad (London: Routledge, 2008), 62–63.
72   Keener, *Gospel of Matthew*, 428; Davies and Allison, *Matthew*, 2:630. J. D. M. Derrett "Thou art the Stone, and Upon This Stone …" *DRev* 106.365 (1988): 276–85 believes Matt 16:18

that the temple is in view since it is located in Zion, and 1 Pet 2:6–8 evidences this understanding by citing the passage in a temple context. This passage, as well as Rom 9:33, also joins Isa 28:16 to another Isaian stone (8:14), which, again, is in a temple context. Several similarities between Isa 8 and 28 exist and the two seem to describe the same situation.[73] The proposed allusion of Matt 16:18 to Isa 28:16 fares quite well with Hays' criteria for an allusion. An allusion to Isa 27:13 in Matt 24:31 and a citation of Isa 29:13 in Matt 15:8–9, not to mention frequent other references to Isa 28:16 in the NT (Rom 9:33, 10:11, 1 Pet 2:6) demonstrate the proposed allusion satisfies the criteria of availability and recurrence, and even has "popular familiarity." In fact, 1QS 8:4–8 also references Isa 28:16 and then describes itself as a figurative temple. There is sufficient volume with significant similarities. Opposing a storm that comes because of a covenant with death (מָוֶת; ᾅδης) and sheol (שְׁאוֹל; θάνατος),[74] but will not being able to destroy it (vv 15–18) would correspond to the church's conflict and victory over the πύλαι ᾅδου. Some have suggested that the Aramaic saying originally referred to a storm (סער or שׂער) instead of a gate (שַׁעַר).[75] This would increase the volume of the allusion since Isa 28 refers to a storm (שׁוֹט שׁוֹטֵף; καταιγίς, vv 15, 17, 18). There is certainly thematic coherence too, as Matthew applies many of Isaiah's deliverance motifs.[76] Thus, sufficient indication indicate the validity of this proposed allusion and thus portrays the building of Matt 16:18 as a temple.

---

    alludes to Isa 28:16, but especially Isa 54 to argue that πέτρα refers to a precious stone. He notes the messianic understanding of 28:16 but does not discuss if or how a messianic text can be applied to Peter. Hillyer, "Rock-Stone Imagery," 80 too sees a parallel between Peter and the one who believes in v 16. As with most allusions, the direction of this reasoning could be reversed: temple construction being behind Matt 16:18 would contribute to the likelihood that an allusion is being made to the temple image of Isa 28:16.

73 Snodgrass, "The Christological Stone Testimonia," 27–28.

74 Based on other usage, one would expect the LXX to have θάνατος then ᾅδης. It is not clear why the order is seemingly reversed.

75 Craig A. Evans, *Matthew* (NCBC; Cambridge: Cambridge University, 2012), 314; The Syriac records a variant, "bar," so there is at least some uncertainty from a textual critical perspective (Stephen Hero, "The Gates or the Bars of Hades? A Note on Matthew 16:17–19," *NTS* 7 (1981): 411–14). However, the text seems to implicitly contrast the gates of Hades with the gates of the kingdom, to which Peter is given the keys (Joel Marcus, "The Gates of Hades and the Keys of the Kingdom (Matt 16:18–19)" *CBQ* 15.3 (1988): 443–55).

76 The last three of Hays' criteria are more difficult, but less significant. One difficulty that arises is later uses of Isa 28:16 to make Christ the foundation stone (following the NT, as in *Epist. Barn.* 6:2 and *Ambr. De Offic.* 1:42). But this complication touches the nerve of this project, that there are times when the Matthean Jesus takes passages which are easily and naturally used of the messiah but does not make the expected application.

A fourth reason for seeing temple imagery behind Matt 16:18 can be found in the significance of Jesus being portrayed as both the messiah and as the one who would build this new edifice. Certainly the central idea of this pericope (16:13–28) is the revelation of Jesus as the messiah, and this suggests that the following image of Jesus' building activity utilizes the view in the first century of the messiah as a temple builder discussed previously (see 4.2.3).

Fifth, the location in Caesarea Philippi may also confirm this interpretation. Witherington argues that another allusion is stronger and so would distract from a reference to the temple, stating

> Neglected in the discussions by Schweizer and many others is the fact that at Caesarea Philippi an underground stream surfaced and can still be seen today. There were traditions that this was one of the gates to the underworld and the river Styx. Both the saying of Peter and the saying of Jesus take on especial relevance and poignancy if they were given in the locale of all these shrines to other sons of the gods and next to the river though to go into the underworld, and it seems to me that the other parallels are frankly more remote.[77]

He also states, "The problem with this conclusion is that the term 'temple' does not come up here,"[78] but this reasoning contradicts the majority of intertextual theories. The possibility of an allusion being more overt does not discredit its existence. To say so is to rule out the very category of allusion. The connection between πύλαι ᾅδου and the entrance to the cave of Pan has been noticed by others.[79] On the one hand, it is uncertain if Matthew's readers (probably in Antioch) would have known this tradition of the grotto of the Greek god Pan and the elaborate temple to Caesar.[80] But on the other hand, the two references are not exclusive since allusions often converge multiple images or backgrounds at once. Instead, Witherington's explanation fits nicely with the approach advocated here – Jesus' temple outdoes the pagan ones.

---

77   Witherington, *Matthew*, 318.
78   Witherington, *Matthew*, 318. See also his *What Have They Done with Jesus: Beyond Strange Theories and Bad History-Why We Can Trust the Bible* (New York: Harper Collins, 2006), 63.
79   E.g. Mary K. Milne and Mark Allan Powell, "Caesarea Philippi," *The HarperCollins Bible Dictionary*: Revised and Updated, ed. Mark Allan Powell, (New York: HarperCollins, 2011), 113; Michael S. Heiser, *The Unseen Realm: Recovering the Supernatural Worldview of the Bible* (Bellingham, WA: Lexham, 2015), 113–15; Elaine A. Phillips, "Peter's Declaration at Caesarea Philippi" in *Lexham Geographic Commentary on the Gospels*, ed. Barry J. Beitzel (Bellingham, WA: Lexham, 2017), 286–96.
80   John Francis Wilson, *Caesarea Philippi: In Search for the Lost City of Pan* (London: I. B. Taurus, 2004), 206 n61.

Thus, the presence of the temple motif elsewhere in Matthew, the cohesion which comes from connecting the stone to the cosmic stone of Rabbinic Judaism, the allusion to Isa 28:16, the messiah as temple builder motif, and the allusion to the pagan shrine of Pan, when taken together, strongly suggest the edifice which Jesus builds in Matt 16:18 is a figurative temple.

4.3.2 Matt 16:18 Portrays the Disciples as the Eschatological Temple Foundation

Since we should connect the πέτρα of Matt 16:18 to the messianic temple foundation, who (or what) is this rock? Jesus' saying clearly plays on the name Πέτρος. The most common understanding of this word play is that Peter is the rock on which Jesus will build, though there are variations on this approach, such as Peter being the rock in his confession,[81] Peter being a representative of the band of apostles,[82] and Peter being a representative of all believers.[83] These nuances are outside of our purview, though I see Peter being a representative of the apostles as the most likely option. The interpretation that πέτρα is Πετρός is likely since the text considers him immediately before and after the logion in question and it would be unlikely for the referent to change without indication.[84] Moreover, the connective καί most naturally continues or expands the identification given before, instead of contrasting it (i.e. "*You* are Peter, *but* [καί]*on this Rock* I will build"?). We will also see support for this view from the messianic import of 16:19.

To be sure, identifying Peter as the rock has received pushback. Even a moderate survey and brief interaction with all major viewpoints would require a monograph on its own, but one loud voice of protest can be considered.[85]

---

81 Nolland, *Gospel of Matthew*, 669.
82 David Turner, "*Primus inter pares?* Peter in the Gospel of Matthew" in *New Testament Essays in Honor of Homer A. Kent Jr.*, ed. G. T. Meadors (Winona Lake, IN: BMH, 1991), 179–201; B. Viviano, "The Gospel according to Matthew" in *The New Jerome Biblical Commentary*, ed. R. Brown et al. (Englewood Cliffs, NJ: Prentice Hall, 1990), 660.
83 E.g. John Calvin, *Commentary on a Harmony of the Evangelists Matthew, Mark, and Luke*, transl. William Pringle (Bellingham, WA: Logos Bible Software, 2010), 2:291.
84 This is not meant to imply that only Peter fits in this role. 18:18 suggests Matthew sees the other disciples fitting this role as well. If the argument is correct and the messianic foundation stone is flexible enough to include Jesus and Peter, surely there is room for it to be stretched even further to include others.
85 Another proposal is that Jesus is referring to himself (R. C. H. Lenski, *The Interpretation of St. Matthew's Gospel* (Minneapolis: Augsburg, 1961), 625–27; John F. Walvoord and Charles H. Dyer, *Matthew* (Chicago: Moody, 2013), 222; Max Wilcox, "Peter and the Rock: A Fresh Look at Matthew XVI. 17–19" *NTS* 22 (1975): 73–88), though this is a minority opinion. Much of what is said in response to Caragounis applies to this viewpoint as well. Robert Gundry, *Peter: False Apostle and Apostate according to Matthew*, 20–21 presents a

Caragounis' *Peter and the Rock* argues at length that the rock in Matt 16:18 is not Peter but Peter's confession.[86] Space only allows for a response to his three most salient points. First, Caragounis mounts an argument that the demonstrative pronoun directs attention away from Peter. Furthermore, Caragounis argues concerning πέτρα and Πέτρος, that though some usage (particularly earlier Greek literature) suggests differentiation, examples demonstrate the two can be used interchangeably.[87] Thus, the fact that Jesus does not use Πετρός in both locations demonstrates he has someone/something besides Peter in mind.[88] In response, the clear references to Peter before and after must also be factored in. That Jesus inserts an image of constructing a temple answers the objections about the use of the demonstrative pronoun and the nature of a word play. In 16:18b, Jesus paints a picture of a builder constructing an edifice on a foundation of rock. Πέτρος, in this text, is an actual person. Πέτρα indicates a foundation stone, which symbolically represents Peter. In other words, by saying "this rock" Jesus does depart from the second person and pointing to something – the figurative image of a foundation stone. The sense is the

unique argument against Peter being the rock, but it has not gained much acceptance. He argues that 16:18 alludes to 7:24–27, where the foundation is Jesus' words. He claims that this excludes temple imagery, but some (e.g. N. T. Wright, *Jesus and the Victory*, 292) have seen it in 7:24–27 too, so that might only increase volume of the allusion. But even if the allusion to 7:24–27 is granted, this does not require the referent to be the same. We have already seen similarities between 16:18 and 21:42, which create a louder echo than the one to 7:24–27. But in 21:42 the referent is Jesus. Gundry does not account for the flexibility of the imagery. After all, Peter and Jesus' words are not entirely exclusive – one only has to imagine Peter communicating Jesus' words.

86 Chrys C. Caragounis, *Peter and the Rock* (BZNW; Berlin: de Gruyter, 1990). Caragounis is selected because he is the most thorough. Ancient writers who see the rock as Peter's confession or his faith include John Chrysostom, Origen, Eusebius, Ambrose, Theodore of Mopsuestia, and Luther (Wilkins, *Matthew*, 563). Modern examples include Allen C. Willoughby, *A Critical and Exegetical Commentary on the Gospel According to St. Matthew*, 3rd ed. (ICC; Edinburgh: T&T Clark, 1912), 176; Alan McNeile, *The Gospel According to St. Matthew* (London: Macmillan, 1915), 241; W. Mundle, "Πέτρα," in *NIDNTT*, 3:384–85; A. B. Bruce, "Synoptic Gospels" in *Expositor's Greek Testament* (Grand Rapids: Eerdmans, 1976), 1:224; Randolph V. G. Tasker, *The Gospel According to St. Matthew: an Introduction and Commentary* (Grand Rapids: Eerdmans, 1961), 162).

87 "So far it would seem that the difference in meaning between πέτρα (= 'rock', 'cliff') and πέτρος (= 'stone') is preserved intact. But there are other passages where πέτρα seems to be used as 'stone' and πέτρος as 'cliff' or 'rock.'" (Caragounis, *Peter and the Rock*, 10.)

88 "That Matthew chose to use Πέτρος and πέτρα, two different words, whose very collocation marks a conscious juxtaposition, indicates clearly his intention to contradistinguish the two terms" (Caragounis, *Peter and the Rock*, 90). For Caragounis' argument to work here, it would have to be demonstrated that, not only were the two terms occasionally used interchangeably, but that this was extremely common. However, as he notes, there are still times when πέτρα and πέτρος refer to bedrock and a stone respectively.

foundation stone but the referent is Peter. To illustrate with another temple text, John 2:19 records Jesus saying Λύσατε τὸν ναὸν τοῦτον. Like Matt 16:18, we again have οὗτος. However, the third person, "otherness" of the pronoun points away to a metaphorical temple. The sense of ναὸν τοῦτον is third person – the temple; the referent, in this example, is first person – Jesus. Similarly, the use of οὗτος does not require the symbolic referent to be outside of the conversation. Moreover, to insist that Peter can only be in view if he is addressed by name or second person pronouns demands too much from metaphorical speech.[89] To insist, as Caragounis does, that Peter as the referent would require saying Σὺ εἶ Πέτρος, καὶ ἐπὶ σὲ οἰκοδομήσω μου τὴν ἐκκλησίαν[90] ignores the use of metaphorical speech.[91]

Second, Caragounis also argues that focusing on Peter's role means we have misunderstood the overall purpose of the pericope – it means confusing the central idea of Peter's confession of Jesus with Jesus' confession of Peter.[92] However, though he is undoubtedly correct that the main idea of the pericope is Jesus' identity as the messiah, this does not mean that every line of the text bears directly on this subject. While Jesus is the focus, it is not "sheer muddle"[93] for the subject matter to shift momentarily to consider the importance of Peter as an implication of his accurate confession. Thus, Caragounis' observations that Peter having the keys of the kingdom does not require him to be the stone are beside the point. Instead, the significance is that v 19 demonstrates the

---

[89] Turner, *Matthew*, 406. One can also recall Jesus' self-reference in the third person (e.g. Matt 16:27, 28) to see that the use of the third person does not imply a third-party is in view.

[90] Caragounis, *Peter and the Rock*, 89.

[91] Similarly, objections are given that had Jesus meant Jesus, he would have clarified as much. Lenski writes "If by 'this rock' Jesus had Peter himself in mind, he could easily have said ἐπὶ σοῦ, 'on thee' will I build my church; or, 'on thee, Peter,' adding his name" (Lenski, *Interpretation of St. Matthew's Gospel*, 625). One can always wish that Jesus would have clarified the exact nature of the imagery, but this cuts both ways. One could easily argue that had Jesus meant himself, he would have said ἐπὶ μου, 'on me' will I build my church." Similarly, Quarles argues "If attention were being shifted from Simon as the rock to another rock, one would have expected the remote demonstrative pronoun (ἐκείνη)" (Charles L. Quarles, *Matthew* (EGGNT; Nashville: B&H Publishing, 2017), 188). Thus, reasoning "had Jesus meant the other position, he would have said …" can be used by either side of the argument. Instead, interpreters must base their case on what stands written.

[92] This "not only destroys the progression of thought in the pericope and impairs its structure, it also deprives the text of its cohesion and coherence. Then, having (according to the theory) moved the focus from Jesus to Peter, to conclude the pericope by re-moving the focus back to Jesus and indicating that his Messiahship was at the heart of the story, is nothing else but sheer muddle" (Caragounis, *Peter and the Rock*, 95).

[93] Caragounis, *Peter and the Rock*, 95.

subject matter has shifted to Peter. Moreover, a change of topic is not the only explanation of the asyndeton in v 19[94] (if it is the original).[95]

Third, Caragounis argues that Matthew, the NT, and the early church saw Jesus as the foundation stone, not Peter.[96] This is perhaps the weakest part of Caragounis' argument, which is especially unfortunate since it seems to be the driving force behind his project. He writes that Paul's later statements "are difficult to reconcile with any view that Paul accepted Peter as the foundation of the Church. In fact, Paul declares unequivocally that there is only one foundation, and that is Christ (1 Cor 3:11)."[97] He then argues the same point regarding 1 Peter. But this argument collapses if Peter represents the twelve, a point which Caragounis grants elsewhere.[98] That this perspective is correct is suggested by the use of the plural pronoun in the question Ὑμεῖς δὲ τίνα με λέγετε εἶναι (16:15). Certainly examples of the apostles performing a critical role in the church abound. Eph 2:20 and Rev 21:14 specifically described them as part of the foundation. The reference to James, Cephas, and John as στῦλοι in Gal 2:9 fits in well here. Wenham plausible explores reasons for thinking Paul has a Matt 16:18 tradition in mind there.[99] Moreover, much of the current research has demonstrated a high view of the disciples in Matthew as replacement leaders of God's people with a significant eschatological function. But even outside of allusions, Matthew (e.g. 19:28) clearly elevates the twelve to some kind of special status. Furthermore, the observation that elsewhere Jesus is called the foundation would not prohibit Peter and/or the twelve being the foundation here,[100] as this requires too much precision and consistency from

---

94 "Asyndeton is a vivid stylistic feature that occurs often for emphasis, solemnity, or rhetorical value (staccato effect), or when there is an abrupt change in topic" (Daniel B. Wallace, *Greek Grammar beyond the Basics: An Exegetical Syntax of the New Testament* (Grand Rapids, MI: Zondervan, 1996), 658). Given the significant reference to the "keys of the kingdom," "solemnity" is probably the correct choice.

95 Several mss have either καί or δέ, including B², C, K, W, Γ, Δ, and D.

96 "Where is the evidence during the first century that the Christian Church thought of Peter as the rock of the universal Church? The answer is simply that there is no such evidence" (Caragounis, *Peter and the Rock*, 102).

97 Caragounis, *Peter and the Rock*, 102.

98 Caragounis, *Peter and the Rock*, 108.

99 David Wenham, *Paul: Follower of Jesus or Founder of Christianity?* (Grand Rapids: Eerdmans, 1995), 200–05. Caragounis, *Peter and the Rock*, 101 states that this reference is sarcastic, given Paul's opposition to Peter in chapter 2. However, Paul treats this group favorably at this point, as evidenced in 2:10.

100 In fact, the incongruency of Jesus being the expected Rock and the link here with Peter has cast doubt by some on its historicity. Seitz claims "In view of the long persisting primitive tradition in which Christ himself is claimed as the church's one foundation, the Matthean interpolation in its present form proves to be nothing more than an exceedingly insecure,

metaphorical speech.[101] In fact, if other uses like 1 Cor 3:10 determine the symbolism of Matt 16:18, this would prove too much since it would rule out his own suggestion that the rock is a confession, not Christ himself. In light of the ease of the reading, as well as the weakness of arguments against the identification, and the case for identifying Πέτρος as the πέτρα seems "rock solid."

4.3.3 The Image of the Eschatological Temple Foundation Was Seen as Messianic

If this is the case, what is the significance of the foundation stone? Though some Jewish people saw the temple *builder* as the messiah, the imagery becomes complicated in that first century Judaism, particularly the kind represented by Matthew and his audience, would have seen the temple *foundation* as a messianic image as well. Many references to a rock in the First Testament are metaphors for YHWH himself. This is so frequent that the LXX often translates צור with θεός (e.g. Deut 32:4, Pss 18:31, 62:2). This may explain why the messiah could so easily be linked with stone and rock imagery.[102] For example, Justin's *Dialogue with Trypho* (36) has Trypho the Jew simply conceding that "Christ is called a Stone." The messianic connotations only increase when the picture goes from just a stone to specifically the temple foundation. This can be seen in other NT references (e.g. 1 Cor. 3:10, Eph 2:20), but we have already discussed the most important text for our research – Matt 21:42. This text clearly depicts Jeus' messianic vocation as the once-rejected-now-chosen stone (most likely cornerstone) of an eschatological temple. However, one more text warrants consideration at this point since it also clearly demonstrates the messianic connotations associated with a foundation stone – Isa 28:16. We saw earlier that Matt 16:18 alludes to this prophetic text. If so, the discussion below is exceptionally relevant. But even if one views this allusion as unlikely, we should still consider this text because we have already seen that the image behind

---

late fabrication, to build upon which would be to build on sand. In contrast to this stands the unshakable consensus of testimony to the more ancient tradition concerning the rock on which the church and its faith was founded, and that rock was Christ" (Oscar J. F. Seitz, "Upon This Rock: A Critical Re-Examination of Matt 16:17–19" *JBL* 69.4 (Dec 1950): 340. Similarly, Wilcox, "Peter and the Rock," 73–88 argues that for these reasons the original saying must have had Jesus as the rock, but Matthew's redaction is a play on words to be connected with σκάνδαλον εἶ ἐμοῦ (16:23).

101 E.g., "the lion" is both Jesus (Rev 5:5) and Satan (1 Pet 5:8)!
102 Jeremias, "Λίθος," 4:273. This connection only expanded in later Christian literature. Snodgrass, "The Christological Stone," 5 explains, "The post-apostolic Church found the OT to be an abundant quarry from which nearly every rock or stone, from the one Jacob used as a pillow (Gen. 28:11f.) to that which killed Goliath (1 Sm. 17:49), could be understood of Jesus."

Matt 16:18 is that of eschatological temple construction and Isa 28:16, along with its reception history, demonstrates the messianic import of this portrayal.

Originally, Isa 28:16 does not have much to commend a messianic reading, as it is in the context of the folly of Jerusalem's leaders relying on a treaty with Egypt. With many parallels to Isa 8, it would not be surprising for readers to connect the stone here with the stone there, specified as יְהוָה צְבָאוֹת (v 13). The MT has vocalized יסד with the perfect יִסַּד, perhaps parallel to Isa 14:32.[103] Thus, a reference to the past establishment of Zion's temple may have originally been in view. But many English translations agree with the LXX (ἐμβαλῶ) and vocalize יסד as a participle, יֹסֵד ("I am laying") which would allow for a future (and thus eschatological) reference. The messianic use of Isa 28:16 may be seen as early as the LXX. Whereas the MT has הַמַּאֲמִין לֹא יָחִישׁ, "the one who believes will not make haste," the LXX has ὁ πιστεύων ἐπ' αὐτῷ οὐ μὴ καταισχυνθῇ, "the one who believes in him will not be ashamed." The inclusion of ἐπ' αὐτῷ makes the object of faith the previous temple stone. Though the LXX may have more of an interest in the messiah here, the additional prepositional phrase does not contribute much. The Targum has באלי and contains the same variant, though 1QIsa[a] follows the MT. But later messianic uses follow the LXX here. Dekker rightly concludes "While a definitive decision in the matter remains difficult to achieve, it is nevertheless possible that the Septuagint translation already presupposed a Messianic interpretation of the stone referred to in 28:16. Whatever the truth may be, the Septuagint's addition of ἐπ' αὐτῷ has evidently facilitated a Messianic interpretation of the said biblical text."[104]

This also influenced the treatment of 8:14, in which the LXX adds ἐὰν ἐπ' αὐτῷ πεποιθὼς ᾖς,[105] which demonstrates how easily the two texts were linked. It has been suggested that 1QS 8:4ff also demonstrates an early link between the two.[106] In fact, Rom 9:33 and 1 Pet 2:6–7 also connect these texts and understand both passages as messianic. The former conflates the two texts ('Ἰδοὺ τίθημι ἐν Σιὼν λίθον προσκόμματος καὶ πέτραν σκανδάλου, καὶ ὁ πιστεύων ἐπ' αὐτῷ οὐ καταισχυνθήσεται)[107] and the latter connects them with a line of its own

---

103 Tull, *Isaiah*, 428.
104 Jaap Dekker, *Zion's Rock-Solid Foundations: An Exegetical Study of the Zion Text in Isa 28:16* (OtSt; Leiden: Brill, 2007), 13.
105 Silva, *NIDNTTE*, 3:120.
106 Steve Moyise, "Isaiah in 1 Peter" in *Isaiah in the New Testament: The New Testament and the Scriptures of Israel*, ed. M. J. J. Menken and Steve Moyise (LNTS; London: T&T Clark, 2005), 179.
107 J. Ross Wagner, "Isaiah in Romans and Galatians" in *Isaiah in the New Testament: The New Testament and the Scriptures of Israel*, ed. M. J. J. Menken and Steve Moyise (LNTS; London: T&T Clark, 2005), 122–23 suggests "The identity of the 'stone' in Romans is open to a number of readings – God, Christ, the law – and the polyvalence of this metaphor

text and Ps 118:22 ('Ἰδοὺ τίθημι ἐν Σιὼν λίθον ἀκρογωνιαῖον ἐκλεκτὸν ἔντιμον, καὶ ὁ πιστεύων ἐπ' αὐτῷ οὐ μὴ καταισχυνθῇ. ὑμῖν οὖν ἡ τιμὴ τοῖς πιστεύουσιν, ἀπιστοῦσιν δὲ λίθος ὃν ἀπεδοκίμασαν οἱ οἰκοδομοῦντες, οὗτος ἐγενήθη εἰς κεφαλὴν γωνίας καὶ λίθος προσκόμματος καὶ πέτρα σκανδάλου).

Later Jewish and Christian texts also employ a messianic interpretation of Isa 28:16. The Targum gives a messianic interpretation of Isa 28:16, "Therefore, thus says the Lord God, 'Behold, I appoint in Zion a king, a strong, mighty king' (מֶלֶךְ תַּקִּיף גִּבָּר), and the one who believes will conquer."[108] The text was often used messianically by early Christians. For example, *Epist. Barn.* 6:2–4 cites the LXX of Isa 28:16 exactly, though the remainder of the verse has been reworded to have more of a soteriological twist. *Epist. Barn.* 6:2–4 connects this Isa 28:16 with other popular messianic texts – Isa 50:7 (LXX ἀλλὰ ἔθηκα τὸ πρόσωπόν μου ὡς στερεὰν πέτραν καὶ ἔγνων ὅτι οὐ μὴ αἰσχυνθῶ),[109] 8:14, and Ps 118:22–23. Given the connections between Isa 28:16, 8:14 and Ps 118:22–23 that we have already seen, the take in *Epist. Barn.* is hardly surprising. Ambrose of Milan, *On the Duties of the Clergy* 1.29.142, and Iranaeus, *Against Heresies* 3.21.7 further demonstrate a messianic understanding of the verse.

Dekker examines early Christian occurrences of Isa 28:16 and concludes,

> It is hardly surprising against such a background that the Zion text of 28:16 was likewise applied to Christ in the Alexandrian tradition as a more or less obvious given. Cyril of Alexandria's commentary on the book of Isaiah represents a clear witness in this respect (5th century). Even the Antiochian tradition, with its strong preference for a literal-historical interpretation, would appear to have commonly included the Messianic interpretation of the stone referred to in 28:16. Theodoret of Cyrus' comment on Isa 28:16 is no less Messianic in this regard than that of his Alexandrian colleague Cyril (5th century).[110]

Thus, the foundation stone of Isa 28:16 was widely conceived as messianic, and there is no reason to doubt this perception would not have been shared by Matthew and his readers. If the allusion to Isa 28:16 in Matt 16:18 is certain, then it evokes messianic stone imagery. The backdrop of temple imagery only strengthens the case since not only was the temple stone of Isa 28:16

---

may be intention. Indeed, all three referents are brought together by Paul in Rom. 10:2–3." This is possible, but the prevalence of the rock being Christ in the NT (e.g. 1 Cor 10:4) suggests that at the least, the messianic interpretation is predominant.

108   Translation mine.
109   Isa 50:8–9 has just been quoted in *Epis. Barn.* 6:1–2.
110   Dekker, *Zion's Rock-Solid Foundations*, 48.

understood messianically, but the motif in general was as well. Moreover, the previous discussion of Matt 21:42 demonstrates the way that Jesus occupies the space of eschatological temple foundation. Matthew and his readers would have understood both the eschatological temple foundation and its builder as messianic images. Yet Matthew uses both images in Matt 16 and switches these roles in ch 21. We can conclude then that Matt 16:18 evokes the picture of temple construction with the result that the foundation expresses messianic expectations, yet Jesus puts Peter (and probably, by extension the rest of the apostles) in this position.

4.4 Matt 7:24–27 Portrays the Disciples as Messianic Temple Builders

So far we have examined Matt 21:42–43 and 16:18 to see how messianic categories regarding eschatological temple construction imagery (builder and foundation, respectively) are used of the disciples. For both instances, the flow of argumentation came in three stages: first to establish that the text evokes images of eschatological temple construction, then to situate the disciples' role in this scene, and finally to demonstrate that this role in eschatological temple construction imagery was traditionally viewed as messianic. But Matt 21:42–43 and 16:18 are not the only places in Matthew which describe the building of a structure on a foundation. The Parable of the Two Builders in 7:24–27 famously concludes the Sermon on the Mount as the final of three "two-ways" images (narrow/wide gate in 7:13–14; good/bad tree in 7:15–16; wise/foolish builder in 7:24–27). Might this parable be classified with the previous two passages discussed in this chapter in portraying the disciples in messianic terms via eschatological temple construction imagery?

The case is not as clear as the other two, but still the possibility is worth exploring. An argument can be constructed similarly to the other cases, specifically Matt 21:42–43 since both rely on the builder figure. The third step has already been established – we have already seen that the eschatological temple builder is a messianic concept in 4.1.3. The second step comes quite easily as there only two explicit mappings in the metaphor:

Πᾶς οὖν ὅστις ἀκούει μου τοὺς λόγους τούτους καὶ ποιεῖ αὐτούς,	ὁμοιωθήσεται[111]	ἀνδρὶ φρονίμῳ, ὅστις ᾠκοδόμησεν αὐτοῦ τὴν οἰκίαν ἐπὶ τὴν πέτραν (v 24).
πᾶς ὁ ἀκούων μου τοὺς λόγους τούτους καὶ μὴ ποιῶν αὐτοὺς	ὁμοιωθήσεται	ἀνδρὶ μωρῷ, ὅστις ᾠκοδόμησεν αὐτοῦ τὴν οἰκίαν ἐπὶ τὴν ἄμμον (v 26).

---

111   The variant ὁμοιώσω αὐτόν does not affect the argument.

Thus, Jesus' disciples are clearly portrayed as those building a "house." However, this scenario is not quite the same as the other passages examined in this chapter or previous ones. So far we have only considered places where the Twelve / the disciples / the apostles are in view. The extent to which these are transferrable figures and Matthew expects all future disciples (cf. 28:18–20) to apply those teachings to themselves is a matter of debate.[112] But 7:24–27 clearly casts a wide net with its two-fold repetition of πᾶς in vv 24 and 26. However, this too must be seen in light of Matthew's description of the setting in 5:1 as the "sermon" is directed to the disciples.[113] The potentially larger referent for the builders is significant for the overall research of this project, since, if the argument of this section is successful, it means the company of those who are in the disciple band and share in Jesus' fulfillment of the messianic vocation predicted in the First Testament stretches wider than the apostles and potentially includes all followers of Jesus' teaching. But though this observation means 7:24–27 might be in a different category than the other case studies examined here, the question must still be raised if the argumentation used earlier also works here.

While the second two links in the chain of argumentation are solid, the first is by far the weakest link and thus requires the most attention. Does the Parable of the Two Builders evoke eschatological temple construction imagery? If this domino falls, so do the other two and we have another instance of Jesus mapping a messianic image to the disciples. Several commentators have seen a connection to the temple here. N. T. Wright comments,

> Like the good revolutionary that he is, Jesus finishes by offering a critique of alternative movements and a dire warning that his way of being Israel is the only way by which his followers may avoid ultimate disaster (7:24–7), a disaster which will be not merely personal, but also national. The house built on the rock, in first-century Jewish terms, is a clear allusion to the Temple. Unless Israel follows the way that Jesus is leading, the greatest national institution of all is in mortal danger.[114]

Kenneth Bailey understands the Parable of the Two Builders as portraying Jesus as the temple's cosmic stone and wonders,

---

112 See discussion in Wilkins, *Discipleship in the Ancient World*, 246; Donaldson, "Guiding Readers," 30–49.
113 See 5.4.1.2 for elaboration of the intended audience of the Sermon on the Mount.
114 Wright, *Jesus and the Victory of God*, 292.

Was Jesus, like Isaiah, 'discerning the time' politically and looking forward to the coming inevitable clash with Rome and expressing his convictions, like Isaiah, as to who would prove the stronger?... It is easy to see how 'There is a storm coming and the temple will fall when it strikes' could be garbled into 'he has threatened to destroy the temple.'[115]

Michael Knowles similarly sees a temple reference in the parable.

In the context of Jesus' ministry, the Parable of the Two Builders conveys a challenge to 'build a house' on a foundation equivalent to that on which God's own house is set ... Even more to the point, since Matthew and Luke probably wrote in the immediate aftermath of the fall of Jerusalem and the destruction of its temple – the city and "house" of God – the doubles both could attest to the fact, to quote Luke, that "the ruin of *that* house was great."[116]

Though the above writers represent those who see this allusion, most commentators do not.[117] A reference to the temple would be admittedly opaque, especially since the parable describes αὐτοῦ τὴν οἰκίαν. The antecedent of αὐτοῦ being the builder obscures a temple reference (one would expect a reference to "God's house" or even just "the house"). Furthermore, the feminine οἰκία, instead of the masculine οἶκος would be strange too since the former is never used in the LXX to refer to the temple – though it occurs around 260 times[118] – nor does the NT use the feminine for the temple, though it occurs 93 times in our corpus. However, there are indications that the temple is in view.

4.4.1   *The Prevalence of Temple Imagery*

If the Sermon on the Mount regularly points to the temple, it is more likely that the reference to a house at the conclusion would continue this motif. Though reference is made to the literal temple cult, particularly going to the altar (5:23–24), several more, subtle, temple references occur in various ways in

---

115 Kenneth E. Bailey, "The Parable of the Two Builders" in *Literary Structure and Rhetorical Strategies in the Hebrew Bible*, ed. L. J. de Regt, J. de Waard, and R. P. Fokkelman (Assen, The Netherlands: Van Gorcum, 1996), 19.

116 Michael Knowles, "'Everyone Who Hears These Words of Mine': Parables on Discipleship" in *The Challenge of Jesus' Parables*, ed. Richard N. Longenecker (Grand Rapids: Eerdmans, 1990), 290, emphasis original.

117 E.g. it is specifically denied in Davies and Allison, *Matthew*, 1:721 and Klyne R. Snodgrass, *Stories with Intent: A Comprehensive Guide to the Parables of Jesus* (Grand Rapids: Eerdmans, 2008), 335.

118 Silva, *NIDNTTE*, 3:471. Silva also explores frequent occurrence of the masculine οἶκος for the temple in the LXX.

the Sermon on the Mount. There are references to Jerusalem (5:35, cf. Ps 48:2) and the New Jerusalem (5:14),[119] which would indirectly call to mind the temple since that is the main attraction of the city, so much so that Jerusalem can function as metonymy for the temple.[120] The prayer in 6:9–10 may allude to David's prayer of dedication of the temple in 1 Chron 29:10–12, as indicated not only by the similar notions of "our Father" and his will and rule extending over heaven and earth, but also since later scribes inserted elements of 1 Chron 29:11–12 as a doxology (Matt 6:13).[121] Welch summarizes his monograph with a chart entitled "Temple Themes and Temple-Related Texts in the Sermon on the Mount" that spans four pages and lists 119 parallels.[122] Many will rightly find much of these a stretch, but several are at least plausible and have been noticed by commentators, such as the τῷ κρυπτῷ (6:6) being the "chamber of secrets" in Herod's temple.[123] However, since these echoes are quieter (or at least about as loud) as the one to the temple in 7:24–27, exploring these allusions will not help the argument here much. If the reasons discussed below do not convince one to see a temple reference in 7:24–27, many of the other temple references will probably not be persuasive either. Still, acknowledging the potential temple motif

---

119   This connection was initially made in Joachim Jeremias, *Jesus' Promise to the Nations* (London: SCM, 1958), 66–67 and adopted in Gerhard von Rad, "Die Stadt auf dem Berge," *EvT* (1948–49): 439–47 and then more fully explored in Ken Campbell, "The New Jerusalem in Matt 5.14" *SJT* 31.4 (1978): 335–63. Other adherents include Hans Dieter Betz, *The Sermon on the Mount: A Commentary on the Sermon on the Mount, including the Sermon on the Plain* (Minneapolis: Fortress Press, 1995), 161–62; Crispin H. T. Fletcher-Louis, "The Destruction of the Temple and the Relativization of the Old Covenant: Mark 13: 31 & Matthew 5: 18" in *Eschatology in Bible and Theology: Evangelical Essays at the Dawn of a New Millennium*, ed. K. E. Brower and M. W. Elliott (Downers Grove, IL: InterVarsity, 1997), 145–70; David Garland, *Reading Matthew: A Literary and Theological Commentary on the First Gospel* (Macon, GA: Smyth & Helwys, 2001), 60; Melvin Tinker, "The Servant Solution: The Co-Ordination of Evangelism and Social Action," *Them* 32.2 (2006): 6–32. The main argument against seeing οὐ δύναται πόλις κρυβῆναι ἐπάνω ὄρους κειμένη as a reference to eschatological Jerusalem (e.g. Isa 60) is πόλις being anarthrous (e.g. France, *Gospel of Matthew*, 176). The presence of the article would make the reference more likely, but the absence of the article does not necessarily communicate indefiniteness (see Wallace, *Greek Grammar*, 243).

120   Jon D. Levenson, *Creation and the Persistence of Evil: The Jewish Drama of Divine Omnipotence* (San Francisco: Harper & Row, 1988), 89–90; Beale, *The Temple and the Church's Mission*, 25.

121   Metzger, *A Textual Commentary*, 14.

122   John W. Welch, *The Sermon on the Mount in Light of the Temple* (Burlington, VT: Ashgate, 2009), 184–87.

123   Welch, *The Sermon*, 122; Joachim Jeremias, *Jerusalem in the Time of Jesus: An Investigation into Economic and Social Conditions During the New Testament Period* (Philadelphia: Fortress, 1969), 133; Geza Vermes, *Jesus the Jew: A Historian's Reading of the Gospels* (Philadelphia: Fortress, 1973), 78; Luz, *Matthew 1–7*, 300–01; Morris, *Gospel according to Matthew*, 138; France, *The Gospel of Matthew*, 236; cf. m. Šeqal 5.6.

more or less running throughout the Sermon on the Mount should alert us to the possibility of seeing the temple reference in its conclusion.

4.4.2 The Possible Allusion to Isa 28 Would Support This Building Being the Temple

The collocation of a rock foundation and the attack of natural disasters has suggested to some a connection to Isa 28:15–18.[124] The proposed allusion satisfies Hays' major criteria.[125] We have already seen the likelihood that this text is evoked in Matthew (16:18), so there is clearly availability, recurrence, and historical plausibility (in fact, the occurrence of this allusion in Matt 16:18 means this this section and the following mutually confirm one another). There is also sufficient volume of similarities: there is a connection with an unreliable refuge in a storm (Isa 28:15, 17, 18)[126] in contrast to a secure one with an emphasis on its foundation (v 16). There is also thematic coherence, as both passages are in the context of unworthy leaders in Israel (Isa 28:7. Matt 7:15–20). This places emphasis on Jesus' unique authority (μου τοὺς λόγους τούτους in v 24). The point thus goes beyond something like that in 1 Enoch 94:6–7, where a house and its foundation are built in sin but will be overthrown. Instead, the thrust is that one must obey Jesus' own ethical system as indicated in the Sermon on the Mount – all other systems, though they might claim to be virtuous, will fail (cf. Matt 7:22 where those who exorcise demons are not allowed entrance into the kingdom).

Another possible intertextual background is Ezek 13:10–12, which depicts builders (οἰκοδομεῖ in 13:10, cf. ᾠκοδόμησεν in Matt 7:24, 26) who plaster a wall instead of fixing its faults to illustrate the actions of false prophets (Ezek 13:2). In Ezekiel 13, a storm comes with three elements[127] and the passage emphasizes its fall by repeating πίπτω four times (Ezek 13:10, 11 – twice, 14). The result is that the foundations (θεμέλια) are exposed (13:14). This is clearly foolish behavior on the part of the builders, though the text does not specifically bring that out like Matt 7:24–27. However, the builders' error is lack of proper attention to problems in the wall, as opposed to choosing an unsuitable foundation

---

124　Turner, *Matthew*, 222; France, *Gospel of Matthew*, 297; Margaret Baker, "Isaiah" in *Eerdman's Commentary on the Bible*, ed. James D. Dunn and John Williams Rogerson, 517; Evans, *Matthew*, 181; Jeremias, *Parables*, 194.

125　However, I am not aware of any early references in the early history of interpretation that connect Matt 7:24–27 with Isa 28:15–18.

126　The storm in v 17 is more vivid in the MT (וְיָעָה בָרָד מַחְסֵה כָזָב וְסֵתֶר מַיִם יִשְׁטֹפוּ) than the LXX (καὶ οἱ πεποιθότες μάτην ψεύδει· ὅτι οὐ μὴ παρέλθῃ ὑμᾶς καταιγίς), though neither is as close is the account in Ezek 13.

127　ἔσται ὑετὸς κατακλύζων, καὶ δώσω λίθους πετροβόλους εἰς τοὺς ἐνδέσμους αὐτῶν, καὶ πεσοῦνται, καὶ πνεῦμα ἐξαῖρον in Ezek 13:11; cf. Matt 7:25, 27 καὶ κατέβη ἡ βροχὴ καὶ ἦλθον οἱ ποταμοὶ καὶ ἔπνευσαν οἱ ἄνεμοι καὶ προσέπεσαν τῇ οἰκίᾳ ἐκείνῃ.

(the foundation being exposed communicates that the building has completely collapsed, not that there was a problem with it). The reference to Isa 28:15–18 is more likely since it contrasts an unreliable building with a trustworthy one and because it places central importance on the foundation. Furthermore, Ezek 13 does not come close to the kind of popular familiarity that Isa 28 enjoyed in the first century. However, if Ezek 13 is a more likely reference (or an additional one), then this would also provide a reason for seeing a reference to the temple since the collapse of Ezekiel's wall is eventually linked with the destruction of Jerusalem in Ezek 13:16.

4.4.3 *The Connection to Matt 16:18 Suggests This Building Is the Temple*

Several commentators see a link between the Two Builders Parable and Matt 16:18,[128] which would strongly suggest we should see the wise man's house as a reference to the temple. Though several commentators have denied the link,[129] Gundry demonstrates this connection at length.[130] He notes that ancient audiences would have listened to long stretches, perhaps even all of Matthew, in single settings and that "it takes less than an hour for an oral reading from the earlier passage to the later one."[131] Moreover, if connections like Matt 16:23 and 4:19[132] and 1:23 and 28:20 are possible, this proposal cannot be dismissed as being too far apart. He also relies on the work of Bigane,[133] that exegetes since Origen connected Matt 7:24–25 to 16:18. Gundry then suggests that not only do both passages have the similarity of a rock foundation for a building, but that the storm of 7:24–27 corresponds to the attacking gates of hades in 16:18.[134]

---

128   E.g. Betz, *Sermon on the Mount*, 563–64; Evans, *Matthew*, 181; Carter, *Matthew and the Margins*, 193; Turner, *Matthew*, 222; France, *Gospel according to Matthew*, 297; Carleston and Evans, *From Synagogue to Ecclesia*, 358; McKelvey, *The New Temple*, 193; Caragounis, *Peter and the Rock*, 107.
129   E.g. Turner, *Matthew*, 406; Snodgrass, *Stories with Intent*, 335; Wilkins, *Concept of a Disciple*, 190; Witherington, *Matthew*, 406.
130   Gundry, *Peter*, 21–23.
131   Gundry, *Peter*, 21.
132   Gundry, *Peter*, 22 points to several textual variants to support an early connection.
133   John E. Bigane III, *Faith, Christ or Peter: Matthew 16:18 in Sixteenth Century Roman Catholic Exegesis* (Washington D.C.: University Press of America, 1981), 81. Similarly, McKelvey, *The New Temple*, 193 argues, "The thought of the text (16:18) resembles that of Matt. 7.24 par., and the fact that a definite connection between Matt. 16:18 and Matt. 7.24 is made in the long recension of Ignatius' epistle to the Philadelphians ('God established his church upon the rock ... against which the floods and winds have beaten but have not been able to overcome it') suggests that πέτρα in Matt. 16.18 stands for the ground upon which the foundation is laid."
134   Gundry's overall purpose in this discussion is to exclude Peter from being the foundation of the church in 16:18, since his thesis is that Matthew presents him as a false disciple. By

The use of temple imagery elsewhere in the Sermon on the Mount and the connections to Isa 28:15–19 and Matt 16:18 favor a temple reference in 7:24–27. Yet, the expression ᾠκοδόμησεν αὐτοῦ τὴν οἰκίαν, with the builder owning the house and the feminine οἰκία, suggest a general house is in view. But though factors point in different directions for this last case study and it is not as clear as the first two, this is a time when the whole is greater than the sum of its parts and the clearer cases of 16:18 and 21:42–43 suggest we should hesitatingly include it with the others.

4.5 Conclusion

In this chapter we have examined three places in Matthew which demonstrate non-messianic mapping. Of course, in two of these (21:42–43 and 16:18), the Matthean Jesus *does* use a messianic hermeneutic of Scripture. But this usage signals two significant observations. First, it reveals how both the image of temple builder and that of temple stone carry messianic connotations. Second, it indicates the presence of an eschatological temple construction context. Both of these observations result in messianic images mapping to the disciples (this places each section of this chapter in our second category, "Messiah → (role) disciples"). It is Matthew's messianic use of the eschatological temple concept which informs us that when these same images are used elsewhere of the disciples, these have messianic freight. According to the gospel of Matthew, the image of an eschatological temple builder carries messianic implications (16:18). But this image is also used of the disciples in 21:42–43, and, perhaps, in 7:24–27. Similarly, the image of an eschatological temple foundation carries messianic implications (21:42–43). But this image is also used of Peter in 16:18.

To summarize, each of the three passages examined in this chapter create a blend in which Jesus maps a messianic image to the disciples. Each passage has its own complications regarding how this blend is constructed. For 21:42–43, the source domain does not specifically map builders into the blend. Yet Matthew's redaction clearly shows that he wants to draw some implication

connecting the two passages, Gundry can observe that the stone of 7:24–25 is not Peter, but Jesus' words, implying that the same would be true of 16:18. However, Jesus only maps the doer/not doers of his words and the wise/foolish builders. Nothing is said to correspond to the foundation. Second, even if Jesus had specifically said his teaching was the rock, a link between the passages does not require that all the symbolism must be consistent. We have already seen in this chapter how flexible Matthew's building language can be. However, though the overall purpose of Gundry's argumentation breaks down, his discussion of the link between 7:24–27 and 16:18 is solid.

from Ps 118:22 for the disciples. Though Matthew is not free to simply add a figure not mentioned in the source text, the builders are constructed in the blend via the governing principle of Pattern Completion – if a group of builders rejects a stone, but it ends up being used in the final product, the implication is that a new group of builders has arrived on the scene. From there, the OT, its understanding in the first century, and most significantly the gospel of Matthew itself show us eschatological temple builders are to be understood messianically.

For 16:18, seeing how the building in view was an eschatological temple formed the largest hurdle (though a minority also has problems with seeing Peter in any role as the πέτρα). Jesus clearly maps the disciples (specifically Peter) into the blend from the target domain. He also maps a builder from the source domain, but the difficulty was in demonstrating that this source domain is not the image of general construction, but that the source is the OT, as understood in the first century, of eschatological temple construction. We saw this not only by considering the significance of the temple motif in Matthew and later Rabbinic parallels to the "cosmic stone," but also by the likely allusion to Isa 28:16 and, most significantly, to the context of Jesus' identity as messiah. Since there was a kind of Judaism which believed the messiah would be an eschatological temple builder, and Jesus' building of a structure centers around him being the messiah, this strongly suggests that structure is the eschatological temple.

Similarly, Matt 7:24–27 also maps followers of Jesus from the target into blend and maps builders from a source. Again, the difficulty lies in knowing if the source domain is only a general building image or if it comes from an eschatological-temple context. The case is far less clear for Matt 7:24–27 than for the other two with evidence pointing in opposite directions. Still, the temple references throughout the Sermon on the Mount, and especially the web of connections created with Isa 28:16 and Matt 16:18, indicate that the source domain is probably from a temple context.

Each of the cases studied here – Matt 21:42–43, 16:18, and 7:24–27 – mutually authenticate one another and demonstrate the Matthean Jesus' use of eschatological construction imagery to categorize the disciples in messianic terms. For each text we have seen that Jesus evokes imagery of eschatological temple construction and that the disciples' role in this scene was traditionally reserved for the messiah. By repeating the motif yet having Jesus and the disciples switch roles, Matthew paints the two in strikingly similar colors.

CHAPTER 5

Matthew's Non-Messianic Use of the Herald in Isa 61:1–3

5.1 Introduction

The previous three case studies have examined occasions of a non-messianic hermeneutic in Matthew by considering figures which have significant messianic potential but are mapped to the disciples. In each, a text/image has varying levels of messianic features itself, but the history of interpretation demonstrates how easily the messiah could be read into the passages. But in each of the case studies we have seen a non-messianic hermeneutic since Matthew maps these potentially messianic images to the disciples.

The case study of this chapter will break from the above pattern in two significant ways. First, after considering the textual features of Isa 61:1–3 and then its history of interpretation, the messianic potential of our source domain will be seen not to be as high as the others studied. Though scholarship has often depicted both of these as clearly messianic, we will see reasons for challenging this description as both the textual features of Isa 61:1–3 and its use in later, relevant Jewish literature can easily go in other directions. But though the passage does not require a messianic interpretation, we will also see that Matthew could have taken it that way. However, we will find that Matthew's allusions to this text in 5:3–4 and 11:5, though not identical, line up with a set of uses which can be labelled "eschatological" but not "messianic."

Second, our consideration of Matthew's use of Isa 61 will also part company from the above case studies in the way it demonstrates a non-messianic hermeneutic. In the above cases, the fulfillment was non-messianic because the images mapped to the disciples, but this is not so clearly the case regarding the use of Isa 61. Instead, we will see that Matthew evokes Isa 61:1–3, and though he could have made much of the herald figure to demonstrate Jesus' messianic identity, he does not make this emphasis because his interests lie elsewhere – the nature of the eschatological blessings themselves. In the previous case studies, we had examined occasions when the Matthean Jesus creates a conceptual blend in which he:

(1) maps a messianic figure from a source domain
and (2) maps the disciples from the target domain to that figure.

However, as noted in the introduction, the other way a non-messianic blending occurs is when the Matthean Jesus maps various elements into the blend, but does not *explicitly* map the messianic figure into the blend. This very well may be the case here as no element of Matt 5:3–4 or 11:5 obviously links Jesus to the herald of Isa 61. However, Blending Theory commends attending to the new imaginative world created through governing principles by the juxtaposition of the Matthean text and the source of the allusion. This will open the door for the possibility that a potentially messianic herald of Isa 61, while not explicitly mapped into the blend, could still be present. If the herald does emerge in the blend, however, we will see reasons for why this figure would map *both* to Jesus *and* the disciples. Thus, as has been true with other case studies, we want to allow room for a variety of mapping schemes and not force Matthew's hermeneutic into a mold. Yet this chapter, though it has significant differences with the others, is in the same category in that it evokes a passage with messianic potential and yet this messianic image does not map exclusively to Jesus.

5.2 Ambiguities in the Original Context

For some, the fact that Jesus alludes to Isa 61 in connection to his ministry demonstrates his identity as the messiah since that text has sufficient messianic indications.[1] However, the messianic features of Isa 61:1–2 are far from certain. The LXX reads

> Πνεῦμα κυρίου ἐπ' ἐμέ, οὗ εἵνεκεν ἔχρισέν με· εὐαγγελίσασθαι πτωχοῖς[2] ἀπέσταλκέν με, ἰάσασθαι τοὺς συντετριμμένους τῇ καρδίᾳ, κηρύξαι αἰχμαλώτοις ἄφεσιν καὶ τυφλοῖς ἀνάβλεψιν, καλέσαι ἐνιαυτὸν κυρίου δεκτὸν καὶ ἡμέραν ἀνταποδόσεως, παρακαλέσαι πάντας τοὺς πενθοῦντας.

The MT reads:

> רוּחַ אֲדֹנָי יְהוִה עָלָי יַעַן מָשַׁח יְהוָה אֹתִי לְבַשֵּׂר עֲנָוִים שְׁלָחַנִי לַחֲבֹשׁ לְנִשְׁבְּרֵי־לֵב לִקְרֹא לִשְׁבוּיִם דְּרוֹר וְלַאֲסוּרִים פְּקַח־קוֹחַ: לִקְרֹא שְׁנַת־רָצוֹן לַיהוָה וְיוֹם נָקָם לֵאלֹהֵינוּ לְנַחֵם כָּל־אֲבֵלִים:

---

[1] Davies and Allison, *Matthew*, 1:438–9. See resources footnoted in this section for further examples.
[2] Codex Sinaiticus reads ταπεινοῖς.

Four features of this text might point to a messianic figure. First, the speaker is said to have God's Spirit on him. Isaiah uses this concept elsewhere to describe a Davidic ruler (11:2) and YHWH's servant (42:1). Some see the repetition of this idea as forming an intertextual connection, linking the herald figure of Isa 61 with more messianic contexts.[3] However, the same concept is applied to restored Israel (32:15, 44:3) and to a preacher / prophet with his "seed" (59:21). This last occurrence seems particularly significant since this possible intertextual connection is the closest at hand to Isa 61:1–2. Though the proximity of one text to another is often not considered by allusion theorists, it seems reasonable to assume an audience is more likely to make connections with a text just read (or heard) moments earlier as opposed to a longer period of time. But the Spirit-anointed figure in 59:21 hardly refers to a single messianic figure. The mention of a coming of a deliver (גּוֹאֵל; ὁ ῥυόμενος) in 59:20 would better fit that position (cf. Rom 11:26 where it is used messianically). But v 21 distances the Spirit-anointed figure from this deliverer by shifting from the third person to describe the latter to the second person to describe the former רוּחִי אֲשֶׁר עָלֶיךָ. Moreover, the text promises the prophet and his "seed" God's "word," and this "word" cannot be separated from the presence of the Spirit. This plurality makes it unlikely that *the* messiah is in view.

Furthermore, similarities between figures do not require them to be identical.[4] For example, we will shortly see Isa 40:1 and 61:2 have intertextual links. An allusion is likely present since the rhetorical stress of 40:1 is so high, inviting comparison. But on the other hand, the connection does not mean the figures mutually interpret one another or should be equated. At least this was not the approach of Matthew and Luke who apply the former context (40:1–3) to John, but not the latter. This observation alone should warn interpreters that Isaian figures are not coterminous simply because they share similar features. Thus, that Matthew would have interpreted the Spirit's presence upon the herald in messianic terms is certainly possible, but not required.

---

3 Motyer, *The Prophecy of Isaiah*, 499; Childs, *Isaiah*, 502; Gary Smith, *Isaiah 40–66*, (NAC; Nashville: Broadman & Holman, 2009), 629; R. B. Chisholm, "The Christological Fulfillment of Isaiah's Servant Songs," *BSac* 163 (2006): 387–404; Abi T. Ngunga, *Messianism in the Old Greek of Isaiah: An Intertextual Analysis* (Göttingen: Vandenhoeck & Ruprecht 2012) 193–205. The repetition of other words / concepts may connect our text with the servant passages, including עני (49:13), אסר (42:7, 49:9), פקח (42:7), רצון (49:8), and כהה (42:3).

4 Andrew Abernethy, *The Book of Isaiah and God's Kingdom: A Thematic-Theological Approach* (Downers Grove, IL: InterVarsity, 2016), 120 also observes that similarities do not require the figures to be coterminous. He sees chapters 1–39 as describing a Davidic ruler, 40–55 a servant, and 56–66 a messenger, whose identities as literary figures should not be confused. Beers, *The Followers of Jesus*, 44–45 has argued in her monograph that though Isa 61 is a "non-traditional servant song," the figure is applied to both Jesus and his followers.

Second, the presence of the Spirit is due to the speaker being "anointed" (מָשַׁח; ἔχρισεν). What significance should be attached to this? Bird argues "The word 'anointed' has obvious messianic connotations, and when Jesus declares that God has anointed him with the Spirit he is making a *de facto* messianic claim."[5] Yet, to what extent this is intended to create expectations of a definite מָשִׁיחַ / χριστός is unclear, as the verb is used elsewhere more generally.[6] It is sometimes used of consecrating priests (e.g. Lev 7:36, Num 35:25), but mostly in establishing a king (e.g. Jud 9:8, 1 Sam 10:1, 15:1, 1 Kgs 1:34). However, Elisha is said to have been anointed as well (1 Kgs 19:16, 1 Chron 16:20, cf. Ps 105:15 = 1 Chron 16:22 which may present בִּמְשִׁיחָי in parallelism with וְלִנְבִיאַי).[7] Sirach 48:8 uses the word for both kings and prophets. *DCH* categorizes this word along with Isa 61:1 and 1 Kgs 19:16 as anointing as a prophet.[8] 1QM 11:7–8 and 4Q266 5 also use the word in apposition with the plural חוֹזֵי ("seers"). Block claims that besides the psalms, only Dan 9:27 uses the verb in an eschatological, messianic context,[9] and even this represents a comparatively optimistic viewpoint over the past century.[10] In Isaiah, Cyrus is described as "anointed" (45:1).[11] It

---

5   Michael Bird, *Jesus is the Christ: The Messianic Testimony of the Gospels* (Downers Grove, IL: InterVarsity, 2013), 83, emphasis his.

6   *HALOT* 643; Joseph A. Fitzmyer, *The Dead Sea Scrolls and Christian Origins* (Grand Rapids: Eerdmans, 2000), 75. John C. Poirier, "Jesus as an Elijianic Figure in Luke 4:16–30," *CBQ* 71.2 (2009): 353 argues that this unique prophetic anointing connects the מבשׂר of Isa 61 to Elijah. He further argues that since this was normally reserved for priests, the Elijianic figure in Isa 61 takes that role as well (cf. 1 Kings 18:20–35 On the other end of the spectrum W. C. van Unnik, "Jesus the Christ" *NTS* 8 (1963): 113 argues Luke uses Isa 61 in Luke 4 to explain the usage of χριστός to his Hellenist readers.

7   Tremper Longman notes the possibility that the form is "A, what's more B" here ("The Messiah: Exploration in the Law and Writings" in *The Messiah in the Old and New Testament*, ed. Stanley E. Porter [Grand Rapids: Eerdmans, 2007], 14). The LXX (Ps 104:15) reads Μὴ ἅπτεσθε τῶν χριστῶν μου καὶ ἐν τοῖς προφήταις μου μὴ πονηρεύεσθε.

8   *DCH*, 5:516.

9   Daniel I. Block, "My Servant David: Ancient Israel's Vision of the Messiah" in *Israel's Messiah in the Bible and the Dead Sea Scrolls*, ed. Richard S. Hess and M. Daniel Carroll (Grand Rapids, Baker, 2003), 25.

10   See e.g. Matthew Novenson's survey, "Messiah Language in Ancient Judaism" in *Christ Among the Messiahs: Christ Language in Paul and Messiah language in Ancient Judaism* (Oxford: Oxford University Press, 2012), 34–63.

11   Ngunga, *Messianism in the Old Greek*, 204–05 notes that the LXX uses τῷ χριστῷ μου Κύρῳ instead of לִמְשִׁיחוֹ. However, his attempts to bolster the messianic nature "anointed" in Isa 61 because of this fall flat. He claims, "our translator read his *Vorlage* and produced his text [to make] the protagonist of Isa 61:1–3a the only individual messianic figure within the LXX-Isaiah with the 'anointing' upon him. This description, read against the translator's way of ignoring king Cyrus (the 'Lord's anointed' according to the MT) as a messianic figure, strongly suggests that the figure depicted in LXX - Isa 61:1–3a was understood ... as a Jewish messiah" (205). Yet, the simplest explanation is that the translator starts YHWH's

is a mistake to confuse the etymology of מָשִׁיחַ / χριστός with the actual figure as understood by authors such as Matthew.[12] Again, while we can imagine Matthew making this hermeneutical move, the original text does not require it.

Third, one mission of the figure is לִקְרֹא לִשְׁבוּיִם דְּרוֹר; κηρῦξαι αἰχμαλώτοις ἄφεσιν. The only other occurrences of דְּרוֹר in the MT refer to the Jubilee (Lev 25:10, Jer 34:8, 15, 17, Ezek 46:17). Thus, the nature of קרא here may go beyond simple proclamation and be used as a speech-act in which the speaker produces the Jubilee, a prerogative of kings.[13] This would support a messianic interpretation. However, if one is reading Isa 61 in the Old Greek, this allusion to Jubilee does not have the same effect since ἄφεσις occurs often in other contexts. Though it still can bear the meaning "release" like דְּרוֹר (e.g. Lev. 25:28), it can also have the associated meaning "debt remission" (e.g. Deut 15:1–2), or notably in Matthew's context, the meaning "forgiveness" (Matt 26:28, so also 1 Enoch 12:5, 13:4, 6, Odes 13:77). This meaning of ἄφεσις is not attested elsewhere in the LXX, but one must be careful to not require too much sophistication from the perspective of Matthew, as if he would have kept track of how they used ἄφεσις in contrast to the LXX. The object of the verb in Isa 61:1, לִשְׁבוּיִם; αἰχμαλώτοις indicates the idea of "release" is in view, but the wide usage of ἄφεσιν in other contexts compared to the more limited occurrences of דְּרוֹר obscure an intertextual connection to the year of Jubilee.

Fourth, speaking comfort may extend beyond proclamation and include reversing the exile (or exile-like) conditions. The figure's purpose is לְנַחֵם כָּל־אֲבֵלִים; παρακαλέσαι πάντας τοὺς πενθοῦντας. In most occurrences of נחם (piel) in Isaiah, the verb goes beyond proclamation and is paralleled with concepts like גאל (52:9) and speaks of restoration. Of all the other passages, 57:18

---

direct speech τῷ χριστῷ. Regardless of the explanation, Ngunga's attempt to thereby heighten the messianic overtones of χριστῷ, can hardly be maintained as the shift from "his" to "my" does not distract from his position as "anointed one."

[12] E.g. Longman attempts to "associate as specifically messianic texts those passages that anticipate a future leader of God's people who is connected to a role in which the ritual of 'anointing' is found" ("The Messiah," 14–15). On the contrary, Oegema, *The Anointed and His People*, 294–99 reviews messianic texts from 300 BCE to 200 CE, concluding the majority refer to one of the following passages: Gen 49:10, Num 24:17, 2 Sam 7:12–13, Isa 11:1–2, Amos 9:11, or Dan 7:13–14. Novenson, *Christ Among the Messiahs*, 58 significantly observes that none of these texts contain a form of מׁשח/χρίω.

[13] John D. W. Watts, *Isaiah 34–66*, (WBC; Dallas: Nelson, 1987), 303. Chisholm, "The Christological Fulfillment," 402; Walter J. Houston, "'Today in Your Very Hearing,': Some Comments on the Christological Use of the Old Testament" in *The Glory of Christ in the New Testament: Studies in Christology in Memory of George Bradford Caird*, ed. L. D. Hurst and N. T. Wright (Clarendon: Oxford, 1987), 46.

has the most lexical correspondence[14] and is nearest to hand. There too receiving comfort is not hearing a message, but having one's situation changed. However, נחם (piel) also occurs elsewhere (22:4, 40:1, 51:19, and 57:6) without this connotation. 40:1 is a particularly strong contender for an allusion since the rhetorical stress is so high, famously beginning the second major section of Isaiah. Moreover, YHWH is the subject in the former set of נחם references, whereas 61:1–3 considers an agent sent by YHWH, which aligns it with the latter set of references. We can conclude with Goldingay,

> Comfort is another expression taken up from Isaiah 40–55. The chapters indeed began (40:1) with YHWH's commissioning comfort for Jerusalem. There the verb 'comfort' (nāḥam piel) denoted words that bring comfort; it can also denote action that comforts (e.g. 49:13; 51:3; 52:9). In the present context, initially it might be unclear which form of comfort the prophet describes, but if so, the rest of these two lines makes clear that the reference is to words or signs of comfort.[15]

Furthermore, this argument also requires dependence on the Hebrew text, since παρακαλέω has a wider semantic range and is used in a greater variety of contexts.[16]

Isa 61:1–3 certainly has other complications, but the above have been briefly presented to demonstrate substantial ambiguity exists in the text, so that legitimate understandings of the figure range from the simple office of a prophet[17]

---

14   וָאֲשַׁלֵּם נִחֻמִים לוֹ וְלַאֲבֵלָיו; παρεκάλεσα αὐτόν, καὶ ἔδωκα αὐτῷ παράκλησιν ἀληθινήν.
15   John Goldingay, *A Critical and Exegetical Commentary on Isaiah 56–66* (ICC; London: Bloomsbury, 2014), 304.
16   Ngunga, *Messianism in the Old Greek*, 193–205, in its effort to promote the messianism of Isa 61:1–3, fails to notice the effect of this shift in semantic range here, as also with ἄφεσιν.
17   R. N. Whybray, *Isaiah 40–66*, (CBC; Grand Rapids: Eerdmans, 1975), 240; Goldingay, *Isaiah*, 629; Paul A. Smith, *Rhetoric and Redaction in Trito-Isaiah*, 30; Claus Westermann, *Isaiah 40–66: A Commentary* (VTSup; Philadelphia: Westminster, 1969), 299 (though on p. 365 he says the text should also be compared with 42:1–4 and 49:1 and contrasts with Isaiah's call in ch 6). George A. F. Knight, *The New Israel* (Grand Rapids: Eerdmans, 1985), 50 claims it is both Trito-Isaiah and the nation of Israel. Paul D. Hanson, *The Dawn of the Apocalyptic: The Historical and Sociological Roots of Jewish Apocalyptic Eschatology*, Rev. ed (Philadelphia: Fortress, 1979), 60–67, 225, says it refers to a Levitical-visionary group opposing the Zadokites. Christopher R. Seitz, "Isaiah 40–66," in *The New Interpreter's Bible: A Commentary in Twelve Volumes*, ed. Leander E. Keck (Nashville: Abingdon, 2001), 6:505 views it as referring to Isaiah, but "as a servant follower of the martyred servant of 52:13–53:12." W. A. M. Beuken, "Servant and Herald of Good News: Isaiah 61 as an Interpretation of Isaiah 40–55," in *The Book of Isaiah: Le Livre D'Isaie: les oracles et leurs relectures unité et complexité de l'ouvrage*, ed. Jacques Vermeylen, (Leuven: University Press, 1989), 411–42

to a definite future messianic figure,[18] regardless if that messiah is to be understood in royal, prophetic, or priestly terms.[19]

5.3 Diversity in Relevant Jewish Literature

The variety of interpretations found in relevant Jewish literature reinforce the above complexities. Unfortunately, Second Temple literature which also refers to Isa 61 is sometimes cited as proof that Matthew (or the canonical gospels in general) simply reiterates contemporary messianic exegesis.[20] This approach fails on two fronts: its omission of non-messianic interpretations from consideration and its questionable reading of the alleged messianic uses. To demonstrate the diversity within Second Temple Judaism, six texts are considered below: Sirach 48; Tg. Isa 61, 1QH^a 23:14–15, 11Q13, 4Q521, and Luke 4.

5.3.1 *Sirach 48*

Jesus ben Sira shows a non-messianic and non-eschatological interpretation of Isa 61:2 when he alludes to the text in his short treatment of Isaiah, Ἡσαίας ὁ προφήτης ὁ μέγας καὶ πιστὸς ἐν ὁράσει αὐτοῦ ... πνεύματι μεγάλῳ ἴδεν τὰ ἔσχατα, καὶ παρεκάλεσεν τοὺς πενθοῦντας ἐν Σειών· ἕως τοῦ αἰῶνος ὑπέδειξεν τὰ ἐσόμενα καὶ τὰ ἀπόκρυφα πρὶν ἢ παραγενέσθαι αὐτά (Sir 48:22, 24–25). The case for an

    argues the figure is flexible so that though he is presented as the servant, he is one of his offspring (44:2–3, 53:10). So also Childs, *Isaiah: A Commentary*, 50; Abernethy, *The Book of Isaiah and God's Kingdom*, 162; and Joseph Blenkinsopp, *Isaiah 56–66: A New Translation with Introduction and Commentary* (AB; New York: Doubleday, 2003), 221. Randall Heskett, *Messianism with the Scriptural Scrolls of Isaiah* (London: T&T Clark, 2007), 225–38 reviews 50 authors. He concludes the text is ambiguous but "provides warrants for messianic interpretation" (266).

18 Walter Kaiser, *The Messiah in the Old Testament* (Grand Rapids: Zondervan, 1995), 183. France, *Jesus and the Old Testament*, 134; Oswalt, *The Book of Isaiah 40–66*, 565. Watts, *Isaiah 34–66*, 305 sees three speakers present in ch. 61 – a preacher (vs. 1–3), a healer (vs. 4–7), and YHWH (vs. 8–11).

19 For this reason, the term "messianic" may be unhelpful in some contexts. Abernethy, *The Book of Isaiah and God's Kingdom*, 119 therefore prefers "agent." Poirier argues for a priestly messiah and reviews arguments to the contrary. "Jesus as an Elijianic Figure," 349–63.

20 Bird, *Jesus is the Christ*, 83–84, in discussion of Luke 4:16–30. Mark L. Strauss, *The Davidic Messiah in Luke-Acts: The Promise and Its Fulfillment in Lukan Christology* (Sheffield: Sheffield Academic, 1995), 233; Darrell Bock, *From Proclamation to Prophecy: Lucan Old Testament Christology* (Sheffield: Sheffield Academic, 1987), 109; Craig A. Evans, "Prophet, Sage, Healer, Messiah, and Martyr: Types and Identities of Jesus," in *Handbook for the Study of the Historical Jesus*, ed. Tom Holmén and Stanley E. Porter (Leiden: Brill, 2010), 2:1237.

allusion here to Isa 61 is quite strong with so much thematic coherence. Ben Sira is discussing the prophet Isaiah and Isa 61 is written in the first person. The volume is also quite loud, having παρακαλέω and πενθέω in common, as well as Σειών as a modifier of "mourners."[21] In this usage, the herald is not an eschatological figure. The use of the first person is thought to point back to the author, whom Ben Sira understands as the historical Isaiah. Instead, the eschatological connection is with his foretelling not only τὰ ἔσχατα, but the events that led up to (ἕως) it.[22] On the one hand παρακαλέω could refer to aspects of Isaiah's ministry such as encouraging Hezekiah and Israel to be faithful during the Assyrian invasion (cf. Isa 24:18), understanding καί as a simple connective and the two clauses paratactically. On the other hand, by being surrounded by descriptions of Isaiah as a prophet of the end times, it is more likely that παρακαλέω should be understood as comforting Israel by pointing to her future renewal and salvation. This takes καί as hypotaxis, "to introduce a result that comes from what precedes"[23] with the possible translation "by his great spirit he saw the end times and thus comforted the mourners in Zion."

5.3.2 *Tg Isa 61:1*

A non-messianic and non-eschatological interpretation of Isa 61:1 can also be seen in its Aramaic translation (with tradition perhaps dating back to the first or second century CE).[24] Targum Jonathan translates the beginning אֲמַר נְבִיָא רוּחַ נְבוּאָה מִן קֳדָם יוי אֱלֹהִים עֲלָי ("the prophet says, 'the spirit of prophecy from the LORD God is on me'"). Here, not only is the speaker identified as the נְבִיָא, which occurs often in Targum Isaiah,[25] but the spirit which he receives is given

---

21   The following illustrates the volume of the proposed allusion:
    Sir 48:24
    παρεκάλεσεν τοὺς πενθοῦντας ἐν Σειών·
    Isa 61:2–3
    παρακαλέσαι πάντας τοὺς πενθοῦντας, δοθῆναι τοῖς πενθοῦσιν Σειὼν αὐτοῖς δόξαν ἀντὶ σποδοῦ
22 GNT reads "and he predicted things that would happen between then and the end of time." Cf. Donald Slager, "Preface," in *A Handbook on Sirach*, ed. Paul Clarke et al., United Bible Societies' Handbooks (New York: United Bible Societies, 2008), 973.
23 BDAG, 495. Cf. A. T. Robertson, *A Grammar of the Greek New Testament in the Light of Historical Research* (Logos Bible Software, 2006), 426.
24 Bruce Chilton, *The Isaiah Targum: Introduction, Translation, Apparatus and Notes* (The Aramaic Bible; Wilmington, Del: Glazier), 1987. See discussion in Paul V. Flesher and Bruce Chilton, "Introduction to the Targum of Isaiah" in *Targums: A Critical Introduction* (Waco, TX: Baylor, 2011), 173–75.
25 Flesher, *Targums: A Critical Introduction*, 176 argues "The Targum's meturgemanin preface *some of their most innovative and creative renderings* with the introductory formula [אֲמַר נְבִיָא]" (emphasis his).

an additional modifier – רוּחַ נְבוּאָה. The theme of true prophecy is significant for *Targum Isaiah* inasmuch as it sees the departure of the Shekinah to imply the cessation of prophecy.[26] Thus, the Targumist sees Isa 61 as referring to Isaiah's legitimacy as a prophet. Sanders rightly judges, "He understood the passage as indeed rabbinic Judaism after him had understood it ... as a reflection by the prophet on his own vocation and hence the source of his authority ... For him Isaiah was here saying something about his own vocation. That's the peshat; and there's an end of it."[27] The dating of sources like Targum Jonathan is notoriously difficult and Sanders argues that the Targum is a reaction against Christian messianic interpretations of Isa 61.[28] However, this seems unlikely since the theme of the prophetic office runs throughout the Targum of Isaiah. Instead, there is no reason to think the targumist sees anything eschatological or messianic in this text.

5.3.3 *Tg Num 25:12*

Consideration should also be given to Tg Num 25:12, since some see an allusion to Isa 61:1–3 there as well.[29] If so it may also understand the text as about the prophetic office in general since Phineas is under consideration. Still, there may be an eschatological flavor since it states מלאך קיים ויחי לעלם למבשרא גאולתא בסוף יומיא ("An enduring messenger [or "messenger of the covenant"[30]] will live forever to herald redemption in the end of days").[31] However, the only indication of allusion seems to be למבשרא, making this a faint echo at best.

---

26 Flesher, *Targums: A Critical Introduction*, 176.
27 James A. Sanders, "From Isaiah 61 to Luke 4" in *Christianity, Judaism and Other Greco-Roman Cults, Part 1: New Testament*, ed. Jacob Neusner (Eugene, OR: Wipf and Stock, 2004), 85. He then notes that later rabbinic interpretation restricts this text only to Isaiah and replaces "anoints" with "appoints." This interpretation continued in later Jewish tradition (e.g. Rashi). J. Rosenberg, *Isaiah (Volume 2): New English Translation of Text, Rashi and Commentary* (New York: Judaica, 1983), 478.
28 Sanders, "From Isaiah 61," 86.
29 Davies and Allison, *Matthew*, 1:438; David W. Pao and Eckhard J. Schnabel, "Luke," in *Commentary on the New Testament Use of the Old Testament*, ed. G. K. Beale and D. A. Carson (Grand Rapids: Baker Academic, 2007), 288.
30 See "קיימ" in Comprehensive Aramaic Lexicon Project, *Targum Lexicon* (Cincinnati, OH: Hebrew Union College, 2004). "Enduring" or "living" slightly fits the context better since the emphasis is on the messenger living forever.
31 Comprehensive Aramaic Lexicon Project, *Targum Pseudo-Jonathan to the Pentateuch* (Cincinnati, OH: Hebrew Union College, 2005), Nu 25:12. Translation mine.

5.3.4   *1QHᵃ 23:14–15*

The Dead Sea Scrolls also record non-messianic understandings of Isa 61 and emphasize the application of this passage in the context of prophecy. Joseph explains, "the Qumran corpus attests to a significant increase in identifying prophets as 'anointed ones,' reflecting 'a widening belief in the important role played by the holy spirit in the prophetic experience.' Isaiah 61 seems to have been the fountainhead of this development."[32] We can begin by considering 1QHᵃ 23:14–15[33] which clearly alludes to Isa 61:1–3:[34]

> to raise up the herald of good news (מבשר) according to your truth, [and to tel]l of your goodness, to proclaim good news (לבשר) to the poor (ענוים) according to the abundance of your compassion, [and to s]atisfy from the fountain of k[nowledge all the contr]ite in spirit and those who mourn (ואבלים) (that they may have) eternal joy (לשמחת עולם).[35]

Here the author praises God for revealing truth to such a lowly one as him so that he can be God's servant and preach his word (cf. lines 9–13). This text speaks of the blessings that come with being a true prophet.[36] Comforting the mourning is accomplished by receiving knowledge.[37] Though it is used self-referentially, this text still has similarities with Sirach and *Targum Jonathan* in not being messianic. However, the authorship of the psalms in the *Hodayot*

---

32   Simon J. Joseph, *Jesus, the Essenes, and Christian Origins: New Light on Ancient Texts and Communities* (Waco: Baylor, 2018), 79; citing John R. Levison, *The Spirit in First-Century Judaism* (AGJU; Leiden: Brill, 1997).

33   18.14–15 in the older, Sukenik system. For discussion, see Eileen M. Schuller, "Recent Scholarship on the Hodayot 1993–2010" in *CBR* 10.1 (2011): 126.

34   Julie A. Hughes, *Scriptural Allusions and Exegesis in the Hodayot* (Leiden: Brill, 2006), 75–79, 152, 147, 152–3, 168, 179 discusses other allusions to Isaiah 61 in the Thanksgiving Hymns, but they concern the imagery of a garden, not a מבשר. She also argues that 1QH 16:5–18:36 is meditation of Isa 40–66, including the theme of the suffering servant.

35   Translation from Eileen M. Schuller and Carol A. Newsom, *Society of Biblical Literature: Early Judaism and its Literature, Volume 36: Hodayot (Thanksgiving Psalms): A Study Edition of 1QHa* (Atlanta: SBL, 2012), 71.

36   Blenkinsopp argues the speaker identifies himself both as a servant and prophet, concluding "there are solid grounds for the conclusion that the profile of the Isaian Servant formed a significant aspect of the self-image of the author of the hymns." He sees the author as having both an eschatological approach while maintaining personal application. Joseph Blenkinsopp, *Opening the Sealed Book: Interpretations of the Book of Isaiah in Late Antiquity* (Grand Rapids: Eerdmans, 2006), 271.

37   The text only has כאי and the נ must be supplied for נבאי. Cf. line 14 – "(you) open the f[oun]tain of truth to the (human) vessel."

is controversial. Douglas argues at length that the Teacher of Righteousness is the author,[38] while others remain agnostic.[39] This complexity has ramifications regarding the extent to which the prophet is in some sense eschatological. If he is the Teacher of Righteousness, he precedes a time of trial, which occurs before the eschaton. Thus, though the speaker might play a specific role in the community's eschatology, it does not seem to be one of "messiah."[40] However, as with much DSS research, this view too has its detractors, most famously by Wise.[41]

5.3.5   *11Q13 2:9*

Other texts do demonstrate a clear eschatological use of Isa 61, yet even these do not provide as clear a precedent for a messianic use as is sometimes claimed. In 11Q13 (11QMelch) 2:9, הואה הקץ לשנת הרצון למלכי צדק alludes to Isa 61, which contains the only occurrence of שנת הרצון in the MT.[42] If so, then Melchizedek plays an important role in this text's interpretation of Isa 61. This passage also presents him as both the herald as well as the one to whom the שנת הרצון

---

38   Michael C. Douglas, "Power and Praise in the Hodayot: A Literary Critical Study of 1QH 9:1–18:14" (PhD diss, University of Chicago, 1998). See also his article, "The Teacher Hymn Hypothesis Revisited: New Data for an Old Crux" *DSD* 6.3 (1999): 239–66. This view was originally advocated by Eliezer Susenik, *The Dead Sea Scrolls of Hebrew University* (Jerusalem: Magnes, 1954).

39   Hughes, *Scriptural Allusions and Exegesis*, 15–17; Carol A. Newsom, *The Self as Symbolic Space: Constructing Identity and Community at Qumran* (Leiden: Brill, 2004), 287–300. Trine Hasselbach's monograph argues against categorizing the Hodayot into "leadership hymns" and "community hymns" since they are eventually collected into the same corpus, creating a "hybrid figure" as the speaker (*Meaning and Context in the Thanksgiving Hymns: Linguistic and Rhetorical Perspectives on a Collection of Prayers from Qumran* (EJL; Atlanta: SBL Press, 2015), esp. 270–75).

40   Emile Puech, "Resurrection: The Bible and Qumran" in *The Bible and the Dead Sea Scrolls: Volume Two: The Dead Sea Scrolls and the Qumran Community*, ed. James H. Charlesworth (Waco, TX: Baylor, 2006), 272. This observation precludes him from being the messiah (Fitzmyer, *Dead Sea Scrolls*, 104; Michael A. Knibb, "The Teacher of Righteousness – A Messianic Title?" in *A Tribute to Geza Vermes: Essays on Jewish and Christian Literature and History*, ed. Philip R. Davies and Richard T. White (JSOTSup; Sheffield: Sheffield Academic, 1990), 51–65, esp. 59–60.

41   Michael O. Wise, *The First Messiah: Investigating the Savior Before Jesus* (San Francisco: HarperCollins, 1999).

42   רָצוֹן occurs two other times in the MT to modify a time, both in Isaiah. 49:8 has בְּעֵת רָצוֹן ("acceptable time") and 58:5 has וְיוֹם רָצוֹן לַיהוָה ("and the acceptable day to YHWH"). The similarity between this latter text and Isa 61:2 may explain why Jesus connects the two in Luke 4:18–19. The allusion to Isa 61 may also be suggested by line 13, possibly referring to וְיוֹם נָקָם לֵאלֹהֵינוּ. Merrill Miller, "The Function of Isa 61:1–2 in 11Q Melchizidek" *JBL* 88.4 (1969): 468.

belongs (replacing YHWH in the MT). The text further extols him by assigning him the role of אלהים in Pss 86:1; 7:8–9 and 82:2, executing vengeance on his enemies and Belial (2:10–16). However, the identification of Melchizedek is disputed. Most identify him as an angelic power, usually Michael,[43] while others argue for YHWH.[44] Rainbow advocates a messianic identification, arguing that other positions overly rely on reconstructions of the lacunae.[45] However, his argument has not gained much acceptance. For our purposes, his proposal is unhelpful because it mostly rests on a messianic reading of other allusions in 11Q13 (particularly Isa 61) and argues this informs the identity of Melchizedek. Thus, relying on Rainbow's study would be arguing in a circle for our purposes. The wisest course seems to be Fitzmyer's agnostic position here.[46]

---

43   Emil Schurer, *The History of the Jewish People in the Age of Jesus Christ* (rev. Geza Vermes and Fergus Millar with Matthew Black and Martin Goodman; 4 vols. (Edinburgh: T&T Clark, 1973–87), 3:449–51; George J. Brooke, "Melchizedek (11QMelch)," *The Anchor Bible Dictionary*, ed. David Noel Freedman; 6 vols (New York: Doubleday, 1992), 4:687–88; L. W. Hurtado, "Principal Angels" in *The Oxford handbook of the Dead Sea Scrolls*, ed. Timothy H. Lim and John J. Collins (Oxford: Oxford University Press, 2010), 550–62, esp. 555. A. S. van der Woude, "Melchisedek als himmlische Erlösergestalt in den neugefundenen eschatologischen Midraschim aus Qumran Höhle, XI," *OtSt* 14 (1965): 367–72. William Horbury rightfully notes that the common distinction between an angelic messiah and a human one are not necessarily exclusive categories since "it can be envisaged that past monarchs may attain angelic status as spirits in the hands of God" ("Messianism in the Old Testament and Pseudepigrapha" in *King and Messiah in Israel and the Ancient Near East*, ed. J. Day (JSOTSup; Sheffield: Sheffield Academic, 1998), 433.

44   Franco Manzi, *Melchisedek e l'angelologia nell'epistola agli Ebrei e a Qumran* (AnBib; Rome: Pontifical biblical Institute, 1997), 206 argues Melchizedek in 11Q13 refers to YHWH. Rick Van de Water, "Michael or Yhwh?: Toward Identifying Melchizedek in 11Q13" in *JSP* 16.1 (2006): 75–86 attempts to merge both YHWH and an intermediary, comparable to Philo's λόγος.

45   Paul Rainbow, "Melchizedek as a Messiah at Qumran," *BBR* 7 (1997): 179–94. He also points to the following for agreement: Jean Carmignac, "Le document de Qumran sur Melchisédeq," *RevQ* 7 (1970): 343–78; Anders Hultgård, "The Ideal 'Lévite', the Davidic Messiah, and the Saviour Priest in the Testaments of the Twelve Patriarchs" in *Ideal Figures in Ancient Judaism*, ed. John J. Collins and George W. E. Nickelsburg (SBLSCS; Chico: Scholars Press, 1980) 93–110, esp. 93; David Flusser, "Melchizedek and the Son of Man," in *Judaism and the Origins of Christianity* (Jerusalem: Magnes Press, Hebrew University, 1988) 186–92. Horbury, "Messianism in the Old Testament Apocrypha," 428 hesitatingly accepts a messianic identity of Melchizedek, though he argues there can be significant overlap between angelic deliverers and human messiahs in Second Temple literature.

46   Joseph A. Fitzmyer, "Further Light on Melchizedek from Qumran Cave 11," in *Essays on the Semitic Background of the New Testament* (London: G. Chapman, 1971), 32.

5.3.6 4Q521

4Q521 (the so-called Messianic Apocalypse) also alludes to Isa 61:1–3.[47] 2:1–2, 5–12 read

> For the heavens and the earth will listen to his anointed one [למשיחו], and all that is in them will not turn away from the precepts of the holy ones ... For the Lord [אדני] will consider the pious, and call the righteous by name, and his spirit will hover upon the poor [ענוים], and he will renew the faithful with his strength. For he will honour the pious upon the throne of an eternal kingdom, freeing prisoners [אסורים], giving sight [פוקח] to the blind [עורים], straightening out the twis[ted.] And for[e]ver shall I cling [to those who h]ope, and in his mercy [...] and the frui[it of ...] ... not be delayed. And the Lord [אדני] will perform marvelous acts such as have not existed, just as he sa[id] [for] he will heal the badly wounded and will make the dead live, he will proclaim good news to the poor [ענוים יבשר].[48]

4Q521 shares verbal similarity with Isa 61:1–3, as indicated in the quotation above.[49] Isa 61 is similarly given an eschatological interpretation, but with no recourse to the year of Jubilee. Instead, it is a pastiche of Scripture describing great actions that will occur in the end time. However, here the subject of the verbs is not Melchizedek, but Adonai (not the grammatical subject, but the only viable antecedent from the previous 7 lines).[50] Collins argues that since God nowhere else is the subject of בשר, an agent is implied. Because other actions include raising the dead and healing,[51] he concludes an Elijah figure

---

47   This was first identified by E. Puech, "Une Apocalypse Messianique (4Q521)," *RevQ* 15 (1992): 475–519.

48   Translation from Martínez and Tigchelaar, *The Dead Sea Scrolls Study Edition*.

49   It alludes to other biblical texts as well. John J. Collins lists Ps 146:5b–8 as the most prominent. "A Herald of Good Tidings: Isaiah 61:1–3 and Its Actualization in the Dead Sea Scrolls" in *The Quest for Context and Meaning: Studies in Biblical Intertextuality in Honour of James A. Sanders*, ed. C. A. Evans and S. Talmon (BINS; Leiden: Brill, 1997), 234. See J. D. Tabor and M. O. Wise, "On Resurrection and the Synoptic Gospel Tradition: A Preliminary Study" *JSP* 10 (1992): 150–61 for several possible allusions.

50   Fitzmyer, *Dead Sea Scrolls*, 95 argues against a messianic interpretation from this.

51   Kvalbein argues these are figurative and that the text does not consider resurrection. (von Hans Kvalbein, "Die Wunder der Endzeit: Beobachtungen zu 4Q521 und Matth 11, 5p" in *ZNW* 88.1–2 [1997]: 113–9). In response see Albert L. A. Hogeterp, "Belief in Resurrection and its Religious Settings in Qumran and the New Testament," in *Echoes from the Caves: Qumran and the New Testament*, ed. F. Garcia Martinez (STDJ; Leiden: Brill, 2009), 309–13, who describes Kvalbein's approach as existing "differently from all other scholarly proposals" (312).

as a prophetic messiah accomplishes this role.[52] However, Wold observes that other prophetic figures like Ezekiel (based on of 4QPseudo-Ezekiel) could fulfill this role and so it is unnecessary to postulate a singular specific agent here even if one is required.[53] Moreover, this depends on an obscurity about the subject of בשר. As seen in Isa 61:1–3 itself, the verb is used in parallelism with other proclamation verbs like קרא, which often have God as the subject. Collins' thesis may have some merit since מׁשיחו is mentioned in verse 1.[54] Bird also argues that messianic agency is implied since v 1 states "heaven and earth will listen to His messiah," which he claims "indicates that the Messiah is the one who preaches, heals, and raises the dead."[55] However, מׁשיחו is in parallelism to "holy ones" in v 2 whose commandments are also obeyed, which suggests מׁשיחו may be a defective plural.[56] In any case, by the time the reader gets to verse 5, the emphasis is solely on אדני as the one who performs these actions. It is best to concur with Martínez when he states "Was der Text uns lehrt, ist dies, das in der Endzeit, in der Zeit des 'messias,' Gott wie versprochen wunderbare Taten vollbringen und die Auferweckung der Toten [natürlich Treuen] eines dieser Wunderwerke sein wird."[57]

From our consideration of extra-biblical uses of Isa 61, we have seen a variety of interpretations. 4Q521 is the closest to an explicit messianic usage, but even this is not as clear as is sometimes claimed. Nor should we say that such an approach dominated the hermeneutical landscape. We must proceed to the NT to see how Luke, then Matthew, use the text themselves instead of assuming they reiterate "contemporary exegesis."

---

52   Collins, "A Herald of Good Tidings," 234–6. Similarly Géza Xeravits, *King, Priest, Prophet: Positive Eschatological Protagonists of the Qumran Library* (STDJ; Leiden: Brill, 2003), 98–110 and J. Zimmermann, *Messianische Texte aus Qumran. Konigliche, priesterliche und prophetische Messiasvorstellungen in den Schriften von Qumran* (Tübingen: Mohr Siebeck, 1998). The presence of a messiah is often assumed for 4Q521, evidenced by its name, the "Messianic Apocalypse," dating to Puech's work. John C. Poirier "The End Time Return of Elijah and Moses at Qumran" *DSD* 10.2 (2003): 226–37 argues that Isa 61 does predict the return of Elijah, not as a prophetic messiah, but as a priestly one (cf. 61:6). Hogeterp well observes that "the messianic identification ... is subject to divergence of scholarly argument" ("Belief in Resurrection," 311).
53   Benjamin Wold, "Agency and Raising the Dead in Pseudo-Ezekiel and 521 2 ii" in *ZNW* 1/103 (2012): 1–19.
54   It also occurs in a highly fragmentary passage, fragment 9. There is also a reference to "all her messiahs" in fragment 8. Collins, *The Scepter and the Star*, 133.
55   Bird, *Are You the One Who is to Come?*, 103.
56   Collins, *The Scepter and the Star*, 137.
57   García Martínez, "Messianische Erwartungen in den Qumranshcriften," 185.

5.3.7 Luke 4:16–30

Though there is no reason to think Matthew had access to the material which informs Luke's Nazareth sermon, Luke 4:16–30 is relevant for our study since it contains the clearest occasion of the canonical gospels describing Jesus's use of Isa 61[58] in the NT and since here too a messianic interpretation seems unlikely.[59] The Lukan Jesus certainly gives the text an eschatological interpretation, coming to fulfillment (πεπλήρωται) at that time (σήμερον).[60] He also clearly interprets the text self-referentially.[61] The herald figure is foregrounded in the quotation, and then Jesus maps himself into that space, as a prophet, confirmed by his general maxim (v 24) and the examples of Elijah and Elisha (vv 25–27). This theme of Jesus as a prophet runs throughout Luke (e.g. 7:16, 39, 24:19, 21) and is traditionally seen as a major feature of Lukan Christology.[62] This usage comports well with the strain of interpretation seen at Qumran which emphasized the prophetic office resulting from the anointing of the spirit.

Though Jesus sees Isa 61 as eschatological and about a prophet, does this mean he also sees one specific messianic figure there?[63] Strauss argues that in 4:16–30, Luke is presenting Jesus as *the* eschatological prophet since he elsewhere links the title χριστός with the Moses-like figure predicted in

---

[58] The text is much closer to the LXX, agreeing at three junctures against the MT: uses the title κυριός instead of אֲדֹנָי יְהוָה; it adds a relative pronoun (οὗ) after the first clause, and replaces the second object of קרא with an infinitive phrase (τυφλοῖς ἀνάβλεψιν). However, it deviates from the LXX in omitting the phrase ἰάσασθαι τοὺς συντετριμμένους τὴν καρδίαν, (Rahlfs has τῇ καρδίᾳ, but Codex Vaticanus has the accusative form). Some significant witnesses include the clause, but its omission is most likely the original reading. (See Metzger, *A Textual Commentary*, 114.) Luke also uses κηρύσσω instead of καλέω (LXX). Luke also inserts a clause from Isa 58:6 and changes ἀποστέλλω to the infinitive. Luke stops before καὶ ἡμέραν ἀνταποδόσεως, though this has been variously interpreted. One of the more distinctive proposals is by Jeremias, *Jesus' Promise to the Nations*, 43–45 that this phrase was reserved for the gentiles and that his rejection at Nazareth is because his listeners were angry he omitted their judgment. See discussion in James R. Edwards, *The Gospel According to Luke* (PNTC; Grand Rapids: Eerdmans, 2015), 139.

[59] Nolland, *Luke*, 1:192.

[60] Edwards, *The Gospel according to Luke*, 138 extends this "today" back to Jesus' birth.

[61] This leads to later Christian usage, such as *Barn.* 14:5–9, which identifies the speaker of Isa 61 as "the Lord Jesus" (v 5), whom the Father was charging (v 6).

[62] E.g. Richard J. Bauckham, "Christology," *Dictionary of Jesus and the Gospels*, 2d ed., ed. Joel B. Green, Jeannine K. Brown, and Nicholas Perrin (Downers Grove, IL; IVP Academic, 2013), 131.

[63] Strauss, *The Davidic Messiah*, 230 seems to assume as much, writing "The eschatological context and the unique status Jesus claims for himself in the present passage (v. 21) indicate that this is no general prophetic call, but that of an eschatological figure."

Deut 18:15–18 (Acts 3:20–23, 7:37).⁶⁴ But though Luke's overall portrayal of Jesus includes being the messianic prophet, that does not imply each reference to him as prophet must be seen in this light. Other Lukan passages, like 7:36–50 (cf. 5.3.8), positively portray Jesus as a prophet without necessarily saying anything about him being *the* prophet.

Green also argues for a prophetic messiah from the repetition of "me," writing "Given the repeated first person singular references in 4:18 ("me" – 3×), the 'fulfillment' of which Jesus speaks must be rooted in his person: He is the one anointed by the Spirit, the herald of the good news, who brings in the new era."⁶⁵ Yet the repetition of "me" is not Lukan, but from the LXX. Moreover, singular pronouns do not always denote a unique fulfillment. In Isa 61:10, for example, first person singular pronouns describe not one individual but many, probably the עֲנָוִים of v 1.⁶⁶

Strauss argues for a royal messiah since the other occurrences of χρίω in Luke-Acts are in royal contexts (Acts 4:27, 10:38), as in Jesus' endowment with the Spirit (Luke 3:22, though the word does not occur there).⁶⁷ The remainder of his arguments, however, depend on the messianic features discussed earlier in the original text of Isa 61:1–3⁶⁸ or on the similarity with 11Q13.⁶⁹ However, all of these arguments can be disregarded since they are from within the citation of Isa 61 itself and not from the surrounding context in Luke 4. As we have seen, the messianic interpretation of Isa 61:1–3 was not the only one on the market in the first century and the data he posits for a messianic use can be taken in other directions.

Some of Bock's arguments overlap with Strauss' but he also argues from the insertion of Isa 58:6, writing "The prophetic picture (Isa. 61) is joined to a liberation portrait (Isa. 58). The insertion points us to the messianic Christology."⁷⁰ On the one hand, if the context of Isa 58 is meant to inform the citation from chapter 61, the figure would be a liberator and not only a preacher. But on the other hand, it is far from clear how a text about Israel's obligation to the

---

64   Strauss' tone is tentative however – "[this] suggests that the function of the eschatological prophet may be implicitly in view in Lk 4:16–30" (*The Davidic Messiah*, 230).
65   Green, *The Gospel of Luke*, 210, 213.
66   The repetition of the headdress imagery (פְּאֵר) probably recalls vs. 3, linking "me" with the עֲנָוִים.
67   Strauss, *The Davidic Messiah*, 232; Cf. Robert H. Stein, *Luke* (NAC; Nashville: Broadman & Holman, 1992), 156.
68   Strauss, *The Davidic Messiah*, 232–33. So also Houston, "'Today in Your Very Hearing,'" 46.
69   Strauss, *The Davidic Messiah*, 233. He cites Sanders' argument noted above that the Targum counters the messianic interpretation, perhaps as a bias against Christian interpretation.
70   Darrell Bock, *Proclamation from Prophecy and Pattern: Lucan Old Testament Christology* (Sheffield: Sheffield Academic, 1987), 109; cf. Bock, *Luke*, 1:409.

disenfranchised requires the agent be the messiah. The condemnation described in ch 58 is due to the *nation's* failure to perform what YHWH expected *them* to do. Fulfilling the command ἀπόστελλε τεθραυσμένους ἐν ἀφέσει (58:6) does not require one to be the messiah.

Turning to the context of Luke 4:16–30, there are four features of the text which, when considered together, suggest Jesus only uses the text eschatologically. (1) His use of the proverb about prophets (v 24), as well as his use of both Elijah (vv 25–6) and Elisha (v 27) suggest he is speaking about the role of a prophet in general.[71] (2) The actions ascribed to the figure in Isa 61 are done by other individuals in Luke-Acts. In Luke-Acts, agents of εὐαγγελίζω includes angels (Luke 1:19, 2:10), John the Baptist (3:18), the apostles (9:6), and the early Christ followers in Acts (e.g. 8:12).[72] Similarly, ἀποστέλλω is used with other recipients, such as angels (Luke 1:19, 26), John the Baptist (7:27), and Jesus' followers (Luke 9:2, 52. 10:1, 3, 11:49, some of whom are named ἀπόστολοι – 6:13).[73] Luke-Acts also contains many examples of others besides Jesus conducting a miraculous ministry, e.g. Luke 9:1–2, 10:7, and Acts 9:12–18 (bestowing sight). These result from the endowment of the Spirit (e.g. Acts 1:8), though the passage which has the most textual proximity highlights the Spirit's presence in Jesus (Luke 3:21–22). (3) Though it is not determinative, a uniquely messianic message at the beginning of Jesus' ministry would be out of line with him preaching the nearness of the kingdom, not directly himself. Since Jesus is not at this stage declaring that he is the messiah, we would not expect an overt self-referential use of a messianic text. (4) Though the progress of events in Luke 4:16–30 is debated,[74] the audience responds positively in v 22.[75] Their change to animosity probably comes from Jesus challenging their "in-group"

---

71 Noted by Bock, *Proclamation from Prophecy*, 109.
72 David Seccombe, "Luke and Isaiah" *NTS* 27.2 (1981): 254.
73 Luke 1:19, 26 and 27 have God as the agent, whereas Jesus is the one who sends his followers.
74 See summary and interaction in Monique Cuany, "'Physician, Heal Yourself!' – Jesus' Challenge to His Own: A Reexamination of the Offense at Nazareth in Light of Ancient Parallels (Luke 4:16–30)" *NovT* 58.4 (2016): 348–54.
75 V 22 begins πάντες ἐμαρτύρουν αὐτῷ. This could be either a dative of advantage or disadvantage ("against him"). Similarly, ἐθαύμαζον could be understood positively or negatively (BDAG, 444–45). Commentators usually take these positively because of the expression τοῖς λόγοις τῆς χάριτος. I. Howard Marshall, *The Gospel of Luke: A Commentary on the Greek Text* (NIGTC; Exeter: Paternoster Press, 1978), 185; Robert A. Stein, *Luke* (NAC; Nashville: B&H, 1993), 157. Based on other uses of χαρίς in Luke-Acts, this probably speaks of his powerfully persuasive words. John Nolland, "Grace as Power," *NovT* 28.1 (1986): 26–31. Whether their response is acceptance (Joseph A. Fitzmyer, *The Gospel According to Luke: A New Translation with Introduction and Commentary* (New York: Doubleday, 1970), 1:528) or merely being impressed (Nolland, *Luke*, 1:198), does not significantly affect our argument.

assumptions.[76] Their initial reception of Jesus' message is best understood if he were communicating that the time of God's visitation had come (but only for those who were qualified as the "poor"), as opposed to presenting himself as messiah.[77] Though he eventually argues for a messianic use of Isa 61 in Luke 4 (based on textual features of Isa 61:1–3), Bock concedes "There is nothing inherently messianic in the subsequent explanation of the OT text ... It is likely that the audience in the synagogue saw nothing more here than a prophetic eschatological claim."[78]

5.3.8 Luke 7:22

Luke 7:22 parallels the use considered below in Matt 11:5 and so many of the comments in our later discussion of that text will apply here. But the passage warrants a brief consideration by itself since the Lukan form is clearer than the Matthean that Isa 61 is only being used eschatologically and not messianically. Luke 7:22 and Matt 11:5 differ in that the former has less occurrences of καί than the latter. The Lukan pericope also lacks the reference to the "works of the messiah" (cf. Matt 11:2). This means the messianic concerns of John's questions are less predominate, though the title "the coming one" (Luke 7:19, 20) is messianic (see discussion in 5.4.2). As we will see though, John's question being about the messiah does not mean that Jesus' answer must be in the same category. John asks a question about the messiah, but Jesus answers with a statement about the nature of the eschaton. This seems to especially be the case in Luke 7 since there, the previous pericope concerns the raising of the widow's son (7:11–17). A mere five verses after this account (v 22), Jesus informs John that νεκροὶ ἐγείρονται. Clearly the pericope of 7:11–17 is intended to exemplify this action. But there, the raising of the dead results in the people's response, Προφήτης μέγας ἠγέρθη ἐν ἡμῖν and Ἐπεσκέψατο ὁ θεὸς τὸν λαὸν αὑτοῦ (v 16). This supports the earlier contention regarding Luke 4, that the miracles of Isa 61, while showing that Jesus is a [great] prophet, do not require people seeing him as *"the"* prophet (i.e. the messiah).

---

76   Edwards, *Luke*, 140; Green, *The Gospel of Luke*, 218. Jeffrey S. Siker, "'First to the Gentiles': A Literary Analysis of Luke 4:16–30," *JBL* 111 (1992): 73–90. Sanders, "From Isaiah 61," 97–105 uses comparative midrash to compare Jesus' approach with that at Qumran. The former he labels "eschatological prophetic" and the latter "eschatological constitutive" (98).
77   Cuany, "Physician, Heal Yourself!" 351.
78   Bock, *Luke*, 1:406. His argument for a messianic use rests on connecting features of the citation to other messianic sections of Luke, such as the baptism, (407–10).

5.4 The Contexts of Matthew's Uses Do Not Suggest an Exclusively Messianic Hermeneutic

5.4.1 *Matt 5:3–4*

5.4.1.1 Matt 5:3–4 Does Allude to Isa 61:1–3

Many commentators see Matt 5:3–4 (Μακάριοι οἱ πτωχοὶ τῷ πνεύματι, ὅτι αὐτῶν ἐστιν ἡ βασιλεία τῶν οὐρανῶν. Μακάριοι οἱ πενθοῦντες, ὅτι αὐτοὶ παρακληθήσονται) as an allusion to Isa 61:1–3.[79] Since the following discussion depends on the legitimacy of this allusion, we can consider a few relevant criteria from Hays' list. Concerning volume, the two texts share the words πτωχός,[80] παρακαλέω and πενθέω.[81] However, volume extends beyond repetition of words and depends on "distinctiveness, prominence, or popular familiarity of the precursor texts"[82] as well as "rhetorical stress."[83] Given the references to Isa 61:1–3 in Luke 4, as well as the relevant Jewish literature considered earlier, it does seem to have "popular familiarity." Moreover, Isa 61:1–3 occupies a prominent place in so called "trito-Isaiah" as the center of a large chiasm.[84] Concerning "recurrence," Matt 11:5 alludes even more clearly to the text. Furthermore, Matt 5 has "contextual allusive density" since the Sermon on the Mount alludes to the OT throughout, with the clearest and closest being to Ps 37:11 in Matt 5:5. Concerning the fourth criterion, "thematic coherence," Matt 5–7 centers around the major theme of God's redemption of Israel through the motif of return from exile. Matt 1–4 carefully establishes this background,[85] and 5:3–4 may link the Sermon on the Mount with this theme by repeating the mourning/comforting concept of 2:18 (though the Greek is ὀδυρμός/ παρακαλέω).[86]

---

79 Nolland, *The Gospel of Matthew*, 201; Blomberg, "Matthew," 20; Osborne, *Matthew*, 166–167; France, *The Gospel of Matthew*, 165–166; Luz, *Matthew*, 1:193; Keener, *The Gospel of Matthew*, 166; Turner, *Matthew*, 149; Witherington, *Matthew*, 120; Evans, *Matthew*, 105; Carson, "Matthew," 130; Hagner, *Matthew*, 1:92; Davies and Allison, *Matthew*, 1:436–9. UBS5 identifies the allusion between Matt 5:4 and Isa 61:2–3, but not Matt 5:3 and Isa 61:1.

80 As noted above, Sinaiticus reads ταπεινοῖς instead of πτωχοῖς.

81 Some manuscripts, as early as the second century, have v 5 before v 4. This would obscure, but not erase, the link to Isa 61:1–2. However, this reading is unlikely to be original. See Metzger, *A Textual Commentary*, 10.

82 Hays, *Conversion*, 36.

83 Hays, *Conversion*, 37.

84 Goldingay, *Isaiah 56–66*, 152.

85 Piotrowski, *Matthew's New David*, 201 explores each of the fulfillment citations in light of their source contexts and argues that these function as "framing in discourse" to establish a return from exile motif.

86 Blomberg suggests Matt 2:18 implies (to the observant Jew) the context of Jer 31:15, which proceeds to command in the next verse that Israel should stop weeping because the

Isaiah also powerfully uses this motif, including ch 61.[87] Moreover, the Sermon on the Mount invites comparison with the Scriptures of Israel, claiming some element of continuity (5:17–19) and contrast (at least with a tradition of interpretation of the Scriptures in the "antitheses" of 5:21–48). Concerning "history of interpretation," the Apostolic Fathers see Jesus as the fulfillment of Isa 61:1–3, though this is normally in light of the Nazareth sermon in Luke 4 (as early as *Epist Barn* 14:7).

Though factors like the above persuade many commentators that Matt 5:3–4 alludes to Isa 61, some disagree in at least viewing it as the primary allusion.[88] N. T. Wright argues that the makarisms of 5:3–10 parallel the woes of ch 23 and in light of Matthew's New Moses motif, this evokes blessings and curses of Deut 27–30.[89] However, though Wright correctly connects the beatitudes with return from exile theme, this does not advantage the proposal of Deut 27–30 over Isa 61 since, as has just been noted, the latter passage also utilizes the return from exile motif. Since both proposals share this feature, the only evidence to suggest Deut 27–30 is the primary allusion is the chiasm in Matthew, and this proposed chiasm has received criticism.[90] This is not to say an allusion to Mt. Ebal and Mt. Gerizim does not exist, but that if it does, the primary reference to Isa 61 is not supplanted.[91]

Quarles similarly argues that the beatitudes continue the New Moses motif and evoke Deuteronomy, though he suggests the allusion is to 33:29 and not the alternatives in chs 27–30.[92] Unlike Wright, Quarles does specifically reject Isa 61 as a major allusion, giving three reasons: (1) a comparison with the Lukan version (6:20–26) demonstrates that the proposed allusion to Isa 61 was not a result of redacting Q, (2) the Isaian context does not contain

---

return from exile is certain. If so, this would heighten the link between 2:18 and 5:3–4. "Matthew," 10.

[87] Bradley Gregory, "The Post-exilic Exile in Third Isaiah: Isaiah 61:1–3 in Light of Second Temple Hermeneutics," *JBL* 126.3 (2007): 475–496 goes so far as to argue that trito-Isaiah is the first theological use the return from exile image. Though there is thematic coherence, this criterion cannot be used to falsify a proposed allusion since "it would be possible for an author deliberately to use the same language in a difference sense (i.e. an antithetical or contrastive allusion)" (Thompson, *Clothed with Christ*, 32).

[88] Michel Talbot, "Heuruex les Doux, car ils heriteront la terre" (Paris: J. Gabalda, 2002), 361–67 also argues against Isa 61 as an allusion, but his argument is not considered here since it has not proved influential.

[89] N. T. Wright, *The New Testament and the People of God* (Minneapolis: Fortress Press, 1993), 388.

[90] Charles L. Quarles, "The Blessings of the New Moses: An Examination of the Theological Purpose of the Matthean Beatitudes" in *JSHJ* 13 (2015): 316–21.

[91] Nor does Wright deny the Isaian allusion – it seems to be a matter of emphasis.

[92] Quarles, "The Blessings of the New Moses," 307–37.

a form of the μακαρ- root, and (3) because Isaiah's servant theme would be an interruption of the New Moses motif which occurs both before and after the beatitudes (specifically in the so-called "antithesis").[93] In response, only Matthew has παρακληθήσονται and Luke's use of πενθέω is negative, in contrast to Matthew and Isaiah. Thus from a redaction perspective, Guelich's argument that Matthew *is* highlighting an allusion should not be dismissed.[94] Moreover, even if Matthew has not redacted his material to introduce the allusion, this does not mean it does not exist. Redaction criticism is best understood as a positive test to detect emphasis, not a negative test to deny what remains in the text.[95] Concerning his second objection, identifying allusions only requires correspondence between some elements of the new context and the source. A lack of parallel would not discredit a suggested allusion. Furthermore, though μακάριοι does not loudly echo Isa 61, there is a quieter resonance with εὐαγγελίζω / בשׂר as even the Hebrew word probably has connotations of "*good news.*"[96] However, some do not see בשׂר as inherently carrying a positive connotation, but as neutral.[97] But even with this understanding the context of Isa 61 surely ensures a positive use. The announcement of Isa 61 is a cause of celebration and this joyful news of eschatological reversal resonates with Matt 5, especially v 12 (χαίρετε καὶ ἀγαλλιᾶσθε). Quarles' third (and main) argument is also answered, as with the response to Wright above, by the presence of the return from exile motif in Isa 61. Since our text concerns the end of exile, it would cohere well with Matthew portraying Jesus as a new Moses who brings the people into the land. Moreover, sudden shifts in imagery occur frequently (e.g. see our discussion of Matt 9:35–36 which turns on a dime from shepherding to harvesting imagery), so even if an allusion to Isa 61 introduces

---

93 Quarles, "The Blessings of the New Moses," 311–12.
94 Robert A. Guelich, "The Matthean Beatitudes: 'Entrance-Requirements' or Eschatological Blessings?" *JBL* 95.3 (1976): 427. Furthermore, the existence of Q has been called into question by some scholars (e.g. ed. Mark Goodacre and Nicholas Perrin, *Questioning Q: A Multidimensional Critique*, (Downers Grove, IL: InterVarsity, 2004)). Nothing in this work depends on a particular compositional theory. But even if one granted the existence of Q and the task of redaction criticism, Quarles' argument is still not necessary.
95 This is a common critique. See, e.g., Mark Goodacre, "Redaction Criticism," *Dictionary of Jesus and the Gospels*, 2d ed., ed. Joel B. Green, Jeannine K. Brown, and Nicholas Perrin (Downers Grove, IL: IVP Academic, 2013), 770.
96 Matthew Seufert, "Isaiah's Herald" *WTJ* 77 (2015): 220–22. Both positive and neutral listings are given in Wilhelm Gesenius and Samuel Prideaux Tregelles, *Gesenius' Hebrew and Chaldee Lexicon to the Old Testament Scriptures* (Bellingham, WA: Logos Bible Software, 2003), 146 and Francis Brown, Samuel Rolles Driver, and Charles Augustus Briggs, *Enhanced Brown-Driver-Briggs Hebrew and English Lexicon* (Oxford: Clarendon Press, 1977), 142.
97 *HALOT*, 163; *DCH*, 2:267.

completely new imagery, this in no way diminishes its likelihood. Moreover, the strong allusion to Ps 36:11 (37:11 ET) in Matt 5:5 demonstrates Matthew is not bound to adhere exclusively to new Moses imagery. With these objections briefly answered, we can safely conclude with the majority of commentators that there is an echo of Isa 61:1–2 in Matt 5:3–4.

5.4.1.2 The Significance of the Allusion

If we are to read Matt 5:3–4 against the backdrop of Isa 61, what connections should be made? First, the πτωχοί of v 3 map to the πτωχοί; עֲנָוִים of Isa 61:1 (Rahlfs' reading is εὐαγγελίσασθαι πτωχοῖς ἀπέσταλκέν με; Sinaiticus reads ταπεινοῖς instead of πτωχοῖς). The parallelism in Isa 61 suggests that the "poor" there should be understood as those who are downtrodden and disenfranchised. The addition of τῷ πνεύματι intensifies the state of poverty, "making the reference to poverty more comprehensive: 'those whose poverty reaches even to their inner spirits.'"[98] Such an interpretation is to be preferred since it maintains the ethos of the OT text and there is no indication this has been changed. Matt 5:3 promises that these ones have ἡ βασιλεία τῶν οὐρανῶν. Nothing in Isa 61 precisely corresponds to this expression, but, following the insights of Chilton,[99] we can see how the general promises of salvation in Isa 61 would roughly fit this description of God's kingdom.

Second, οἱ πενθοῦντες in Matt 5:4 maps to several elements in Isa 61. The most prominent is toward the end of 61:2 because of its proximity to παρακαλέω (παρακαλέσαι πάντας τοὺς πενθοῦντας), which corresponds to the same verb in Matt 5:3. But the immediate context in Isaiah contains more uses of the mourning concept. 60:20 promises ἀναπληρωθήσονται αἱ ἡμέραι τοῦ πένθους σου and 61:3, continuing v 2, states δοθῆναι τοῖς πενθοῦσιν Σιων δόξαν ἀντὶ σποδοῦ, ἄλειμμα εὐφροσύνης τοῖς πενθοῦσιν. This helps to clarify the identity of the "mourners" as those who are going through hardship rather than those who mourn over sin.[100]

Third, it may be that αὐτοὶ κληρονομήσουσιν τὴν γῆν in v 5 finds resonance with Isa 60:21, δι' αἰῶνος κληρονομήσουσιν τὴν γῆν. This would be secondary to the louder allusion (or even unintroduced quotation) to Ps 36:11, οἱ δὲ πραεῖς κληρονομήσουσιν γῆν. Still, since Isa 61 has clearly been brought to the reader's

---

98 Suggested as an option in Nolland, *The Gospel of Matthew*, 199. For a full exploration, see Mark Allen Powell, "Matthean Beatitudes: Reversals and Rewards of the Kingdom" *CBQ* 58.3 (July 1996): 260–79. Such an understanding of πνεῦμα corresponds to the use in 60:3, πνεύματος ἀκηδίας, which is replaced with καταστολὴν δόξης. The use of "spirit" here hardly means "spiritually humble." Contra Morris, *Gospel According to Matthew*, 95–96.

99 E.g. Bruce D. Chilton, *The Glory of Israel: The Theology and Provenience of the Isaiah Targum* (JSOTSup; Sheffield: JSOT Press, 1983), 77–80.

100 Contra Morris, *Gospel According to Matthew*, 97.

mind before, this connection too may be intended. If so, this would reinforce γῆ as "land" rather than "earth" since Isa 60 sees the "land" in connection "boundaries" (ὅριον) "walls" (τεῖχος) and "gates" (πύλη) in v 18, which suggest territory in Israel, not the entire planet, is in view.[101]

The above brief exploration of correspondences demonstrate how identifying the intertextual mappings add insight and depth to the Matthean beatitudes. But though there is some kind of mapping between Isa 61 and Matt 5, these concern the identity of those who are blessed (οἱ πτωχοί; οἱ πενθοῦντες) and the nature of these blessings (αὐτοὶ παρακληθήσονται; κληρονομήσουσιν τὴν γῆν). However, Jesus does not explicitly map the spirit endowed herald of Isa 61:1 into the blend. Unlike the quotation in Luke 4 which includes this earlier portion of the Isaian text (πνεῦμα κυρίου ἐπ' ἐμὲ οὗ εἵνεκεν ἔχρισέν με), Matt 5 only specifically attends to the identity of those who receive the blessings and the nature of those blessings. Though the Lukan Jesus' use of Isa 61:1–3 is clearly self-referential, this is not the case for the Matthean Jesus. Due to the passive voice of the second line of each element of the Beatitudes, v 4 only says the mourners will be comforted, but does not specify the one who does this comforting. This passive obscures a link to Isa 61 in which the herald is the one sent to comfort. Remarkably, Matthew does not specify or directly link Jesus with this herald figure.

However, some see the allusion as evoking the herald and thus signaling Jesus' messianic identity.[102] We have discussed before the difficulty of knowing how much of the referred-to text an allusion evokes (see 1.3.1.3). What satisfies one interpreter as sufficient warrant does not always satisfy another, and much here depends on one's hermeneutical presuppositions. The argument at this stage will proceed by noting our fork in the road about whether or not the herald figure is evoked, and then explore each path to see where it takes us. The result will be that, regardless of which direction we take at this juncture, we will arrive at some version of Matthew evidencing a non-messianic hermeneutic.

---

101   Recall that the Topology Principle states that "Other things being equal, set up the blend and the inputs so that the useful topology in the inputs and their outer-space relations [the way elements relate independently of the blend] is reflected by inner-space relations [the new relationships which are at play within the blend]." (Fauconnier and Turner, *The Way We Think*, 326). In other words, the relationships from the sources should be preserved as closely as possible in the constructed blend. Since there is no indication otherwise ("other things being equal"), this means we should apply Isaiah's description of YHWH as reversing exilic like conditions for the oppressed to Matthew's beatitudes.

102   Davies and Allison, *Matthew*, 1:438; Osborne, *Matthew*, 166; Witherington, *Matthew*, 120; Keener, *The Gospel of Matthew*, 166; Evans, *Matthew*, 105.

If we consider the source domain of Isa 61:1–3 and see that the elements which are directly mapped into the blend are the recipients of the blessings (οἱ πτωχοί; οἱ πενθοῦντες) and the content of these blessings (αὐτοὶ παρακληθήσονται; κληρονομήσουσιν τὴν γῆν), but decide that the Spirit-anointed herald is not mapped into the blend, but is left in the "generic space," what can we conclude? From our consideration of the textual features of Isa 61:1–2 and our exploration into some later uses of relevant Jewish literature, we saw that it was entirely possible, though far from necessary for Matthew to have viewed this figure in messianic terms. Certainly the one who can see the messiah in Isa 42:1–4 (cf. Matt 12:18–21) and in Isa 53:4 (cf. Matt 8:17), let alone in Hos 11:1 (cf. Matt 2:15), could have also seen him in Isa 61:1–2 from what we have seen in the early part of this chapter. But the fact that this connection is not explicitly made demonstrates that the description of Matthew's hermeneutic as "Christocentric" (cf. 1.2.1) should be nuanced. If Matthew is a "Christological maximalist," seeing the messiah in every possible place, resorting to artificial exegesis so as to provide as much prophetic support as possible for Jesus' messianic identity, then the "oversight" in Matt 5:3–4 is hard to explain. Instead, what concerns the Matthean Jesus in these Beatitudes is that the long-awaited promises of the eschaton are "at hand" and to explicate the advantage this will have for those who are poor, mourn, etc. The hermeneutic of fulfillment here is better described as "broadly eschatological" than narrowly messianic. The prophecy of Isa 61:1–3 can be announced as being realized in Matt 5:3–4 because of the proclamation of 4:17. At this stage of Matthew's telling of the story, what matters is that the time has come for God's kingdom to arrive. The spotlight does not fall on the agency of Jesus as the messiah who is necessary to usher in these promises. Thus, if we take a more "minimalistic" trajectory, the mapping scheme is non-messianic in that nothing from a potentially messianic source domain gets mapped to Jesus because the interest lies elsewhere, namely the content of the eschaton's blessings and those who will receive them.

But what if we take the other path? What if we grant that, though Jesus makes no explicit mappings of the herald in Isa 61, the figure nonetheless ends up in the blend? We have seen how Blending Theory provides some explanation about how this would be the case, as it emphasizes the imaginative new world created by the juxtaposition of two domains and people's tendency to "fill in the gaps" as emerging structures are created through the use of governing principles. Recall that the Pattern Completion Principle states

> Other things being equal, complete elements in the blend by using existing integrated patterns as additional inputs. Other things being equal,

use a completing frame that has relations that can be the compression versions of the important outer-space vital relations between the inputs.[103]

This addresses "elaboration" / "running the blend" in creating an emergent structure. 1.3.2.2 considered a political ad example and the Pattern Completion Principle explains why the audience ends up picturing Bush as Byrd's murderer. Similarly, this principle suggests that the hearers of our allusion are to "run the blend" and complete the picture. The passive voice pattern of the beatitudes obscures the "agent."[104] But though Matt 5:4 says the mourners "will be comforted," the Pattern Completion Principle suggests that this prompts a discovery of the identity of the comforter. The Topology Principle, that relationships outside the blend should be preserved as much as possible inside the blend,[105] suggests that this role is to be fulfilled by the Spirit-anointed herald.[106] According to Blending Theory at least, it is entirely feasible that our allusion maps the herald figure into the blend indirectly.

If we grant that the herald figure has been indirectly mapped into the blend (via the governing principles of Pattern Completion and Topology), to whom does he map? Jesus would be the first to come to mind as he is the one actively preaching in Matt 5–7. Though they do utilize the explanations of Blending Theory, the mind's tendency to run the blend best explains how the interpreters noted above end up seeing this as a messianic use of Isa 61. However, there is no reason to see only Jesus occupying this role. Instead, there are good reasons to see the Sermon on the Mount as foregrounding the missional role of the disciples. 5:1–2 presents the disciples as the intended audience by creating a separate space for them in distinction from the crowds. Though this element of "learner" continues to an extent in Matthew (the disciples are the intended recipients of each of Matthew's five main discourses),[107] Wilkins has

---

103 Fauconnier and Turner, *The Way We Think*, 328.
104 This departs from the previously used sense of "agent" as "instrument." The grammatical term "subject" would not be accurate. I am using language from functional grammar here. See Paul R. Kroeger, *Analyzing Syntax: A Lexical-functional Approach* (Cambridge: Cambridge University Press, 2004) 9.
105 Fauconnier and Turner, *The Way We Think*, 326.
106 The introduction also discussed the Integration Principle, which says the blend should be coherent and memorable. Though this principle sometimes causes minimization of the other principles, this does not seem to be the case for the allusion to Isa 61:1–3 in Matt 5:3–4. Instead, the resulting scene of God endowing a herald with the Spirit so that he pronounces blessings on those in exilic like conditions is coherent and easily memorable.
107 This is clear in 5:1, 10:1, and 18:1. Though the crowds listen to the parables (13:2, 34), Jesus clarifies that their intended audience is only the disciples (13:10, 36). If the eschatological discourse includes ch 23, then the audience is the crowds and the disciples (23:1). But

persuasively argued that "the emphasis in the common use of the term was not upon 'learning,' or upon being a 'pupil,' but upon adherence to a great master ... μαθητής carried the general / technical associations of adherent, with the type of discipleship determined by the one leading."[108]

While several Matthean texts elucidate the kind of discipleship Jesus demands, the most relevant here is 4:18–20. Not only does this text demand attention because "the initial appearance of a character is often important, for it creates expectations that readers carry with them into the rest of the story,"[109] but also because of its proximity to 5:3–4. With only three verses between this pericope and the opening of the Sermon on the Mount, Matthew surely intends it to remain in the audience's mind as they encounter the first occurrence of μαθητής (5:1).[110] 4:19 describes the followers of Jesus as "fishers of people" (4:19).[111] Moreover, the Sermon on the Mount proceeds to describe the disciples as in line with prophets (5:12)[112] who are πρὸ ὑμῶν. This phrase seems to mean more than "chronologically prior," which would have gone without saying.[113] They are also "salt" and "light" (5:13–16), and in contrast to the false prophets of Israel (7:15–20). Thus, if the herald figure is in view, the

---

though there are connections, discourse proper should be seen as beginning in ch 24, making only the disciples the audience (24:3).

108   Wilkins, *Discipleship in the Ancient World*, 11–90. Similarly, Donaldson, "Guiding Readers," 33 argues "The distinctive character of discipleship for Matthew is determined by (1) the person to whom disciples give their allegiance and (2) the nature of the relationship established between disciples and teacher."

109   Donaldson, "Guiding Readers," 35. Warren Carter, "Matthew 4:18–22 and Matthean Discipleship: An Audience-Oriented Perspective" in *CBQ* 59.1 (1997): 62 also sees the text as strategic for understanding discipleship.

110   "The essential characteristics of discipleship appear already in the calling of the first disciples at 4:18–22" (David R. Bauer, "The Major Characters of Matthew's Story: Their Function and Significance" in *Interpretation* 46.4 (1992): 361–62. Cf. Donald Senior, *The Gospel of Matthew* (IBT; Nashville: Abingdon, 1997), 64; Osborne, *Matthew*, 165.

111   If Matthew thinks of the disciples as only consisting of the four in Matt 4:18–22 is hard to tell. The selection of the 12 is just prior to the sermon in Luke (4:12–20). Matt 10:2–4 only records their names, with no account of the calling of the other eight. But regardless if μαθηταί includes more than the four individuals of 4:18–22, that literary description extends to the general quality of discipleship expected throughout Matthew. The likelihood that this alludes to texts like Jer 16:15–16 which portray fisherman as eschatological judges is unlikely since the work is positive in Matthew. There is a possibility that the allusion is ironic, but this would decrease the clarity of the reference. Still, if such passages are being evoked, it would reinforce an aspect of this research in which the disciples are foretold eschatological agents working alongside Jesus.

112   Turner, *Israel's Last Prophet*, 178 describes these verses as "the crucial text on the disciples as rejected prophets." He devotes a chapter in his monograph to this motif (177–224).

113   Contra BDAG, 864.

Sermon on the Mount's description of their missional role would include them occupying that space as well. Guelich rightly observes that the "material on the missionary nature of discipleship immediately follows the declaration in the Beatitudes of the 'good news' set in the context of Isaiah 61. Disciples are not only those who hear and respond to the good news but become by the very nature of discipleship messengers of this good news."[114] This line of interpretation can also be found in Calvin's comments on Isaiah,

> As Christ explains this passage with reference to himself, (Luke 4:18) so commentators limit it to him without hesitation, and lay down this principle, that Christ is introduced as speaking, as if the whole passage related to him alone. The Jews laugh at this, as an ill-advised application to Christ of that which is equally applicable to other prophets. My opinion is, that this chapter is added as a seal to the former, to confirm what had hitherto been said about restoring the Church of Christ ... This chapter ought, therefore, to be understood in such a sense, that Christ, who is the Head of the prophets, holds the chief place, and alone makes all those revelations; but that Isaiah, and the other prophets, and the apostles, contribute their services to Christ, and each performs his part in making known Christ's benefits. And thus we see that those things which Isaiah said would be accomplished by Christ, have now been actually accomplished.[115]

Thus, according to Blending Theory, the herald figure emerges in the blend and the allusion maps him both to Jesus and to the disciples. Earlier, when we considered the option of simply leaving the herald figure in the generic space, we had concluded the mapping was non-messianic since Jesus is not mapped into the blend. Matthew's hermeneutic is non-messianic in that the herald figure does not map to him because it maps to no one. However, if we take this second path and follow the suggestions of Blending Theory, then we also end up with a non-messianic mapping. But here, both Jesus and the disciples likely map into the blend and the herald figure maps to both. Again, we are not particularly concerned with Matthew's messianic mappings, a feature of his hermeneutics that is well established. It should come as no surprise that

---

114   Robert A. Guelich, *The Sermon on the Mount: A Foundation for Understanding* (Waco, TX: Word, 1982), 128. For a similar understanding, particularly stressing the applicability of Isa 61 to the mission of the disciples, see Edward Young, *Isaiah* (Grand Rapids: Eerdmans, 1972), 3:458.

115   John Calvin, *Commentary on the Book of the Prophet Isaiah*, transl. William Pringle (Bellingham, WA: Logos Bible Software, 2010), 4:303.

one who believes Jesus is the messiah would map potentially messianic texts to him. Instead, the contribution our research seeks to make is to observe that there are some mappings which land on individuals besides Jesus. And if we take this direction at the fork in the path, such seems to be the case with the disciples in Matt 5:3–4.

5.4.2   Matt 11:5

The second[116] primary allusion to Isa 61:1–3 is in Matthew 11:5.[117] In contrast to 5:3–4, the use of Isa 61 here is clearly in a messianic context. In both the Matthean and Lukan contexts, John the Baptist has sent messengers to ask Σὺ εἶ ὁ ἐρχόμενος ἢ ἕτερον προσδοκῶμεν; (Matt 11:3).[118] The title ὁ ἐρχόμενος is messianic,[119] though it evokes "no figure of a specific strand of eschatological expectation ... [but] bringing to expression in a nonspecific manner the essence of all Jewish eschatological hope."[120] Two additional features might show a messianic context (besides the same arguments seen previously from the discussion of Luke 4 and the history of Isaiah 61's interpretation[121]). First, Matthew has added the phrase τὰ ἔργα τοῦ Χριστοῦ in his account (11:2) as

---

116   Matt 3:16–17 might be seen as an allusion to Isa 61:1–3 (e.g. Turner, *Matthew*, 119), but this work is not concerned with such faint echoes. The loud volume of Isa 42:1 would probably drown out any echo to Isa 61. E.g., Davies and Allison, *Matthew*, 1:337 entertain the possibility that the reference to Isa 42:1 is a quotation.

117   Matthew's fourfold repetition of καί finds a stronger parallel in the fourfold use of καί in Isa 29:18–19 than τότε ... καί ... τότε ... καί in 35:5–6 (see discussion below of other allusions).

118   Luke records the question twice (7:19, 20) with the only difference from Matthew being ἄλλον instead of ἕτερον. Nolland suggests Luke has made the change (*Luke 1–9:20*, 328). Hanna Stettler, "Die Bedeutung der Täuferanfrage in Matthäus 11, 2–6 par Lk 7,18–23 für die Christologie," *Bib* 89.2 (2008): 176 sees all changes made by Luke.

119   Silva, *NIDNTTE*, 2:285.

120   Nolland, *Luke*, 1:329 and *Gospel of Matthew*, 450–51. He discusses other messianic suggestions and points to Gen 49:10 and Hab 2:3 as potentially forming the background of waiting for the messiah. Evans, *Matthew*, 234 also points to Ps 118:26, Zech 9:9, 14:5 and 4Q252 5:3 (which discusses Gen 49:10), though these only contain the idea of "coming" and not of "waiting." Morris, *The Gospel according to Matthew*, 274 argues the expression was not a "recognized messianic title," but that is how Matthew uses it. Luz states "Matthew is probably thinking of John's saying about the stronger one 'who comes after him' (3:11), that is, of the Son of Man. That means that here, as in the reference in 3:11 to the one who will judge by fire" (Luz, *Matthew 1–8*, 133).

121   E.g. Peter Mallen, *The Reading and Transformation of Isaiah in Luke-Acts* (LNTS; London: T&T Clark, 2008), 167; Bird, *Jesus is the Christ*, 84; Carson, "Matthew," 262; Bock, *Proclamation from Prophecy*, 112.

what compels John the Baptist to send his disciples.[122] Second, the concluding makarism (Matt 11:6 = Luke 7:23) emphasizes not stumbling because of Jesus.[123] Stettler puts it quite strongly, "Der Makarismus in v. 6 besagt, dass an der Stellung zu ihm das Heil eines jeden Menschen hängt. Auch das kommt einer messianischen Selbstaussage gleich."[124]

But though the question concerns Jesus' messianic identity,[125] this does not require Jesus' response to be a direct answer.[126] While the messianic context of these features is clear, Isa 61 is nonetheless best understood as only being used eschatologically. Verse 5 evokes several Isaian texts. However, deciding between 29:18–19 and 35:5–6 is difficult. Each text consists of four promises of reversal, with the first of these three finding parallels in Matt 11:5, as illustrated in the following diagram:

TABLE 4 Possible Allusions to Matt 11:5

Isa 29:18–19 (LXX)	Matt 11:5	Isa 35:5–6 (LXX)
καὶ ἀκούσονται ἐν τῇ ἡμέρᾳ ἐκείνῃ κωφοὶ λόγους βιβλίου… ὀφθαλμοὶ τυφλῶν βλέψονται καὶ ἀγαλλιάσονται πτωχοὶ διὰ κύριον ἐν εὐφροσύνῃ καὶ οἱ ἀπηλπισμένοι τῶν ἀνθρώπων ἐμπλησθήσονται εὐφροσύνης	τυφλοὶ ἀναβλέπουσιν καὶ χωλοὶ περιπατοῦσιν, λεπροὶ καθαρίζονται καὶ κωφοὶ ἀκούουσιν καὶ νεκροὶ ἐγείρονται καὶ πτωχοὶ εὐαγγελίζονται	τότε ἀνοιχθήσονται ὀφθαλμοὶ τυφλῶν καὶ ὦτα κωφῶν ἀκούσονται τότε ἁλεῖται ὡς ἔλαφος ὁ χωλός καὶ τρανὴ ἔσται γλῶσσα μογιλάλων ὅτι ἐρράγη ἐν τῇ ἐρήμῳ ὕδωρ καὶ φάραγξ ἐν γῇ διψώσῃ

---

122 For a discussion of sources and how this might fit with Q, see Stephen Witetschek, "What Did John Hear? The Reconstruction of Q 7:18–19 and its Implications" *NovT* 56 (2014): 245–60. Evans, *Matthew*, 234; Lidija Novacovic, *Messiah, the Healer of the Sick: A Study of Jesus as the Son of David in the Gospel of Matthew* (Tübingen: Mohr Siebeck, 2003), 184 writes "Matthew's redaction phrase [τὰ ἔργα τοῦ Χριστοῦ] secures a reply to the personal aspect of John's inquiry."

123 "Only in this beatitude [v 6] is the christological focus explicit (but indirectly the christological focus is just as strong in Mt. 5:11)." Nolland, *The Gospel of Matthew*, 452.

124 Stettler, "Die Bedeutung," 195.

125 The difficulty this poses in light of John's perception of Jesus in Matt 3 is discussed by Morris, *Matthew*, 274–75, who concludes he was asking about the kind of messiah Jesus was. So also Turner, *Matthew*, 290–91.

126 Silva, *NIDNTTE*, 4:482.

If a choice had to be made, 29:18–19 is slightly preferable since βλέψονται (29:18) is closer to Matthew's ἀναβλέπουσιν than ἀνοιχθήσονται (35:5), and since πτωχοί (29:19) would nicely form a bridge to πτωχοί in 61:1.[127] However, if Matthew has something like the MT in mind, the occurrence in 35:5 of פקח (LXX ἀνοίγω) might form this bridge to difficult פְּקַח־קוֹחַ in 61:1 (LXX ἀνάβλεψις). Furthermore, Isa 26:19 may also be in view. This would require combining elements of two phrases, though they are still near each other: ἀναστήσονται οἱ νεκροί, καὶ ἐγερθήσονται οἱ ἐν τοῖς μνημείοις. Yet a choice between these options may not be necessary and Jesus may simply be alluding to an overall Isaian theme.[128] In any case, though Isa 26:19, 29:18–19, and 35:5–6 are all eschatological, *none* are messianic. None contain specific information about an agent but only describe what kind of activity can be expected in the eschaton. This alone demonstrates the texts which Jesus uses to answer John's messianic question must not necessarily address that question directly. We can conclude with France, "The passages in Isaiah most obviously alluded to in Jesus' list of miracles in v. 5 (Isa 35:5–6; cf. 26:19; 29:18) concern the eschatological blessings brought by God himself, and do not envisage a separate Messiah figure."[129]

Why call these texts to mind then? It seems that though Jesus does not allude to "messianic proof texts" here, he does evoke eschatological passages which have messianic implications. Jesus' reply responds to John's incorrect assumptions about the nature of the kingdom and the time of judgment. This is especially clear in the Matthean version, which has added the detail of John being in prison (11:2).[130] John had understood ὁ ἐρχόμενος (cf. 3:11) as one who would "clean out his threshing floor" and "burn up the chaff with unquenchable

---

[127] This was a common exegetical practice. Sanders illustrates this with the repetition of ἄφεσις in Isa 61:1 and 58:6 in Luke 4. James A. Sanders, "Isaiah in Luke" *Int* 36.2 (1982): 151. This is Hillel's second *midot, gezera sawa*. Craig A. Evans and L. Novakovic, "Midrash," *Dictionary of Jesus and the Gospels*, 2d ed., *Edition*, ed. Joel B. Green, Jeannine K. Brown, and Nicholas Perrin, (Downers Grove, IL: IVP Academic, 2013), 589. Though the healing of lepers is often seen to be without an Isaian allusion, Evans argues for Isa 53:4, comparing *b. Sanh. 98*. (*Matthew*, 235).

[128] So Nolland, *Luke 1–9:20*, 330.

[129] France, *The Gospel of Matthew*, 423 n17. See also Stettler, "Die Bedeutung," 179. Bock, *From Prophecy to Fulfillment*, 113 makes a similar observation about Isa 29 and 35, but because of his interpretation of Luke 4:16–30 does not apply a similar understanding to Isa 61 here. Contra Morris, *The Gospel according to Matthew*, 277, "But Jesus is using words that will evoke recollections of messianic prophecy: the blind, the deaf, and the lame (also the dumb) are the subject of prophecy (Isa. 35:5–6)." However, this statement may be using "messianic" as a rough equivalent for "eschatological." Unfortunately, the two are not always distinguished.

[130] Luke's record of this is much farther removed (3:20).

fire" (3:12). Now in prison, it seems as if this would not happen.[131] Jesus addresses this misunderstanding about the nature of the eschaton instead of directly answering his surface question. Moreover, this answer suggests to John that he "cannot assume that his captivity will end because of Jesus' ministry; suffering continues even while the kingdom is present and the expected figure has arrived."[132]

Furthermore, the works done by Jesus do not in themselves uniquely identify him as *the* messiah. Not only does the broad portrait of the apostles in Luke-Acts confirm this (see above under discussion of Luke 4:16–30), but the immediate context of Matthew includes the sending of the twelve (Matt. 10:1, 7–8). Though the passive voice in Jesus' response (Matt 11:5=Luke 7:22) is explained by the Isaian allusions, it also significantly hides the agent. The immediate context of Matt 10 includes the disciples as those who preach and perform miracles. In fact, their message (10:7) is the same as Jesus' (4:17, so also with John in 3:2) and their miraculous works (10:8) closely parallel Jesus' (chs 8–9).[133] Kynes discusses the parallels in ch 10 and concludes

> The mission of the Twelve is portrayed as an extension of Jesus' own mission ... the messianic works ... appear to include the deeds of the disciples for the list of deeds expected in the time of the Messiah ... describes their activity, too. In the mission given to them Jesus' disciples share in that presence of the kingdom which is evident in his ministry.[134]

Whether in word or deed, "it is enough for a disciple to be like his lord" (10:25). Thus, performing the actions of 11:5 does not prove that one is the messiah, since the context just prior to 11:2–6 emphasizes that others besides the messiah accomplish them. Instead, they demonstrate the arrival and nature of the eschaton. John's question is ultimately answered since Jesus is clearly the

---

131 France, *The Gospel of Matthew*, 423–5; Luz, *Matthew*, 133; Blomberg, *Matthew*, 185; Osborne, *Matthew*, 415. Osborne also notes that 35:4 and 61:2 include themes of judgment. Thus, if the wider context of these passages are being evoked, then Jesus' criticism of John is lessened. Alternatively, it may be that Jesus is "studiously avoiding mention of judgment even when citing texts that intermingle blessing and judgment, suggest[ing] that the judgment is delayed, even while the promised blessings are being fulfilled in his ministry" (D. A. Carson, "Do the Prophets and the Law Quit Prophesying before John? A Note on Matthew 11:13," in *The Gospels and the Scriptures of Israel*, ed. Craig A. Evans and William R. Stegner (JSNTSup; Sheffield: Sheffield Academic, 1994), 180–81.

132 Brian C. Dennert, *John the Baptist and the Jewish Setting of Matthew* (WUNT; Tübingen: Mohr Siebeck, 2015), 204. Dennert also notes that the response to John's situation has relevance for Jesus' followers who can expect similar persecution (200).

133 Nolland, *The Gospel of Matthew*, 417 sees a chiasm in 10:8 with 8:2–4 and 9:18–26.

134 Kynes, *A Christology of Solidarity*, 75–77.

essential figure in accomplishing these works. Without him, the disciple band and the mission of ch 10 would be nothing. However, the way Isa 61 addresses John's messianic question is indirect because of the three contextual factors described above – similarity with the other Isaian texts in 11:5, the thought flow of the pericope concerning the nature of the eschaton, and the immediately prior position of mission discourse.[135]

At this point, we are faced with a dilemma similar to Matt 5:3–4 regarding whether or not we should see the herald figure indirectly mapped into the blend. But the results are the same in 11:5 as our previous discussion. If the allusion does not evoke the herald figure, then we have a non-messianic mapping in that a potentially messianic text is evoked but attention is given elsewhere and nothing maps to Jesus. In this case, Jesus has decided to use Isa 61 as he uses Is 29 and 35 – eschatologically but not messianically. On the other hand, if we follow the insights of Blending Theory, suggesting the herald figure is intended to be indirectly mapped into the blend, then there is no reason Jesus exclusively occupies the space of the herald. The surrounding context demonstrates that the disciples to are on God's eschatological mission, performing the same role as the herald of Isa 61.

5.5 Conclusion

The investigations of this chapter into the textual features of Isa 61:1–3 and its use in Sir 48, *Tg Isa*, 1QH[a] 23, *Tg Num*, 11Q13, 4Q521, Luke 4, Luke 7, Matt 5, and Matt 11 can be used to construct a metaphorical conversation of readers of Isa 61. The original text speaks of a herald whom the Spirit of YHWH empowers to play a key role in the process of restoring the עֲנָוִים. However, there are insufficient indicators in the surrounding context to determine with certainty if Isaiah has in mind a messiah figure. Subsequent history of interpretation shows how uncertain this text is. Ben Sira considers the herald and sees him as a description of the historical Isaiah. Targum Jonathan, as would be expected

---

135   This interpretation contrasts Matthew W. Bates, *The Birth of the Trinity: Jesus, God, and the Spirit in the New Testament and Early Christian Interpretations of the Old Testament* (Oxford: Oxford University Press, 2015), 94–96. He argues for a prosopological understanding based on 11Q13 and 4Q521, as well as Irenaeus, *Epid.* 53, Origen, *Comm. Jo.* 6. 196, Tertullian, *Prax.* 11, and *Barn.* 14.7–9, so in Isa 61:1–3, "the Spirit had inspired Isaiah to step into a future theodramatic role and from this provisional platform in the divine economy, to perform a speech in the character (*prosōpon*) of the anointed herald of God" (94). However, even if there are good reasons to see the herald figure evoked in the NT contexts (Bates is considering Luke 4), we have seen that the disciples can be excluded, which would deny the possibility of a "theodramatic role."

from a translation, does not significantly contribute to the conversation. There is not enough to tell if this reader of Isa 61 would have agreed with Ben Sira or if he would have seen the figure as eschatological, but he does emphasize that the person occupies the role of prophet. 1QH^a 23 uses the passage self-referentially, but debates about the author make it unclear as to whether or not this is the Teacher of Righteousness. This person is considered an important eschatological figure, but it is unlikely that this was seen as the messiah. 11Q13 also picks up the herald and sees him as someone significant, Melchizedek, whom the majority of scholars take as an angelic power, though some take as YHWH and even fewer as the messiah. 4Q521 can be seen as continuing the conversation, but though the text speaks of a messiah (or messiahs) earlier, by the time it uses the allusion to Isa 61 only God is portrayed as actualizing the promises. It is possible, but by no means certain, that the earlier messiah(s) are assumed as his agents. When Luke 4 speaks in the conversation, it too presents its own view of the herald, claiming that the figure maps to Jesus of Nazareth. Yet that pericope presents Jesus as a prophet, but not necessarily the messiah. Such a use lines up well with the allusion in Luke 7:22.

When Matthew chimes in, he is clearly in agreement with those who understand Isa 61 eschatologically and as being fulfilled at his present time. His explicit interests lie in using the text to pronounce the nature of the promised blessings (having the kingdom, being comforted, inheriting the land) and the recipients of those blessings (the poor in spirit, those who mourn). Unlike the reference in Luke 4, neither Matt 5 nor 11 explicitly picks up the herald figure and connects him with anyone in his narrative. In this sense, Matthew's hermeneutic is non-messianic in that neither the potentially messianic herald, not Jesus, are overtly mapped into the blend. We also considered the possible route taken by several commentators and suggested by Blending Theory that Isa 61's herald figure is subtly, or indirectly, present in the blend via the governing principles of Pattern Completion and Topology so that an emergent structure arises in which there is a figure who accomplishes these tasks. If, for example, the mourners are comforted, this implies a comforter. If the poor have the gospel preached to them, this suggests a preacher. The herald of Isa 61 provides this role. But though this figure clearly maps to Jesus, there is no sufficient reason to see him as the sole occupant of this space. Instead, the context of both Matt 5 and 11 provide evidence that disciples also are on God's eschatological mission and fulfill the same role as Jesus of the herald in Isa 61. From this perspective, Matthew's hermeneutic is non-messianic, not in that the herald does not map to Jesus. He does. But the non-messianic hermeneutic can be seen in that herald's additional mappings to Jesus' disciples, who, because of their proximity to Jesus, participate in his mission and role and thus can be clothed in the same messianic imagery from Isa 61.

CHAPTER 6

Conclusion

6.1 Variety within the Case Studies Reveals Matthew's Overall Hermeneutic

Since our aim has been to investigate Matthew's general hermeneutic of fulfillment, we have not spent as much time as we could on only one of his allusions to the Old Testament. If, for example, we only considered the use of eschatological shepherding imagery, this would be insufficient to make claims about Matthew's wider use of the Hebrew Bible. If we had only considered one case study, we could be excused in thinking that Matthew anomalously had broken from his normal pattern. Instead, we have seen four studies in the above chapters, each having its own sub-studies, all of which establish Matthew's practice of using messianic texts in non-messianic ways. Other scholars have observed a non-messianic use of messianic texts elsewhere (though, to the best of my knowledge, not in Matthew), but one of the unique contributions of this work is to connect several such instances in order to describe Matthew's overall approach to the fulfillment of Scripture.

Our approach in the above studies has been inductive, attempting to craft descriptions which best fit the data and this has resulted in a variety of non-messianic mappings. On the one hand, we have seen some consistency in the case studies. We have explored times when the Matthean Jesus creates a conceptual blend in which he evokes a messianic text as a source domain and:

(1) maps various elements into the blend, but does not explicitly map the messianic figure himself.

OR

(2) maps a messianic figure from a source domain
(3) and maps the disciples from the target domain to that figure.

The more minimalist understanding of the allusion to Isa 61 fits the description of (1), but the more maximalist view of this allusion, as well as the other case studies fit comfortably in steps (2) and (3). Yet, there have been variations within this broad framework. We have seen Matthew pick up a potentially messianic passage but not explicitly map the figure in question into the blend in the allusion to Isa 61:1–3 in Matt 5:3–4 and 11:5. However, in that case, we noted that the difficulty of knowing how much of a source text Matthew intends to be relevant for an allusion and, taking our lead from Blending Theory, considered the possibility that the herald figure is subtly mapped into the blend. If this route is taken, the works done by the herald figure are accomplished by both Jesus and his followers, a point which both surrounding contexts emphasize. In this situation, the messianic figure maps with referential opacity to both Jesus and the disciples in the same allusion. In the other case studies, the potentially messianic figures map to Jesus in one part of Matthew, but to the disciples in another part. The eschatological shepherd maps to Jesus in Matt 15:24 and 25:31–46, and to the disciples in 10:6. The temple stone maps to Jesus in 21:42, but to Peter in 16:18. The temple builder maps to Jesus in 16:18, but to the disciples in 21:42. In the second case study, especially with Ps 80 in view, there was a double mapping of the son. Jesus is the son as one who suffers with the vine, but the role of caring for the future prosperity of the vine goes to the replacement farmers. There, we saw more than referential opacity. The same figure has different roles, each of which is accomplished by different agents.

Furthermore, not only have we seen variety in the way there has been a double mapping, but we have also seen variety in the ways and clarity with which the element in the source text could have been viewed as messianic. Both textual features and the history of interpretation demonstrate that Ezek 34, Jer 23, Ps 118, and the temple builder of 2 Sam 7 have a high degree of messianic potential. Isa 61 and especially Isa 5 were not so evidently messianic. From the text of Isa 61 the herald figure may or may not be a figure arriving in the eschaton, and even if he were eschatological he may not be the messiah. These different possibilities manifested themselves in the history of interpretation. Isa 5 had far less messianic potential, but even then later usage of the image shows how easily issues of eschatology and agency played a part in the milieu surrounding Isa 5. But Matthew could have used all these passages, despite their varying amount of potential, to inform his readers of Jesus' messianic identity. The fact that he does not used them in this way shows us something more than Matthew missing low-hanging fruit. Instead, the variety of uses in the above case studies suggests Matthew is not as routinely interested in exploiting the OT for reasons to support his view of Jesus as often as some scholars claim. More than that, Matthew has a practice of mapping messianic figures to both Jesus and the disciples.

We have also seen a variety in the clarity and ways Matthew maps the disciples into the blend. Chapter 2's discussion of eschatological shepherd imagery provided the most direct reference to the disciples as they, the listed apostles (Matt 10:1–4), are commissioned by Jesus to search for the lost sheep in 10:6.

CONCLUSION 215

Chapter 3's examination of the use of Isaiah' vineyard was also quite emphatic about the disciples' place in the blend as the logic of the parable precludes the son figure from having any abiding role in the vineyard due to his murder. Instead, there is a clear transfer of roles as the old farmers are disposed of and new ones are hired. Elements of eschatological temple building in chapter 4, though not without complications, also have a relatively clear mapping of the disciples into the blend. Though there have been a few detractors regarding the identity of the rock on which Jesus builds his church, the majority of modern interpreters rightly see this as some kind of reference to Peter. Matt 7:24–27 fitting in the temple building motif was something of an anomaly as those envisioned as building on a rock form a wider circle than the twelve disciples/apostles in the other instances. This suggests that Matthew may be comfortable describing even Jesus' followers outside of the apostolic band in messianic terms. But the other allusions in chapter 4 and especially chapter 5 have a much more subtle way of getting the disciples into the blend. Though the quote from Psalm 118:22–23 does not specifically mention new builders, we can see how they could easily get there through the governing principle of Pattern Completion. Their presence is likely in temple building blend of Matt 21:42 since they were just mapped into the vineyard blend of 21:33–41 (which envelopes the temple building blend by continuing in v 43) as the replacement farmers. Deciding if the disciples are in the blend created by alluding to Isa 61:1–3 in Matt 5:3–4 and 11:5 is more difficult. We noted the challenge of knowing how much a source text eventually is relevant for understanding the target text, but explored the possibility that there too, the disciples, along with Jesus, end up in the blend.

The variety of ways Matthew maps the messianic figure and the disciples into the blend (or left in the generic space), as well as the different ways a double mapping / referential opacity connects the messianic figure and the disciples, shows that we are concerned with a spectrum of cases. This has two significant effects. First, it means the above examples reinforce one another. If, for example, we had only considered the temple building blend in Matt 21:42, we may not have detected that this informs us of the disciples' role. But since they are mapped into the blend elsewhere (and significantly in the preceding vineyard blend), the likelihood they are here highly increases. The clearer precedents clarify the more difficult ones. Second, this spectrum of case studies shows that the resulting non-messianic hermeneutic does not stem from an obscurity in either Matthew's understanding of the source text or a unique feature in the Matthean alluding text, but manifests a generality of his fulfillment hermeneutic.

6.2 Matthew's Hermeneutic May Occur Elsewhere

This generality from a range of different case studies raises questions regarding the hermeneutics of other biblical authors and the uniqueness of Matthew's approach. Because of its strong emphases on fulfillment and discipleship (and to have a manageable scope of study), we have restricted ourselves to the Gospel of Matthew. But no step of our argumentation implies our findings would not also apply to other authors of the NT. While we have seen differences in the ways various authors handle particular texts, we have also seen variety in the way Matthew himself uses Scripture. Thus, the noted differences, say between Matthew's use of Isa 61 and Luke's, do not suggest the latter's hermeneutic should not be described as broadly eschatological.

While forming a case for the hermeneutics of other authors would require examining sufficient case studies from their corpa, we have observed a couple which scholars have already been investigated, namely Luke's use of Isaian servant imagery and Revelation's use of Psalm 2 (cf. 1.2.4). Other areas of inquiry come to mind for inquiry, such as the parallel Synoptic accounts for the case studies seen here; the snake crusher of Gen 3:15 in Rom 16:20; the eschatological farmers and builders in 1 Cor 3; the warrior of Isa 59 in Eph 6; the herald of Isa 52 in Rom 10:15 (cf. Eph 6:15); Joshua / conquest imagery in Hebrews (e.g. 13:5–6, cf. Josh 1:5 and Ps 118:6); or the delivered singer of Ps 40 with a new song in texts like Rev 5:9 and 14:3. Messianic connotations of the above may often have been overlooked because the mapping scheme targets the disciples. But if a hermeneutic like the one proposed here spills over to other NT authors, this may well account for such phenomena. We have not constructed an argument for other authors, but the evidence may head in that direction.

6.3 The Case Studies Demonstrate "Messianic" Should Be Stretched to "Eschatological"

Though the above four case studies are broad enough to suggest we are dealing with Matthew's hermeneutic in general, still we have only been able to consider a small slice of Matthew's seemingly ubiquitous use of the First Testament. This calls for caution even as we proceed to draw conclusions about Matthew's overall hermeneutic of fulfillment. While the case studies have explored different instances of Matthew's non-messianic use of messianic texts, this data does not imply a messianic hermeneutic cannot be found in Matthew. Far from it. Matthew frequently uses the Hebrew Bible in order to bolster his fundamental conviction that Jesus is the messiah. In fact, we have had occasion to briefly consider some of these instances in order to set the stage for Matthew's surprising non-messianic use. For example, we can be certain that Matthew sees the eschatological shepherd as the messiah because of his messianic use in 25:31–46. Our argument has frequently required a messianic use to establish that the text or image in question was seen by Matthew as messianic in other places. Moreover, both scholarly and popular works have well documented Matthew's overwhelmingly messianic use of the OT outside of the relatively small scope here. Furthermore, Matthew's practice of using non-messianic texts for messianic purposes highlights the unexpected times when he uses messianic texts for non-messianic purposes.

Yet Matthew's references to the Hebrew Bible which easily fit in the category "messianic," do not mean this is an adequate description of all his uses of fulfillment texts. It is one piece of the puzzle – a very large piece – but still it does not comprise the whole. The above four case studies, then, do not supplant the category "messianic," but supplement it. These are instances which do not fit the normal use of "messianic" and so call for nuancing our understanding so that the bounds of the category are stretched to include both the prevalent messianic uses of the First Testament as well as the ones exemplified in the above case studies. The label "broadly eschatological" accomplishes this purpose nicely as it emphasizes the ushering in of the kingdom promises and leaves the question of agency open. Sometimes the spotlight does not fall upon any agency, even though we can easily imagine Matthew having a messianic interpretation of the text (e.g. the allusions to Isa 61 in Matt 5:3–4 and 11:5). If we describe Matthew's approach in using the OT as "messianic," we are left with the difficulty of why he does not explicitly map such figures into the blend but remain in the generic space. At other times, Matthew is concerned with agency, but Matthew maps the expected messianic figure to the disciples as well as Jesus. In many other occasions, Matthew goes to lengths to establish that Jesus is the key agent whom God uses to bring in his kingdom. Labeling Matthew's hermeneutic as "messianic" works well for this last category, but not for the first two. A more appropriate label for his use of fulfillment texts which accounts for wider scope of data is to label his hermeneutic as "broadly eschatological."

6.4 Possible Explanations

If the above four case studies suffice to inform us of Matthew's hermeneutical approach in general such that messianic imagery can be expanded from mapping exclusively to Jesus to having a kind of referential opacity in which it also maps to the disciples, how can this be explained? Two features of Matthew's gospel can account for this phenomenon. First, the ministry of Matthew's Jesus centers around the central proclamation "repent, for the kingdom of heaven is at hand" (4:17). Though Jesus' messianic identity becomes more prominent (as far as the unfolding narrative is concerned) after Caesarea Philippi, it is by no means Matthew's exclusive interest. Instead, the primary emphasis focuses on the arrival and nature of the kingdom along with its implications. It is God who ultimately fulfills the OT's kingdom hope, and this means Matthew is not always necessarily concerned with the agent(s) he uses to accomplish these purposes. Thus, the approach advocated here of a "broadly eschatological" hermeneutic fits well with the overall purpose of Matthew not so much being to persuade readers that Jesus is the messiah, but to explain the way in which the kingdom has been (and will be) ushered in. Certainly Matthew eagerly seeks to present Jesus as the messiah and son of God. But this can hardly be his whole purpose. A way of describing Matthew's purpose which accounts for this as well as the other material in the gospel is to see it as "kingdom-centric." Thus, if Matthew's overall purpose is kingdom focused, why should we not expect him to read and apply the Scriptures from that same vantage point?

Second, Matthew can map his figures with a kind of referential opacity so that messianic texts and images are connected to both Jesus and his followers because of his theology of discipleship. Though figures besides Jesus occupy messianic space, these are not arbitrary agents whom God uses alongside of Jesus. Instead, only their proximity to the messiah grants them in such a position. Our first case study brought this out the most directly, as Jesus commissions the apostles with his authority to search for the lost sheep of the house of Israel. The statement in 10:25, ἀρκετὸν τῷ μαθητῇ ἵνα γένηται ὡς ὁ διδάσκαλος αὐτοῦ, applies in its immediate context to suffering and yet this demonstrates wider logic of the Mission Discourse. However, though other Matthean texts considered in this research are not as explicit, each in its own way has indications that the disciples only come to occupy the same messianic mapping as Jesus because of their connection to him. In our examination of the Wicked Tenant Parable in chapter 3, the replacement farmers are those who will hand over the crop at the proper time (cf. the previous parable which compares two children – the latter represents those who repented, specifically at the ministry of John – see 21:32). However, this should also be understood in light of the rejection of the current leaders being due to their hostility to the son. The importance of proximity to Jesus is not nearly as prominent here as in the Mission Discourse, and yet the ultimate reason one group is rejected and the other put in its place in the Wicked Tenant Parable centers around how one relates to the son. God patiently suffers with the current religious establishment until they cross the line of killing his son. Similarly, the citation of Ps 118:22–23, considered in the first section of chapter 4, also frames the central issue as how one reacts to the stone by either rejecting it or building with it. The new builders are only legitimate because they build on (or with) the once-rejected stone. In the other two Matthean passages examined in chapter 4, proximity to Jesus clearly is of utmost importance for being mapped into a messianic blend. Jesus describes Peter as the temple foundation because of his conviction that Σὺ εἶ ὁ Χριστὸς ὁ υἱὸς τοῦ θεοῦ τοῦ ζῶντος (16:16) and those who build on the rock (7:24–27) are explained in v 24, Πᾶς οὖν ὅστις ἀκούει μου τοὺς λόγους τούτους καὶ ποιεῖ αὐτούς.[1]

Thus, though there are indications in each of the case studies examined here that messianic imagery can be applied only because of one's proximity to Jesus, Matt 10 stands head and shoulders above the rest in explicating the nature of this relationship. Matthew certainly would not allow any of the disciples to share the description "messiah." None but Jesus in his glories shall wear that honored title. Yet the Gospel as a whole portrays the messiah as on a mission, a mission which calls for participation (e.g. 9:36–38). Though this emerges elsewhere in Matthew, the Mission Discourse in particular portrays the disciples as doing several of the same messianic actions as Jesus – preaching the message of the kingdom, performing miracles, pronouncing judgment, offering forgiveness. If one is concerned that the argumentation of this research could be used in reverse, to demonstrate the invalidity of these proposed allusions because of the uncomfortable closeness it creates between Jesus and the disciples, the Mission Discourse alone suffices to show that it is Matthew himself who brings this surprising proximity to our attention.

The categories of cognitive linguistics prove particularly helpful in considering both the closeness and distance between Jesus and the disciples. Due to his conviction that only Jesus is the messiah, and yet his view that the disciples are sent out by Jesus to participate in Jesus' own mission, the mapping of messianic texts and images to the disciples should be described as "role" and not "identity." However, though we can utilize the crisp terminology of cognitive linguistics, Matthew does not have this luxury. Perhaps this explains why the phenomenon considered here falls in the realm of allusion and not citation. Granted, we have considered one citation (Matt 21:42 // Ps 118:22–23), but we could not have arrived at our conclusions if we had not been attentive to the surrounding allusions. Though it is not altogether clear why the non-messianic hermeneutic established in this research does not emerge in a study of Matthew's quotations, one possible explanation for this is that allusions

---

[1] The earlier placement of μου may be intended to bring out the centrality of Jesus.

provide Matthew with the kind of ambiguity necessary to distance himself from identifying the disciples as the messiah. Again, Jesus exclusively bears this title in Matthew. Thus, it may be that a citation in which the disciples are explicitly linked with a well-known messianic figure would make Matthew fear that too strong of a connection would be made and thus betray his fundamental conviction about the uniqueness of Jesus. Making these sorts of connections via allusion may provide the right amount of distance and ambiguity to communicate that the disciples share in this role, but not in this identity. While it is difficult to know with certainty *why* this happens, we have seen *that* it does and the above explanation is at least a viable explanation.

By considering a variety of situations, the case studies of this research signal that the description of Matthew's hermeneutic of fulfillment as "messianic" must be nuanced as it is too narrow to fit all the data. When one attends to allusions, options of other agency, whether only by God or also through the disciples as messianic agents, must be considered and a broader eschatological hermeneutic demands a place at the table. This description of Matthew's hermeneutic of fulfillment opens up possibilities and reveals fresh options when considering other issues in Matthew. Who knows what may emerge if the broader eschatological paradigm presented here were considered in studying other topics, like the significant allusions to the "son of man" of Dan 7 (who also has corporate aspects; cf. 7:27), the Elijah/Elisha typology (for John – Matt 11:14; Jesus – Matt 8:1–4, 14–15; disciples – Matt 8:22), the comparison of Peter to Eliakim (Matt 16:19), or even the examples in other corpa (6.2)? Space has not allowed such investigations to be made here. But the above case studies demonstrate that research into topics like these should at least allow for the possibility of a broadly eschatological hermeneutic. We have already seen and have reason to think we will continue to see the Matthean Jesus map a messianic image to others besides himself because he summons them to the honor and responsibility of participating in his own messianic vocation.

Bibliography

Abasciano, Brian J. *Paul's Use of the Old Testament in Romans 9.1–9: An Intertextual and Theological Exegesis*. London: T&T Clark, 2005.

Abernethy, Andrew. *The Book of Isaiah and God's Kingdom: A Thematic-Theological Approach*. Downers Grove, IL: InterVarsity, 2016.

Adam, Sean A. and Seth M. Ehorn, editors. *Composite Citations in Antiquity: Volume One: Jewish, Graeco-Roman, and Early Christian Uses*. LNTS. New York: T&T Clark, 2016.

Adam, Sean A. and Seth M. Ehorn, editors. *Composite Citations in Antiquity: Volume Two: New Testament Uses*. LNTS. New York: T&T Clark, 2018.

Adna, J. *Jesu Stellung zum Tempel: Die Tempelaktion and das Tempelwort als Ausdruck seiner messianischen Sendung*. WUNT. Tübingen: Mohr Siebeck, 2000.

Akpunonu, Peter D. *The Vine, Israel, and the Church*. New York: Peter Lang, 2004.

Aland, Barbara et al., editors. *The Greek New Testament*, Fifth Revised Edition. Stuttgart, Germany: Deutsche Bibelgesellschaft, 2014.

Alexander, Ralph H. "Ezekiel." In *The Expositor's Bible Commentary: with the New International Version*, edited by Frank E. Gaebelein, 6:736–996. Grand Rapids: Zondervan, 1986.

Allen, Leslie C. *Ezekiel*. WBC. Nashville: Thomas Nelson, 1994.

Allen, Leslie C. *Jeremiah: A Commentary*, edited by William P. Brown, Carol A. Newsom, and David L. Petersen. OTL. Louisville, KY: Westminster John Knox Press, 2008.

Allen, Leslie C. *Psalms 101–150*. WBC. Nashville: Word, Thomas Nelson, 2002.

Allison, Dale. *The New Moses: A Matthean Typology*. Minneapolis: Fortress Press, 1993.

Arndt, William, Frederick W. Danker, Walter Bauer, and F. Wilbur Gingrich. *A Greek-English Lexicon of the New Testament and Other Early Christian Literature*. Third Edition. Chicago: University of Chicago Press, 2000.

Atkinson, Kenneth R. "On the Use of Scripture in Development of Militant Davidic Messianism at Qumran: New Light from *Psalm of Solomon 17*." In *The Interpretation of Scripture in Early Judaism and Christianity: Studies in Language and Tradition*, edited by Craig A. Evans, 106–23. JSPSS. Sheffield: Sheffield Academic, 2000.

Bailey, Kenneth E. "The Parable of the Two Builders." In *Literary Structure and Rhetorical Strategies in the Hebrew Bible*, edited by L. J. de Regt, J. de Waard, and R. P. Fokkelman. Assen, The Netherlands: Van Gorcum, 1996.

Baker, Margaret. "Isaiah." In *Eerdman's Commentary on the Bible*, edited by James D. Dunn and John Williams Rogerson, 489–352. Grand Rapids: Eerdmans, 2003.

Baldwin, Joyce G. "*Semah* as a Technical Term in the Prophets." *VT* 14 (1964): 93–97.

Balz, Horst Robert, and Gerhard Schneider. *Exegetical Dictionary of the New Testament*. Grand Rapids: Eerdmans, 1990.

Barber, Michael P. "Jesus as the Davidic Temple Builder and Peter's Priestly Role in Matthew 16:16–19." *JBL* 132.4 (2013): 935–53.

Barclay, John M. G. *Paul and the Gift*. Grand Rapids: Eerdmans, 2015.

Barton, Stephen C. *Discipleship and Family Ties in Mark and Matthew*. SNTSMS. Cambridge: Cambridge University Press, 1994.

Basser, Herbert W. *The Gospel of Matthew and Judaic Traditions: A Relevance-based Commentary*. Leiden: Brill, 2015.

Bates, Matthew W. *The Birth of the Trinity: Jesus, God, and the Spirit in the New Testament and Early Christian Interpretations of the Old Testament*. Oxford: Oxford University Press, 2015.

Bates, Matthew W. *The Hermeneutics of the Apostolic Proclamation: The Center of Paul's Method of Scriptural Interpretation*. Waco: Baylor: 2012.

Bauckham, Richard J. "Christology." *Dictionary of Jesus and the Gospels*. Second Edition. Edited by Joel B. Green, Jeannine K. Brown, and Nicholas Perrin, 125–34. Downers Grove, IL: IVP Academic, 2013.

Bauckham, Richard. "The Messianic Interpretation of Isa 10:34 in the Dead Sea Scrolls, 2 Baruch and the Preaching of John the Baptist." *DSD* 2.2 (1995): 208.

Bauer, David R. "The Major Characters of Matthew's Story: Their Function and Significance." *Interpretation* 46.4 (1992): 357–67.

Baxter, Wayne. "From Ruler to Teacher: The Extending of the Shepherd Metaphor in Early Jewish and Christian Writings." In *Early Christian Literature and Intertextuality: Volume 1: Thematic Studies*, edited by H. Daniel Zacharias and Craig A. Evans, 208–24. London: T&T Clark, 2009.

Baxter, Wayne. *Israel's Only Shepherd: Matthew's Shepherd Motif and His Social Setting*. London: T&T Clark, 2012.

Beale, Gregory K. *The Book of Revelation: A Commentary on the Greek Text*. NIGTC. Grand Rapids: Eerdmans, 1999.

Beale, Gregory K. "Did Jesus and the Apostles Preach the Right Doctrine from the Wrong Texts? Revisiting the Debate Seventeen Years Later in the Light of Peter Enn's Book *Inspiration and Incarnation*." *Them* 32.1 (Oct 2006): 18–43.

Beale, Gregory K. *Handbook on the New Testament Use of the Old Testament: Exegesis and Interpretation*. Grand Rapids: Baker, 2012.

Beale, Gregory K. *The Temple and the Church's Mission: A Biblical Theology of the Dwelling Place of God*. NSBT. Downers Grove, IL: IVP Academic, 2004.

Beale, Gregory K. and Donald A. Carson, eds. *Commentary on the New Testament Use of the Old Testament*. Grand Rapids: Baker Academic, 2007.

Beasley-Murray, George R. *John*. WBC. Nashville: Thomas Nelson, 1999.

Beaton, Richard. *Isaiah's Christ in Matthew's Gospel*. SNTSMS: Cambridge: Cambridge University Press, 2002.

BIBLIOGRAPHY

Beers, Holly. *The Followers of Jesus as the 'Servant': Luke's Model from Isaiah for the Disciples in Luke-Acts*. LNTS: London: T&T Clark, 2016.

Beetham, Christopher A. *Echoes of Scripture in the Letter of Paul to the Colossians*. Biblical Interpretation. Leiden: Brill, 2008.

Begg, Christopher T. "The Identity of the Princes in Ezekiel 19: Some Reflections." *ETL* 65.4 (1989): 358–69.

Ben-Porat, Ziva. "The Poetics of Literary Allusion." *PTL* (1976): 105–28.

Beuken, W. A. M. "Servant and Herald of Good News: Isaiah 61 as an Interpretation of Isaiah 40–55." In *The Book of Isaiah: Le Livre D'Isaie: les oracles et leurs relectures unité et complexité de l'ouvrage*, edited by Jacques Vermeylen, 411–42. Leuven: University Press, 1989.

Bigane III, John E. *Faith, Christ or Peter: Matthew 16:18 in Sixteenth Century Roman Catholic Exegesis*. Washington D.C.: University Press of America, 1981.

Bird, Michael F. *Are You the One Who is to Come? The Historical Jesus and the Messianic Question*. Grand Rapids: Baker Academic, 2009.

Bird, Michael F. "Jesus and the 'Parting of the Ways.'" In *Handbook for the Study of the Historical Jesus: How to Study the Historical Jesus*, edited by Tom Holmén and Stanley E. Porter, 1183–1215. Leiden: Brill, 2011.

Bird, Michael F. *Jesus is the Christ: The Messianic Testimony of the Gospels*. Downers Grove, IL: InterVarsity, 2013.

Black, Matthew. "The Christological Use of the Old Testament in the New Testament." *NTS* 18.1 (1971): 1–14.

Blenkinsopp, Joseph. *Ezekiel*. Interpretation. Louisville: Westminster John Knox, 1990.

Blenkinsopp, Joseph. *Isaiah 56–66: A New Translation with Introduction and Commentary*. AB. New York: Doubleday, 2003.

Blenkinsopp, Joseph. *Opening the Sealed Book: Interpretations of the Book of Isaiah in Late Antiquity*. Grand Rapids: Eerdmans, 2006.

Block, Daniel I. *The Book of Ezekiel: Chapters 1–24*. NICOT. Grand Rapids: Eerdmans, 1997.

Block, Daniel I. *The Book of Ezekiel: Chapters 25–48*. NICOT. Grand Rapids: Eerdmans, 1998.

Block, Daniel I. *Beyond the River Chebar: Studies in the Kingship and Eschatology in the Book of Ezekiel*. Cambridge: James Clarke & Co, 2013.

Block, Daniel I. "Bringing Back David: Ezekiel's Messianic Hope." In *The Lord's Anointed: Interpretation of Old Testament Messianic Texts*, edited by Philip E. Satterthwaite, Richard S. Hess and Gordon J. Wenham, 167–88. Grand Rapids: Baker, 1995.

Block, Daniel I. "My Servant David: Ancient Israel's Vision of the Messiah." In *Israel's Messiah in the Bible and the Dead Sea Scrolls*, edited by Richard S. Hess and M. Daniel Carroll, 17–56. Grand Rapids, 2003.

Blomberg, Craig L. "Degrees of Reward in the Kingdom of Heaven?" *JETS* 35.2 (June 1992): 159–72.

Blomberg, Craig L. "Matthew." In *Commentary on the New Testament Use of the Old Testament*, edited by Gregory K. Beale and Donald A. Carson, 1–109. Grand Rapids: Baker Academic, 2007.

Blomberg, Craig L. *Matthew*. NAC. Nashville: Broadman & Holman Publishers, 1992.

Blomberg, Craig L. "Reflections on Jesus' View of the Old Testament." In *The Enduring Authority of the Christian Scriptures*, edited by Donald A. Carson, 669–701. Grand Rapids: Eerdmans, 2016.

Bobichon, Philippe. "Composite Features and Citations in Justin Martyr's Textual Composition." In *Composite Citations in Antiquity: Volume One: Jewish, Graeco-Roman, and Early Christian Uses*, edited by Sean A. Adam and Seth M. Ehorn, 158–81. LNTS. New York: T&T Clark, 2016.

Boccaccini, Gabriele. *Middle Judaism: Jewish Thought, 300 B.C.E. to 200 C.E.* Minneapolis: Fortress, 1991.

Bock, Darrell and James Charlesworth. *Parables of Enoch: A Paradigm Shift*. London: Bloomsbury, 2013.

Bock, Darrell. *Proclamation from Prophecy and Pattern: Lucan Old Testament Christology*. Sheffield: Sheffield Academic, 1987.

Bockmuehl, Markus. *The Remembered Peter*. WUNT. Tübingen: Mohr Siebeck, 2010.

Boda, Mark J. *The Book of Zechariah*. NICOT. Grand Rapids: Eerdmans, 2016.

Borig, Rainer. *Der wahre Weinstock: Untersuchungen zu Jo 15, 1–10*. SANT. München: Kösel, 1967.

Brodie, Thomas L. *The Gospel according to John: A Literary and Theological Commentary*. Oxford: Oxford University, 1995.

Brooke, George J. "4Q500 1 and the Use of Scripture in the Parable of the Vineyard." *DSD* 2.3 (1995): 287–88.

Brooke, George J. "Melchizedek (11QMelch)." In *The Anchor Bible Dictionary*, edited by David Noel Freedman, 4:687–88. New York: Doubleday, 1992.

Brown, Francis, Samuel Rolles Driver, and Charles Augustus Briggs. *Enhanced Brown-Driver-Briggs Hebrew and English Lexicon*. Oxford: Clarendon Press, 1977.

Brown, Jeannine K. *The Disciples in Narrative Perspective*. AcBib. Leiden: Brill, 2002.

Brownlee, William H. "Ezekiel's Poetic Indictment of the Shepherds." *Harvard Theological Review* 51.4 (1958): 191–203.

Bruce, A. B. "The Synoptic Gospels." *Expositor's Greek Testament: Volume 1*, 1–651. Grand Rapids: Eerdmans, 1901.

Bruce, F. F. "New Wine in Old Wine Skins: III. The Corner Stone." *ExpTim* 84.8 (1973): 231–35.

Brueggemann, Walter. *Psalms*. NCBC. Cambridge: Cambridge University Press, 2014.

Brunson, Andrew C. *Psalm 118 in the Gospel of John: An Intertextual Study on the New Exodus*. WUNT. Tübingen: Mohr Siebeck, 2003.

Cadbury, Henry J. "The Titles of Jesus in Acts." In *The Beginnings of Christianity*, edited by F. J. F. Jackson and K. Lake, 5:369–70. London: Macmillan, 1933.

Cahill, M. "Not a Cornerstone! Translating Ps 118, 22 in the Jewish and Christian Scriptures." *RB* 106 (1999): 345–57.

Calvin, John. *Commentary on a Harmony of the Evangelists Matthew, Mark, and Luke*, vol. 2. Translated by William Pringle. Bellingham, WA: Logos Bible Software, 2010.

Calvin, John. *Commentary on the Book of the Prophet Isaiah*. Translated by William Pringle. Bellingham, WA: Logos Bible Software, 2010.

Campbell, Ken. "The New Jerusalem in Matt 5.14." *SJT* 31.4 (1978): 335–63.

Caragounis, Chrys C. *Peter and the Rock*. BZNW. Berlin: de Gruyter, 1990.

Carlston, Charles E. and Craig Evans. *From Synagogue to Ecclesia*. WUNT. Tübingen: Mohr Seibeck, 2014.

Carmignac, Jean. "Le document de Qumran sur Melchisédeq." *RevQ* 7 (1970): 343–78.

Carson, Donald A. "Do the Prophets and the Law Quit Prophesying before John? A Note on Matthew 11:13." In *The Gospels and the Scriptures of Israel*, edited by Craig A. Evans and William R. Stegner, 179–94. JSNTSup. Sheffield: Sheffield Academic, 1994.

Carson, Donald A. *The Gospel according to John*. PNTC. Grand Rapids: InterVarsity Press, 1991.

Carson, Donald A. "Matthew." In *The Expositor's Bible Commentary: Volume 8*, edited by Frank E. Gaebelein, 1–599. Grand Rapids: Zondervan, 1984.

Carter, Warren. "Matthew 4:18–22 and Matthean Discipleship: An Audience-Oriented Perspective." *CBQ* 59.1 (1997): 58–75.

Carter, Warren. *Matthew and the Margins: A Socio-Political and Religious Reading*. JSNTSup. Sheffield: Sheffield Academic, 2000.

Chae, Young. *Jesus as the Eschatological Davidic Shepherd: Studies in the Old Testament, Second Temple Judaism, and in the Gospel of Matthew*. Tübingen: Mohr Siebeck, 2006.

Chaney, Marvin L. "Whose Sour Grapes? The Addressees of Isaiah 5:1–7 in the Light of Political Economy." *Semeia* 87 (1999): 105–18.

Charles, Robert H. *The Apocrypha and Pseudepigrapha of the Old Testament in English: with introductions and critical and explanatory notes to the several books*. Oxford: Clarendon Press, 1913.

Charlesworth, James J. *The Old Testament Pseudepigrapha*. 2 Volumes. London: Yale University Press, 1983.

Chester, Andrew J. *Messiah and Exultation: Jewish Messianic and Visionary Traditions and New Testament Christology*. WUNT. Tübingen: Mohr Siebeck, 2007.

Childs, Brevard S. *Isaiah: A Commentary*. OTL. Louisville, KY: Westminster John Knox Press, 2001.

Chilton, Bruce D. *The Glory of Israel: The Theology and Provenience of the Isaiah Targum*. JSOTSup. Sheffield: JSOT Press, 1983.

Chilton, Bruce D. *The Isaiah Targum: Introduction, Translation, Apparatus and Notes*. The Aramaic Bible. Wilmington, Del: Glazier, 1987.

Chisholm, Robert B. "The Christological Fulfillment of Isaiah's Servant Songs." *BSac* 163 (2006): 387–404.

Cienki, Alan J., Barbara Josephine Luka, and Michael B. Smith. *Conceptual and Discourse Factors in Linguistic Structure*. San Diego: CSLI Publications, 1995.

Clifford, Richard J. Jr. *The Cosmic Mountain in Canaan and the Old Testament*. Eugene, OR: Wipf & Stock, 2010.

Clines, David J. A., ed. *The Dictionary of Classical Hebrew*. 8 volumes. Sheffield, England: Sheffield Academic Press; Sheffield Phoenix Press, 1993–2011.

Collins, John J. "A Herald of Good Tidings: Isaiah 61:1–3 and Its Actualization in the Dead Sea Scrolls." In *The Quest for Context and Meaning: Studies in Biblical Intertextuality in Honour of James A. Sanders*, edited by Craig A. Evans and S. Talmon, 225–40. BIS. Leiden: Brill, 1997.

Collins, John J. "Messianism in the Maccabean Period." In *Judaisms and Their Messiahs at the Turn of the Christian Era*, edited by Jacob Neusner, William S. Green, and Ernest S. Frerichs, 97–110. Cambridge: Cambridge University Press, 1987.

Collins, John J. *The Scepter and the Star: Messianism in light of the Dead Sea Scrolls*. Grand Rapids: Eerdmans, 2010.

Comprehensive Aramaic Lexicon Project. *Targum Lexicon*. Cincinnati, OH: Hebrew Union College, 2004.

Comprehensive Aramaic Lexicon Project. *Targum Pseudo-Jonathan to the Pentateuch*. Cincinnati, OH: Hebrew Union College, 2005.

Conzelmann, Hans. *1 Corinthians: A Commentary on the First Epistle to the Corinthians*. Translated by James W. Leitch. Hermeneia. Philadelphia: Fortress, 1975.

Cooper, Ben. *Incorporated Servanthood: Commitment and Discipleship in the Gospel of Matthew*. London: Bloomsbury, 2013.

Cooper, Lamar E. *Ezekiel*. NAC. Nashville: Broadman & Holman Publishers, 1994.

Coulson, Seana and Todd Oakley. "Blending Basics." *Cognitive Linguistics*, 11 3/4 (2000): 1–22.

Craigie, Peter C. *Jeremiah*. WBC. Dallas: Word, 1991.

Cuany, Monique. "'Physician, Heal Yourself!' – Jesus' Challenge to His Own: A Reexamination of the Offense at Nazareth in Light of Ancient Parallels (Luke 4:16–30)." *NovT* 58.4 (2016): 348–54.

Dasma, Alinda. "The Merkabah as a Substitute of Messianism in Targum Ezekiel?" *VT* 62.4 (2012): 515–33.

Davies, W. D., and Dale C. Allison Jr. *A Critical and Exegetical Commentary on the Gospel according to Saint Matthew*. Vol. 1–3. ICC. London: T&T Clark International, 2004.

Day, John. "The Development of Belief in Life after Death in Ancient Israel." In *After the Exile: Essays in Honour of Rex Mason*, edited by John Barton and David J. Reimer, 231–57. Macon, GA: Mercer University Press, 1996.

de Moor, Johannes C. "The Targumic Background of Mark 12:1–12: The Parable of the Wicked Tenants." *JSJ* (1998): 63–80.

Dearman, J. Andrew. *Jeremiah and Lamentations*. NIVAC. Grand Rapids: Zondervan, 2002.

deClaissé-Walford, Nancy, Rolf A. Jacobson, and Beth LaNeel Tanner. *The Book of Psalms*. NICOT. Grand Rapids: Eerdmans, 2014.

Deeley, Mary K. "Ezekiel's Shepherd and John's Jesus: A Case Study in the Appropriation of Biblical Texts." In *Early Christian Interpretation of the Scriptures of Israel: Investigations and Proposals*, edited by C. A. Evans and J. A. Sanders, 252–65. JSNTSup. Sheffield: Sheffield Academic, 1997.

Deines, Roland. "Did Matthew Know He Was Writing Scripture?" (Part 1). *EuroJTh*. 22.2 (2013): 101–09.

Deines, Roland. "Did Matthew Know He Was Writing Scripture?" (Part 2). *EuroJTh*. 23.1 (2014): 3–12.

Dekker, Jaap. *Zion's Rock-Solid Foundations: An Exegetical Study of the Zion Text in Isa 28:16*. OtSt. Leiden: Brill, 2007.

Dennert, Brian C. *John the Baptist and the Jewish Setting of Matthew*. WUNT. Tübingen: Mohr Siebeck, 2015.

Derrett, J. Duncan M. "The Stone that the Builders Rejected." In *Studies in the New Testament*, 2:64–65. Leiden: E. J. Brill, 1977.

Derrett, J. Duncan M. "Thou art the Stone, and Upon This Stone …" *DRev* 106.365 (1988): 276–85.

DesCamp, Mary Therese. *Metaphor and Ideology: Liber Antiquitatum Biblicarum and Literary Methods Through a Cognitive Lens*. Leiden: Brill, 2007.

Docherty, Susan E. "New Testament Scriptural Interpretation in its Early Jewish Context." *NovT* 57.1 (2015): 1–19.

Dodd, Charles H. *According to the Scriptures: The Sub-Structure of New Testament Theology*. London: Nisbet, 1952.

Doering, Lutz. "The Epistle of Baruch and Its Role in 2 Baruch." In *Fourth Ezra and Second Baruch: Reconstruction after the Fall*, edited by Matthias Henze and Gabriele Boccaccini, 151–73. Leiden: Brill, 2013.

Donaldson, Terrence L. "Guiding Readers – Making Disciples: Discipleship in Matthew's Narrative Strategy." In *Patterns of Discipleship in the New Testament*, edited by Richard N. Longenecker, 30–49. Grand Rapids: Eerdmans, 1996.

Donaldson, Terence L. *Patterns of Discipleship in the New Testament*. Grand Rapids: Eerdmans, 1996.

Douglas, Michael C. "Power and Praise in the Hodayot: A Literary Critical Study of 1QH 9:1–18:14." PhD dissertation: University of Chicago, 1998.

Douglas, Michael C. "The Teacher Hymn Hypothesis Revisited: New Data for an Old Crux." *DSD* 6.3 (1999): 239–66.

Duff, Paul B. "The March of the Divine Warrior and the Advent of the Greco-Roman King: Mark's Account of Jesus' Entry into Jerusalem." *JBL* 111.1 (1992): 55–71.

Duguid, Iain. *Ezekiel and the Leaders of Israel*. VTSup. Leiden: Brill, 1994.

Duguid, Iain. "Messianic Themes in Zechariah 9–14" in *The Lord's Anointed: Interpretation of Old Testament Messianic Texts*. Edited by Philip E. Satterthwaite, Richard S. Hess, and Gordon J. Wenham. Grand Rapids: Baker, 1995.

Dunn, James D. G. *Jesus Remembered: Christianity in the Making*. Grand Rapids: Eerdmans, 2003.

Eco, Umberto. *Semeiotics and the Philosophy of Language*. Bloomington: Indiana University Press, 1986.

Edwards, James R. *The Gospel According to Luke*. PNTC. Grand Rapids: Eerdmans, 2015.

Eliav, Yaron A. "The Temple Mount in Jewish and Early Christian Traditions: A New Look." In *Jerusalem: Idea and Reality*, edited by Tamar Mayer and Suleiman A. Mourad, 65–84. London: Routledge, 2008.

Enns, Peter. *Inspiration and Incarnation: Evangelical and the Problem of the Old Testament*, Second Edition. Grand Rapids: Baker Academic, 2015.

Eubank, Nathan. "What Does Matthew Say about Divine Recompense? On the Misuse of the Parable of the Workers in the Vineyard (20:1–16)." *JSNT* 35.3 (March 2013): 242–63.

Evans, Craig A. "Jesus' Parable of the Tenant Farmers in Light of Lease Agreements in Antiquity." *JSP* 14 (1996): 65–83.

Evans, Craig A. "How Septuagintal is Isa 5:1–7 in Mark 12:1–9?" *NovT* 45.2 (2003): 105–10.

Evans, Craig A. "Listening for Echoes of Interpreted Scripture." In *Paul and the Scriptures of Israel*, edited by Craig A. Evans and James A. Sanders, 47–51. JSNTSup. London: Bloomsbury, 1993.

Evans, Craig A. "Prophet, Sage, Healer, Messiah, and Martyr: Types and Identities of Jesus." In *Handbook for the Study of the Historical Jesus*, edited by Tom Holmén and Stanley E. Porter, 1217–44. Leiden: Brill, 2010.

Evans, Craig A. "The Messiah in the Dead Sea Scrolls." In *Israel's Messiah in the Bible and the Dead Sea Scrolls* edited by Richard S. Hess, M. Daniel Carroll, 85–101. Eugene, OR: Wipf & Stock, 2003.

Evans, Craig A. and James A. Sanders, editors. *Paul and the Scriptures of Israel*. JSNTSup. Sheffield: Sheffield Academic, 1993.

Evans, Craig A. *Matthew*. NCBC. Cambridge: Cambridge University, 2012.

BIBLIOGRAPHY

Evans, Craig A. *Jesus and His Contemporaries: Comparative Studies.* AGJU. Leiden: Brill, 2001.

Evans, Craig A. and L. Novakovic. "Midrash." In *Dictionary of Jesus and the Gospels.* Second Edition. Edited by Joel B. Green, Jeannine K. Brown, and Nicholas Perrin, 588–94. Downers Grove, IL: IVP Academic, 2013.

Evans, Vyvyan and Melanie Green. *Cognitive Linguistics: An Introduction.* Edinburgh: Edinburgh Press, 2006.

Fauconnier, Gilles and Mark Turner. "Conceptual Integration Networks." *Cognitive Science* 22.2 (1998): 133–87.

Fauconnier, Gilles and Mark Turner. *The Way We Think: Conceptual Blending and the Mind's Hidden Complexities.* New York: Basic Books, 2002.

Feinberg, Charles L. *Jeremiah: A Commentary.* Grand Rapids: Zondervan, 1982.

Ferreira, Johan. *Johannine Ecclesiology.* JSNTSup. Sheffield: Sheffield Academic, 1998.

Fitzmyer, Joseph A. *Essays on the Semitic Background of the New Testament.* London: G. Chapman, 1971.

Fitzmyer, Joseph A. *The Dead Sea Scrolls and Christian Origins.* Grand Rapids: Eerdmans, 2000.

Fitzmyer, Joseph A. *The Gospel According to Luke: A New Translation with Introduction and Commentary.* Anchor. New York: Doubleday, 1970.

Fitzmyer, Joseph A. *The One Who is To Come.* Grand Rapids: Eerdmans, 2008.

Flashman, Richard H. "Passover in the Writings." In *Messiah in the Passover*, edited by Darrell L. Block and Mitch Glaser, 47–56. Grand Rapids: Kregel, 2017.

Flesher, Paul V. M. and Bruce D. Chilton. *The Targums: A Critical Introduction.* Leiden: Brill, 2011.

Fletcher-Louis, Crispin H. T. "The Destruction of the Temple and the Relativization of the Old Covenant: Mark 13: 31 & Matthew 5: 18." In *Eschatology in Bible and Theology: Evangelical Essays at the Dawn of a New Millennium*, edited by K. E. Brower and M. W. Elliott, 147–50. Downers Grove, IL: InterVarsity, 1997.

Flusser, David and S. Safrai. שירי דוד החיצוניים in עיונים במקרא, edited by B. Uffenheimer, 83–105. Tel Aviv, 1970.

Flusser, David. "Melchizedek and the Son of Man." In *Judaism and the Origins of Christianity.* 186–92. Jerusalem: Magnes Press, Hebrew University, 1988.

Foster, Paul. "Echoes without Resonance: Critiquing Certain Aspects of Recent Scholarly Trends in the Study of the Jewish Scriptures in the New Testament." *JSNT* 38.1 (2015): 96–111.

France, Richard T. *Jesus and the Old Testament: His Application of Old Testament Passages to Himself and His Mission.* Downers Grove, IL: InterVarsity Press, 1971.

France, Richard T. "The Formula-Quotations of Matthew 2 and the Problem of Communication." *NTS* 27.2 (1981): 233–251.

France, Richard T. *The Gospel of Matthew.* NICNT. Grand Rapids: Eerdmans, 2007.

France, Richard T. *Matthew: Evangelist and Teacher*. Grand Rapids: Zondervan, 1989.
Fretheim, Terrence E. *Jeremiah*. SHBC. Macon, GA: Smyth & Helwys, 2002.
Frey, Jörg. "The Reception of Jeremiah and the Impact of Jeremianic Traditions in the New Testament: A Survey." In *Jeremiah's Scriptures: Production, Reception, Interaction, and Transformation*, edited by Hindy Najman and Konrad Schmid, 499–543. JSJSup. Leiden: Brill, 2016.
Gamble, Harry Y. *Books and Readers in the Early Church: A History of Early Christian Texts*. New Haven: Yale, 1995.
Garland, David. *Reading Matthew: A Literary and Theological Commentary on the First Gospel*. Macon, GA: Smyth & Helwys, 2001.
Gelston, A. "A Sidelight on the 'Son of Man.'" *SJT* 22 (1969): 189–96.
Gelston, A. *Biblia Hebraica Quinta: The Twelve Minor Prophets: Volume 13*. Stuttgart: Deutsche Bibelgesellschaft, 2010.
Gesenius, Wilhelm and Samuel Prideaux Tregelles. *Gesenius' Hebrew and Chaldee Lexicon to the Old Testament Scriptures*. Bellingham, WA: Logos Bible Software, 2003.
Giovino, Mariana. *The Assyrian Sacred Tree: A History of Interpretations*. Fribourg, Switzerland: Academic Press, 2007.
Goldingay, John. *A Critical and Exegetical Commentary on Isaiah 56–66*. ICC. London: Bloomsbury, 2014.
Goldingay, John. *Psalms 42–89*. BCOTWP. Grand Rapids: Baker, 2007.
Goldingay, John. *Psalm 90–150*. BCOTWP. Grand Rapids: Baker, 2008.
Goldstein, Jonathan A. "How the Authors of 1 and 2 Maccabees Treated the 'Messianic' Promises." In *Judaisms and their Messiahs at the Turn of the Era*, edited by Jacob Neusner, W. S. Green, and E. S. Frerichs, 69–96. Cambridge: Cambridge University, 1987.
Gomola, Aleksander. *Conceptual Blending in Early Christian Discourse: A Cognitive Linguistic Analysis of Pastoral Metaphors in Patristic Literature*. Berlin: de Gruyter, 2018.
Goodacre, Mark and Nicholas Perrin, editors. *Questioning Q: A Multidimensional Critique*. Downers Grove, IL: InterVarsity, 2004.
Goodacre, Mark. "Redaction Criticism." In *Dictionary of Jesus and the Gospels*. Second Edition. Edited by Joel B. Green, Jeannine K. Brown, and Nicholas Perrin, 767–71. Downers Grove, IL: IVP Academic, 2013.
Goodrich, John K. "Rule of the Congregation and Mark 10:32–52: Glory and Greatness in Eschatological Israel." In *Reading Mark in Context: Jesus and Second Temple Judaism*, edited by Ben C. Blackwell, John K. Goodrich, and Jaston Maston, 166–73. Grand Rapids: Zondervan, 2018.
Gosse, Bernard. "Le Psaume 80 Dans Le Cadre Du Psautier Et Ezechiel 17." *Scandinavian Journal of the Old Testament*, 19.1 (2005): 52.

Grant, Robert M. "The Coming of the Kingdom." *JBL* 67 (1948): 297–303.
Gray, Arthur. "The Parable of the Wicked Husbandmen." *HibJ* 19 (1920–21): 42–52.
Greenberg, Moshe. *Ezekiel 1–20*. AB. Garden City: Doubleday, 1995.
Gregory, Bradley. "The Post-exilic Exile in Third Isaiah: Isaiah 61:1–3 in Light of Second Temple Hermeneutics." *JBL* 126.3 (2007): 475–496.
Guelich, Robert A. "The Matthean Beatitudes: 'Entrance-Requirements' or Eschatological Blessings?" *JBL* 95.3 (1976): 427.
Guelich, Robert A. *The Sermon on the Mount: A Foundation for Understanding*. Waco, TX: Word, 1982.
Guenter, Kenneth E. "Blessed is He Who Comes': Psalm 118 and Jesus's Triumphal Entry." *BSac* 173 (Oct–Dec 2016): 425–47.
Gundry, Robert H. *Peter-False Disciple and Apostate according to St. Matthew*. Grand Rapids: Eerdmans, 2015.
Gundry, Robert H. *The Use of the Old Testament in St. Matthew's Gospel, With Special Reference to the Messianic Hope*. NovTSup. Leiden: Brill, 1967.
Hagner, Donald A. *Matthew*. WBC. 2 Volumes. Nashville: Thomas Nelson, 1995.
Hall, Christopher A., editor. *Ancient Christian Texts: Commentary on Jeremiah: Jerome*. Translated by Michael Graves. Downers Grove, IL: InterVarsity, 2012.
Halliday, Michael A. K. *An Introduction to Functional Grammar*. London: Arnold, 1985.
Hallo, William W. and K. Lawson Younger Jr. editors. *The Context of Scripture: Canonical Compositions from the Biblical World*. Leiden: Brill, 2003.
Hamilton Jr., James M. "'The Virgin Will Conceive': Typological Fulfillment in Matthew 1:18–23." In *Built Upon the Rock: Studies in the Gospel of Matthew*, edited by Daniel M. Gurtner and John Nolland, 228–47. Grand Rapids: Eerdmans, 2008.
Hanson, Paul D. *The Dawn of the Apocalyptic: The Historical and Sociological Roots of Jewish Apocalyptic Eschatology*, Revised Edition. Philadelphia: Fortress, 1979.
Hasselbach, Trine. *Meaning and Context in the Thanksgiving Hymns: Linguistic and Rhetorical Perspectives on a Collection of Prayers from Qumran*. EJL. Atlanta: SBL Press, 2015.
Hatina, Thomas R. *In Search of a Context: The Function of Scripture in Mark's Narrative*. JSNTSup. London: Sheffield, 2002.
Hayes, Elizabeth R. "The One Who Brings Justice: Conceptualizing the Role of 'The Servant' in Isaiah 42:1–4 and Matthew 12:15–21." In *Let Us Go Up to Zion: Essays in Honour of H. G. M. Williams on the Occasion of his Sixty-Fifth Birthday*, edited by Iain Provain and Mark Boda, 143–51. SVT. Leiden: Brill, 2012.
Hayes, Elizabeth R. *The Pragmatics of Perception and Cognition in MT Jeremiah 1:1–6:30: A Cognitive Linguistics Approach*. BZAW. Berlin: de Gruyter, 2008.
Hays, Richard B. *Conversion of the Imagination: Paul as Interpreter of Israel's Scripture*. Grand Rapids: Eerdmans, 2005.
Hays, Richard B. *Echoes of Scripture in the Gospels*. Waco, TX: Baylor, 2016.

Hays, Richard B. *Echoes of Scripture in the Letters of Paul*. New Haven: Yale University Press, 1989.

Hays, Richard B. "The Righteous One as Eschatological Deliverer." In *Apocalyptic and the New Testament: Essays in Honor of J. Louis Martyn*, edited by J. Marcus and M. L. Soards, 191–225. JSNTSup. Sheffield: JSOT Press, 1989.

Hays, Richard B., Stefan Alkier and Leroy A. Huizenga, editors. *Reading the Bible Intertextually*. Waco, TX: Baylor, 2009.

Heil, John P. "The Double Meaning of the Narrative of Universal Judgment in Matthew 25.31–46." *JSNT* 69 (1998): 3–14.

Heil, John P. "Ezekiel 34 and the Narrative Strategy of the Shepherd and Sheep Metaphor in Matthew." *CBQ* 55 (1993): 698–708.

Heiser, Michael S. *The Unseen Realm: Recovering the Supernatural Worldview of the Bible*. Bellingham, WA: Lexham, 2015.

Hengel, Martin. "Das Gleichnis von den Weingärtnern Mic 12.1–12 im Lichte der Zenonpapyri und der rabbinischen Gleichnisse." *ZNW* 59 (1968): 1–39.

Henning, Bruce. "The Apostles as the Messiah's Kingly and Prophetic Shepherds of Jer 23." *BBR* 29.2 (2019): 154–173.

Henze, Matthias. *Jewish Apocalypticism in Late First Century Israel: Reading 'Second Baruch'*. Tübingen: Mohr Siebeck, 2011.

Hero, Stephen. "The Gates or the Bars of Hades? A Note on Matthew 16:17–19." *NTS* 7 (1981): 411–14.

Heskett, Randall. *Messianism with the Scriptural Scrolls of Isaiah*. London: T&T Clark, 2007.

Hieke, Thomas. "Psalm 80 and Its Neighbors." *BN* 86 (1997): 39.

Hill, David. "'Son of Man' in Psalm 80 v 17." *NovT* 15.4 (1973): 261–69.

Hillyer, C. N. "'Rock-Stone' Imagery in I Peter." *TynBul* 22 (1971): 58–81.

Hirsch, E. D. Jr. *Validity in Interpretation*. New Haven: Yale Press, 1967.

Hogeterp, Albert L. A. "Belief in Resurrection and its Religious Settings in Qumran and the New Testament." In *Echoes from the Caves: Qumran and the New Testament*, edited by F. Garcia Martinez, 299–320. STDJ. Leiden: Brill, 2009.

Holladay, W. L. *Jeremiah 1: A Commentary on the Book of the Prophet Jeremiah Chapters 1–25*. Hermeneia. Philadelphia: Fortress, 1986.

Hollander, John. *The Figure of Echo: A Mode of Allusion in Milton and After*. Berkeley: University of California Press, 1984.

Hooker, Morna D. *Jesus and the Servant: The Influence of the Servant Concept of Deutero-Isaiah in the New Testament*. London: SPCK, 1959.

Horbury, William. *Jewish Messianism and the Cult of Christ*. London: SCM, 1998.

Horbury, William. *Messianism Among Jews and Christians*. Second Edition. London: Bloomsbury, 2016.

Horbury, William. "Messianism in the Old Testament Apocrypha." In *King and Messiah in Israel and the Ancient Near East: Proceedings of the Oxford Old Testament Seminary*, edited by John Day, 401–32. JSOTSup. Sheffield: Sheffield Academic, 1998.

Hossfeld, Frank Lothat, Erich Zenger, and Linda M. Maloney. *A Commentary on Psalms 51–100*. Heremeneia. Minneapolis: Fortress, 2005.

Houston, Walter J. "'Today in Your Very Hearing,': Some Comments on the Christological Use of the Old Testament." In *The Glory of Christ in the New Testament: Studies in Christology in Memory of George Bradford Caird*, edited by L. D. Hurst and N. T. Wright, 37–50. Clarendon: Oxford, 1987.

Howe, Bonnie. *Because You Bear This Name: Conceptual Metaphor and the Moral Meaning of 1 Peter*. Leiden: Brill, 2006.

Hughes, Julie A. *Scriptural Allusions and Exegesis in the Hodayot*. STDJ. Leiden: Brill, 2006.

Huizinga, Leroy A. "The Old Testament in the New, Intertextuality and Allegory." *JSNT* 28.1 (Sep 2015): 17–35.

Hultgård, Anders. "The Ideal 'Lévite,' the Davidic Messiah, and the Saviour Priest in the Testaments of the Twelve Patriarchs." In *Ideal Figures in Ancient Judaism*, edited by John J. Collins and George W. E. Nickelsburg, 93–110. SBLSCS. Chico: Scholars Press, 1980.

Hummel, Horace D. *Ezekiel 1–20*. Concordia Commentary. St. Louis: Concordia, 2005.

Hurtado, Larry W. "Principal Angels." In *The Oxford handbook of the Dead Sea Scrolls*, edited by Timothy H. Lim and John J. Collins, 550–62. Oxford: Oxford University Press, 2010.

Hutchison, John C. "The Vine in John 15 and Old Testament Imagery in the 'I am' Statements," *BSac* 168 (Jan–March, 2011): 63–80.

Instone-Brewer, David. *Techniques and Assumptions in Jewish Exegesis before 70 CE*. TSAJ. Tübingen: Mohr Siebeck, 1992.

Irwin, William. "What is an Allusion?" *Journal of Aesthetics and Art Criticism* 59.3 (2001): 287–293.

Iser, Wolfgang. *Prospecting: From Reader Response to Literary Anthropology*. Baltimore: John Hopkins, 1989.

Jeremias, Joachim. *Jerusalem in the Time of Jesus: An Investigation into Economic and Social Conditions During the New Testament Period*. Philadelphia: Fortress, 1969.

Jeremias, Joachim. *Jesus' Promise to the Nations*. London: SCM Press, 1958.

Jeremias, Joachim. *The Eucharistic Words of Jesus*. London: SCM Press, 1966.

Jones, Ken. *Jewish Reactions to the Destruction of Jerusalem in A.D. 70: Apocalypses and Related Pseudepigrapha*. Leiden: Brill, 2011.

Joseph, Simon J. *Jesus, the Essenes, and Christian Origins: New Light on Ancient Texts and Communities*. Waco: Baylor, 2018.

Josephus, Flavius. *The Works of Josephus: Complete and Unabridged*. Translated by William Whiston. Peabody: Hendrickson, 1987.

Joyce, Paul M. "King and Messiah in Ezekiel." In *King and Messiah in Israel and the Ancient Near East: Proceedings of the Oxford Old Testament Seminar*, edited by John Day, 323–37. London: Bloomsbury, 2013.

Joyce, Paul M. *Ezekiel: A Commentary*. LHBOTS. New York: T&T Clark, 2007.

Juel, Donald. *Messiah and Temple: The Trial of Jesus in the Gospel of Mark*. SBLDS. Missoula: Scholars Press, 1977.

Juel, Donald. *Messianic Exegesis: Christological Interpretation of the Old Testament in Early Christianity*. Philadelphia: Fortress Press, 1992.

Kaiser, Otto. *Isaiah 1–12: A Commentary*. Translated by John Bowden. OTL. Philadelphia: Westminster, 1983.

Kaiser, Walter C. Jr. "The Messiah of Psalm 80." *BSac* 174 (Oct–Dec 2017): 287–93.

Kaiser, Walter C. Jr. *The Messiah in the Old Testament*. Grand Rapids: Zondervan, 1995.

Kaiser, Walter C. Jr. *The Uses of the Old Testament in the New*. Eugene, OR: Wipf and Stock, 2001.

Kaminsky, J. S. *Corporate Responsibility in the Hebrew Bible*. Sheffield: Sheffield Academic, 1995.

Kee, Howard C. "Messiah and the People of God." In *Understanding the Word: Essays in Honor of Bernhard W. Anderson*, edited by James T. Butler, Edgar W. Conrad, and Ben C. Ollenburger, 341–58. JSOTSup. Sheffield: JSOT Press, 1985.

Keener, Craig S. *The Gospel of Matthew: A Socio-Rhetorical Commentary*. Grand Rapids, MI: Eerdmans, 2009.

Keil, Carl Friedrich and Franz Delitzsch. *Commentary on the Old Testament*. Peabody, MA: Hendrickson, 1996.

Kellum, L. S. "Farewell Discourse." In *Dictionary of Jesus and the Gospels*. Second Edition. Edited by Joel B. Green, Jeannine K. Brown, and Nicholas Perrin, 265–69. Downers Grove: IVP Academic, 2013.

Kessler, Stephen. *Theories of a Metaphor Revised: Against a Cognitive Theory of Metaphor: An Apology for Classical Metaphor*. Berlin: Logos Verlag, 2018.

Kim, Mitchell. "Respect for Context and Authorial Intention: Setting the Epistemological Bar." In *Paul and Scripture: Extending the Conversation*, edited by Christopher D. Stanley, 115–29. ECL. Atlanta: SBL, 2012.

Kim, Seyoon. "Jesus-The Son of God, the Stone, the Son of Man, and the Servant: The Role of Zechariah in the Self-Identification of Jesus." In *Tradition and Interpretation in the New Testament: Essays in Honor of E. Earle Ellis*, edited by Gerald F. Hawthorne and Otto Betz, 134–49. Tübingen: Mohr Siebeck, 1987.

Kingsbury, Jack D. "The Parable of the Wicked Husbandmen and the Secret of Jesus' Divine Sonship in Matthew: Some Literary-Critical Observation." *JBL* 105.4 (1986): 643–55.

BIBLIOGRAPHY

Kirk, J. R. Daniel. "Conceptualizing Fulfillment in Matthew." *TynBul* 59.1 (2008): 77–98.

Kittel, Gerhard, Geoffrey W. Bromiley, and Gerhard Friedrich, editors. *Theological Dictionary of the New Testament*. Grand Rapids, MI: Eerdmans, 1964–1988.

Kloppenborg, John S. "Egyptian Viticultural Practices and the Citation of Isa 5:1–7 in Mark 12:1–9." *NT* 44 (2002): 134–59.

Kloppenborg, John S. "Isa 5:1–7 LXX and Mark 12:1, 9, Again." *NovT* 46 (2004): 12–19.

Knibb, Michael A. *The Ethiopic Book of Enoch: Introduction, Translation and Commentary*. Oxford: Oxford University, 1978.

Knibb, Michael A. "The Teacher of Righteousness – A Messianic Title?" In *A Tribute to Geza Vermes: Essays on Jewish and Christian Literature and History*, edited by Philip R. Davies and Richard T. White, 51–65. JSOTSup. Sheffield: Sheffield Academic, 1990.

Knight, George A. F. *The New Israel*. Grand Rapids: Eerdmans, 1985.

Knowles, Michael. "'Everyone Who Hears These Words of Mine': Parables on Discipleship." In *The Challenge of Jesus' Parables*, edited by Richard N. Longenecker, 286–305. Grand Rapids: Eerdmans, 1990.

Knowles, Michael. *Jeremiah in Matthew's Gospel: The Rejected Prophet Motif in Matthean Redaction*. JSNTSup. Sheffield: Sheffield Academic, 1993.

Koehler, Ludwig, Walter Baumgartner, M. E. J. Richardson, and Johann Jakob Stamm. *The Hebrew and Aramaic Lexicon of the Old Testament*. 2 Volumes. Leiden: E. J. Brill, 1994–2000.

Koester, Craig R. *Symbolism in the Fourth Gospel: Meaning, Mystery, Community*. Minneapolis: Fortress Press, 1995.

Konradt, Matthias. *Israel, Church, and Gentiles in the Gospel of Matthew*. Translated by Kathleen Ess. Waco, TX: Baylor, 2014.

Köstenberger, Andreas. *The Gospel of John*. BECNT. Grand Rapids: Baker, 2004.

Köstenberger, Andreas. "Hearing the Old Testament in the New: A Response." In *Hearing the Old Testament in the New Testament*, edited by Stanley E. Porter, 255–94. Grand Rapids: Eerdmans, 2006.

Köstenberger, Andreas. *A Theology of John's Gospel and Letters: The Word, the Christ, the Son of God*. Grand Rapids: Zondervan, 2015.

Kövecses, Zoltán. *Metaphor: A Practical Introduction*, Second Edition. Oxford: Oxford University Press, 2010.

Kroeger, Paul R. *Analyzing Syntax: A Lexical-functional Approach*. Cambridge: Cambridge University Press, 2004.

Kunjummen, Raju D. "The Things Concerning Himself, Beginning with Moses: The Messiah's Suffering and Subsequent Glory." In *Reflections from the Emmaus Road: Essays in Honor of John H. Fish III, David A. Glock, and David J. MacLeod*, edited by Franklin S. Jabini, Raju D. Kunjummen, and Mark R. Stevenson, 167–183. Dubuque, IA: Emmaus Bible College, 2018.

Kuyvenhoven, Rosalie. "Jeremiah 23:1–8: Shepherds in Diachronic Perspective." In *Paratext and Megatext as Channels of Jewish and Christian Tradition: The Textual Markers of Contextualization*, edited by August A. den Hollander, Ulrich B. Schmid, Willem Frederick Smelik, 1–36. JCPS. Leiden: Brill, 2003.

Kynes, William L. *A Christology of Solidarity: Jesus as the Representative of His People in Matthew*. Lanham, MD: University Press of America, 1991.

Lakoff, George and Mark Johnson. *Metaphors We Live By*. Chicago: University of Chicago Press, 1980.

Lakoff, George. "The Contemporary Theory of Metaphor." In *Metaphor and Thought*, Second Edition, edited by Andrew Ortony, 202–51. Cambridge: Cambridge University Press, 1993.

Lakoff, George. *Women, Fire, and Other Dangerous Things: What Categories Reveal about the Mind*. Chicago: University of Chicago Press, 1987.

Lambert, Wilfred. *Babylonian Wisdom Literature*. Winona Lake, IN: Eisenbrauns, 1996.

Laniak, Timothy S. *Shepherds after My Own Heart: Pastoral Traditions and Leadership in the Bible*. NSBT. Downers Grove, IL: InterVarsity, 2006.

Lanier, Gregory R. "The Curious Case of צמח and ἀνατολή: An Inquiry into Septuagint Translation Patterns." *JBL* 134.3 (2015): 505–27.

Lanier, Gregory R. *Old Testament Conceptual Metaphors and the Christology of Luke's Gospel*. LNTS. London: T&T Clark, 2018.

Lasor, W. L. "Prophesy, Inspiration, and *Sensus Plenior*," *TynBul* 29 (1978): 49–60.

Le Peau, Andrew T. *Mark Through Old Testament Eyes: A Background and Application Commentary*. Grand Rapids: Kregel, 2017.

Lee, Suk Yee. *An Intertextual Analysis of Zechariah 9–10: The Early Restoration Expectations of Second Zechariah*. New York: Bloomsbury, 2015.

Lenski, R. C. H. *The Interpretation of St. Matthew's Gospel*. Minneapolis: Augsburg, 1961.

Levenson, Jon D. *Creation and the Persistence of Evil: The Jewish Drama of Divine Omnipotence*. San Francisco: Harper & Row, 1988.

Levey, Samson. "Targum to Ezekiel." *HUCA* 46 (1975): 139–158.

Levey, Samson. *The Targum of Ezekiel: Translated, with a Critical Introduction, Apparatus, and Notes*. The Aramaic Bible. Edinburgh: T&T Clark, 1987.

Levison, John R. *The Spirit in First-Century Judaism*. AGJU. Leiden: Brill, 1997.

Liddell, Henry George, Robert Scott, Henry Stuart Jones, and Roderick McKenzie. *A Greek-English Lexicon*. Oxford: Clarendon Press, 1996.

Lied, Liv Ingebord. *The Other Lands of Israel: Imaginations of the Land in 2 Baruch*. JSJSup. Leiden: Brill, 2008.

Lindars, Barnabas. *New Testament Apologetic: The Doctrinal Significance of the Old Testament Quotations*. London: SCM Press, 1961.

Litwak, Kenneth D. "Echoes of Scripture? A Critical Survey or Recent Works on Paul's Use of the Old Testament." *CRBS* 6 (1998): 260–88.

Longman III, Tremper. "The Messiah: Exploration in the Law and Writings." In *The Messiah in the Old and New Testament*, edited by Stanley E. Porter, 13–34. Grand Rapids: Eerdmans, 2007.

Lundbom, Jack R. *Jeremiah 21–36: A New Translation with Introduction and Commentary.* AB. New York: Doubleday, 1999.

Lundhaug, Hugo. *Images of Rebirth: Cognitive Poetics and Transformational Soteriology in the Gospel of Philip and the Exegesis of the Soul.* NHMS. Leiden: Brill, 2010.

Luz, Ulrich. *Matthew 1–7: A Commentary on Matthew 1–7.* Hermeneia. Minneapolis, MN: Fortress Press, 2007.

Macaskil, Grant. *Union with Christ in the New Testament.* Oxford: Oxford University, 2013.

Mallen, Peter. *The Reading and Transformation of Isaiah in Luke-Acts.* LNTS. London: T&T Clark, 2008.

Manning, Gary T. Jr. "Shepherd, Vine and Bones: The Use of Ezekiel in the Gospel of John." In *After Ezekiel: Essays on the Reception of a Difficult Prophet*, edited by Paul M. Joyce and Andrew Mein, 25–44. New York: T&T Clark, 2011.

Manning, Gary T. Jr. *Echoes of a Prophet: The Use of Ezekiel in the Gospel of John and in Literature of the Second Temple Period.* LNTS. London: T&T Clark, 2004.

Manzi, Franco. *Melchisedek e l'angelologia nell'epistola agli Ebrei e a Qumran.* AnBib. Rome: Pontifical Biblical Institute, 1997.

Marcus, Joel. "The Gates of Hades and the Keys of the Kingdom (Matt 16:18–19)." *CBQ* 15.3 (1988): 443–55.

Marcus, Joel. *The Way of the Lord: Christological Exegesis of the Old Testament in the Gospel of Mark.* SNTW. London: T&T Clark, 2004.

Marshall, I. Howard. *The Gospel of Luke: A Commentary on the Greek Text.* NIGTC. Exeter: Paternoster Press, 1978.

Martínez, Florentino G. "Messianische Erwartungen in den Qumranschriften." *Jahrbuch für biblische Theologie* 8 (1993): 171–208.

Martínez, Florentino G. and Eibert Tigchelaar. *The Dead Sea Scrolls Study Edition. Vol. 2: 4Q274–11Q31.* Leiden: Brill, 1998.

McCasland, Vernon. "Matthew Twists the Scriptures." *JBL* 80 (1961): 143–48.

McConnell, Richard S. *Law and Prophecy in Matthew's Gospel: The Authority and Use of the Old Testament in the Gospel of St. Matthew.* Basel: Friedrich Reinhardt, 1969.

McKane, William. *Jeremiah 1–25: A Critical and Exegetical Commentary.* ICC. London: T&T Clark, 1986.

McKelvey, R. J. "Christ the Cornerstone." *NTS* 8.4 (1964): 352–59.

McKelvey, R. J. *The New Temple: The Church in the New Testament.* Oxford Theological Monographs. London: Oxford University, 1969.

McNeile, Alan. *The Gospel According to St. Matthew.* London: Macmillan, 1915.

Meier, John P. *A Marginal Jew: Volume 3: Companions and Competitors*. ABRL. New York: Doubleday, 2001.

Menken, Maarten J. J. "Composite Citations in the Gospel of Matthew." In *Composite Citations in Antiquity: Volume Two: New Testament Uses*, edited by Sean A. Adams and Seth M. Ehorn 34–61. LNTS. New York: T&T Clark, 2018.

Menken, Maarten J. J. "Deuteronomy in Matthew's Gospel." In *Deuteronomy in the New Testament*, edited by Steve Moyise and Maarten J. J. Menken, 42–62. LNTS. London: T&T Clark, 2007.

Menken, Maarten J. J. *Matthew's Bible: The Old Testament Text of the Evangelist*. Belgium: Leuven, 2004.

Metzger, Bruce Manning, United Bible Societies. *A Textual Commentary on the Greek New Testament, Second Edition a Companion Volume to the United Bible Societies' Greek New Testament (4th Rev. Ed.)*. London; New York: United Bible Societies, 1994.

Meyer, Ben. *The Aims of Jesus*. London: SCM, 1979.

Meyers, Carol L. and Eric M. Meyers. *Haggai, Zechariah 1–8: A New Translation with Introduction and Commentary*. AB. Garden City: Doubleday, 1995.

Millard, Alan. *Reading and Writing in the Time of Jesus*. Sheffield: Sheffield Academic Press, 2001.

Miller, Jean. *Les citations d'accomplissement dans l'Évangile de Matthieu: Quand Dieu se rend present en toute humanité*. AnBib. Rome: Editrice Pontificio Istituto Biblico, 1999.

Miller, Merrill. "The Function of Isa 61:1–2 in 11Q Melchizedek." *JBL* 88.4 (1969): 468.

Miller, Merrill. *Scripture and Parable: A Study of the Biblical Features in the Parable of the Wicked Husbandmen and Their Place in the History of Tradition*. Ph. D. Dissertation: Columbia University, 1974.

Milne, Mary K. and Mark Allan Powell. "Caesarea Philippi." In *The HarperCollins Bible Dictionary (Revised and Updated)*, edited by Mark Allan Powell, 113. New York: HarperCollins, 2011.

Mitchell, David C. *The Message of the Psalter: An Eschatological Programme in the Book of Psalms*. JSOTSup. Sheffield: Sheffield Academic, 1997.

Montanari, Franco. *The Brill Dictionary of Ancient Greek*. Leiden: Brill, 2015.

Moo, Douglas J. *The Old Testament in the Gospel Passion Narratives*. Sheffield: Almond Press, 1983.

Moo, Douglas J. "The Problem of Sensus Plenior." In *Hermeneutics, Authority, and Canon*, edited by D. A. Carson and J. D. Woodbridge, 179–211. Grand Rapids: Zondervan, 1986.

Moo, Douglas J. and Andrew David Naselli. "The Problem of the New Testament's Use of the Old Testament" in *The Enduring Authority of the Christian Scriptures*, edited by Donald A. Carson, 702–46. Grand Rapids: Eerdmans, 2016.

Moran, William L. "Gen 49:10 and its use in Ezek 21:32." *Bib* 39.4 (1958): 405–25.

Morris, Leon. *The Gospel according to Matthew*. PNTC. Downers Grove: InterVarsity Press, 1992.

Motyer, J. Alec. *The Prophecy of Isaiah: An Introduction and Commentary*. Downers Grove, IL: InterVarsity, 1993.

Mowery, Robert L. "Son of God in Roman Imperial Titles and Matthew." *Bib* 83 (2002): 100–110.

Mowery, Robert L. "Subtle Differences: The Matthean 'Son of God' References." *NovT* 32 (1990): 193–200.

Mowinckel, Sigmund. *He That Cometh: The Messiah Concept in the Old Testament and Later Judaism*. Translated by G. W. Anderson. New York: Abingdon, 1954.

Moyise, Steve. *Evoking Scripture: Seeing the Old Testament in the New*. London: T&T Clark, 2008.

Moyise, Steve. "Isaiah in 1 Peter." In *Isaiah in the New Testament: The New Testament and the Scriptures of Israel*, edited by M. J. J. Menken and Steve Moyise, 175–88. LNTS. London: T&T Clark, 2005.

Mundle, W. "Πέτρα." In *New International Dictionary of New Testament Theology*, edited by Colin Brown, 3:384–85. Grand Rapids: Zondervan, 1986.

Newsom, Carol A. *The Self as Symbolic Space: Constructing Identity and Community at Qumran*. Leiden: Brill, 2004.

Ngunga, Abi T. *Messianism in the Old Greek of Isaiah: An Intertextual Analysis*. Göttingen: Vandenhoeck & Ruprecht 2012.

Nickelsburg, George W. E. "Salvation without and with a Messiah" in *Judaisms and their Messiahs at the Turn of the Christian Era*, edited by Jacob Neusner, William S. Green, and Ernest Frerichs, 49–68. Cambridge: Cambridge University, 1987.

Nickelsburg, George W. E. *1 Enoch 1: A Commentary on the Book of Enoch, Chapters 1–36; 81–108*. Hermeneia. Minneapolis: Fortress, 2001.

Nolland, John. "Grace as Power," *NT* 28.1 (1986): 26–31.

Nolland, John. *The Gospel of Matthew: A Commentary on the Greek Text*. NIGTC. Grand Rapids: Eerdmans, 2005.

Nolland, John. *Luke*. 3 volumes. WBC. Nashville, TN: Thomas Nelson, 1989–1993.

Nolland, John. "The King as Shepherd: The Role of Deutero-Zechariah in Matthew." In *Biblical Interpretation in Early Christian Gospels: Volume 2: The Gospel of Matthew*, edited by Thomas R. Hatina, 133–46. LNTS. London: T&T Clark, 2008.

Novacovic, Lidija. *Messiah, the Healer of the Sick: A Study of Jesus as the Son of David in the Gospel of Matthew*. Tübingen: Mohr Siebeck, 2003.

Novakovic, Lidija. "Matthew's Atomistic Use of Scripture: Messianic Interpretation of Isaiah 53.4 in Matthew 8.17." In *Biblical Interpretation in Early Christian Gospels: Volume 2: The Gospel of Matthew*, edited by Thomas R. Hatina, 147–62. LNTS. London: T&T Clark, 2008.

Novenson, Matthew. *Christ Among the Messiahs: Christ Language in Paul and Messiah language in Ancient Judaism*. Oxford: Oxford University Press, 2012.

Novenson, Matthew. *The Grammar of Messianism: An Ancient Jewish Political Idion and Its Users*. Oxford: Oxford University Press, 2017.

Odell, Margaret S. *Ezekiel*. SHBC. Macon, GA: Smyth & Helwys, 2005.

Oegema, Gerbern. *The Anointed and His People: Messianic Expectations from the Maccabees to Bar Kochba*. JSPSup. Sheffield: Sheffield Academic, 1998.

Olmstead, Wesley G. "A Gospel for a New *Nation*: Once More, the ἔθνος of Matt 21.43." In *Jesus, Matthew's Gospel and Early Christianity: Studies in the Memory of Graham Stanton*, edited by Daniel M. Gurtner, Joel Willitts, and Richard A. Burridge, 115–32. LNTS. London: T&T Clark, 2011.

Olmstead, Wesley G. *Matthew's Trilogy of Parables: The Nation, the Nations, and the Reader in Matthew 21:28–22:14*. SNTSMS. Cambridge: Cambridge University, 2003.

Olson, Daniel C. *A New Reading of the Animal Apocalypse of 1 Enoch: 'All Nations Shall Be Blessed': With a New Translation and Commentary*. SVTP. Leiden: Brill, 2013.

Onyenali, Rowland. *The Trilogy of Parables in Mt 21:28–22:14: From a Matthean Perspective*. ATS. Frankfurt am Main: Peter Lang, 2013.

Oropeza, B. J. and Steve Moyise, editors. *Exploring Intertextuality: Diverse Strategies for New Testament Interpretation of Texts*. Eugene, OR: Cascade, 2016.

Oropeza, B. J. and Max Lee, editors. *Practicing Intertextuality: Jewish and Greco-Roman Exegetical Techniques in the New Testament*. Eugene, OR: Cascade, forthcoming.

Osborne, Grant R. *Matthew*. ZECNT. Grand Rapids: Zondervan, 2010.

Oswalt, John. *The Book of Isaiah: Chapters 1–39*. NICOT. Grand Rapids: Eerdmans, 1986.

Overman, J. Andrew. *Church and Community in Crisis: The Gospel According to Matthew*. Valley Forge: Trinity Press, 1996.

Overmann, J. Andrew. *Matthew's Gospel and Formative Judaism: The Social World of the Matthean Community*. Minneapolis: Ausburg, 1990.

Pao, David W. and Eckhard J. Schnabel. "Luke." In *Commentary on the New Testament Use of the Old Testament*, edited by Gregory K. Beale and Donald A. Carson, 251–415. Grand Rapids: Baker Academic, 2007.

Perri, Carmela. "On Alluding." *Poetics* 7.3 (1978): 289–307.

Perriman, A. "The Corporate Christ: Re-assessing the Jewish Background." *TynBul* 50.2 (1999): 241–63.

Perrin, Nicholas. *Jesus and the Temple*. Grand Rapids: Baker, 2010.

Petterson, Anthony R. *Behold Your King: The Hope for the House of David in the Book of Zechariah*. New York: T&T Clark, 2009.

Petterson, Anthony R. *Haggai, Zechariah & Malachi*. ApOTC. Downers Grove, IL: InterVarsity, 2015.

Phillips, Elaine A. "Peter's Declaration at Caesarea Philippi." In *Lexham Geographic Commentary on the Gospels*, edited by Barry J. Beitzel, 286–97. Bellingham, WA: Lexham, 2017.

Piotrowski, Nicholas G. *Matthew's New David at the End of Exile: A Socio-Rhetorical Study of Scriptural Citations*. NovTSup. Leiden: Brill: 2016.

Piotrowski, Nicholas G. "'Whatever You Ask' for the Missionary Purposes of the Eschatological Temple: Quotation Typology in Mark 11–12." *SBJT* 21.1 (2017): 97–121.

Poirier, John C. "The End Time Return of Elijah and Moses at Qumran." *DSD* 10.2 (2003): 226–37.

Poirier, John C. "Jesus as an Elijianic Figure in Luke 4:16–30." *CBQ* 71. 2 (2009): 349–63.

Pomykala, Kenneth. *Davidic Dynasty Tradition in Early Judaism: Its History and Significance for Messianism*. Atlanta: Scholars Press, 1995.

Pond, Eugene W. "Who are the Sheep and the Goats in Matthew 25:31–46?" *BSac* 159 (July–Sept 2002): 288–301.

Porter, Stanley E. "Allusions and Echoes." In *As It Is Written: Studying Paul's Use of Scripture*, edited by Stanley Porter and Christopher Stanley, 29–40. Atlanta: Society of Biblical Literature, 2008.

Porter, Stanley E. "The Use of the Old Testament in the New Testament: A Brief Comment on Methodology and Terminology." In *Early Christian Interpretation of the Scriptures of Israel: Investigations and Proposals*, edited by Craig A. Evans and James A. Sanders, 79–96. JSNTSup. Sheffield: Sheffield Academic, 1997.

Powell, Mark Allen. "Matthean Beatitudes: Reversals and Rewards of the Kingdom." *CBQ* 58.3 (July 1996): 260–79.

Powery, Emerson. *Jesus Reads Scripture: The Function of Jesus' Use of Scripture in the Synoptic Gospels*. BibInt. Leiden: Brill, 2003.

Puech, Emile. "Une Apocalypse Messianique (4Q521)." *RevQ* 15 (1992): 475–519.

Puech, Emile. "Resurrection: The Bible and Qumran." In *The Bible and the Dead Sea Scrolls: Volume Two: The Dead Sea Scrolls and the Qumran Community*, edited by James H. Charlesworth, 247–81. Waco, TX: Baylor, 2006.

Quarles, Charles L. "The Blessings of the New Moses: An Examination of the Theological Purpose of the Matthean Beatitudes." *JSHJ* 13 (2015): 316–21.

Quarles, Charles L. *Matthew*. EGGNT. Nashville: B&H Publishing, 2017.

Quek, Tze-Ming. "'I will give Authority over the Nations': Psalm 2.8–9 in Revelation 2.26–27." In *Early Christian Literature and Intertextuality: Volume 2: Exegetical Studies*, edited by Craig A. Evans and H. Daniel Zacharias, 175–187. LNTS. London: T&T Clark, 2009.

Rainbow, Paul. "Melchizedek as a Messiah at Qumran." *BBR* 7 (1997): 179–94.

Rice, Sally and John Newman. *Empirical and Experimental Methods in Cognitive/ Functional-Research*. San Diego: CSLI Publications, 2010.

Ridgway, John K. "A Correlation between Healing and Peace in Matt 10:1–16, Jesus' Commission to the Twelve." *Proceedings*, 11 (1991): 108.

Riesenfeld, Harald. *The Gospel Tradition*. Translated by E. M. Rowley and R. A. Kraft. Philadelphia: Fortress, 1970.

Robertson, A. T. *A Grammar of the Greek New Testament in the Light of Historical Research*. Bellingham, WA: Logos Bible Software, 2006.

Rogers, T. J. "Shaking the Dust off the Markan Mission Discourse." *JSNT* 272 (2004): 169–92.

Rosenberg, J. *Isaiah (Volume 2): New English Translation of Text, Rashi and Commentary*. New York: Judaica, 1983.

Ross, Allen P. *A Commentary on the Psalms: Volume 3*. Grand Rapids: Kregel, 2016.

Rothfuchs, Willhelm. *Die Erfüllungszitate des Matthäus-Evangeliums: Eine biblische-theogische Untersuchung*. BWANT. Stuttgart: Kohlhammer, 1969.

Rowe, Robert D. *God's Kingdom and God's Son: The Background to Mark's Christology from Concepts of Kingship in the Psalms*. AGJU. Leiden: Brill, 2002.

Runeson, Anders. *Divine Wrath and Salvation: The Narrative World of the First Gospel*. Minneapolis: Fortress, 2016.

Sailhamer, John H. "Hosea 11:1 and Matthew 2:15" *WTJ* 63 (2001): 87–96.

Sailhamer, John H. *The Meaning of the Pentateuch: Revelation, Composition, and Interpretation*. Downers Grove, IL: InterVarsity, 2010.

Saldarini, Andrew. *Matthew's Christian-Jewish Community*. Chicago: University of Chicago Press, 1994.

Sanders, James A. "From Isaiah 61 to Luke 4." In *Christianity, Judaism and Other Greco-Roman Cults, Part 1: New Testament*, edited by Jacob Neusner, 46–6. Eugene, OR: Wipf and Stock, 2004.

Sanders, James A. "Isaiah in Luke." *Int* 36.2 (1982): 144–55.

Sawyer, John F. A. *Sacred Languages and Sacred Texts*. London: Routledge, 1999.

Schellenberg, R. S. "Eschatology." In *Dictionary of Jesus and the Gospels*. Second Edition. Edited by Joel B. Green, Jeannine K. Brown, and Nicholas Perrin, 232–39. Downers Grove, IL: IVP Academic, 2013.

Schmeller, T. "Der Erbe des Weinbergs: Zu den Gerichtsgleichnissen Mk 12,1–2 und Jes 5,1–7." *MTZ* 46.2 (1995): 183–201.

Schnabel, E. J. "Apostle." In *Dictionary of Jesus and the Gospels*. Second Edition. Edited by Joel B. Green, Jeannine K. Brown, and Nicholas Perrin, 34–45. Downers Grove, IL: IVP Academic, 2013.

Schreiner, Patrick. *Matthew, Disciple and Scribe: The First Gospel and Its Portrayal of Jesus*. Grand Rapids: Baker Academic, 2020.

Schreiner, Patrick. "Peter, the Rock: Matthew 16 in light of Daniel 2." *CTR* 13.2 (2016): 99–117.

Schuller, Eileen M. "Recent Scholarship on the Hodayot 1993–2010." *CBR* 10.1 (2011): 119–62.

Schuller, Eileen M. and Carol A. Newsom. *Hodayot (Thanksgiving Psalms): A Study Edition of 1QHa*. EJL. Atlanta: SBL, 2012.

Schurer, Emil. *The History of the Jewish People in the Age of Jesus Christ*. Revised by Geza Vermes and Fergus Millar with Matthew Black and Martin Goodman. Edinburgh: T&T Clark, 1973–87.

Schutter, William L. *Hermeneutic and Composition in 1 Peter*. WUNT; Tübingen: Mohr Siebeck, 1989.

Scott, J. M. "Exile and Restoration." In *Dictionary of Jesus and the Gospels*. Second Edition. Edited by Joel B. Green, Jeannine K. Brown, and Nicholas Perrin, 251–58. Downers Grove, IL: IVP Academic, 2013.

Seccombe, David. "Luke and Isaiah." *NTS* 27.2 (1981): 252–59.

Seitz, Christopher R. "Isaiah 40–66." In *The New Interpreter's Bible: A Commentary in Twelve Volumes*, edited by Leander E. Keck, 6:309–552. Nashville: Abingdon, 2001.

Seitz, Oscar J. F. "Upon This Rock: A Critical Re-Examination of Matt 16:17–19." *JBL* 69.4 (Dec 1950): 340.

Senior, Donald. *The Gospel of Matthew*. IBT. Nashville: Abingdon, 1997.

Senior, Donald. "The Lure of the Formula Quotations: Re-assessing Matthew's Use of the Old Testament with the Passion Narrative as Test Case." In *The Scriptures in the Gospels*, edited by C. M. Tuckett, 89–115. BETL. Leuven: Leuven University, 1997.

Seufert, Matthew. "Isaiah's Herald." *WTJ* 77 (2015): 220–22.

Shäfer, Peter. "Tempel und Schopfung: Zur Interpretation einiger Heiligtumstraditionen in der rabbischen Literatur." In *Studien zur geschichte und Theologie des rabbinischen Judentums*, 122–33. AGJU. Leiden: Brill, 1978.

Shepherd, Michael. *A Commentary on the Book of the Twelve: The Minor Prophets*. Grand Rapids: Kregel Academic, 2018.

Sheppard, Gerald. "More on Isaiah 5:1–7 as a Juridical Parable" *CBQ* (1981): 45–47.

Shultz, Richard L. *The Search for Quotations: Verbal Parallels in the Prophets*. JSOTSup. Sheffield: Sheffield Academic, 1999.

Siker, Jeffrey S. "'First to the Gentiles': A Literary Analysis of Luke 4:16–30." *JBL* 111 (1992): 73–90.

Silva, Moisés, editor. *New International Dictionary of New Testament Theology and Exegesis*. 5 volumes. Grand Rapids: Zondervan, 2014.

Sim, David. *The Gospel of Matthew and Christian Judaism*. Edinburgh: T&T Clark, 1998.

Slager, Donald. "Preface." In *A Handbook on Sirach*, edited by Paul Clarke et al., vii–viii. United Bible Societies' Handbooks. New York: United Bible Societies, 2008.

Smith, Gary. *Isaiah 40–66*. NAC. Nashville: Broadman & Holman, 2009.

Smith, Paul Allan. *Rhetoric and Redaction in Trito-Isaiah: the Structure, Growth, and Authorship of Isaiah 56–66*. VTSup. Leiden: Brill, 1995.

Snodgrass, Klyne R. "The Christological Stone Testimonia in the New Testament." PhD Dissertation: University of St. Andrews, 1973.

Snodgrass, Klyne R. "The Parable of the Wicked Husbandmen: Is the *Gospel of Thomas* Version the Original?" NTS 21 (1975): 142–44.
Snodgrass, Klyne R. *The Parable of the Wicked Tenants: An Inquiry into Parable Interpretation*. WUNT. Eugene, OR: Wipf and Stock, 2011.
Snodgrass, Klyne R. *Stories with Intent: A Comprehensive Guide to the Parables of Jesus*. Grand Rapids: Eerdmans, 2008.
Speiser, E. A. "Background and Function of the Biblical Nasi." CBQ 25.1 (1963): 111–17.
Sperber, A. *The Aramaic Bible*. Leiden: Brill, 1974.
Stanley, Christopher D. *Arguing with Scripture: The Rhetoric of Quotations in the Letters of Paul*. New York: T&T Clark, 2004.
Stanton, Graham N. "5 Ezra and Matthean Christianity in the Second Century." JTS 28.1 (1977): 67–83.
Stanton, Graham N. "Once More: Matthew 25:31–46." In *A Gospel for a New People: Studies in Matthew*, 207–31. Edinburgh: T&T Clark, 1992.
Steen, Gerard. "Metaphor and Language and Literature: A Cognitive Perspective." In *Language and Literature* 9:3 (2000): 261–77.
Stein, Robert A. *Luke*. NAC. Nashville: B&H, 1993.
Stettler, Hanna. "Die Bedeutung der Täuferanfrage in Matthäus 11,2–6 par Lk 7,18–23 für die Christologie." Bib 89.2 (2008): 173–200.
Stone, Michael E. "The Messiah in 4 Ezra." In *Judaisms and their Messiahs at the Turn of the Christian Era*, edited by Jacob Neusner, William S. Green and Ernest Frerichs, 209–24. Cambridge: Cambridge University, 1987.
Stone, Michael E. and Matthias Henze. *4 Ezra and 2 Baruch: Translations, Introductions, and Notes*. Minneapolis: Fortress, 2013.
Stovell, Beth M. *Mapping Metaphorical Discourse in the Fourth Gospel: John's Eternal King*. LBS. Leiden: Brill, 2012.
Strack, H. and P. Billerbeck. *Kommentar zum Neuen Testament aus Talmud und Midrash*. 3 volumes. Munchen: Beck, 1926.
Strauss, Mark L. *The Davidic Messiah in Luke-Acts: The Promise and Its Fulfillment in Lukan Christology*. Sheffield: Sheffield Academic, 1995.
Strauss, Mark L. *Four Portraits, One Jesus: A Survey of Jesus and the Gospels*. Grand Rapids: Zondervan, 2011.
Strecker, Georg. *Der Weg der Gerechtigkeit: Untersuchung zur Theologie des Matthäus*. FZPhTh. Göttingen: Vandenhoeck & Reuprecht, 1971.
Streett, Andrew. "From Marginal to Mainstream: The Adamic Son of Man and the Potential of Psalm 80." CTR 13.2 (2016): 77–98.
Streett, Andrew. *The Vine and the Son of Man: Eschatological Interpretation of Psalm 80 in Early Judaism*. Philadelphia: Fortress Press, 2014.
Subramanian, J. Samuel. *The Synoptic Gospels and the Psalms as Prophecy*. LNTS. London: T&T Clark, 2007.
Susenik, Eliezer. *The Dead Sea Scrolls of Hebrew University*. Jerusalem: Magnes, 1954.

Sweeney, Marvin A. "Jeremiah's Reflection on the Isaian Royal Promise: Jeremiah 23:1–8 in Context." In *Uprooting and Planting: Essays on Jeremiah for Leslie Allen*, edited by John Goldingay, 308–21. LHBOTS. New York: T&T Clark, 2007.

Tablert, Charles H. *Matthew*. Paideia Commentary on the New Testament. Grand Rapids: Baker Academic, 2010.

Tabor, J. D. and Michael O. Wise. "On Resurrection and the Synoptic Gospel Tradition: A Preliminary Study." *JSP* 10 (1992): 150–61.

Talbot, Michel. *Heuruex les Doux, car ils heriteront la terre*. Paris: J. Gabalda, 2002.

Tasker, Randolph V. G. *The Gospel According to St. Matthew: An Introduction and Commentary*. Grand Rapids: Eerdmans, 1961.

Tate, Marvin. *Psalms 50–100*. WBC. Nashville, TN: Thomas Nelson, 1990.

Telford, W. R. *The Barren Temple and the Withered Tree*. JSNTSup. Sheffield: JSOT, 1980.

Terrien, Samuel. *The Psalms: Strophic Structure and Theological Commentary*. Eerdmans' Critical Commentary. Grand Rapids: Eerdmans, 2003.

Thompson, J. A. *The Book of Jeremiah*. NICOT. Eerdmans: Grand Rapids, 1980.

Thompson, Michael B. *Clothed with Christ: The Example and Teaching of Jesus in Romans 12:1–15:3*. Eugene, OR: Wipf and Stock, 2011.

Thomson, J. G. S. S. "The Shepherd Ruler Concept in the OT and Its Application in the NT." *SJT* 8.4 (1955): 409–10.

Tinker, Melvin. "The Servant Solution: The Co-Ordination of Evangelism and Social Action." *Them* 32.2 (2006): 6–32.

Toussaint, Stanley. *Behold Your King: A Study of Matthew*. Grand Rapids: Kregel, 1980.

Trebilco, Paul R. *Self-Designations and Group Identity in the New Testament*. Cambridge: Cambridge University Press, 2002.

Trilling, Wolfgang. *Das Wahre Israel: Studien zur Theologie des Matthäus-Evangeliums*. SANT. München: Kösel, 1964.

Tucker, Gene M. "The Book of Isaiah." In *The New Interpreter's Bible*, edited by L. E. Keck et al., 6:25–305. Abingdon: Nashville, 2001.

Tull, Patricia K. *Isaiah 1–39*. SHBC. Macon, GA: Smyth & Helwys, 2010.

Turner, David L. "'His Glorious Throne': The Future of Israel and the Gentiles according to Matthew." Paper presented at SBL 11/19/2016.

Turner, David L. *Israel's Last Prophet*. Minneapolis: Fortress Press, 2015.

Turner, David L. *Matthew*. BECNT; Grand Rapids: Baker Academic, 2008.

Turner, David L. "*Primus inter pares?* Peter in the Gospel of Matthew." In *New Testament Essays in Honor of Homer A. Kent Jr.*, edited by G. T. Meadors, 179–201. Winona Lake, IN: BMH, 1991.

Twelftree, Graham H. *In the Name of Jesus: Exorcism Among Early Christians*. Grand Rapids: Baker Academic, 2007.

Twelftree, Graham H. "ΕΙ ΔΕ ... ΕΓΩ ... ΕΚΒΑΛΛΩ ΤΑ ΔΑΙΜΟΝΙΑ! ... [Luke 11:19]." In *Gospel Perspectives, Vol. 6: The Miracles of Jesus*. Edited by David Wenham and Craig Blomberg. Sheffield: JSOT Press, 1986.

Unger, Merrill F. *Zechariah: Prophet of Messiah's Glory*. Eugene, OR: Wipf & Stock, 2014.
van de Water, Rick. "Michael or Yhwh?: Toward Identifying Melchizedek in 11Q13." *JSP* 16.1 (2006): 75–86.
van der Woude, A. S. "Melchisedek als himmlische Erlösergestalt in den neugefundenen eschatologischen Midraschim aus Qumran Höhle, X." *OtSt* 14 (1965): 367–72.
van Groningen, Gerard. *Messianic Revelation*. Eugene, OR: Wipf and Stock, 1990.
van Hecke, Pierre. "Metaphor and Conceptual Blending." In *Metaphor in the Hebrew Bible*, edited by Pierre van Hecke, 215–32. Leuven: Leuven University Press, 2005.
van Unnik, W. C. "Jesus the Christ." *NTS* 8 (1963): 101–16.
vanTine, Jarrett. "The Restoration of Israel's Priesthood as the Framework for Matthean Ethics." SBL Presentation, Boston, MA, November 21, 2017.
Vermes, Geza. *Jesus the Jew: A Historian's Reading of the Gospels*. Philadelphia: Fortress, 1973.
Violet, Bruno. *Die Apokalypsen des Esra und des Baruch in deutscher Gestalt, II*. Leipzig: J. C. Hinrichs, 1924.
Viviano, B. "The Gospel according to Matthew." In *The New Jerome Biblical Commentary*, edited by R. Brown et al., 630–74. Englewood Cliffs, NJ: Prentice Hall, 1990.
von Hans, Kvalbein. "*Die Wunder de Endzeit: Beobachtungen zu 4Q521 und Matth 11, 5p.*" In *ZNW* 88.1–2 (1997): 113–19.
von Rad, Gerhard. "Die Stadt auf dem Berge." *EvT* (1948–49): 439–47.
von Thaden, Robert H. Jr. *Sex, Christ, and Embodied Cognition: Paul's Wisdom for Corinth*. ESEC. Atlanta: SBL Press, 2017.
Wagner, J. Ross. "Isaiah in Romans and Galatians." In *Isaiah in the New Testament: The New Testament and the Scriptures of Israel*, edited by M. J. J. Menken and Steve Moyise, 117–32. LNTS. London: T&T Clark, 2005.
Wagner, J. Ross. *Heralds of the Good News: Isaiah and Paul in Concert in the Letter to the Romans*. Leiden: Brill, 2003.
Wagner, J. Ross. "Psalm 118 in Luke-Acts: Tracing a Narrative Thread." In *Early Christian Interpretation of the Scriptures of Israel: Investigations and Proposals*, edited by Craig A. Evans and James A. Sanders, 154–78. JSNT. Sheffield: Sheffield Academic, 1997.
Wagner, J. Ross. *Reading the Sealed Book: Old Greek Isaiah and the Problem of Septuagint Hermeneutics*. Waco, TX: Baylor, 2013.
Wallace, Daniel B. *Greek Grammar beyond the Basics: An Exegetical Syntax of the New Testament*. Grand Rapids: Zondervan, 1996.
Wallace, Howard N. "Tree of Knowledge and Tree of Life." In *The Anchor Yale Bible Dictionary*, edited by David Noel Freedman, 6:656–60. New York: Doubleday, 1992.
Walton, John H. and D. Brent Sandy. *The Lost World of Scripture: Ancient Literary Culture and Biblical Authority*. Downers Grove, Il. IVP Academic, 2013.
Walvoord, John F. "The End Times." In *Understanding Christian Theology*, edited by Charles R. Swindoll and Roy B. Zuck. Nashville: Thomas Nelson, 2003.

BIBLIOGRAPHY 247

Walvoord, John F. and Charles H. Dyer. *Matthew*. Chicago: Moody, 2013.
Walvoord, John F. *Matthew: Thy Kingdom Come*. Chicago: Moody, 1974.
Watson, Francis. *Paul and the Hermeneutics of Faith*, Second Edition. London: Bloomsbury, 2015.
Watts, John D. W. *Isaiah 1–33*, Revised Edition. WBC. Grand Rapids: Zondervan, 2018.
Watts, John D. W. *Isaiah 34–66*. WBC. Dallas: Nelson, 1987.
Watts, Rikki E. "Mark." In *Commentary on the New Testament Use of the Old Testament*, edited by Donald A. Carson and Gregory K. Beale, 111–249. Grand Rapids: Baker Academic, 2007.
Watts, Rikki E. "The Lord's House and David's Lord: The Psalms and Mark's Perspective on Jesus and the Temple." *BibInt* (2007): 307–322.
Watts, Rikki E. *Isaiah's New Exodus in Mark*. Grand Rapids: Baker, 1997.
Welch, John W. *The Sermon on the Mount in Light of the Temple*. Burlington, VT: Ashgate, 2009.
Wenham, David. *Paul: Follower of Jesus or Founder of Christianity?* Grand Rapids: Eerdmans, 1995.
Weren, W. J. C. *Studies in Matthew's Gospel: Literary Design, Intertextuality and Social Setting*. BibInt. Leiden: Brill, 2014.
Whybray, R. N. *Isaiah 40–66*. CBC. Grand Rapids: Eerdmans, 1975.
Wilcox, Max. "Peter and the Rock: A Fresh Look at Matthew XVI. 17–19." *NTS* 22 (1975): 73–88.
Wildeberger, Hans. *Isaiah 1–12*. CC. Translated by Thomas H. Trapp. Minneapolis: Fortress, 1991.
Wilkins, Michael J. *Discipleship in the Ancient World and Matthew's Gospel*. Second Edition. Eugene, OR: Wipf and Stock, 2015.
Wilkins, Michael J. *Matthew*. NIVAC. Grand Rapids: Zondervan, 2009.
Williams, Gary R. "Frustrated Expectations in Isaiah V 1–7: A Literary Interpretation." *VT* 35.4 (1985): 459–65.
Williamson, H. G. M. *Isaiah 1–5: A Critical and Exegetical Commentary*. ICC. London: T&T Clark, 2006.
Williamson, H. G. M. *Variations on a Theme: King, Messiah and Servant in the Book of Isaiah*. Didsbury Lectures. Carlisle: Paternoster Press, 1998.
Willis, John T. "The Genre of Isaiah 5:1–7." *JBL* 96 (1977): 337–62.
Willis, John T. "Yahweh Regenerates his Vineyard: Isaiah 27." In *Formation and Intertextuality in Isaiah 24–27*, edited by J. Todd Hibbard and Hyun Chul Paul Kim, 201–08. AIL. Atlanta: SBL, 2013.
Willitts, Joel. *Matthew's Messianic Shepherd King: In Search of the Lost Sheep of the House of Israel*. BZNW. Berlin: Walter de Gruyter, 2007.
Willoughby, Allen C. *A Critical and Exegetical Commentary on the Gospel According to St. Matthew*, Third edition. ICC. Edinburgh: T&T Clark, 1912.

Wilson, John Francis. *Caesarea Philippi: In Search for the Lost City of Pan*. London: I. B. Taurus, 2004.

Wise, Michael O. *The First Messiah: Investigating the Savior Before Jesus*. San Francisco: HarperCollins, 1999.

Wise, Michael O., Martin G. Abegg Jr., and Edward M. Cook, editors. *The Dead Sea Scrolls: A New Translation*. New York: HarperOne, 2005.

Witetschek, Stephen. "What Did John Hear? The Reconstruction of Q 7:18–19 and its Implications." NT 56 (2014): 245–60.

Witherington, Ben, III. *Jesus, Paul and the End of the World: A Comparative Study in New Testament Eschatology*. Downers Grove, IL: InterVarsity, 1999.

Witherington, Ben, III. *John's Wisdom: A Commentary on the Fourth Gospel*. Louisville: Westminster John Knox, 1995.

Witherington, Ben, III. *Matthew*. SHBC. Malcon, GA: Smyth and Helwys, 2006.

Witherington, Ben, III. *What Have They Done with Jesus: Beyond Strange Theories and Bad History-Why We Can Trust the Bible*. New York: Harper Collins, 2006.

Witmer, Amanda. *Jesus, The Galilean Exorcist: His Exorcisms in Social and Political Context*. London: Bloomsbury, 2012.

Wold, Benjamin. "Agency and Raising the Dead in Pseudo-Ezekiel and 521 2 ii." ZNW 1/103 (2012): 1–19.

Wolters, Albert M. *Zechariah*. HCOT. Leuven: Peeters, 2014.

Wright, N. T. "Jerusalem in the New Testament." In *Jerusalem, Past and Present in the Purposes of God*, edited by Peter W. L. Walker, 53–77. Grand Rapids: Baker, 1994.

Wright, N. T. *Jesus and the Victory of God*. London: SPCK, 1996.

Wright, N. T. *The New Testament and the People of God*. London: SPCK, 1993.

Xeravits, Géza. *King, Priest, Prophet: Positive Eschatological Protagonists of the Qumran Library*. STDJ. Leiden: Brill, 2003.

Young, Edward. *Isaiah, Volume III*. Grand Rapids: Eerdmans, 1972.

Zacharias, H. Daniel. "Matthew's Presentation of the Son of David: Davidic Tradition and Typology in the Gospel of Matthew." PhD Dissertation; University of Aberdeen, 2015.

Zacharias, H. Daniel. *Matthew's Presentation of the Son of David: Davidic Tradition and Typology in the Gospel of Matthew*. T&T Clark Biblical Studies. London: Bloomsbury, 2017.

Zimmerli, Walther. *Ezekiel: A Commentary on the Book of the Prophet Ezekiel*. Hermeneia. Philadelphia: Fortress Press, 1979.

Zimmermann, J. *Messianische Texte aus Qumran. Königliche, priesterliche und prophetische Messiasvorstellungen in den Schriften von Qumran*. WUNT. Tübingen: Mohr Siebeck, 1998.

Zinken, Jörg. "Ideological Imagination: Intertextual and Correlational Metaphors in Political Discourse." *Discourse & Society* (2003): 507–23.

Modern Author Index

Abasciano, Brian J.   20, 22, 23
Abernethy, Andrew   182, 185
Adam, Sean A.   38
Adna, J.   155, 156
Akpunonu, Peter D.   114, 122
Alexander, Ralph H.   51
Allen, Leslie   70, 71, 73, 77, 49
Allison, Dale C.   47–48, 45, 61, 64, 78, 128, 161, 162, 174, 181, 188, 198, 202, 207
Atkinson, Kenneth R.   59

Bailey, Kenneth   173
Baker, Margaret   176
Baldwin, Joyce G.   76
Barber, Michael P.   77, 161
Barclay, John M. G.   28
Barton, Stephen C.   9
Basser, Herbert W.   126, 130
Bates, Matthew   24
Bauckham, Richard J.   111, 194
Bauer, David R.   205
Baxter, Wayne   48, 65, 71
Beale, G. K.   17, 26, 145, 161, 175
Beasley-Murray, George R.   122, 125
Beaton, Richard   7
Beers, Holly   13–14, 182
Beetham, Christopher A.   20
Begg, Christopher T.   106
Ben-Porat, Ziva   26, 28
Betz, Hans Dieter   177
Beuken, W. A. M   185–86
Bigane III, John E.   177
Billerbeck, P.   146
Bird, Michael F.   60, 157, 183, 185, 193, 207
Black, Matthew   118, 46
Blenkinsopp, Joseph   104, 185, 189
Block, Darrell   104, 105, 107, 108, 49, 50, 53, 62, 68, 73, 183
Blomberg, Craig   2, 79, 198, 128, 146, 153, 210
Bobichon, Philippe   38
Boccaccini, Gabriele   58
Bock, Darrell   60, 185, 195, 196, 197, 207, 209
Bockmuehl, Markus   161
Boda, Mark   85, 87, 156
Borig, Rainer   122

Briggs, Charles Augustus   200
Brodie, Thomas   122
Brooke, George J.   146, 191
Brown, Francis   200
Brownlee, William H.   68
Bruce, A. B.   166
Bruce, F. F.   160
Brueggemann, Walter   114
Brunson, Andrew C.   145, 148
Bühner, J. A.   67

Cadbury, Henry   3–4, 25
Cahill, M.   153, 158, 159
Calvin, John   165, 206
Campbell, Ken   175
Caragounis, Chrys C.   166–69
Carlston, Charles E.   6, 81, 177
Carmignac, Jean   191
Carson, Donald A.   4, 56, 118, 122, 198, 207, 210
Carter, Warren   78, 130, 177, 205
Chae, Young   45, 56, 58, 63
Chaney, Marvin L.   99
Charles, Robert H.   110, 111, 112
Charlesworth, James   60
Chester, Andrew J.   155
Childs, Brevard S.   99, 101, 182, 186
Chilton, Bruce   187, 201
Chisholm, R. B.   182, 184
Cienki, Alan J.   30
Clifford, Richard J.   107
Collins, John J.   54, 76, 192, 193
Conzelmann, Hans   134
Cooper, Ben   9, 51, 52, 104
Coulson, Seana   33, 34
Craigie, Peter C.   71, 72, 73, 74, 70
Cuany, Monique   196, 197

Dasma, Alinda   55
Davies, W. D.   45, 61, 64, 78, 128, 161, 162, 174, 181, 188, 198, 202, 207
Day, John   101
De Moor, Johannes C.   147
Dearman, J. Andrew   71
deClaissé-Walford, Nancy   76, 114

Deeley, Mary K. 56
Deines, Roland 19
Dekker, Jaap 170, 171
Delitzsch, Franz 70, 71, 87, 101, 114
Dennert, Brian c. 210
Derrett, J. D. M. 154, 162
DesCamp, Mary Therese 28
Docherty, Susan E. 18, 116
Dodd, Charles H. 10–11, 26
Doering, Lutz 112
Donaldson, Terrence L. 10, 173, 205
Douglas, Michael C. 190
Driver, Samuel Rolles 200
Duff, Paul B. 154
Duguid, Ian 87, 104
Dunn, James D. G. 18
Dyer, Charles H. 165

Eco, Umberto 27
Edwards, James R. 194, 197
Ehorn, Seth M. 38
Eliav, Yaron 162
Enns, Peter 25
Eubank, Nathan 79
Evans, Craig A. 6, 23, 81, 84, 96–97, 108, 132, 163, 177, 185, 198, 202, 207, 208, 209
Evans, Vyvyan 29, 30, 31

Fauconnier, Gilles 33, 34, 35, 36, 37, 38, 39, 202, 204
Feinberg, Charles L. 70, 71, 73
Ferreira, Johan 123
Fitzmyer, Joseph 155, 183, 190, 191, 192, 196
Flashman, Richard H. 143
Flesher, Paul V. 187
Fletcher–Louis, Crispin H. T. 175
Flusser, David 147, 191
Foster, Paul 19, 20
France, Richard 3, 6, 8, 17, 26, 45, 62, 91, 153, 161, 175, 176, 177, 185, 198, 209, 210
Fretheim, Terrence E. 74, 77
Frey, Jörg 74

Gamble, Harry Y. 18
Garland, David 175
Gelston, Anthony 83, 86, 117, 118
Genesius, Wilhelm 200
Giovino, Mariana 106–07

Goldingay, John 76, 114, 115, 185, 198
Gomola, Aleksander 29, 34
Goodacre, Mark 200
Goodrich, John K. 79
Gosse, Bernard 114, 117
Grant, Robert M. 154
Gray, Arthur 127
Green, Joel B. 195
Green, Melanie 29, 30, 31
Greenberg, Moshe 51
Gregory, Bradley 199
Grundmann, Walter 79
Guelich, Robert A. 200, 206
Guenter, Kenneth E. 144
Gundry, Robert H. 7, 22, 48, 64, 161, 171, 177

Hagner, Donald A. 134, 198
Halliday, Michael A. K. 30
Hamilton, James M. 4
Hanson, Paul D. 185
Hasselbach, Trine 190
Hatina, Thomas R. 25, 26
Hayes, Elizabeth R. 29, 40
Hays, Richard B. 8, 16, 19, 20, 22, 24, 27, 46, 47, 63, 75, 98, 132, 198
Heike, Thomas 114
Heil, John P. 48, 61, 81
Heiser, Michael S. 164
Hengel, Martin 132
Henning, Bruce 68
Henze, Matthias 110, 112
Hero, Stephen 163
Heskett, Randall 185
Hill, David 117, 118
Hillyer, C. N. 161, 162, 163
Hirsch, E. D. 20
Hogeterp, Albert L. A. 192
Holladay, W. L. 95
Hollander, John 27
Hooker, Morna 85
Horbury, William 51, 139, 191
Hossfeld, Frank Lothat 114
Houston, Walter J. 184, 195
Howe, Bonnie 28
Hughes, Julie A. 189, 190
Huizinga, Leroy A. 16
Hultgard, Anders 191
Hummel, Horace D. 107–08

MODERN AUTHOR INDEX

Hurtado, L. W. 191
Hutchison, John C. 122

Instone–Brewer, David 26
Irwin, William 18
Iser, Wolfgang, 21

Jeremias, Joachim 145, 146, 169, 175, 194
Johnson, Mark 29, 31
Jones, Ken 110
Joseph, Simon J. 189
Joyce, Paul M. 51, 52, 108
Juel, Donald 25, 155

Kaiser Jr., Walter 4, 26, 117, 185
Kaiser, Otto 99
Kaminsky, J. S. 13
Kee, Howard 124
Keener, Craig 45, 61, 98, 130, 153, 162, 198, 202
Keil, Carl Freidrich 70, 71, 87, 101, 114
Kellum, L. S. 121
Kessler, Stephen 29
Kim, Mitchell 20
Kim, Seyoon 156
Kingsbury, Jack D. 128
Kirk, Daniel 3
Klein, George L. 87
Kloppenborg, John S. 94, 97
Knibb, Michael A. 58, 190
Knight, George A. F. 185
Knowles, Michael 68, 174
Koester, Craig R. 56
Konradt, Matthias 10, 78, 98, 130, 131
Köstenberger, Andreas 97, 122, 123, 143
Kövesces, Zoltán 29, 31, 32
Krämer, H. 153
Kroeger, Paul R. 204
Kunjummen, Raju D. 13
Kuyvenhoven, Rosalie 68
Kvalbein, von Hans 192
Kynes, William L. 11–12, 150, 151–52, 210

Lakoff, George 29, 30, 32, 29, 31
Lambert, Wilfred 48
Laniak, Timothy S. 51, 70
Lanier, Gregory R. 29, 75, 102, 150
Lasor, William 4
Le Peau, Andrew T. 17

Lenski, R. C. H. 165, 167
Levenson, Jon D. 175
Levey, Samson 55
Levison, John R. 189
Lied, Liv Engebord 109, 110, 112
Lindars, Barnabas 7
Longman, Tremper 183, 184
Luka, Barbara Josephine 30
Lundhaug, Hugo 29, 36, 37, 71, 73, 74
Luz, Ulrich 8, 15 91, 175, 198, 207, 210

Macaskil, Grant 155
Mallen, Peter 207
Maloney, Linda M. 114
Manning, Gary T. 56, 107, 122
Manzi, Franco 191
Marcus, Joel 25, 131, 144, 149, 163
Marshall, I. Howard 196
Martinez, F. Garcia 192, 193
McCasland, Vernon 3
McConnell, Richard S. 7
McKane, William 72, 73, 74
McKelvey, R. J. 153, 159, 177
McNeile, Alan 166
Meier, John P. 10
Menken, Maarten J. J. 22, 38
Metzger, Bruce Manning 60, 150, 175, 194, 198
Meyer, Ben 86, 155, 161, 162
Meyers, Carol L. 159
Meyers, Eric M. 159
Millard, Alan 18
Miller, Jean 7
Miller, Merril 127, 190
Milne, Mary K. 164
Mitchell, David C. 144
Montanari, Franco 64
Moo, Douglas 4, 20, 26
Moran, William 108
Morris, Leon 91, 175, 201, 207, 208, 209
Motyer, J. Alec 97, 101, 182
Mowerly, Robert L. 135
Mowinckel, Sigmund 50
Moyise, Steve 16, 17, 26, 170
Mundle, W. 166

Newman, John 30
Newsom, Carol A. 189, 190
Ngunga, Abi T. 182, 183–4, 185

Nickelsburg, George W. E.   57, 58
Nolland, John   2, 9, 22, 45, 60, 64, 78, 84, 89, 90, 101, 147, 153, 161, 165, 194, 196, 198, 201, 207, 208, 209, 210
Novakovic, Lidija   3, 26, 208, 209
Novenson, Matthew   15, 183, 184

Oakley, Todd   33, 34
Odell, Margaret S.   103, 105, 106, 108
Oegma, Gerbern S.   75, 184
Olmstead, Wesley G.   128, 130
Olson, Daniel C.   58
Onyenali, Rowland   128
Oropeza, B. J.   16
Osbourne, Grant   2, 91, 128, 131, 198, 202, 205, 210
Oswalt, John   99, 185
Overmann, J. Andrew   8, 130

Pao, David W.   188
Perri, Carmela   16–19
Perriman, A.   13
Perrin, Nicholas   155, 157, 158
Petterson, Anthony Robert   85, 87, 155, 156, 157, 158
Phillips, Elaine A.   164
Piotrowski, Nicholas   7, 8, 9, 22, 144, 154, 198
Poirier, John C.   183, 193
Pomykala, Kenneth   54
Pond, Eugene W.   61
Porter, Stanley E.   19, 20
Powell, Mark Allan   164, 201
Powery, Emerson   2
Puech, Emile   190, 192

Quarles, Charles L.   167, 199–200
Quek, Tze-Ming   13

Rainbow, Paul   191
Rengstorf, K. H.   67
Rice, Sally   30
Ridgway, John K.   90
Riesenfeld, Harald   134
Robertson, A. T.   187
Rogers, T. J.   91
Ross, Allen   76, 113, 117
Rothfuchs, Willhelm   7

Rowe, Robert D.   118
Runeson, Anders   24

Safrai, S.   147
Sailhamer, John H.   5, 14
Saldarini, Andrew   130
Sanders, James A.   188, 197, 209
Sandy, Brent D.   18
Sawyer, John F. A.   18
Schellenber, R. S.   123
Schlatter, A.   12
Schmeller, Von Thomas   94, 100
Schnabel, Eckhard J.   67, 188
Schreiner, Patrick   6–7, 45, 161
Schuller, Eileen M.   189
Schurer, Emil   191
Schutter, William L.   147
Scott, J. M.   74
Seccombe, David   196
Seitz, Christopher R.   168–69, 185
Senior, Donald   3, 7, 205
Seufert, Matthew   200
Shäfer, Peter   161
Shepherd, David   157
Shepherd, Michael   5
Sheppard, Gerald   98
Shultz, Rihard L.   68
Siker, Jeffrey S.   197
Silva, Moisés   52, 67, 79, 153, 170, 174, 207, 208
Sim, David   18, 130
Slager, Donald   187
Smith, Gary   182
Smith, Michael B.   30
Snodgrass, Klyne   118, 146, 148, 163, 174, 177
Snyder, Bob   22–23
Speiser, E. A.   51
Sperber, A.   75
Stanley, Christopher D.   18
Stanton, Graham   56, 60, 61, 151
Steen, Gerard   29
Stein, Robert H.   195, 196
Stettler, Hanna   207, 208, 209
Stone, Michael E.   55, 110
Stovell, Beth M.   29, 30
Strack, H. P.   146
Strauss, Mark   80, 185, 194, 195
Strecker, Georg   7

Streett, Andrew 116, 117, 118, 119, 124, 125
Subramanian, J. Samuel 143
Suk, Yee Lee 87
Susenik, Eliezer 190
Sweeney, Marvin A. 75, 77
Swindoll, Charles R. 50

Talbert, Charles H. 130
Talbot, Michel 199
Tabor, J. D. 192
Tasker, Randolph V. G. 166
Tate, Marvin E. 114
Telford, W. R. 154
Thompson, J. A. 70, 73
Thompson, Michael B. 22, 199
Thomson, J. G. S. S. 71
Tinker, Melvin 175
Toussaint, Stanley 61
Trebilco, Paul R. 10
Tregelles, Samuel Prideaux 200
Trilling, Wolfgang 151
Tucker, Gene M. 100
Tull, Patricia K. 99, 170
Turner, David 2, 45, 63, 78, 80, 98, 101, 130, 131, 165, 167, 176, 177, 198, 205, 208
Turner, Mark 33, 34, 35, 36, 37, 38, 39, 202, 204
Twelftree, Graham H. 89, 90

Unger, Merrill 85

Van de Water, Rick 191
Van der Woude, A. S. 191
Van Groningen, Gerard 71
Van Hecke, Pierre 33
Van Unnik, W. C. 183
Van–Tine, Jarret 77
Vermes, Geza 175
Violet, Bruno 112
Viviano, B. 165
Von Rad, Gerhard 175
Von Thaden Jr., Robert H. 29

Wagner, J. Ross 26, 101, 145, 170
Wallace, Daniel B. 168, 175
Wallace, Howard N. 106
Walton, John H. 18
Walvoord, John F. 50, 61, 165
Watson, Francis 15, 19, 21, 28
Watts, John D. 96, 102, 147, 154, 184, 185
Watts, Rikki E. 25, 143
Welch, John W. 175
Wenham, David 168
Weren, W. J. C. 22, 94, 126, 132
Westermann, Claus 185
Whybray, R. N. 185
Wilcox, Max 165, 169
Wildeberger, Hans 96, 100
Wilkins, Michael J. 10, 153, 166, 173, 177, 205
Williams, Gary R. 96
Williamson, H. G. M. 40, 101
Willis, John T. 96, 100
Willitts, Joel 45, 48, 78, 81
Willoughby, Allen C. 166
Wilson, John Francis 164
Wise, Michael O. 190, 192
Witetschek, Stephen 208
Witherington III, Ben 78, 122, 177, 161, 164, 198, 202
Witmer, Amanda 89
Wold, Benjamin 193
Wolters, Albert M. 85, 87
Wright, N. T. 118, 155, 157, 161, 166, 173, 199

Young, Edward 206

Zacharias, H. Daniel 19, 45
Zenger, Erich 114
Zeravits, Geza 193
Zimmerli, Walther 49, 52, 106
Zimmermann, J. 193
Zinken, Jörg 30
Zuck, Roy B. 50

Subject Index

Agency 46
   Agency in 2 Baruch 36–40 111
   Agency in Ezekiel's Vines 105–06
   Agency in Isa 5:1–7 97–99
   Agency in John 15 122–23
   Agency in Matt 21:33–45 127–33
   Agency in Ps 80 115–16
Allusions (see also Criteria of an Allusion)
   Bonus Points 17
   Contrastive Allusions 23
   Definition of Allusion 16–20
   Function of an Allusion 25–28
   Maximalist Approaches to Allusions 26–28
   Metonymy 27
   Minimalist Approaches to Allusions 25–26
Apostles
   Apostles as "sent ones" 67
   Apostles as Eschatological Temple Builders 149–55
   Apostles as Healers 65–66
   Apostles as Oppressors 88–91
   Apostles as Prophets 80–81

Capstone v. Cornerstone 152–53, 158–60
Cognitive Linguistics 28–41
Cognitive Metaphor Theory / Conceptual Metaphor Theory 29–32
   Blend, Definition of 32–33
   Blending Theory 32–41
   Cross–Domain Mapping 30
   Elaboration 204
   Emergent Structure 33–36, 130, 203
   Entailments 31
   Generic Space 32, 203, 206, 215
   Governing Principles 35–36, 130, 152, 179, 181, 203
      Integration Principle 36
      Pattern Completion Principle 35–36, 66, 130, 152, 179, 203–04, 215
      Running the Blend 35–36, 66, 130, 152, 204
      Topology Principle 35, 202
   Multi–Scope Blends 36–38, 41
   Pattern Completion Principle 35–36, 66, 130, 152, 179, 203–04, 215
   Partial Metaphorical Utilization 31
   Referential Opacity 39–40, 215, 218
   Running the Blend 35–36, 66, 130, 152, 204
   Source Domain 30
   Vital Relations 38–40, 41, 139–40, 219
Contrastive Allusions 23
Cosmic Tree 106–07
Criteria of an Allusion 20–24
   Availability 20–22
   Clustering 22
   Contextual Allusive Density 23, 198
   Contextual Verbal Coherence 22
   Historical Probability 24
   History of Interpretation 24
   Priming 22
   Recurrence 22
   Satisfaction 24
   Thematic Coherence 23
   Volume 22

Definition of Messianic Text 15
Disciples
   Disciples as Eschatological Temple Builders 149–55
   Disciples as Isaiah's heralds 204–15
   Disciples as Oppressors 88–91
   Disciples as Prophets 80–81
   Disciples as under a "yoke" 12

Encyclopedia of Production 27
Entailments 31
Eschatology Themes
   Eschatology and Messianic Themes in 2 Baruch 36–40 111–12
   Eschatology Themes in Ezekiel's Vine 106
   Eschatology Themes in Isa 5:1–7 99–100
   Eschatology Themes in John 15 123
   Eschatology Themes in Matt 21:33–45 133–34
   Eschatology Themes in Ps 80 116
Exile Motif in Matthew 74
Exorcism as Spiritual Battle 89–90

SUBJECT INDEX

First in the Kingdom   78
Fulfillment   2–5
Function of an Allusion   25–28

Greatest in the Kingdom   78
Grotto of Pan   164

Hermeneutics
   Approaches to Matthew's Hermeneutic
     3–5
   Atomistic Hermeneutics   25
   Authorial Intent   17–20
   Christological Hermeneutic in Matthew
     3–5
   Ecclesiological Hermeneutic in Matthew
     7–9
   Gaps of Meaning   21
   Locus of Meaning   17–20

Identification of Allusion   20–24
Identity v. Role   138
Inferences   31
Integration Network Theory (see Cognitive Metaphor Theory)   32–41
Intertextual Blending   36
Intertextual Metaphor   30
Invariance Principle   32

Leader v. Prince   51
Literary Criticism   19

Matthean Community   18–19
Matthew's Theology of Discipleship   9–13
Matthew's Version of the Old Testament
   21–22
Maximalist Approaches to Allusions   26–28
Melchizedek   190–91
Messianic References
   Branch   75–77, 116–18, 156–57
   Coming One   207
   Cornerstone   85
   David   50
   Shepherd   49
   Son of Man   117
   Temple Builder   155–60
   Temple Foundation   169–72
Messianic Themes
   Messianic Themes in Ezekiel's Vines
     107–08

Messianic Themes in Isa 5:1–7   101–02
Messianic Themes in Isa 61:1–3   181–97
Messianic Themes in John 15   123–24
Messianic Themes in Matt 21:33–45
   135–36
Messianic Themes in Ps 80   116–17
Messianic Themes in Psalm 118   144–48
Metalepsis   27
Method   14–41
Minimalist Approaches to Allusions   25–26
Mourners   201
Multi–Scope Blends   36–38, 41

Partial Metaphorical Utilization   31
Peter as the "Rock" in Matt 16:18   165–69
Poor   201

Recurrence   198
Referential Opacity   39–40, 215, 218

Sensus Plenior   4
Shepherd Imagery
   Shepherd Imagery for General Leadership
     70–73
   Shepherd Imagery for Kings   70
   Shepherd Imagery for Prophets   71–73
   Shepherding Imagery for Eschatological
     Figures   73–77
Source Domain   30
Summary of Thesis   1–2, 42–44

Target Domain Override   30, 32
Teacher of Righteousness   190
Temple Imagery
   Temple Builder   155–60
   Temple Foundation   169–72
   Temple Imagery in Matt 16:18   161–72
   Temple Imagery in Psalm 118   144–48
   Temple Imagery in the Sermon on the
     Mount   174–76
The Words of Heavenly Lights   53n29
Thematic Coherence   198
Twelve Phylarchs   78

Vital Relations   38–40, 41, 139–40, 219

Ancient Sources Index

Old Testament

Genesis
- 3:15 — 216
- 28:10–22 — 162
- 28:11f — 169
- 35:18 — 79
- 37:20 — 132
- 49:8–12 — 108
- 49:10 — 76, 184, 207
- 49:11 — 96
- 49:22 — 117

Exodus
- 3:7 — 86
- 5:6 — 86
- 5:10 — 86
- 5:13 — 86

Leviticus
- 7:36 — 183
- 25:10 — 184
- 25:28 — 184

Numbers
- 24:17 — 47–48, 78, 184
- 35:25 — 183

Deuteronomy
- 15:1–2 — 184
- 18:15–18 — 195
- 27–30 — 199
- 32:4 — 169
- 32:32 — 96

Joshua
- 1:5 — 216

Judges
- 4:21–22 — 85
- 5:26 — 85
- 9:8 — 183
- 16:14 — 85
- 20:2 — 85

1 Samuel
- 10:1 — 183
- 14:38 — 85
- 15:11 — 183
- 16:1 — 102
- 16:13 — 102
- 17:48 — 169

2 Samuel
- 5:2 — 46, 70
- 7 — 13, 156, 214
- 7:5, 8 — 51
- 7:12 — 51
- 7:12–13 — 184
- 7:12–14 — 51
- 7:13–14 — 76
- 14:15 — 98

1 Kings
- 1:39 — 102
- 2:19 — 79
- 5–6 — 156
- 11:34 — 52
- 19:16 — 183
- 22:17 — 47–48, 78

2 Kings
- 17:13–14 — 127

1 Chronicles
- 16:22 — 183
- 16:29 — 183
- 17 — 156
- 17:1–14 — 51
- 17:6 — 70
- 29:10–12 — 175

2 Chronicles
- 18:16 — 47–48, 78
- 26:15 — 85
- 36:15 — 127

Esther
- 10:3 — 79

ANCIENT SOURCES INDEX

Psalms		5	122, 214, 41
2	58–59, 120, 216	5:1–7	96–103
2:8	135	5:5	104
2:8–9	13, 191	5:6	95
8:3	129	5:8–30	97
17:7	117	5:9	95, 104
18:31	169	8:14	163, 170, 171
18:35	117	10:34	111
23	34	11:1	75, 102, 107, 76
37:11	198, 201	11:1–2	184
40	216	11:2	182
44:3	117	11:5	213
45:9	79	11:10	102, 115
48:2	175	14:32	170
62:2	169	19:13	85
78:68–72	107	22:4	185
78:71–72	70	22:23	86
80	113–21, 122, 140	24:18	187
82:2	191	26:14	50
86:1	191	26:19	10, 101
89:3–4	51	27	116, 122
92:10	102	27:2–6	107, 98–99, 129, 133
105:15	183	27:2–13	102
110:1	117	27:13	163
116:11	117	28:7	176
116:8	117	28:15–18	176, 177, 178
118	120, 214, 41	28:16	158, 160, 162, 163, 165, 169, 170, 171, 179, 86
118:6	216		
118:16	117	29:13	163
118:22	86, 147, 158, 171, 179,	29:18–19	207, 208, 209
118:22–23	132, 143, 148, 149, 171, 215, 219, 143	30:29	143
		32:15	182
118:26	207	35:4	210
132:17	76, 102	35:5–6	208, 209
146:5–8	192	40:1	182, 185
		40:1–3	182
Proverbs		42	40
19:17	63	42:1	182, 207
26:3	130	42:1–4	203
28:7	130	42:6	147
		42:7	182
Isaiah		44:3	182
2:2–4	107	44:28	70
3:13–15	98–99	44:28–45:1	156
3:14	95, 95, 102, 129	45:1	183
4	116	49:6	147
4:2	101, 102, 124	49:8	182, 190

Isaiah (cont.)

49:9	182
49:13	182, 185
50:7	171
50:8–9	171
51:3	185
51:19	185
52	216
52:9	184, 185
54	163
54:4	203
57:6	185
57:18	184
57:18–21	90
58:5	190
58:6	195, 196, 209
59	216
59:11	71
59:21	182
60:18	202
60:20	201
61	41, 214, 217
61:10	195
61:1–3	180–212, 213, 215
61:2	210

Jeremiah

1:18	71
1:5	71
2:8	72
2:21	95, 194, 122, 124
2:26	71
3:11	74
3:15	71
4:2	74
4:9	71
5:13	95
5:31	71
6:13	71
7:11	68
8:1	71
9:24	74
10:21	71
12:1	74
12:10	71
12:10–11	104, 95
13:13	71
16:15–16	205
17:16	71
20:12	74
22:3	74
22:15	74
22:24–30	70
22:30	74
23	214
23:1–4	73
23:1–6	49, 68–83
23:4	49, 50, 81, 87, 137, 140
23:4–5	50
23:5	107
23:5–6	53, 87
23:9–40	72
23:25	72
25:11–12	73
25:34	71
29:10–14	74
30:9	50
31:15	68, 198
31:31	68
33:14–18	77
33:15	107, 184
34:17	184
34:8	184
49:35–38	88
50:6	71
50:44	71
51:23	95

Ezekiel

7:27	50
12:10–12	51
13:10–12	176
13:11	176
13:14	176
13:16	177
14:22–23	105
15	103–09, 122
15:5–7	103
15:6–8	103
15:10–11	103
15:12–14	103
17	103–09, 122, 124
17:3–4	103
17:12	103
17:16–20	105
17:21	106

ANCIENT SOURCES INDEX

17:22–24	107	Daniel	
17:23	106	2:44	150
17:6–8	111	4:17	113
19	103–09, 122	7	75
19:1	50	7:9–14	60
19:5–20	104	7:13–14	117, 133, 184, 58
19:10–14	106	9:27	183
19:12–14	103	10	89
19:14	103, 122		
21:25	51	Hosea	
22:27	64	3:5	50
31	107	11:1	5, 203
34	45, 47–67, 137, 138, 214		
34:1–10	69	Joel	
34:4	65	4:1–3	60n55
34:5	49		
34:6	65	Amos	
34:8	64, 65	9:11	184
34:10	65		
34:12	65	Micah	
34:16	63, 65	4:1–3	107
34:17–22	73	5:2	46
34:23	51, 62	5:5	70
34:23–24	49–57, 73, 140		
34:29	65	Nahum	
34:31	62	3:18	70
37:15–22	50, 69		
37:24	50, 69	Habakkuk	
37:24–25	52	2:3	207
38:2–3	50	2:4	75
39:1	50		
44:3	52	Zepheniah	
45:7	52	1:16	85
45:8	52	3:6	85
45:16	52		
45:17	52	Zechariah	
45:22	52	3:1	79
46:2	52	3:8	75, 107
46:4	52	3:9	76
46:8	52	4:7	86
46:10	52	4:7–9	157, 162
46:12	52	4:8	159
46:16	52	6:9–15	76
46:17	52, 184	6:12	107
46:18	52	6:12–13	156, 157
48:21	52	9:8–10	87
48:22	52	9:9	207
		9:10	86

Zechariah (cont.)
- 9:13 — 88
- 9:14–16 — 89
- 9:15 — 88
- 9:16 — 88
- 10:2–4 — 83–92, 140
- 10:3 — 88
- 13:7 — 84
- 14:4 — 154
- 14:5 — 207
- 14:11 — 155

Malachi
- 2:7 — 72

New Testament

Matthew
- 1:23 — 177
- 2:5–6 — 3
- 2:6 — 46
- 2:15 — 5, 135, 203
- 2:16–18 — 64
- 2:17 — 71
- 2:18 — 68, 198, 199
- 3:2 — 81, 134, 210
- 3:11 — 207
- 3:12 — 209–10
- 3:16–17 — 207
- 3:17 — 135
- 4:3 — 135
- 4:16 — 218
- 4:17 — 31, 81, 134, 203, 210
- 4:18–20 — 205
- 4:19 — 177
- 5:1 — 173, 204
- 5:1–11 — 91
- 5:3–4 — 198–206, 213, 215, 217
- 5:3–10 — 199
- 5:5 — 198, 201
- 5:9 — 135
- 5:12 — 80, 205
- 5:13–16 — 205
- 5:14 — 175
- 5:17 — 18
- 5:19 — 78, 79
- 5:23–24 — 174
- 5:31 — 79
- 5:35 — 175
- 5:45 — 135
- 6:6 — 175
- 6:9–10 — 175
- 6:13 — 175
- 7:13–14 — 172
- 7:15 — 65, 81
- 7:15–20 — 176, 205
- 7:21–23 — 80
- 7:22 — 72, 176
- 7:24–27 — 172–78, 179, 215, 219
- 7:27 — 220
- 8:1–4 — 220
- 8:14–15 — 220
- 8:17 — 203
- 8:22 — 220
- 8:29 — 90, 135
- 8–9 — 65, 66
- 9:1–10 — 64
- 9:32–34 — 64
- 9:35 — 64, 65, 66
- 9:35–36 — 200
- 9:36 — 45–92
- 9:36–38 — 219
- 10:1 — 66, 67, 210
- 10:1–4 — 214
- 10:2–4 — 66, 205
- 10:4 — 134
- 10:6 — 140, 214, 45–92, 67, 82
- 10:7 — 80, 210
- 10:8 — 80, 210
- 10:11–15 — 90
- 10:15 — 91
- 10:16 — 66
- 10:16–30 — 152
- 10:19–20 — 80
- 10:23 — 66
- 10:24–25 — 67
- 10:25 — 12–13, 210, 218
- 10:27 — 80
- 10:40–41 — 80
- 10:40–42 — 67
- 11:2 — 197, 207, 209
- 11:5 — 197, 207–11, 215, 217
- 11:9 — 81
- 11:11 — 79
- 11:13 — 207

ANCIENT SOURCES INDEX

11:14	220	20:21	79
11:27	135	20:25–27	78
11:28–30	12	21:1–11	161
12	40	21:5	87, 88
12:6	161	21:9	143
12:18–21	203	21:11	81
12:25–29	90	21:12–13	148
13:2	204	21:12–17	154
13:4–12	91	21:13	68
13:10	204	21:14–16	129, 161
13:10–15	128	21:15	129
13:24	204	21:18–22	134, 154, 91
13:35	81	21:21	132, 154
13:36	204	21:23	127, 148
13:39	133	21:25–27	127
13:52	18	21:26	81, 129
13:57	81	21:27	128
14	12	21:28–32	128
14:5	81	21:31–41	161
14:33	135	21:32	218
15:8–9	163	21:33–41	80, 215
15:24	64, 67, 82, 214	21:33–45	93, 125–36
16:3	134	21:33–46	154
16:13–28	164	21:34–37	94
16:14	81	21:38	135
16:15	168	21:41–43	133, 159
16:16	135	21:42	149, 161, 214, 215
16:18	149, 158, 161–72, 176, 177–178, 179, 214	21:42–43	142–160, 172, 178
		21:43	94, 132
16:19	165, 220	21:44	150
16:23	177	21:45–46	130
16:24–26	152	21:46	128
17:5	135	22:1–14	128
17:11–13	81	22:16	128
17:16	91	22:42	135
18:1	204	22:45	135
18:1–4	79	23	199
18:4	78	23:1	204
18:11–14	60	23:2–3	129
18:18	165	23:28	148
19:1	204	23:31–35	64
19:23	79	23:34	81
19:27	78	23:38	154, 161
19:28	131, 168	24:1–2	148
19:28–30	79	24:1–31	161
19:30	78, 79	24:2	154
20:1–16	79, 129	24:3	205
20:16	78, 79	24:31	163

Matthew (cont.)
24:32	134
24:36	135
25	53, 57, 60–61, 82
25:31–46	60, 62n61, 214, 217
25:33	79
25:61	161
26:28	68, 184
26:31	84
26:61	148
26:64	135
26:74	79
27:9	71
27:40	135, 148, 161
27:43	135
27:51–53	134
27:54	135
28:18–20	18, 131, 133, 173
28:19	135
28:20	177

Mark
1:15	134
6:34	48n9, 81
11:27	131
11:28	127
11:29–33	127
11:33	128
12	98
12:1–12	119
12:2	134
12:7	132
12:9	132
12:10–11	147
12:10–12	131

Luke
1:19	196
1:26	196
2:10	196
3:18	196
3:20	209
3:21–22	196
3:22	195
4	207, 211
4:12–20	205
4:16–20	194–97
4:18	195
4:25–27	194
6:13	196
7:16	194
7:19–20	197
7:22	197, 210, 211
7:23	208
7:27	196
7:36–50	195
7:39	194
9:6	196
9:50	196
9:52	196
10:1	196
10:3	196
10:7	196
11:49	196
20:2	127
20:3–8	127
20:9	128
20:16	132
20:17	147
20:18	150
20:19	128
20:28	128
24:19	194
24:21	194
24:25–27	27

John
1:29	65, 122
2:19	167
2:21	122
3:14	122, 123
3:15–16	123
3:36	123
5:24	123
6:32	122
6:47	123
8:28	123
10	56
10:14	65
10:16	56
10:28	123
10:30	56
12:32	123
12:34	123
13–17	121
14:16	122

ANCIENT SOURCES INDEX

15	118	Hebrews	
15:1–8	121–25	1:3	79
17	122–23	1:5	156
17:20	122	13:5–6	216
20:21	122		

1 Peter

Acts		2:5	147
1:8	196	2:6	163
2:33	79	2:6–7	158, 160, 170–71
3:18	147	2:6–8	163
3:20–23	195	2:7	147, 149
4:11	147	3:22	79
4:25	120		
4:27	195	Revelation	
7:37	195	1:3	216
8:12	196	2:26–27	13
9:12–18	196	20:2	100
10:38	195	3:7	86
13:51	91	5:6	76
		5:9	216

Romans

Apocrypha and Pseudepigrapha

8:34	79		
9:6–13	28		
9:33	163, 170	1 Enoch	
10:11	163	12:5	184
10:15	216	13:4	184
11:26	182	13:6	184
16:20	216	53:6	157
		85–90	57
1 Corinthians		89	53
3	216	89:16	57
3:5–17	134	89:31	57
3:10	154	89:39	57
3:11	168–69	89:45	57
		89:48	57
Galatians		89:58	57
2:9	168	90:29	157
		90:37	58
Ephesians		90:37–39	57
1:20	79	94:6–7	176
2:20	169		
6	216	2 Baruch	
6:15	216	29–30	111
		36–40	109–13
Colossians		39:3–5	110
3:1	79	40:1–4	110
		53	111
		74	111

2 Esdras
2:34	55
7:26	55
7:29	56
7:33	55
12:11–12	110
12:32	55
12:34	56

Gospel of Thomas   65, 98

Judith
11:19	47–48

Odes
13:77	184

Psalms of Solomon
17	53, 57, 58–59, 76
17:21	59
17:21–23	157
17:22	59
17:24	58
17:40–41	59

Sibylline Oracles
5:414–27	157
5:432–33	157

Sirach
5:1–2	157
5:5–6	157
24:17	122–21
48:8	183
48:22	186–87
48:24–25	186–87
49:10	211
50:2	85

Testament of Solomon
22:7–23:4	149
23:1–4	144
23:6–8	162

Testament of Daniel
5:10–12	157

Tobit
3	89
13:8	130

Dead Sea Scrolls

1Q13 2:10–16	191
1Q16	116
1Q20 (Genesis Apocryphon) 20:28–29	89
1QH^a 23	211
1QH^a 23:14–15	189
1QIs^a	100
1QM 11:7–8	183
1QM	89
1QS 8:4	170
1QS 8:4–8	163
4Q161 3:18	77
4Q171	116
4Q173	116
4Q174	76, 157
4Q174 3:18–21	13
4Q252 5:3	207
4Q252 5:3–4	76
4Q266 5	183
4Q285	76, 111
4Q471	89
4Q500	95, 148, 153
4Q504	53–54, 54
4Q521	211
4Q521 2:1–2, 5–12	192–93
4QpIs^a	111
4QPseudo-Ezekiel	193
11Q5 (11QPs^a)	89, 116, 145
11Q6	145
11Q11	89
11Q13	211
11Q13 2:9	190–91
CD 4:19–20	154
CD 8:18	154

ANCIENT SOURCES INDEX

Other Jewish Writings

Amidah
- 14 — 157

b. Ber.
- 64a — 154

b. Meg.
- 18a — 157

b. Shabb.
- 114a — 154

b. Yoma
- 53b — 162
- 54b — 162

Josephus
- *The Antiquities of the Jews* 8.354 — 10
- *The Antiquities of the Jews* 15.11.3 — 97
- *Wars of the Jews* 5:120 — 97

Lev. Rab.
- 9.6 — 157
- 37.4 — 147

m. 'Ohal
- 2:3 — 91

m. Ber.
- 5:5 — 67

m. Pesahim
- 5:7 — 143

m. Seqal
- 5.6 — 175

m. Tehar
- 4:5 — 91

m. Yoma
- 5:2 — 162

Midr. Can.
- 1:5 — 154

Midr. Ps
- 18 — 79
- 118.22, 24 — 147

Pes. R.
- 36.1 — 147

Sip. Deut. Piska
- 312 — 130

Songs of David (A.18) — 146, 147

T. Pesahim
- 95b — 143

Targum Ezekiel
- 34:24 — 54
- 37:25 — 54

Targum Isaiah
- 5 — 95, 148
- 53:5 — 157
- 57 — 90
- 61:1 — 187–88
- 61:1–3 — 211

Targum Numbers
- 25:12 — 188

Targum Psalms
- 80:12 — 124
- 118:22–23 — 153
- 118:22 — 145, 147

Targum Zechariah
- 6:12 — 157

Targum Exodus
- 28:30 — 162

Targum Isaiah
- 4:2 — 101–02

Targum Jeremiah
    23:4   71
    23:5   75

y. Ber. 2.3   147

Early Church History

Ambrose of Milan, *On the Duties of the Clergy*
    1:42   163
    1.29.142   171

Epistle of Barnabbas
    6:2   163
    6:2–4   171
    14:7   199
    14:7–9   211

Iranaeus
    Against Heresies 3.21.7   171
    Epid. 53   211

Origen
    Comm. Jo. 6   211

Tertullian
    Prax. 11   211

Printed in the United States
By Bookmasters